SIMILARITY

A PARADIGM FOR CULTURE THEORY

SIMILARITY

A PARADIGM FOR CULTURE THEORY

Edited by
ANIL BHATTI and DOROTHEE KIMMICH

with the assistance of SARA BANGERT

Tulika Books

Published by
Tulika Books
44 (first floor), Shahpur Jat, New Delhi 110 049, India
www.tulikabooks.in

First edition (hardback) 2018

ISBN: 978-93-82381-96-9

Printed at Chaman Enterprises, Delhi 110 002

Contents

Preface to the English Edition

This volume presents the English versions of papers first published in German, under the title *Ähnlichkeit*, in 2015.[1] The English volume is supplemented by three new contributions, by Andreas Kilcher, Uwe Wirth and Ravi Ahuja.

In an interview on his recent novel, *The Golden House*, Salman Rushdie emphasizes the problems associated with the current discourse on identity as follows:

> So, in New York right now, if you talk about identity, most people will assume you're talking about gender issues. In India it seems to me that the identity debate has to do with authenticity of Indianness and religious sectarianism, and identity becomes an aspect of the Hindu–Muslim issue. In England national identity became very big during the whole Brexit debate, but there the people were in a way harking back to some imaginary golden age of England – an idea of an identity that was pre-European and better than European. So it interests me that in these different parts of the world that I've spent a lot of my life thinking about, everybody means different things by identity, so that just became a natural subject.[2]

Rushdie's remarks underscore the point that anti-humanist ideologies are obsessed with purity and origins. As against this, a substantive democratic perspective in our times is based on the development of the critical art of inheritance – how to find, rehabilitate, critically inherit and appropriate cultural heritages, combining past and present, establishing links and out of the plenitude of the world deriving that critical assemblage which will enable us to avoid racist, sexist and cultural othering. This is based on mingling, mixing and emphasizing affiliations, alliances and similarities in the complex search for a possible united front against ontologizing differences and against the rise of anti-humanist social forces.

The concepts of identity and otherness are both becoming ever-more questionable, not least due to global political events of the last few decades. The assumption of distinct cultural identities in the era of greater refugee and migratory flows seems increasingly inadequate. Though the postcolonial critique of identity has also given consideration to alterity and hybridity, this has remained within the paradigm of difference as an overall perspective. For these reasons, it is important to reflect upon whether a concept of 'similarity' can be developed alongside the concept of difference which has hitherto dominated Cultural Studies. The category of similarity, we had suggested in the introduction to the German volume, offers an alternative for examining our increasingly complex cultural world.

'Similarity' is a concept with its own history and affiliations which had been obscured, till recently, by the dominant presence of the research paradigm privileging difference. That is why it was earlier discredited by suggesting that it supported an assimilationist position, leading to a forceful adjustment of cultures, gender or religion. In addition, similarity and thinking in similarity were supposedly part of a premodern way of thinking belonging to other times and places – part of primitive stages of culture or a premodern epoch, and therefore part of a different order of things that was distinct from a rationalist modern epoch in which only exact concepts are valid.

This volume explores the theoretical range of the concept of similarity in historical and systematic terms. It is seen as not only a heuristic concept, but also an argument and an alternative option in cultural practice. The contributions presented here come from literary and cultural studies, from philosophy, political science, sociology, ethnology and history.

Thinking in similarity does in fact oppose the desire to draw precise borders and exact definitions. But this supposed drawback can be an advantage when dealing with complex phenomena of culture where fluid transitions, multiple overlapping and broad spatial borders are a given. The specific epistemological achievement of the category of similarity consists in offering new ways of seeing the diffuse dynamics and fuzzy relations that are characteristic of our complex and entangled contemporary world.

In the German volume we had emphasized that thinking about similarity should not be (mis-)understood as a false form of harmonization or a levelling of differences. Rather, considerations of similarity contain a subversive potential to expose the claimed antagonisms and radical incompatibilities of opposition or difference as nothing more than legitimist ideology. We had drawn attention to the fact that it was by affirming similarity that the ontologizing claims of the caste system as a cosmic order could be exposed. Dr Ambedkar made the criticism, as early as 1936, that the brutal form of systematic exclusion of the Dalits (the so-called untouchables) in the Hindu caste system is also based on a fundamental denial of the possibility of 'fluidity and equity' in social conditions and in social practice.[3] Emphasizing similarity, then, is a subversive form of critique of all attempts to ontologize the appearance of variations in social class or occupation or the body, as manifested in racial, casteist sedimentation of essentialist claims of inherent difference.

We have by now a comprehensive historical archive for dealing with the cultural specifics of our contemporary polyglot, multireligious, pluricultural and syncretic worlds of displacement and migration. Reference to this archive suggests that instead of hard dichotomous structures and hitherto dominant polarities based on notions of difference and alterity, our contemporary cultural processes lead to pluricultural conditions characterized by plurilingual competence, syncretism and heterogeneities that are becoming features of our increasingly complex societies. These processes are characterized by conflicts between heterogeneity and homogeneity in fields of power and domination. Whereas perspectives from participatory democracy celebrate the process of heterogeneity, fascist world-views try to force homogeneity on to the world. Against this background we suggest that the traditional emphasis on the principle of a hermeneutic of understanding difference in culture theory and practice is inadequate for comprehending the processes of space–time transformations which characterize our contemporary world.

Instead of a hermeneutics of difference, we suggest that the perspective of non-hermeneutic dispositions make *similarity* a productive concept for enabling us to come to terms with a complex world of entanglements, shared histories and migrations. It also offers a critique of all forms of exceptionalism, and enforces the need for a new secular, syncretistic perspective beyond all orthodoxies. It disposes us to seeing polyvalent, polycentric, overlapping and transient fields with greater adequacy than traditional hermeneutic approaches. They also replace traditional linearity in favour of a greater emphasis on simultaneity. Critical studies in the humanities then means thinking in analogies and comparisons, seeking affiliations and commonalities, and looking upon cultures as interwoven, shared and 'entangled'. Similarity as a conceptual framework is increasingly being used to analyse situations that were earlier dealt with in terms of ethnic relations, inter-religious relations and intercultural relations. These were traditionally dealt with in binary terms through the hermeneutics of 'self' and 'other'. Instead we pay greater attention to partial overlappings, and partial distances and nearness. This also replaces the traditional emphasis on 'identity'.

In Jewish studies, the concept of similarity is being used to deal with the complex worlds of Eastern Europe. For instance, Karl Hödl says: '"Similarity" may serve as an important category of analysis in Jewish Studies in that it focuses on commonalities without neglecting the differences between Jews and non-Jews.'[4] The reassessment of the Habsburg monarchy is again a result of thinking in commonalities and similarities, as against the dominating paradigm of the nation-state in Europe.[5] This has led, among others, to a revised approach to the Habsburg monarchy, as well as to multilingualism and to the question of identity-based descriptions of large societies.[6] For instance, Pieter Judson writes that his book 'underscores just how similar the Habsburg Empire was to other European states while highlighting moments when it pioneered new ideas about nationhood and new practices of governance. Like every European state, however, it also developed distinctive institutions and practices that make its history unique.'[7] The equation of Indian identity with a Hindu identity is a part of this process of destroying the syncretic, diverse, non-identitarian culture of India that was always based on interactions between many religions, languages and life-worlds, which were in turn based on a functioning play of 'similarity'.[8]

Instead of treating the multinational, multilingual state as a deviation from the norm of the essentially monolingual nation-state, approaches based on analogous reasoning, overlapping, simultaneity of historically diverse social formations and, in general, the theoretical move to affirm non-linear thinking has been significant. By focusing on similarities we again argue against the closure of identity and the drive towards complete sameness, and emphasize that we deal with various kinds of similarities and overlapping processes in our complex worlds. This may well be the background against which we hope this volume will be read.

Acknowledgements

We are grateful to the many colleagues, friends and institutions whose encouragement and help made possible the present English version of the German volume, *Ähnlichkeit: Ein kulturwissenschaftliches Paradigma* (2015). We are grateful to Indira Chandrasekhar for including our project in the publishing plans of Tulika Books.

We thank the authors for cooperating with the process of translating and updating the original contributions to the German edition. We are grateful to the translators Claire Bacher, Joanna White, Allison Brown Mike Zuber, and in particular to Alan Fortuna who is responsible for most of the translations, and who carried out this task with meticulous care and admirable efficiency. Our special thanks are due to the editorial team at Tulika Books for the care with which the manuscript was edited for publication. As was the case during the publication of the German edition, Sara Bangert gave us invaluable help at every stage of the English edition. We are especially grateful to her for assistance over the many years during which our project on 'Similarity' progressed, from its beginnings in the Kulturwissenschaftliches Kolleg of the University of Konstanz through the final stages of our work at the University of Tübingen. We record our gratitude to the Fritz Thyssen Foundation, the Kulturwissenschaftliches Kolleg of the University of Konstanz (especially Jan Kröger), and the Universitätsbund Tübingen/Vereinigung der Freunde der Universität Tübingen (Association of Friends of the University of Tübingen) for their generous funding of the translation.

Notes

1 For reviews of the German volume, see Patrut (2016) and Mühr (2016).

2 From Doshi (2017).

3 Cf. Ambedkar's controversy with Mahatma Gandhi; reprinted in Ambedkar (2014): 347.

4 Hödl (2017).

5 This was already evident in the volume on rethinking Habsburg edited by Johannes Feichtinger and Heidemarie Uhl; cf. Feichtinger and Uhl, eds. (2016). Cf. also Fillafer (2012).

6 For instance, renewed attention to Bolzano's early writings of 1816 is of increased relevance now. Cf. Bolzano (2007). Cf. also Burger (1993) and Csáky (2010).

7 Cf. Judson (2016): 12. But also: 'We need not gravitate to an opposite extreme by asserting central and eastern Europe's blanket "Similarity" to the rest of Europe. Rather, we need to understand the history of this region – its institutions and its economic, social, political, and cultural development – within, not outside of, a broadly comparative European context' (ibid.).

8 For instance, Mohan Bhagwat, the head of the RSS, the Hindu organization which is the backbone of the BJP, is reported to have asserted that one may follow a different religion, different culture, philosophy, language and style of eating, but everyone living in India is a Hindu: 'Every Hindu is my own brother. In India one may follow a different eating habits, way of worshipping the gods, philosophy, language and culture. But all of them are Hindus. There are many who are Hindu but they are not aware of it. Only those who consider Bharat Mata his own mother are true Hindus.' Cf. 'Everyone living in India is a Hindu: Mohan Bhagwat', *The Hindu*, 25 February 2018; available at http://www.thehindu.com/news/national/everyone-living-in-india-is-a-hindu-mohan-bhagwat/article22852200.ece

References

Ambedkar, B.R. (2014), *Dr Babasaheb Ambedkar: The Annihilation of Caste*, with commentary and edited by S. Anand, and introduced by Arundhati Roy's essay, 'The Doctor and the Saint', New Delhi: Navayana.

Bhatti, Anil and Dorothee Kimmich, eds (2015), *Ähnlichkeit: Ein kulturtheoretisches Paradigma*, Konstanz: Konstanz University Press.

Bolzano, Bernard (2007), 'On the Relations between the Two Peoples of Bohemia: Read on the seventh Sunday after Pentecost, 1816 [July 21]', in *Selected Writings on*

Ethics and Politics, translated by Paul Rusnock and Rolf George, Amsterdam: Rodopi: 96–122.

Burger, Hannelore (1993), 'Der Verlust der Mehrsprachigkeit: Aspekte des Mährischen Ausgleichs', *Bohemia*, 34: 77–89.

Csáky, Moritz (2010), *Das Gedächtnis der Städte: Wien und die urbanen Milieus in Zentraleuropa*, Wien u. a.: Böhlau.

Doshi, Tishani (2017), '"I'm here all by myself": The Salman Rushdie interview', 1 September, available at http://www.thehindu.com/books/interview-with-salman-rushdie-on-the-golden-house/article19600953.ece

Feichtinger, Johannes (2010), *Wissenschaft als Reflexives Projekt: Von Bolzano über Freud zu Kelsen: Österreichische Wissenschaftsgeschichte 1848–1938*, Bielefeld: transcript.

Feichtinger, Johannes *et al.*, eds (2003), *Habsburg postcolonial: Zentraleuropa – Orte Innerer Kolonisierung?* Innsbruck, Wien, München.

Feichtinger, Johannes and Heidemarie Uhl, eds (2016), *Habsburg Neu Denken: Vielfalt und Ambivalenz in Zentraleuropa: 30 kulturwissenschaftliche Stichworte*, Wien u.a.: Böhlau.Patrut, Iulia (2016), in *Zeitschrift für interkulturelle Germanistik* (*ZiG*), 7.

Fillafer, Franz Leander (2012), 'Imperium oder Kulturstatt: Die Habsburgmonarchie und die Historisierung der Nationalkulturen im 19. Jahrhundert', in Philipp Ther, ed., *Kulturpolitik und Theater: Die kontinentalen Imperien in Europa im Vergleich*, München: Oldenbourg and Wien: Böhlau: 27–54.

Hödl, Karl (2017), 'Jewish history beyond binary conceptions: Jewish performing musicians in Vienna around 1900', *Journal of Modern Jewish Studies*, 16, 3: 377–94.

Judson, Pieter (2016), *The Habsburg Empire: A New History*, Cambridge, MA: The Belknap Press of Harvard University.

Mühr, Stefan (2016), in *Acta Germanica*, 44.

Patrut, Iulia (2016), in *Zeitschrift für interkulturelle Germanistik* (*ZiG*), 7.

Ruthner, Clemens (2018), *Habsburgs 'Dark Continent': Postkoloniale Lektüren zur österreichischen Literatur und Kultur im langen 19. Jahrhundert Francke* (Kultur – Herrschaft – Differenz, Bd. 23), Tübingen: Francke.

April 2018
New Delhi and Tübingen

ANIL BHATTI and DOROTHEE KIMMICH

Introduction

Anil Bhatti and Dorothee Kimmich

The idea that the concept of 'similarity' could offer a new, alternative approach to cultural studies arose from preliminary discussions between scholars in India (New Delhi) and Germany (Konstanz, Tübingen).[1] Following these discussions, different conceptions of similarity were considered by scholars from diverse disciplines within the framework of three conferences, supported by the Fritz Thyssen Foundation, the Excellence Cluster 16: 'Cultural Foundations of Integration' at the University of Konstanz, and the Institute of German Studies and the Forum Scientiarum at the University of Tübingen. This volume is a collection of the contributions and papers that emerged from these conferences.

This volume does not seek to present a comprehensive history of similarity or of ideas about similarity. Not only would this require a review of the entirety of philosophical history from Aristotle to Nelson Goodman, it would also demand a survey of many other academic fields in which related concepts, such as mimicry, mimesis, analogy, assimilation and imitation, play central roles; in other words, it would require an overview of knowledge traditions as diverse as art history and psychology, as well as cognitive science and biology.

Instead, this collection seeks to introduce and to explore important and exemplary interpretations of similarity for cultural studies research. The essays presented here thus stem from the relevant disciplines of literary and cultural studies, but also from philosophy, political science, sociology, ethnology and history. The essays are arranged according to their systematic perspectives: the first part of the book deals with conceptual attempts to establish the relevance of similarity for cultural studies research, while the second part is devoted to testing different models of application.

'Similarity' in the History of Knowledge (Dorothee Kimmich)

Why 'similarity'?

'Similarity' is not a new concept, and is not thought of here as a research paradigm lacking its own history and tradition. Quite the contrary: prominent authors stretching from antiquity to the classical modern period have emphasized the importance of similarity as an epistemological guiding principle – and an orienting practice – in central passages of their works. In the twentieth century, however, 'similarity' as a heuristic concept became the focus of more and more scepticism. While it never became completely obsolete, a useful update of the concept of similarity within the framework of cultural studies debates has yet to emerge.

While the concept of distinction, of 'difference', set significant precedents in twentieth-century theory and flourished in a wide variety of scholarly disciplines, concepts of similarity found few supporters. Not only did structuralist and post-structuralist theorems declare difference (and its specifically deconstructivist counterpart, *différance*) to be the paradigm of knowledge organization, cultural studies also operated with the concepts of 'identity' and 'otherness' – and thus sought to identify cultural differences and arrange them into hierarchical systems.[2] Far removed from such considerations, thinking about difference also became a descriptive and analytical concept, and gained political relevance, especially in the context of *gender studies* and *postcolonial studies*.[3]

Cultural differences were not only marked and criticized as distinguishing hierarchical characteristics, they also experienced an enduring ideologization in certain political and scientific contexts: '[I]n the post-Cold War world, the most important distinctions among peoples are not ideological, political, or economic. They are cultural.'[4] The acceptance and impact of this thesis – expressed as a political battle cry by Samuel P. Huntington in the 1990s – have not been limited to the field of political theory. Indeed, to this day it represents, encourages and promotes highly effective political and social practices of cultural differentiation, othering and even discrimination.

The concepts of identity and otherness are both becoming ever-more questionable, not least due to the global political events of the last few decades. Not only have the problems with 'Clash of Civilizations' as an explanatory model and a pattern of action been exposed, but the assumption of distinct cultural identities[5] in the era of postmodern migratory flows seems increasingly inadequate.[6] For these reasons, it is important not only to discuss but also to reflect upon whether a concept of cultural similarity can be developed alongside a concept of cultural difference: a field of 'as-well-as', and thus something like a philosophy of similarities.[7] In doing so, it is important to consider the requirements that such a concept would have to meet, to avoid becoming arbitrary.

What is 'similarity'?

'We cannot easily imagine a more familiar or fundamental notion than this [the notion of similarity], or a notion more ubiquitous in its applications. . . . And yet, strangely, there is something logically repugnant about it', wrote Willard van Orman Quine in his 'Dewey Lectures', held in 1969 at Columbia University, New York.[8] And Quine was no exception. His unease with the concept of similarity was shared by many other philosophers, as well as by linguists, scholars of visual studies, psychologists, cognition theorists, biologists, ethnologists and literary scholars: 'For we are baffled when we try to relate the general notion of similarity significantly to logical terms. . . . The dubiousness of this notion is itself a remarkable fact. For surely there is nothing more basic to thought and language than our sense of similarity.'[9]

In addition to sharing these concerns, many scholars have agreed with Quine's assessment that the term, the concept and even the experience of 'similarity' are not only familiar to us but are global and fundamental – and yet are unsuitable for scientific use. Thus, we clearly have no problems understanding what similarity is in our everyday lives, or how we identify, evaluate, negotiate and use similarities around us. Despite this, a definition of similarity according to classical criteria such as necessary and sufficient conditions seems to be stubbornly elusive.

Similarity is thus 'clearly' a vague term, to phrase it as a paradox. The judgment of the history of philosophy from Aristotle to Quine finds such vague terms to be philosophically unacceptable. In the case of similarity, Nelson Goodman's criticism has been particularly influential – even outside philosophical circles. He describes 'similarity' as 'slippery', and deems it comparatively worthless for philosophy and science: 'Comparative judgments of similarity often require not merely selection of relevant properties but a weighting of their relative importance, and variation in both relevance and importance can be rapid and enormous.'[10] Goodman concludes that 'circumstances alter similarities'.[11] He claims that such contextual dependence precludes an appropriate and satisfying geometric modelling of similarity.

Over the last few decades, a variety of disciplines have repeatedly sought to follow Goodman's criticism and to model similarity in ways beyond the geometrical approach. All of these new approaches begin by formalizing the contextuality of similarity; as Lieven Decock and Igor Douven stressed in their 2011 essay, for instance, 'the main stumbling blocks for the old geometrical model . . . were the fact that it is unable to account for asymmetries in people's similarity judgements as well as for the context-sensitivity of such judgements'.[12]

For both philosophical and, increasingly, cognitive scientific and psychological discussions, models and methods that can be traced back to Wittgenstein's reflections on family resemblance are helpful, such as Lotfi Zadeh's so-called *fuzzy logic* or Eleanor Rosch's 'Prototype Theory'. Such approaches do not seek to precisely define the characteristics, borders and capacities of 'similarity'; instead, they seek to understand and describe its vagueness.[13]

In 1990, George Lakoff observed that philosophical research on vagueness was not 'PC' ('politically correct').[14] He was clearly referring to a specific scientific tradition that he saw as underlying philosophy, linguistics and possibly other empirical sciences. And his observations are certainly consistent with the rejection of similarity by many philosophers: the vagueness of similarity is not 'PC'.

At almost the same time, other disciplines joined and advanced the debates surrounding vague concepts and the vagueness of concepts. The cognitive sciences, semiotics, and especially psychology and linguistics, have come to dominate the field. It is little wonder, then, that discussions about similarity have become particularly relevant to reflections on vagueness. Similarity defines a field of knowledge that connects questions from theories of perception, epistemology, media history and cultural anthropology, and manages to span the distance to an anthropologically connoted aesthetics as well. In this sense, one can view the discourse surrounding similarity to be a sort of 'index fossil' that can be traced through modern discursive formations, drawing a profile line through modern considerations of existential vagueness and fundamental diffusivity.[15]

For the time being, we can at least state this: vague concepts are conceptualized as entities with fluid borders and, to some degree, stable centres. Similarity is not only itself such an entity, it is also the structural principle according to which such entities are organized: precisely according to a higher or lower similarity, with the prototype at the centre of the field.[16] Such a conception rehabilitates similarity as a useful philosophical concept, for instance, in the area of philosophy of identity, 'where it is argued that the so-called paradoxes of identity – puzzle cases involving the possibility of change over time and issues of constitution – can be explained in a uniform and elegant manner by construing the identity predicate as it occurs in those paradoxes in terms of similarity'.[17]

Most recently, similarity has become important in the philosophy of science as well: 'A third case in point, this one from the philosophy of science, is the role attributed to similarity in the so-called semantic conception of theories. . . . The appropriate model–world relation . . . is rather one of similarity in certain respects. . . . Meanwhile, this has become almost common lore among philosophers of science.'[18]

Thus there is now a certain consensus regarding the conceptual description of similarity, if not about a clear definition. Ulrike Hahn, Nick Chater and Lucy B. Richardson memorably expressed a sentiment that most similarity scholars would subscribe to today: '[S]imilarity is determined by the transformation distance between representations: entities which are perceived to be similar have representations which are readily transformed into one another, whereas transforming between dissimilar entities requires many transformations.'[19]

In this definition too, similarity retains an affinity to the spatial modelling of proximity and distance, and a certain connection to a temporal dimension that can be best described as a slower or more rapid, or as a clear or less clear, transformation over time. Today, similarity is no longer considered to be a property of objects, but rather as a more or less subjective, mental, cognitive concept that facilitates, structures and orients our perceptions. For cognitive scientists, questions regarding contextual dependency – the so-called 'perspective' (*Hinsicht*) that judges the relevance of similarity references – remain unanswered.

Furthermore, we can clearly state that until a few decades ago, philosophically analytical scholarly discourse had a tendency to eliminate relationships of similarity from its considerations, primarily for methodological reasons. But this does *not* mean, as many authors themselves would concede, that similarity does not have a meaningful role in many areas of cognition, memory, language and culture. What it does mean, however, is that within a specific and dominant academic context, speaking about similarity causes problems and thus becomes less relevant. For this reason, the discourse around similarity has migrated to other fields.

What is 'similarity' for?

'A philosophy of similarity must lead to an ontology whose fundamental concepts are of the near and the far, of distance and remoteness.'[20] With this statement Robert Spaemann makes it clear that similarity connotes spatial thinking, and thus is in agreement with recent research in cognitive science. An ontology of similarity will have to deal with spatial relationships, and concepts of distance and proximity.

Similarity implies something like qualitative proximity. We might talk about the spatial proximity of objects, the temporal proximity of events, the numerical proximity of quantities, qualitative proximities (such as in colours), and naturally also the emotional proximity of humans, which we call sympathy and empathy. Relationships of similarity are thus useful to describe conditions that imply both relative proximity and relative distance at the same time, and which represent these respective distances as dynamic, as changeable. This is why similarity always includes a dynamic and temporal but not teleological aspect, in addition to spatial characteristics.

Similarity is a 'figure of the continuous',[21] of the transitory. Although it requires the demarcation of differences, it never constitutes a break or an opposition. The concept of similarity connotes evolution, change and metamorphosis, but concepts such as loss of self, adjustment pressure and assimilation can also be described using models of similarity. As a problematic and problem-generating figure of the continual, similarity disrupts the great heuristic divisions of modernity: nature and culture, people and things, foreign (other) and self. In contrast to a philosophical ontology, cultural studies research on similarity must also pose questions about the 'practical', praxeological aspects of similarity. While philosophical ontology asks the question, 'what is similarity?', the cognitive sciences ask the question, 'what is similarity for?' Cultural studies must also pose questions about the practices of similarity: not just the question of how we can *recognize* similarity, but also those about how – and why – we *do* similar things. Questions regarding practices are connected with previously mentioned concepts such as mimesis, mimicry, assimilation, acculturation and imitation, as well as questions about globalization, internationalization, transculturality, migration, and even literature, art and aesthetics.

Similarity arises, declines, and can be more or less clear, important or obvious, according to different aspects and respects. Similarity can be covered up or made more prominent. Relationships of similarity can mark something spontaneous, involuntary, unconscious, even something unwanted and passive. On the other hand, there are political, social and cultural practices of intentional and wilful 'similarizing', but also many examples of forced and violent assimilation.

Our perception of similarity is intuitive, and its criteria are undefinable or are dependent on context. Practices of similarity, including the desire for imitation and the delight at successful mimesis, are innate abilities, but are without doubt also culturally and environmentally dependent. 'Similarity' seems to be semantically symmetrical, but in certain situations proves to be irreversible and asymmetrical. Similarity is a category of perception, and exhibits an irreducible aspect of cultural and individual experience. Similarity organizes knowledge and memory, yet at the same time misleads us with platitudes and commonplaces of all kinds. It is both premodern and postmodern. It overextends philosophy and is a challenge for cultural studies.

'Similarity': Preliminary Thoughts about a *Suchbegriff* or Search Term (Anil Bhatti)

Hermeneutic abstinence or: what is 'similarity' good for?

Thinking about similarity opens different possibilities for dealing with the problems of complex societies than do methodologies focused on differences. In India, for example, a strong methodological preference for associating questions of diversity with a specific form of tolerance has developed over time, fed in part by the experiences of anti-colonialism. Within this context, thinking about tolerance is not based on a paradigm of 'understanding'; instead, it requires a concept of social practice that is based on 'accommodation'. This has led to a preference for the maxim that it is more important to get along with one another than to understand one another. In other words, that it is more important to cultivate the art of social behaviour in conditions of diversity first, and only later seek the logic of understanding behind such behaviour. In short, it has led to a strategy of de-dramatization.

India stands in sharp contrast to Germany where we seek to use a hermeneutic of understanding to arrive at tolerance. Instead, India has developed something like a preference for non-hermeneutic methods to discuss tolerance, a result of historical experiences in a complex, multilingual and multi-religious society that is stratified by caste and class, and that has always contained a latent potential for violence. Such methods do not focus primarily on dichotomies or the drawing of boundaries, but on attempts to find overlapping fields of similarity. In cultural practice this means that the principle of 'this . . . as well as that' is emphasized, as opposed to the principle of 'either–or'. This allows syncretic possibilities to emerge in a society otherwise threatened by fundamentalism.

In such contexts, thinking about similarity should not be (mis) understood as a false form of harmonization or the levelling of differences. Rather, considerations of similarity contain a subversive potential to expose the claimed antagonisms and radical incompatibilities of opposition, differences and so-called 'clashes' as nothing more than ideology. In India, the emphasis on similarity thus represents an important pillar for all secular movements and beliefs. Conversely, a disregard for considerations of similarity foments fanaticism, which often leads to violent riots. Why, for instance, should Hindus and Muslims – who otherwise live and cooperate well together in everyday social practice – suddenly become enemies simply because religious fanatics want to demonstrate the irreconcilable differences between their respective interpretations of Hinduism and Islam?

The destructive potential for violence in fundamentalist movements in both India and Europe, and the necessity of finding new ways of discussing tolerance and integration policies in a world of migration, form the background for the timeliness of 'similarity'. The current relevance of 'similarity' for cultural studies is related to the problems of complex, pluricultural societies that are increasingly characterized by a high level of linguistic, religious and cultural diversity. Often these are migratory societies, such as in Europe today, or they are states whose diversity has grown over the course of history, such as in India. All such societies must deal with processes of transformation that have led to further increases in social diversity. *Pluri*cultural conditions (not *multi*cultural, parallel societies), multilingualism and syncretism mark the tension between the heterogeneity that characterizes large state units (such as in India, and many countries in Africa, Latin America and Asia) and the homogeneity that is often expected of mostly smaller nation-states (such as in Europe). Heterogeneous states have increasingly come under pressure from different forms of fundamentalism to homogenize. Conversely, traditional nation-states are confronted by new challenges that are characterized by processes of heterogenization.

In this often conflict-filled process, largely monolingual and more or less monocultural living environments are becoming pluralized; the emergence of Europe from a range of different nation-states is one example. Recourse to historical experience plays an important role in such processes. In Europe, such experiences include the Habsburg monarchy and Central Europe as a region of great linguistic, confessional and cultural diversity. In India, they refer back to the tradition of syncretism in order to emphasize commonalities in religious and social practice(s). Other previously colonialized regions around the world, such as Africa, offer further points of reference.

In open *pluri*cultural worlds, we increasingly see something like a habitus of indifference towards the supposed relevance of visual differences: an 'indifference towards difference'.[22] The reason for this is that, to a certain extent, people are accustomed to difference in pluricultural situations, and there is no need for difference to be further emphasized or even theoretically safeguarded – even within the context of post-colonialism. By contrast, social practices make us aware of and underline similarities. Such considerations of similarity emphasize relations and networks between people/segments of society; they focus on the overall fabric of society.

Thinking about 'similarity' throws a critical light on theoretical and political preferences for the polarity between identity and difference, and questions concepts such as 'authenticity' and cultural purism. Instead, considerations of similarity place more emphasis on the tentative, the transitory, the unclear – on fluid borders, nuances, minimal deviations, *fuzziness* and vagueness – and define such terms using flexible and polyvalent language.

In the broadest sense, considerations of similarity thus declare scepticism towards the dichotomy between 'self' and 'other'. This dichotomy, hermeneutically favoured in Europe (and especially in Germany), focuses on generating dialogue between multiple, clearly separate entities or positions, in order to achieve something like 'higher' values, such as tolerance of the foreign. These separate entities are usually called 'cultures'. But the dialogue between 'self' and 'foreign' is a binary model that inappropriately simplifies the complexity of the real world – even if it is expanded with the idea of the polylogue to describe polycentric situations. The need for dialogue that such a model necessarily entails requires representatives who can speak on behalf of their respective constituencies. But when it comes to inter-cultural dialogue, representing an entire 'culture' (and speaking on its behalf) is highly problematic.

Considerations of similarity arise out of scepticism towards these dialogic models, which are based on the desire to understand the other: after all, the history of colonialism provides us with many examples of the devastating connection between understanding and oppression.[23] Similarity is thus not a concept of harmonization, but rather a moment of destabilization for supposedly stable, 'natural' dichotomous regimes.

'Pänidentität' or: what is 'similarity'?

The field of translation plays an important role in considerations of similarity, because the concept of partial correspondence and partial variation is well known in both the theory and practice of translation.[24] We know that there are no exact equivalents for many words in different languages. In a passage from his *Parerga and Paralipomena* that remains relevant today, Arthur Schopenhauer wrote: 'and so not all the concepts described by the words of one language are exactly the same as those expressed by the words of another; . . . but they are often concepts that are merely similar and cognate, yet different through some modification'.[25]

The editor of Schopenhauer's work explains that this '*Pänidentität*,' as Schopenhauer expressed it, means 'almost the same' ('*Fastgleichheit*') – which encompasses exactly what we are looking for with considerations of similarity.[26] The overlaps between fixed entities become more flexible and a certain porousness emerges on the boundaries between them; previously discrete domains become permeable. If we call these categories 'circles of similarity' (following Rudolf Carnap[27]) and consider them to be 'cultures' (in a colloquial sense), then we can state that these cultures are no longer 'monads' due to the many overlaps between them.

If one wishes to maintain the coherence and exclusivity of separate cultures, then one must prevent such overlaps. The *cantonments* in colonial India, the *homelands* of apartheid, the prohibitions against fraternization and the fear-laden denial of similarity in racism are examples of such attempts. As Bhimrao Ramji Ambedkar criticized as early as 1936, the brutal form of systematic exclusion of the dalits (the so-called 'untouchables') in the Hindu caste system is also based on a fundamental denial of the possibility of 'fluidity and equity' in social conditions and in social practice.[28]

The idea of similarity and a focus on overlaps can be applied to dissolve rigid dichotomies and cultural hierarchization. In doing so, however, it is not as much about considerations of the *in-between*, the *third space* or hybridity. These are concepts of conditions. Understood as cultural practice, the importance of similarity is that it marks social processes; it is a concept of movement that is conceived as a counter-movement to the dominant hermeneutic of the self and the other.

In addition to approaches from translation studies, the methodological perspective of a 'shared history', introduced to historical scholarship by Sanjay Subrahmanyam, is also important for work on 'similarity'. This perspective deals with concepts such as 'shared', 'connected', 'entangled history' and '*histoire croisée*'; with shared and common history (histories), and their entanglement with one another.[29]

The concept of similarity incorporates many ideas from this line of historical research, particularly its view of cross-border historical interconnections and overlaps. The perspective of a 'shared history' is, for instance, helpful in challenging certain essentializing lines of argumentation within discussions of colonialism. This game of essentializing thought tends to conceive of colonialism as a deformation, as a disruption of a so-called 'inherent' and 'authentic' historical path. Decolonialization, then, is understood as a 'liberation' from external, foreign forces. According to this reading, 'decolonization' thus involves reclamation of the 'pure', 'authentic', 'original roots' of one's 'own' tradition. Behind this view lies an understanding of language, nationality and state as separate, closed units that in many ways can be traced back to Johann Gottfried von Herder.[30]

If we instead deviate from this still dominant view and turn to considerations of historical interconnections, we can evaluate colonialization differently, and understand it as but one part in the contradictory overall development of global interconnections and entanglements. Complex cultural formations such as Europe or India emerge from processes of increasing interconnectedness that arise from this overall development. From this perspective, the economic, political and cultural reordering of the colonial and post-colonial era is seen as a process that leads to a universalist configuration of solidarity and empathy. It is no longer about the reclamation of authenticity. Rabindranath Tagore recognized such trends in India shortly after the First World War, and sought to combine India's liberation from ('external') colonial rule with an 'internal' liberation from the oppression of the caste system.[31] Anti-colonialism, anti-nationalism, cosmopolitanism, and the combination of national and universal history would be part of this double liberation, and it would be a 'project of universalism'.

Jürgen Osterhammel's works are a good example of such a position, which he compares with Christopher Alan Bayly's 2004 study on *The Birth of the Modern World*:

> Both books forgo a regional breakdown into nations, civilizations, or continents. Both regard colonialism and imperialism as a dimension so important that instead of dealing with it in a separate chapter, they keep it in view throughout. Both assume that there is no sharp distinction between what Bayly, in the subtitle of his book, calls 'global connections' and 'global comparisons'; these can and must be combined with each other, and not all comparisons need the protective backup of strict historical methodology. Controlled play with associations and analogies sometimes, though by no means always, yields more than comparisons overloaded with pedantry can do.[32]

The contradiction between concepts of similarity and models of difference made a decisive impact on the ideology of British colonialism. This ideology developed under the constant tension between the recognition of similarities and the assertion of difference. For colonialist ideology, religion and caste became the central categories of difference, which in India led to far-reaching policies of religious homogenization in the form of closed 'religious communities'.[33] Additionally, a politics of *separate electorates* was established, with representatives of each electorate acting as speakers and negotiation partners between religious communities and with the British colonial power. The result was a disastrous division of society between a majority (Hindus) and a minority (Muslims).

This division disrupted many lines of connection in social practice that had softened religious boundaries. For the anti-colonial movement, the essentialization of religious identity in the form of closed *communities* was a major cause of tensions between Hindus and Muslims. For this reason, many efforts to generate social peace within Indian politics have been based on concepts of similarities between these groups, and imply a refusal to accept clear, closed and, moreover, assigned identities.[34]

An instructive older document from the anti-colonial movement – one that remains sadly relevant today – emphasizes the element of proximity in religiously diverse societies that are slowly growing together.[35] The report of the Kanpur Riots Enquiry Committee was written following exceptionally bloody clashes between Hindus and Muslims in the industrial city of Kanpur in 1931 (sixteen years before India gained independence in 1947). The idealistic passion found in the report gives us an impression of the intensity with which the anti-colonial movement sought to generate a unity of action between Muslims and Hindus to counteract the colonial politics of '*divide et impera*'. The idea of a cultural amalgamation of Hindus and Muslims was clearly idealistic, but it was also legitimate for the committee to point out that Muslims and Hindus shared many areas of life within India.[36]

This desire to emphasize the common unifying elements in the practices of India's major religions is illustrated by something that Rabindranath Tagore wrote in his journal in 1932, while travelling through Persia and Iraq:

> All over Asia the cry has arisen that sectarian religion cannot be allowed to wreck the natural basis of community life, bringing dissensions where a common economic, social and historical background should preserve an inevitable continuity of cooperation. When during a farewell feast given to an Englishman of high official position in the Government of Palestine he said, 'Palestine is a Mohammedan country, and its government should therefore, be in the hands of the Mohammedans, on condition that the Jewish and Christian minorities are represented in it' – then Mufti-Haji-el-Husaini of Jerusalem answered, 'For us it is an exclusively Arab, not a Mohammedan question. During your sojourn in this country you have doubtless observed that here there are no distinctions between Mohammedan and Christian Arabs. We regard the Christians not as a minority, but as Arabs.'[37]

Maulana Abul Kalam Azad, one of the most important representatives of the anti-colonial movement, emphasized the significance of commonality and a shared heritage in his address to the Indian National Congress in 1940:

> If Hinduism has been the religion of the people here for several thousands of years, Islam also has been their religion for a thousand years.

> Just as a Hindu can say with pride that he is an Indian and follows Hinduism, so also we can say with equal pride that we are Indians and follow Islam. I shall enlarge this orbit still further. The Indian Christian is equally entitled to say with pride that he is an Indian and is following a religion of India, namely Christianity.
>
> Eleven hundred years of common history have enriched India with our common achievement. Our languages, our poetry, our literature, our culture, our art, our dress . . .[38]

Fundamentalism in India adopted the need for classification and segregation from colonialism; this is equally true for both *Hindutva* and various strains of Islamic fundamentalism. The philosopher Alam Khundmiri highlighted this problem for Muslims after India's independence particularly forcefully: 'Muslims are not one homogeneous cultural group in the entire country, if culture is not confused with religion. There are still strong grounds to believe that India comprises different cultural groups, the bases of which are not merely religion.'[39]

Criticism of Eurocentrism or: why 'similarity'?

Looking at similarities not only gives us a new perspective on the colonial history and structurally associated fundamentalism in a country like India, it also makes it possible to formulate a criticism of Eurocentrism and exceptionalism. As Samir Amin has pointed out, the biases of both Christians and Muslims during the crusades were neither Eurocentric nor Islamocentric, because neither religion had enough power to enforce its vision on a global scale.[40] Eurocentrism is a historical position that is closely associated with the development of capitalism, the expansion of colonial rule, and the evolution of a specific colonialist ideology centred on the uniqueness of Europe or the west.

Referencing his novel, *The Enchantress of Florence* (2008), Salman Rushdie once said in an interview:

> [T]here are ideas which grew up in the West, and in a slightly different form they grew up as well in the East; the idea of freedom, of open discourses, of tolerance, of sexual freedom even to the level of hedonism. . . . So to say that we must now consider them to be culturally specific . . . is a denial of human nature.[41]

Such perspectives are becoming ever more common in scholarly research. Where earlier researchers would draw borders, they now find parallels, see similarities and describe networks of relationships. A new style of argumentation has emerged.

In *The Theft of History*, anthropologist Jack Goody noted that the development of 'Bronze Age civilizations in Asia and Europe ran along roughly parallel lines. How then did many European writers assume quite a different development in the two continents from "Antiquity" onwards, leading eventually to the western "invention" of "capitalism"?'[42] He emphasized that it would be a mistake

> to look at the situation solely in terms of some relatively limited differences in the modes of production when there are so many similarities not only in the economy but in the modes of communication and in the modes of destruction including, eventually, the use of gunpowder. All these similarities, including ones in family structure and culture more generally, were set aside in favour of the 'oriental' hypothesis which stresses the different historical trajectories of east and west.[43]

Goody used similar arguments regarding the Renaissance: 'It is the Renaissance that lies at the centre of my concerns, and here I want to confine my attention to similar activities outside Europe, their comparative neglect and what that implies for European historiography.'[44] He was concerned with the global plurality of '*renaissances*', and wrote that '[f]rom a sociological standpoint renaissances were multiple and not confined to "capitalism" nor to the west. Europe was not alone, nor was it a cultural island.'[45]

If we consistently proceed comparatively and develop a global perspective, we arrive at an approach that calls into question the intellectual seizure of historical events. In addition to the Renaissance, this also applies to the Enlightenment. In one study, historian Sebastian Conrad criticized the position that follows from theories of diffusion – namely, that the Enlightenment was a European invention which was then disseminated to the rest of the world: 'Scholars are now challenging the Eurocentric account of the "birth of the modern world".'[46]

Europeans were not alone in contouring the Enlightenment; international authors from across the globe made contributions. 'Rather than a process of diffusion, the longer history of Enlightenment was the result of its constant reinvention' in different places around the world.[47] Needless to say, this criticism does not apply solely to Eurocentrism, but rather to any form of cultural seizure. Indocentric claims to exclusivity can also be rebutted by comparative studies so that universalistic moments emerge. The interest in parallels, analogies and similarities between philosophies in India and Europe means that 'these cease to be "oriental" or "western" thought and instead become "universal" thought'.[48]

India is no more an island than Europe is. In this respect, comparative research that points to the significant connections between Indian and Greek epics (for instance) is particularly relevant in an era when fundamentalist thought is based on the uniqueness of cultural products. Fernando Wulf Alonso, who wrote just such a large-scale comparative study about the epic in India and Greece, came to the following conclusion:

> Once again, it has been noted that in the past, as in the present, cultural and religious pluralism, from within and without, coupled with every imaginable type of cultural interactions, learning, and creations and reworking has prevailed in the Subcontinent, which, in turn, denotes the impossibility of defending exclusivist and unidirectional models or monotonic identities, either for understanding the moment in history or for proposing that falsification of reality as a model for the present. And it has been corroborated time and again how historical reality proves to be infinitely distant from attempts to reduce it to simple schemas, to the false dichotomy between the 'foreign' and the 'native' which only act to hinder our understanding of the beautiful diversity of the world, our appreciation of the wealth and potential tucked away within the folds of cultural exchanges and interactions which have conveyed, and must continue conveying the history that has made us human.[49]

Conclusion

In summary, it can be said that the theoretical and practical profiling of similarity illustrates the extent to which pluricultural societies depend on supporting social practices of handling complex diversity, rather than on the construction of closed cultures that are able to negotiate with one another through representatives. Research on similarity is about describing the proximate in processes of convergence and divergence; describing asymptotes instead of identities.

Naturally, all of this stands within the larger context of power and the asymmetrical exercise of power in contemporary global politics, because assertions of similarity defy the colonialist moment of domination that turns social differences into ontological differences through the development of colonial authority. It is at least tentatively conceivable that one could refrain from the act of interpretation that seeks to understand other cultures, and that one could tend to remain hermeneutically abstinent, as it were, in pluricultural contexts.

We adhere to the principle that it is more important to get along with one another than it is to understand one another. We can assume that many things are similar in this complex world, and content ourselves with letting indifference take its effect on difference. Thinking about similarity allows us to introduce an 'uncertainty relation' into our analysis. We observe large areas of overlapping more frequently in urban situations where multilingualism has become widespread, and less so in situations where several visible differences confound our ability to judge similarities and overlaps. In this respect, and as mentioned before, considerations of similarity are based on the comprehensive importance of translation as applied to social practice. This focus places the potentialities of transformation, of metamorphosis and of transposition at the centre of social practice. Discretion and civility become important parameters of social interaction, which also allows us to bring an ethical dimension to our everyday lives: we are not exactly the same, but we are also not totally different. In this sense, it is more about a perspective of 'similarity in diversity' than the familiar demand for 'unity in diversity' – ultimately, it is about 'similarity without sameness'.

Similarity could thus be understood as a universalist, humanist perspective to be used as a '*Suchbegriff*' ('search term').[50] This also implies a criticism of the concept of 'a right to difference' that has developed under capitalism. Nationalist and fundamentalist positions both maintain and essentialize this difference. In this way, Samir Amin's polemically shaped 'right to be similar' can be understood as a critical and subversive demand that distinguishing characteristics not become factors of division.[51]

This right to similarity and solidarity, understood in opposition to the absolutization of difference though homogenization, might also imply the demand for a democratic and pluricultural way of life. Considerations of similarity thus also have cultural–political consequences. By opening the door to syncretism, linguistic diversity, multilingualism, pluriculturalism and a social state of uncertainty, work on similarities contributes to the normalization and development of perspectives found outside of the dichotomy between identity and difference.

Thanks

We would like to sincerely thank all the institutions and people who have supported this project in a different ways. This goes for the financial help, organizational support and, above all, for the willingness to engage in discussions and debates that were multilingual, international and pluricultural. We are grateful to the Fritz Thyssen Foundation for the generous initial financing, which made it possible to organize the first two conferences. We would especially like to thank the Kulturwissenschaftliches Kolleg at the University of Konstanz, which contributed more than just funding by providing the framework for our respectivefellowships, thereby creating the intellectual and academic context for this kind of debate. We thank the Alexander von Humboldt Foundation for the Research Award for Anil Bhatti and the University of Tübingen, where he was able to do his research during his time as a Humboldt Award winner. Jochen Bedenk, Sven Sappelt, Nicole Falkenhayner and Christopher Möllmann provided critical organizational support for the conferences in Konstanz, and we owe them many thanks. Alexander Schmitz and Bernd Stieglerin Konstanz carefully and critically edited the original German volume. Britta Fietzke quickly and effectively provided the quite extensive translations, and we are very thankful for this help. But all of this would not have been possible without the efforts of Sara Bangert, who corrected, systematized, compiled, corresponded and generated bibliographies. She has earned our deep and heartfelt thanks.

Notes

1 Cf. Bhatti *et al.* (2011).

2 For example, see DFG Collaborative Research Center 541, 'Identities and Alterities: The Function of Alterity for the Constitution and the Construction of Identity' ('Identitäten und Alteritäten: Die Funktion von Alterität für die Konstitution und Konstruktion von Identität'), Freiburg, 1997–2003.

3 These considerations are not only relevant for questions of cultural theory within the context of transcultural topics, they are also relevant to gender studies, and thus to another area of politics and practice: theories that saw difference as their classificatory and conceptual basis have informed feminist theory. The gender debate that has taken place since the 1980s, and particularly fields like Queer Studies, have started to abandon this concept in favour of experiments with new approaches that are indeed akin to ideas of similarity. Still, no fundamental culture theory concepts exist yet; cf. Dumiche, Gutjahr and Liska, eds (2007).

4 Huntington (1996): 21.

5 Cf. Hall (2008); Zirfas and Jörissen (2007): 243–52. See also Lotman and Uspenskij (1984).

6 Cf. Koschorke (2009); Welsch (1999).

7 Bhatti (2007); Bhatti (2009); Bhatti *et al.* (2003); Bhatti (2010); Assmann and Assmann (1990): 26. See also Brumlik (2000); Ezli (2007); Goody (2010); Kimmich (2009); Kimmich (2010); Tezcan (2010).

8 Quine (2013): 7.

9 Ibid.: 6–7.

10 Goodman (1972): 445.

11 Ibid.

12 Decock and Douven (2011): 66.

13 See note 16. Cf. Zadeh (2005); Rehkämper (2005).

14 Lakoff (1987): 10.

15 Cf. Gamm (1994).

16 Researchers such as Eleanor Rosch have suggested different versions of the prototype theory. Moreover, they have developed a mathematical model based on spatial concepts – the so-called 'Voronoi tessellations' (see this volume's cover art): 'Prototype theory builds on the observation that among the instances of a property, some are more representative than others. The most representative one is the prototype of the property. A Voronoi tessellation of a given space divides that space into a number of cells such that each cell has a centre and consists of

all and only those points that lie no closer to the centre of any other cell than to its own center; the centers of the various cells are called the *generator points* of the tessellation. Given that, by way of mathematical fact, Voronoi tessellations divide spaces into *convex* regions, a Voronoi tessellation of a conceptual space that takes points representing prototypes as generator points carves up that space into natural properties' (Decock and Douven 2011: 71; emphases in original).

[17] Ibid.: 73.

[18] Ibid.

[19] Hahn, Chater and Richardson (2003): 1.

[20] Spaemann (2011): 57.

[21] Descola (2013): 3.

[22] Here we may recall Alan Badiou's evocative ideas on 'indifferent multiplicities', from *L'Être et l'Événement*. I only have the English translation, *Being and Event,* at my disposal. In it Badiou writes: 'If truths exist, they are certainly indifferent to differences' (Badiou 2006: xii). See also the section on Leibniz (ibid.: 315–26). With regard to Leibniz, I would also refer to Vincenzo De Risi's seminal study (De Risi 2007). The definition of similarity offered by Leibniz remains important for the backdrop of our discussion. In the words of Hermann Weyl: 'Leibniz had given the geometric notion of similarity this philosophical twist: Similar, he said, are two things which are indiscernible when each is considered by itself' (Weyl 1983: 127). See also De Risi (2007): 140.

[23] Cf. Todorov (1985).

[24] Cf. the contributions in Renn, Straub and Shimada, eds (2000); Italiano and Rössner, eds (2012). See, in particular, Langenohl (2014) and Wutsdorff (2014).

[25] Schopenhauer (1974): 567.

[26] In the original translation '*Pänidentität*' is translated as 'close identity'. Cf. ibid.; Schopenhauer (1965): 666.

[27] Carnap ([1928] 2003): 180, §111. He also uses the term 'part identical'; see ibid.: 182, §113.

[28] Cf. Ambedkar's controversy with Mahatma Gandhi, reprinted in Ambedkar (2014): 347.

[29] Cf. Subrahmanyam (1997); Bayly (1989); Conrad and Randeria (2002); and the inspiring internet forum www.kakanien.ac.at. Also Haupt and Kocka, eds (2009).

[30] Cf. Herder (1989): 287; Herder (2000); Bhatti (2014).

[31] Rabindranath Tagore (1998): 84.

[32] Osterhammel (2014): xvii.

[33] Metcalf (2008): 134. 'The centrality of religious community, along with that of caste, for the British marked out India's distinctive status as a fundamentally different land.'

[34] For example, cf. Maulana Abul Kalam Azad, mentioned below (see note 38).

[35] Cf. Das and Indian National Congress ([1931] 2005): 76.

[36] Cf. ibid.: 156.

[37] Tagore (2003): 32.

[38] Azad (1991): 23ff. Also: '[O]ur manners and customs, the innumerable happenings of our daily life, everything bears the stamp of our joint endeavour. There is indeed no aspect of our life which has escaped this stamp. Our languages were different, but we grew to use a common language; our manners and customs were dissimilar, but they acted and reacted on each other, and thus produced a new synthesis. Our old dress may be seen only in ancient pictures of bygone days; no one wears it today. . . . This joint wealth is the heritage of our common

nationality, and we do not want to leave it and go back to the times when this joint life had not begun.'

[39] '[T]he distinct cultural identity of Muslims has a restricted meaning so as their distinct religious notions and ethical norms are concerned and beyond that, any mention of a distinct Muslim identity is a myth. The future of Muslims is tied up with the growth of the idea of secularism and the rise of institutions based on this idea.' Also, Ansari, ed. (2001): 280f.

[40] Cf. Amin (2008): 103.

[41] See the book review: Oates (2008).

[42] Goody (2006): 3.

[43] Ibid.: 60: 'At the broadest level, ethnocentricism divides all of us from the others and so helps to define our identity. But it is a bad guide to history, especially to world history.'

[44] Goody (2010): 42.

[45] Ibid.: 274.

[46] Conrad (2012): 1001. 'Such a rereading implies three analytical moves: First, the eighteenth-century cultural dynamics conventionally rendered as "Enlightenment" cannot be understood as the sovereign and autonomous accomplishment of European intellectuals alone; it had many authors in many places. Second, Enlightenment ideas need to be understood as a response to cross-border interaction and global integration. Beyond the conventional Europe-bound notions of the progress of "reason", engaging with Enlightenment has always been a way to think comparatively and globally. And third, the Enlightenment did not end with romanticism: it continued throughout the nineteenth century and beyond. Crucially, this was not merely a history of diffusion; the Enlightenment's global impact was not energized solely by the ideas of the Parisian philosophers. Rather, it was the work of historical actors around the world.'

[47] Ibid.: 1022.

[48] Dragonetti and Tola (2013): 293. See also the research of Harjeet Singh Gill (2007), Theodore Stcherbatsky (1996) and Uma Chattopadhyay (2012). Further inspiration may be found in the articles in Gaier, Kohl and Saviello, eds (2012).

[49] Alonso (2014): 480f. This perspective would, of course, require rigorously stopping the use of the category of 'influence'.

[50] Negt and Kluge (2001): 299. 'So that if one now varies the concept of "substance," then its antithesis becomes either the concept sought after, or the question.'

[51] Cf. Amin (1999): 42.

References

Alonso, Fernando Wulff (2014), *The Mahabharata and Greek Mythology*, translated by Andrew Morrow, New Delhi: Yoga Publications Trust.

Ambedkar, Bhimrao Ramji (2014), *Annihilation of Caste: The Annotated Critical Edition*, edited and with commentary by S. Anand, introduced by Arundhati Roy's essay, 'The Doctor and the Saint', New Delhi: Navayana and London: Verso, 2014.

Amin, Samir (1999), *Spectres of Capitalism: A Critique of Current Intellectual Fashions*, New York: Monthly Review Press.

——— (2008), *Eurocentrism*, translated by Russell Moore, Delhi: Aakar Books; first edition, New York: Monthly Review Press, 1988.

Ansari, M.T., ed. (2001), *Secularism, Islam and Modernity: Selected Essays of Alam Khundmiri*, New Delhi: Sage.

Assmann, Aleida and Jan Assmann (1990), 'Kultur und Konflikt: Aspekte einer Theorie des unkommunikativen Handelns', in Jan Assmann and Dietrich Harth, eds, *Kultur und Konflikt*, Frankfurt am Main: Suhrkamp: 11–48.

Azad, Maulana Abul Kalam (1991), *The Selected Works of Maulana Abul Kalam Azad*, Vol. 1, edited by Ravinder Kumar, New Delhi: Atlantic.

Badiou, Alain (2006), *Being and Event* (*L'Être et l'Événement*), translated by Oliver Feltham, London: Bloomsbury.

Bayly, Christopher Alan (1989), *Imperial Meridian: The British Empire and the World 1780–1830*, London and New York: Routledge.

Bhatti, Anil (2007), '". . . zwischen zwei Welten schwebend . . ." Zu Goethes Fremdheitsexperiment im "West-östlichen Divan"', in Hans-Jörg Knobloch and Helmut Koopmann, eds, *Goethe: Neue Ansichten*, Würzburg: Koenigshausen and Neumann: 103–21.

——— (2009), 'Der Orient als Experimentierfeld: Goethes "Divan" und der Aneignungsprozess kolonialen Wissens', *Goethe-Jahrbuch 2009*, Göttingen: Wallstein: 115–28.

——— (2010), 'Heterogenität, Homogenität, Ähnlichkeit', in Andrea Allerkamp and Gérard Raulet, eds, *Kulturwissenschaften in Europa: eine grenzüberschreitende Disziplin?*, Münster: Westfälisches Dampfboot: 250–56.

——— (2014), 'Heterogeneities and Homogeneities: On Similarities and Diversities', in Johannes Feichtinger and Gary B. Cohen, eds, *Understanding Multi-culturalism and the Habsburg Central European Experience*, New York and Oxford: Berghahn: 17–47.

Bhatti, Anil *et al.* (2003), 'Kulturelle Vielfalt und Homogenisierung', in Johannes Feichtinger, ed., *Habsburg Postcolonial: Machtstrukturen und kollektives Gedächtnis*, Innsbruck: Studien Verlag: 55–68.

——— (2011), 'Ähnlichkeit: Ein kulturtheoretisches Paradigma', *Internationales Archiv für Sozialgeschichte der deutschen Literatur*, 36 (1): 261–75.

Brumlik, Micha (2000), '"Alle Kultur ist ein Bastard – und parasitär": In welchem Verhältnis stehen Mensch, Kultur, Gewalt und Konflikt zueinander?', in Andreas Kämpf, Birgit Meding and Norbert Sievers, eds, *Shortcut Europe: Kultur und Konflikt: Culture and Conflict*, Bonn: Fonds Soziokultur: 25–35.

Carnap, Rudolf ([1928] 2003), *The Logical Structure of the World and Pseudoproblems in Philosophy*, Chicago and La Salle: Open Court.

Chattopadhyay, Uma (2012), *Dishonoured by Philosophers: Upamana in Indian Epistemology*, New Delhi: D.K. Printworld.

Conrad, Sebastian (2012), 'Enlightenment in Global History: A Historiographical Critique', *American Historical Review*, 117 (4): 999–1027.

Conrad, Sebastian and Shalini Randeria (2002), 'Geteilte Geschichten: Europa in einer postkolonialen Welt', in Sebastian Conrad and Shalini Randeria, eds, *Jenseits des Eurozentrismus: Postkoloniale Perspektiven in den Geschichts und Kulturwissenschaften*, Frankfurt am Main and New York: Campus Verlag: 9–49.

Das, Bhagavan and Indian National Congress ([1931] 2005), *The Communal Problem: Report of the Committee appointed by the Indian National Congress (Karachi Session, 1931) to enquire into the Kanpur Riots of March 1931*, New Delhi: National Book Trust.

De Risi, Vincenzo (2007), *Geometry and Monadology: Leibniz's Analysis Situs and Philosophy of Space*, Basel, Boston and Berlin: Birkhäuser.

Decock, Lieven and Igor Douven (2011), 'Similarity after Goodman', *Review of Philosophy and Psychology*, 2 (1), Springer Verlag: 61–75.

Descola, Philippe (2013), *Beyond Nature and Culture*, translated by Janet Lloyd, Chicago: University of Chicago Press.

Dragonetti, Carmen and Fernando Tola (2013), *Indian and Western Philosophies: Unity in Diversity*, New Delhi: Motilal Banarsidass; previously published as *On the Myth of the Opposition between Indian Thought and Western Philosophy*, Hildesheim: Olms, 2004.

Dumiche, Béatrice, Ortrud Gutjahr and Vivian Liska, eds (2007), *Geschlechterdifferenzen als Kulturkonflikte*, Bern: Lang.

Ezli, Özkan (2007), 'Von der Identität zur Individuation: "Gegen die Wand" – eine Problematisierung kultureller Identitätszuschreibungen', in Levent Tezcan and Monika Wohlrab-Sahr, eds, *Konfliktfeld Islam in Europa*, Baden-Baden: Nomos: 283–304.

Gaier, Martin, Jeanette Kohl and Alberto Saviello, eds (2012), *Similitudo: Konzepte der Ähnlichkeit in Mittelalter und Früher Neuzeit*, München: Fink.

Gamm, Gerhard (1994), *Flucht aus der Kategorie: Die Positivierung des Unbestimmten als Ausgang aus der Moderne*, Frankfurt am Main: Suhrkamp.

Gill, Harjeet Singh (2007), *Conceptualism in Buddhist and French Traditions*, Patiala: Publication Bureau, Punjabi University.

Goodman, Nelson (1972), 'Seven Strictures on Similarity', in *Problems and Projects*, Indianapolis and New York: Bobbs Merrill: 437–46.

Goody, Jack (2006), *The Theft of History*, Cambridge: Cambridge University Press.

——— (2010), *Renaissances: The One or the Many?*, Cambridge: Cambridge University Press.

Hahn, Ulrike, Nick Chater and Lucy B. Richardson (2003), 'Similarity as Transformation', *Cognition*, 87 (1): 1–32.

Hall, Stuart (2008), *Rassismus und kulturelle Identität: Ausgewählte Schriften*, Vol. 2, edited by Ulrich Mehlem, Hamburg: Argument-Verlag.

Haupt, Heinz-Gerhard and Jürgen Kocka, eds (2009), *Comparative and Transnational History: Central European Approaches and New Perspectives*, New York and Oxford: Berghahn.

Herder, Johann Gottfried von (1989), *Ideen zur Philosophie der Geschichte der Menschheit*, Frankfurt am Main: Deutscher Klassiker Verlag.

——— (2000), 'Bekehrung der Juden', in *Adrastea*, edited by Günter Arnold, Frankfurt am Main: Deutscher Klassiker Verlag.

Huntington, Samuel P. (1996), *The Clash of Civilizations and the Remaking of World Order*, New York: Simon and Schuster.

Italiano, Federico and Michael Rössner, eds (2012), *Translation, Narration, Media and the Staging of Differences*, Bielefeld.

Kimmich, Dorothee (2009), 'Öde Landschaften und die Nomaden in der eigenen Sprache: Bemerkungen zu Franz Kafka, Feridun Zaimoglu und der Weltliteratur als "littérature mineure"', in Özkan Ezli, Dorothee Kimmich and Annette Werberger, eds, *Wider den Kulturenzwang: Migration, Kulturalisierung und Weltliteratur*, Bielefeld: 297–316.

——— (2010), 'Migration und Literatur: Literatur als Kulturkritik', in Andrea Allerkamp and Gérard Raulet, eds, *Kulturwissenschaften in Europa: eine grenzüberschreitende Disziplin?*, Münster: Westfälisches Dampfboot: 234–49.

Koschorke, Albrecht (2009), 'Wie werden aus Spannungen Differenzen? Feldtheoretische Überlegungen zur Konfliktsemantik', in Heinz Fassmann, Wolfgang Müller-Funk and Heidemarie Uhl, eds, *Kulturen der Differenz – Transformationsprozesse in Zentraleuropa nach 1989: Transdisziplinäre Perspektiven*, Göttingen: V&R Unipress: 271–86.

Lakoff, George (1987), *Women, Fire and Dangerous Things: What Categories Reveal About the Mind*, Chicago: University of Chicago Press.

Langenohl, Andreas (2014), 'Scenes of Encounter: A Transnational Approach to Travelling Concepts in the Study of Culture', in Doris Bachmann-Medick and Ansgar Nünning, eds, *The Trans/National Study of Culture*, Amsterdam: De Gruyter.

Lotman, Jurij and Boris Uspenskij (1984), 'The Role of Dualistic Models in the Dynamics of Russian Culture', in *The Semiotics of Russian Culture*, Ann Arbor: Department of Slavic Languages and Literatures University of Michigan.

Metcalf, Thomas R. (2008), *Ideologies of the Raj*, Cambridge: Cambridge University Press.

Negt, Oskar and Alexander Kluge (2001), *Der unterschätzte Mensch: Gemeinsame Philosophie in zwei Bänden*, Vol. 1, Frankfurt am Main: Zweitausendeins Verlag.

Oates, Joyce Carol (2008), 'In the Emperor's Dream House: *The Enchantress of Florence* by Salman Rushdie', *The New York Review of Books*, 55 (10), 12 June.

Osterhammel, Jürgen (2014), *The Transformation of the World: A Global History of the Nineteenth Century*, Princeton, NJ: Princeton University Press.

Quine, Willard van Orman ([1969] 2013), 'Natural Kinds', in Nicholas Rescher, ed., *Essays in Honour of Carl G. Hempel: A Tribute on the Occasion of His Sixty-Fifth Birthday*, Dordrecht: Springer.

Rehkämper, Klaus (2005), 'Ist der Begriff der bildhaften Ähnlichkeit wirklich undefinierbar?', in Klaus Sachs-Hombach, ed., *Bildwissenschaft zwischen Reflexion und Anwendung*, Köln: Halem: 242–50.

Renn, Joachim, Jürgen Straub and Shingo Shimada, eds (2000), *Übersetzung als Medium des Kulturverstehens und sozialer Integration*, Frankfurt am Main: Campus Verlag.

Schopenhauer, Arthur (1965), 'Parerga and Paralipomena', in *Sämtliche Werke*, Vol. 5, edited by Wolfgang Freiherr von Löhneysen, Stuttgart and Frankfurt am Main: Cotta/Insel.

——— (1974), 'On Language and Words', in *Parerga and Paralipomena: Short Philosophical Essays*, Vol. 2, Oxford: Oxford University Press.

Spaemann, Robert (2011), 'Ähnlichkeit', in *Schritte* über *uns hinaus: Gesammelte Reden und Aufsätze*, Vol. 2, Stuttgart: Klett-Cotta.

Stcherbatsky, Theodore (1996), *Buddhist Logic*, Vols 1 and 2, New Delhi: Munshiram Manoharlal.

Subrahmanyam, Sanjay (1997), 'Connected Histories: Notes towards a Reconfiguration of Early Modern Eurasia', *Modern Asian Studies*, 31 (3).

Tagore, Rabindranath (1998), 'Nationalism in India', in Fred Dallmayr and G.N. Devy, eds, *Between Tradition and Modernity: India's Search for Identity: A Twentieth Century Anthology*, New Delhi: Altamira: 77–90.

——— (2003), *Journey to Persia and Iraq: 1932 (Tagore Travelogues)*, translated from Bengali by Surendranath Tagore and Sukhendu Ray, Santiniketan: Visva-Bharati.

Tezcan, Levent (2010), 'Der Tod der Kultur: Wie Fatih Akin den großen Kulturdialog umgeht', in Ökzan Ezli, ed., *Kultur als Ereignis. Fatih Akins Film 'Auf der anderen Seite' als transkulturelle Narration*, Bielefeld, transcript: 47–70.

Todorov, Tzvetan (1985), *The Conquest of America: The Question of the Other*, Norman, Oklahoma: University of Oklahoma Press.

Welsch, Wolfgang (1999), 'Transculturality: The Puzzling Form of Cultures Today', in Mike Featherstone and Scott Lash, eds, *Spaces of Culture: City, Nation, World*, London and New Delhi: Sage: 194–213.

Weyl, Hermann (1983), *Symmetry*, Princeton, NJ: Princeton University Press.

Wutsdorff, Irina (2014), 'Übersetzungskritik: Sprachkritik. Zum Fall Fritz Mauthner im böhmischen Kontext', *Zeitschrift fürinterkulturelle Germanistik*, 5 (2), special issue: 'Übersetzen: Praktiken kulturellen Transfers am Beispiel Prags', edited by Irina Wutsdorff and Štěpán Zbytovský, Bielefeld, transcript: 39–56.

Zadeh, Lotfi A. (2005), 'Toward a Generalized Theory of Uncertainty (GTU): an outline', *Information Sciences*, Vol. 172: 1–40.

Zirfas, Jörg and Benjamin Jörissen (2007), *Phänomenologien der Identität. Human-, sozial- und kulturwissenschaftliche Analysen*, Wiesbaden: VS Verlag für Sozialwissenschaften.

THEORY

Similarity

Valences of a post-colonial concept

Albrecht Koschorke

I

In many respects, the cultural studies discourse of the past few decades has represented a reaction to fundamental geopolitical shifts. The decolonization that took place after the Second World War was accompanied by a loss of significance for the cultural and ideological leadership of Europe, and then of the west as a whole. It became increasingly implausible to view Christianity, the racist superiority of whites, occidental rationality, or even western achievements such as the Enlightenment and democracy, as the pinnacle of human history (in the sense of the teleological world-historical systems of the nineteenth century). Instead of such models of development, all of which either implicitly or explicitly imposed hegemonic claims, the search began for alternative concepts that respected the worldwide diversity of social systems and developmental paths. The cultural sciences have reacted to the relativization of western universalism by seeking to break up historical hierarchies and encourage encounters between representatives of different cultures under the guise of the experience of *alterity*. But the postcolonial emphasis on alterity is also ironically caught up in colonial ways of thinking. The high regard for heterogeneity, difference and hybridity is plagued by the decisive weakness that it only seeks to invert the importance of powerful dichotomies, while leaving the dichotomous pattern as such untouched. Even the terminological construction of 'post-colonialism' involves a negative reference to the influences of the previous era, thus signalling a stubborn reliance on colonial ways of thinking. This is also reflected in strategies of *alterization*: according to postcolonial thought, in order to appropriately recognize the other in all of her/his otherness, she/he must first be declared to be an other; she/he must to a certain extent be *made different*. Within this framework, even acceptance and understanding are based on an implicit premise of inequality that must first be overcome with significant cultural effort. As a result, postcolonial discourse has tended to *dramatize* the experience of being other – for instance, regarding the diction of subalterns or minorities who seek to establish themselves with their own voices or with respect to the position of mainstream society, in order to acknowledge its own rights in the light of conflicting demands. To a certain extent, this desire to recognize the other always comes too late, because it has already drawn boundaries that must then be overcome.

In contrast, 'similarity' as it is understood here represents a *category of de-dramatization*. On the one hand, similarity distances itself from a programme of assimilation which declares a set developmental norm for universal applicability. On the other, it counters the dramatic emphasis on (ethno-national, religious, cultural, gender) differences, which ultimately lead to an ever-more specific and sensitive *identity politics*, thus substantially weakening the forces of change. In truth, the awareness of similarity floats in a transitional zone between the self and the other, the own and the foreign, thus avoiding the postcolonial and poststructuralist paradoxes popular in cultural studies.[1] 'Similarity' means that something is *somehow* equal and *somehow* different; the concept thus replaces sharp borders and border contradictions with *vagueness*. Admittedly, this also makes the concept harder to work with.

'Similarity' is a vague category also in another respect. In contrast to identity and contradiction, both of which demand rigorous attempts to clearly define an object (and thus require relatively stringent consistency checks), 'similarity' is better suited to a *hermeneutic of the provisional*. When two things are judged to be 'similar', it is not necessary to know and consider everything about the objects; indeed, even important properties can be ignored, because it is not about an exact relation but rather a mixed relationship between congruence and non-congruence within a relatively wide bandwidth of properties. To put it another way: 'similarity' requires *less diacritical energy* than the determination of identity or outright otherness – especially given that the mode of using (primarily) pre-conceptual and approximate background assumptions requires fewer intellectual resources than a recognition of the otherness of the other.[2] The impression of similarity always has something of a 'leave-it-at-that'. The similar is thus often associated with the modal determination of 'kind of', while sameness is either ascertainable or not, without there being any wider margin of discretion here.

This 'hermeneutic convenience' can also be seen positively, and this goes for 'similarity' as an emphatically *civic category*. If I think about the identity of another person, I have to know a lot about them (or think that I know a lot about them) and have to attempt to deeply analyse them. On the other hand, if I articulate the impression that another person is similar to me, this normally implies a certain ignorance; I satisfy myself with what I can see and know, and am not interested in the rest. In contrast to identity, 'similarity' can thus tolerate a certain lack of transparency, and is an adequate mode of perception where people only *partially* encounter one another, find themselves in fluid relationships, networks and forms of *partial inclusion*. It denotes a mode of interpersonal relations under the auspices of undemanding *incomplete information*. This is why the suggestion of similarity fits with a high degree of inattention and anonymity. It civilizes in instances where diversity is perceptible but should not be placed in the spotlight: in situations of multiethnic coexistence, in urban and global-societal contexts.[3]

Using Niklas Luhmann's distinction, we might be able to assign to 'similarity' the role of a *medium*, a 'soft' matrix in which the 'hard' *forms* of identity and difference make their impact under certain circumstances, and at a higher level of social and mental differentiating energy. In order to judge or deny one's own concrete identity – or the concrete identity of another – an act of comparison must first take place; and such comparison takes place within a pre-rational and incompletely explicated *mimetic global context*.[4] To use the vocabulary of action theory: all rigid, socio-cultural distinctions are based on at least a minimum of cultural contact, on cross-border traffic and exchanges between both sides. This implies that even competitors have communicative contact with one another, and join weak, often informal forms of cooperation. From a purely technical perspective, they experience one another as similarly disposed actors. The point at which this social cooperation between social groups breaks apart and shifts towards distinction and even essential incompatibility, towards limiting what can be exchanged (for instance, basic goods and services) and towards taboos that block social exchange (for instance, regarding intermarriages), depends on the respective amount of pressure for distinction or the level of antagonism. In extreme situations, the opponents might even be denied the quality of humanity; they are denied even the most elemental form of similarity.

II

The socio-cultural evolutionary and modernization theories of the nineteenth and twentieth centuries almost universally assigned the property of similarity to a 'place on the other side' – to the 'savages', either from earlier eras or as a residue of pre-modernity. One prominent example is the periodization found in Foucault's *The Order of Things*, according to which 'resemblance played a constructive role in the knowledge of Western culture' until the end of the sixteenth century.[5] At the dawn of modernity, however, 'the cruel reason of identities and differences' prevailed, and relegated similarity to the lower sphere of irrationality, delusions and confusion.[6]

Without meaning to, Foucault here assumed a colonial figure of thought from around 1900. James G. Frazer, who collected and systematized anthropological knowledge of the time, ascribed the phenomenon of magic to the laws of association of ideas, and specifically to two particular, fundamental rules of combination: similarity and contact. According to this view, magical practices are based on the confusion between an association of ideas and factual causal relationships. In the case of the *law of similarity*, the primitive's error arises from the belief 'that things which resemble each other are the same', or 'that like produces like, or, in other words: that an effect resembles its cause'.[7] Still, Frazer made sure to note that civilized rationality is not immune to a reversion back to such delusional relational systems: 'We seem to move on a thin crust which may at any moment be rent by the subterranean forces slumbering below.'[8]

The notion that 'they' can be misled by the conceptual bridge of similarity to believe in magical practices, while 'we' have learned to see things objectively and scientifically, is also perpetuated in situations where its significance has been inverted. One example of this can be found in the work of Lévi-Bruhl: even though he classified the pre-logical, participatory thinking of primitive people as a condition of ignorance, he also mourned the loss of the 'intimate and entire possession' of things that such thought made possible.[9] Such thinking is not far from Walter Benjamin's theory of the mimetic capacities that have been 'lost' in modern man, or that at least live on as 'nothing but a weak rudiment of the formerly powerful compulsion to become similar and also to behave mimetically'[10] – and which have been preserved in language as a great repository of 'earlier powers of mimetic production and comprehension'.[11]

For all of the authors mentioned here, the concept of similarity was used in the service of an ultimately *asymmetrical modern narrative* – whether optimistically as progress from a lower and overcome level of rationality, or nostalgically as a lost capacity to participate in things. Only the field of art has been able to offer a sort of reservation for the similar, both practically and theoretically.[12] Indeed, in the era of colonialism, Europe showed itself to be receptive (particularly in the area of aesthetics) to ways of thinking and forms of presentation from non-European countries. As a result, art (in the broadest sense) was unburdened by the norms of western rationalism and became the only really open channel for *reciprocal* cultural exchange.

The legacy of colonialism can only really be overcome if – to use an expression from Bruno Latour – we advance to a *symmetric anthropology* that handles truth and error, western and non-western, and modern and non-modern thought with the same language and the same categories.[13] Consequently, we must look for approaches that allow for the reconstitution of the history of occidental philosophy (concept of epistemology, ideas of causality) and art history (mimesis) as something other than an 'overcoming of similarity', which almost inevitably contains Eurocentric traits. One contribution might be found in evidence that the symbolic world in modern societies creates a communicative web of weak connections between things that are assumed to be similar, and that precisely because of their low definitional firmness, such connections retain a high degree of plasticity. Principal representatives of such a perspective in modernity include Fritz Mauthner and Ludwig Wittgenstein.[14]

III

A central characteristic of theories of modernization which themselves have inherited Enlightenment ideas of the progress of history is that they postulate a synchronism between technical-industrial, social and cultural developmental logics.[15] The confidence of the post-war period that economic modernization would (sooner or later) lead to a socio-structural and political shift towards western models, such that all developed countries would culturally converge into a secular, enlightened, democratic and individualist modernity, has not materialized. In reality, processes of modernization have shown themselves to be paradoxical because they have proceeded at different speeds in different sectors, and have often even generated counter-tendencies to the accepted principal direction of history.[16] Technical innovations have proceeded more rapidly than social institutions or cultural habits which are anchored deeply in the socialization of people. This has resulted in processes of modernization (if we can even call them that) *on the ground* composed of a tangle of external adoptions, everyday practical appropriations, creative transformations, sluggish resistances and contrary reaction formations – and all of this in a state of perpetual tension between global and local considerations, between standardization and decentralized 'network densification',[17] between globalized conformity and a refocus on local traditions that are considered autochthonous.

It is also possible, however, that criticism of the Eurocentric character of modernity, and the development of concepts such as *multiple modernities* or postmodern diversity, have led the unifying power and technological achievements of modernity to be underestimated. As much as local cultural characteristics have asserted themselves or have even formed under the pressure of overpowering external influences, it is also an unmistakable fact that the general living conditions of people across the globe are converging. Indigenous ways of life that have somehow survived colonialism are condemned to extinction. Mobilization, urbanization, the global interdependence of markets and capital flows, the emergence of a global work force, the distribution of cheap weapons, and the advancement of new information technologies have led to processes of massive social differentiation, on the one hand, but on the other, have also led to a significant reduction in the diversity of human ways of life. In comparison, the emphasis of cultural idiosyncrasies often seems to do nothing but satisfy a compensatory need. From a functionalistic perspective, this 'reflexive strengthening of cultural origins' is a result of the fact that the increasing complexity of a highly interdependent global society 'is no longer capable of being centrally regulated', and thus allows the 'need for sectoral as well as regional and local self-organization' to grow.[18]

The concept of similarity could also fulfil an important heuristic function in the light of this extremely non-uniform situation. It circumvents the exoticization of more distant and rural-local cultures, for which only meagre illustrative material can be found in late modernity, and whose last bastion seems to be folklore and tourism. At the same time, 'similarity' as it is understood here can neither be used in the service of an ideology of assimilation nor in models of normative modernity. Once again, the use of similarity would take on a mediating, plasticizing function. It would do justice to global adaptations without aligning such developments with a specific developmental goal. At the other end of the spectrum, similarity would also serve to weaken pushes towards particularity and otherness, and maintain the prospect of finding a common social basis upon which the inhabitants of global modernity move.

IV

Still, the picture drawn here may be somewhat optimistic. First, it is by no means the case that the use of a certain concept penetrates to the mode of social confrontations; just linguistically re-labelling conflicts does not necessarily change them. More concretely, evidence can be found that the fluid medium of mimetic influences and adaptations in which concrete social forms arise and dissipate does not necessarily have a civilizing effect. In certain cases, the recognition of similarity does not represent a milder, friendlier alternative to conflict-laced patterns of identity; on the contrary, it may constitute the conditions for an escalation of conflict. The fact is that something like mimetic exchange also takes place between enemies: under certain conditions, opponents can enter into a *hostile symbiosis* that is based on similarities that existed before the conflict, and which aligns both parties even more with one another as the struggle between them becomes more bitter. Such cases call for a more in-depth consideration of the role of mimetic desire, which represents a centre of energy in René Girard's culture and conflict theory.[19] But this is not the place for that. Even a less speculative approach than Girard's theory reveals a close connection between mimesis and violence. This can be seen both in microsociological studies of violent situations that indicate the degree to which violent actors time and synchronize their actions to one another,[20] as well as in the semantics of global politics. An analysis of the latter illustrates the way in which even enemies require a common language so that each of them can enter into a form of double-sided monologue that confirms and nourishes the reciprocal image of the enemy.

An especially striking example of this can be found in the immediate political situation involving the war between the United States of America (USA) and Islamist terror groups, and in a broader sense, between 'the west' and 'Islam'.[21] Both sides of the conflict fall back on apocalyptic end-time scenarios shared by the Abrahamic religions – they reciprocally attribute the role of Satan to the other.[22] A study on *Master Narratives of Islamist Extremism* (partially financed by the Pentagon) lists thirteen narrative patterns used by militant Islamists in propaganda videos and public statements.[23] One of the most effective is the story of the Pharaoh, which can be summarized as a story in which 'the arrogant tyrant rejects the Word of God revealed by His prophet, the tyrant is punished, and his body is preserved as a divine warning for future nations to submit to God's Will'.[24] The story is obviously taken from the Book of Exodus, which not only represents *the* centrepiece of Jewish belief and collective thought, but is also the basis of the founding myth of the USA. In other words, the hate towards the USA spread in Islamic countries, their allies and the dictators that have held power for so long derives its eloquence from the exact same mythological sources as the imperial mission of the USA, which sees itself as the land of freedom. The problem here is that there is *too much* underlying agreement between the parties: the opponents are *not different enough* from one another to be able to break out of the mimetic spiral of violent symbolism. In such cases, the communicative *flow* that is generated by similarity is a part of the problem, not the solution. Such similarity does not serve as a medium of civil half-distance, but rather as fertile ground for an escalation of conflict that is not limited to the field of symbolic action.

V

The examples discussed here can be seen as a warning sign – as an urgent recommendation to remember that it is risky to call for the reawakening of a mimetic capacity that has supposedly been lost by modern man. When it comes to updating the concept of similarity, the examples provided above may help with conceptual specification. As a form of thought in a post-postcolonial civil society that does not consider itself to be an arena for conflicting, generally secessionist and political-identity demands, similarity is only appropriate if it cuts its ties with mimetic suggestibility. As strange as it might sound, similarity requires the addition of cosmopolitan detachment in order to cognitively organize the interdependent juxtaposition of global neighbours as 'indifference to difference' (Anil Bhatti). To the extent that it describes weakly defined social relationships based on its hermeneutic vagueness, similarity points towards a world beyond binding, holistic-corporate wholeness – beyond the centralized disposition of modern nation-states and their enclosed territories in which (in contrast to pre-industrial agrarian societies) cultural homogeneity became a demand.[25] The concept of similarity could thus have heuristic potential in any context where the unifying pressure of centrally focused social control mechanisms does not apply, where interdependence and foreignness combine in multifaceted and volatile mixtures, and where the intersection of global deterritorializing and local territorializing dynamics generates a new culture of artefacts.[26] In other words, the preferred area of application for similarity lies in the peripheral zones of contemporary national order – a periphery, however, that is making advances into the centre of this order.

Notes

1 The Constance graduate programme – 'The Figure of the Third' (2003–09) – had a similar thematic thrust. Cf. Koschorke (2010).

2 The writings of Lévinas provide insight into the incredible effort the latter process can take.

3 This is one of Anil Bhatti's primary research interests, and the research and ideas presented in this volume can largely be traced back to his ideas. Two of his publications in particular must be mentioned here: Bhatti *et al.* (2007) and Bhatti (2009).

4 On the concept of mimesis: McKeon (1936–37); Gebauer and Wulf (2003). Unfortunately, the relevant passage in *Ästhetischen Grundbegriffe* is unsuitable.

5 Foucault (2002): 19.

6 Ibid.: 54.

7 Frazer (1911): 54, 174.

8 Ibid.: 236.

9 Lévy-Bruhl (1986): 383f.

10 Benjamin (1979): 69.

11 Benjamin (2005): 722.

12 Cf. Funk, Mattenklott and Pauen, eds (2001).

13 Cf. Latour (1993): 92ff.

14 Multiple references on this can be found in Bhatti *et al.* (2011).

[15] Cf. the concise overview in Mergel (2012).
[16] Loo and Reijen (1997).
[17] Cf. the instructive essay by Lübbe (1996).
[18] Ibid.: 137, 145f.
[19] Cf. Girard (1979).
[20] According to Collins (2011: 26): '[H]umans have evolved to have particularly high sensitivities to the micro-interactional signals given off by other humans. Humans are hard-wired to get caught in a mutual focus of intersubjective attention, and to resonate emotions from one body to another in common rhythms.' This being attuned to one another can even be seen in the 'asymmetrical entrainment' between perpetrators and victims (ibid.: 102ff).
[21] Cf. Koschorke (2005).
[22] For more on the mobilizing effects of apocalyptic narratives in the USA and other western countries, cf. Smith (2005).
[23] Halverson, Goodall Jr. and Corman (2011).
[24] Ibid.: 7.
[25] Cf. Gellner (1983).
[26] The recent anthropological concept of *assemblage* has heavily influenced the latter of these (Collier and Ong 2005: 4): 'As global forms are articulated in specific situations – or territorialized in *assemblages* – they define new material, collective, and discursive relationships.'

References

Benjamin, Walter (1979), 'Doctrine of the Similar', *New German Critique*, special Walter Benjamin issue, 17, Spring, Milwaukee: University of Wisconsin-Milwaukee.

——— (2005), 'On the Mimetic Faculty', in *Walter Benjamin: Selected Writings*, Vol. 2, Part 2: *1931–1934*, edited by Michael W. Jennings, Howard Eiland and Gary Smith, Cambridge, MA and London: Belknap Press.

Bhatti, Anil (2009), 'Culture, Diversity and Similarity: A Reflection on Heterogeneity and Homogeneity', *Social Scientist*, 37 (7–8).

Bhatti, Anil *et al.* (2007), '". . . zwischen zwei Welten schwebend . . .": Zu Goethes Fremdheitsexperiment im West-östlichen Divan', in Hans-Jörg Knobloch and Helmut Koopmann, eds, *Goethe: Neue Ansichten*, Würzburg: Königshausen and Neumann: 103–21.

——— (2011), 'Ähnlichkeit: Ein kulturtheoretisches Paradigma', *Internationales Archiv für Sozialgeschichte der deutschen Literatur*, 36 (1), Bielefeld: De Gruyter: 261–75.

Collier, Stephen J. and Aihwa Ong (2005), 'Global Assemblages, Anthropological Problems', in Stephen J. Collier and Aihwa Ong, eds, *Global Assemblages: Technology, Politics, and Ethics as Anthropological Problems*, Malden, MA: Blackwell: 3–21.

Collins, Randall (2011), *Violence: A Micro-sociological Theory*, Princeton, NJ: Princeton University Press.

Foucault, Michel (2002), *The Order of Things*, London and New York: Routledge.

Frazer, James G. (1911), *The Golden Bough: A Study in Magic and Religion*, Part I: *The Magic Art and the Evolution of Kings*, London: Macmillan.

Funk, Gerald, Gert Mattenklott and Michael Pauen, eds (2001), *Ästhetik des Ähnlichen: Zur Poetik und Kunstphilosophie der Moderne*, Frankfurt am Main: Fischer.

Gebauer, Gunter and Christoph Wulf (2003), *Mimetische Weltzugänge: Soziales Handeln – Rituale und Spiele – Ästhetische Produktionen*, Stuttgart: Kohlhammer.

Gellner, Ernest (1983), *Nations and Nationalism*, Oxford: Blackwell.

Girard, René (1979), *Violence and the Sacred*, Baltimore: John Hopkins University Press.

Halverson, Jeffry R., Harold L. Goodall Jr. and Steven R. Corman (2011), *Master Narratives of Islamist Extremism*, New York: Macmillan.

Koschorke, Albrecht (2005), 'Staaten und ihre Feinde: Ein Versuch über das Imaginäre der Politik', in Jörg Huber, ed., *Einbildungen*, Zürich: Springer: 93–115.

——— (2010), 'Ein neues Paradigma der Kulturwissenschaften', in Eva Esslinger *et al.*, eds, *Die Figur des Dritten: Ein kulturwissenschaftliches Paradigma*, Berlin: Suhrkamp: 9–31.

Latour, Bruno (1993), *We Have Never Been Modern*, translated by Catherine Porter, Cambridge, MA: Harvard University Press.

Lévy-Bruhl, Lucien (1986), *How Natives Think*, translated by Lilian A. Clare, Princeton, NJ: Princeton University Press.

Loo, Hans van der and Willem van Reijen (1997), *Modernisierung: Projekt und Paradox*, Munich: DTV.

Lübbe, Hermann (1996), 'Netzverdichtung. Zur Philosophie industriegesellschaftlicher Entwicklungen', *Zeitschrift für philosophische Forschung*, Vol. 50: 133–50.

McKeon, Richard (1936–37), 'Literary Criticism and the Concept of Imitation in Antiquity', *Modern Philology*, Vol. 34: 1–35.

Mergel, Thomas (2012), 'Modernization', *European History Online* (EGO), Mainz: Institut für Europäische Geschichte (IEG), 21 June; available at http://www.ieg-ego.eu/mergelt-2011-de, accessed on 16 February 2013.

Smith, Philip (2005), *Why War? The Cultural Logic of Iraq, the Gulf War and Suez*, Chicago and London: University of Chicago Press.

On the Humanism of Similarity

Jan Assmann

From antiquity to modernity, the humanist idea has proclaimed a humanism of equality, especially in the twentieth century, as illustrated by the works of authors such as Thomas Mann and Karl Jaspers. This conception has been based on properties shared by all men: what we might call the Platonic ideal of man, represented biblically as the image of God in human beings. The Platonic model postulates that all categories of objects share certain similarities with one another, and that the sum of these similarities exist as an ideal outside of individual differences between objects; the degree to which each object resembles this ideal is the degree to which it is similar to others.

This humanism of equality can be contrasted with Anil Bhatti's call for a concept of similarity[1] and of humanism based on Ludwig Wittgenstein's model of family resemblance.[2] Among other examples, Wittgenstein illustrated his concept of family resemblance using the image of a thread.[3] A thread is made up of several individual fibres, none of which actually runs its entire length. Still, the thread as a whole is capable of holding significant weight. The same principle holds for categories of objects: they are similar and connected to one another not by properties that they all share, but rather by neighbourly intertwining with one another. It seems to me that the concept of similarity could thus solve some of the problems that have derailed the search for commonalities between people, religions and cultures. Because the Wittgensteinian model of commonality was not yet available in the eighteenth century, the Platonic model was able to dominate without rival. Today, in the era of globalization, the question of commonalities between all peoples, cultures and religions is being posed under completely new conditions, and with a whole new level of urgency.

I would like to illustrate the humanism of the eighteenth century using textual examples from Gotthold Ephraim Lessing and his friend Moses Mendelssohn.[4] Both were concerned with how to overcome the inequality between men caused by differences in social class, nation and religion, and which allowed them to be provoked into hate and violence against one another. The model that both men offered was characterized by a concept of 'dual membership', which claimed that every person is a member of a specific religion, nation and class, while at the same time also being a member of humanity as a whole. The idea was to relativize the factors that created unbridgeable differences between men.

Mendelssohn saw the strongest and most problematic factor of difference in the idea of divine revelation as codified in the holy scriptures of various world religions, according to which each competing religion claims to have exclusive access to sacred truths. The problem of divine revelation stems from the fact that it claims to provide absolute and universal truths that are also exclusive, and that divide believers from non-believers. In particular, Mendelssohn saw a misunderstanding in the Christian concept of revelation, and contrasted it with Judaism, which he did not consider to be a revealed religion at all. 'I believe', he wrote,

> . . . Judaism knows of no revealed religion in the sense in which Christians understand this term. The Israelites possess a divine legislation – laws, commandments, ordinances, rules of life, instruction in the will of God . . . but no doctrinal opinions, no saving truths, no universal propositions of reason. These the Eternal reveals to us and to all other men, at all times, through nature and thing, but never through word and script.[5]

Mendelssohn thus made a dual distinction. On the one hand, he distinguished between universal rational principles and particular life rules; on the other, he differentiated between natural and written revelations. According to him, general rational principles refer to 'eternal truths'; according to the Jewish tradition, such truths are revealed to all men at creation and are at least to a certain extent understandable by all men, thanks to the rational faculties given to man by the creator. Such truths thus belong to the realm of rationality and not belief, and (according to Jewish tradition) cannot be and should not be codified in written form. 'They were always entrusted to the living, spiritual teachings, which keep pace with the changes of time and circumstances.' Hence man can, and should, only record 'historical' and not 'eternal' truths, and the laws that were revealed to Moses were nothing more than the former. 'It seems to me that only where historical truths are concerned does it befit the supreme wisdom to instruct men in a human manner, that is, through words and writing.'[6] Accordingly, the historical truth of law only applies to Jews, while eternal truth, never revealed by words and writing and only by nature, applies to humanity as a whole. 'This is the universal religion of mankind, not

Judaism; and the universal religion of mankind, without which men are neither virtuous nor capable of felicity, was not to be revealed there.'[7] This is why Judaism is not concerned with the exclusion of other religions as heathenism: 'Judaism boasts of no exclusive revelation of eternal truths that are indispensable to salvation – no "revealed religion" in the usual sense of that phrase. Revealed religion is one thing, revealed legislation is another.'[8]

Mendelssohn thus differentiated between individual religions (such as Judaism, Christianity and Islam) and the universal human religion, which he understood as a religiosity that all men share though their common participation in God's creation. In this way, every person belongs to two religions: the specific ancestral religion that each person is born into or converts to, and the universal human religion. According to Mendelssohn, this dual membership would generate recognition and peace between religions if only people were made aware of its existence.

Such considerations were about the problem of tolerance, with the question of how to prevent the *clash of religions*. But Mendelssohn did not invoke similarity to deal with such problems. Instead, he used a concept of equality by claiming that nature and rationality are shared by all men: nature reveals the creator to mankind, while rationality allows men to (at least partially) decipher this revelation. His concept of a universal human religion, which he may have adapted from Rousseau's *religion de l'homme*, brought these commonalities together in one idea.

Gotthold Ephraim Lessing was also concerned with the problem of tolerance, and he addressed it using the dialectic of identity and difference in his 'Masonic Dialogues', published in 1778 under the title *Ernst and Falk*.[9] In these dialogues, Lessing claimed that that which connects us also separates us from others. The following passage (slightly abridged) from the second of his five dialogues, illustrates this point:

> FALK. Civil society cannot unite men without dividing them, nor divide them without erecting walls or digging ditches to keep them apart. . . .
>
> May there be men in every state who are beyond popular prejudice and who know exactly when patriotism ceases to be virtuous. . . . [M]en who are not the creatures of the prejudices of the religion they were raised in, who do not believe that everything which they regard as good and true must be good and true. . . . [M]en who are not dazzled by high position and not put off by low, men in whose company the nobleman gladly stoops and the lowly confidently rise. . . .
>
> What would you say if I told you that today men like this exist everywhere; that from now on there are always going to be such men? . . . What if I told you, further, that they do not live ineffectually dispersed,

> like the Church Invisible? . . . I'll get right to the point – these men that we are speaking of are the Freemasons . . . these very men who have taken on the job of re-establishing human solidarity, including this in their proper business.[10]

The problem here (which Lessing claims to solve with the institution of Freemasonry) is not only one that can be put into words; it is perpetual, 'grounded in the nature of man and civil society', and is based on the divisions between men that inevitably accompany their union with one another. More recently, the psychologist Erik H. Erikson has described this dynamic as 'pseudo-speciation'.[11] Lessing named three different factors of such pseudo-speciation: political factors, which divide people into citizens of different countries; religious factors, which divide people into believers of different religions; and social factors, which divide people into members of different classes. According to Lessing, the establishment of a cosmopolitan culture would counteract such factors, and he saw Freemasonry as the bearer of such a culture. His Freemasons would form an international intellectual elite that would put the principle of dual membership into practice by simultaneously belonging to both their nation, social class and faith, as well as a transnational, trans-religious and trans-class secret society that worked towards overcoming these differences through understanding, recognition and tolerance.

Lessing's model was able to do without a postulate of strong commonalities between men, such as Mendelssohn's human religion. Instead, his Freemasons practised communality within the boundaries of their respective individual transnational and trans-religious contacts, without recourse to an idea of a universal common orientation in the sense of a human religion or a world ethos. One could also imagine this model being interpreted using Bhatti's concept of similarity.

Johann Gottfried von Herder, on the other hand, vehemently objected to Lessing's concept. He countered Lessing's Freemasons with the *république des lettres*:

> It has convened, it is visible. Faust or Gutenberg was – how shall I put it? – its Grand Master, or rather its first serving brother. Everything I encounter there raises me above all divisions within civil society, preparing and training me for commerce, not with such and such human beings, but with human beings as such.[12]

Herder also categorically rejected any idea or form of secret society:

> No true light can remain hidden, even if one wanted to hide it; and the purest light is not to be found in the crypt. . . . All such symbols

may once have been good and necessary; as I see it, however, they are no longer so. In our times we have to use the opposite method: *pure, bright, revealed truth*.[13]

Herder is known as a theoretician of difference, as an advocate for the respective specific national character (*Volksgeist*) of each people, and the respective origins of each culture and religion. In his view, however, such differences were also dialectically associated with a particularly strong concept of commonality, which he developed in his *Letters Concerning the Progress of Humanity*. Beyond the differences between men, which he emphasized and admired like no other, Herder was concerned with what he called the 'great, noble building of humanity'.[14]

Herder, Mendelssohn and even Lessing, all considered the common features between men – whether as a human religion, humanity or cosmopolitanism – more in the Platonic sense than in a Wittgensteinian–Bhattian sense; they thought of such features as an idea and not as an interrelationship. In this reading, all people are a part of the human religion or humanity as a whole regardless of how different they might be as members of particular religions, nations and cultures. In the eighteenth century, there was no cosmopolitanism without universalism, and the only way to escape hate, war and intolerance was seen in the appropriation of the foreign into the common. The problem with this form of humanism is that such commonality is so faint, abstract and empty that it has no practical effects. To use Wittgenstein's analogy, it is as if there is one fibre running through the entire thread, but it is so thin that it can neither support any weight nor connect the other fibres together. Thus, such humanism requires further specification, and it was inevitable that this faint idea of humanity would become differently coloured and shaped around the world. As a result, in many cases, cosmopolitanism and colonialism became indistinguishable from one another.

The romanticists, and particularly conservative romanticists such as Ernst Moritz Arndt, Joseph Görres and Johann Jakob Bachofen, passionately protested against this abstract eighteenth-century humanism, which assumed that rationality or the 'spirit' represented the common property of all men. In his book *Der Geist als Widersacher der Seele* (*The Spirit as Adversary of the Soul*, 1929–32), Ludwig Klages collected such voices and declared himself – at the peak of European modernity – the spokesman of this romantic hostility towards the spirit.[15] For these romanticists, Kant's 'emergence from self-imposed immaturity' represented an alienation from the life-giving forces of our native earth, blood and community. In his work *Germania and Europa* (1802), Arndt wrote: I identify in man 'only three of his main forces: these are the body, the soul, and the spirit, which almost all human languages distinguish from one another'.[16] According to Arndt, at its highest level of development the spirit grimly rages against the body and the soul. If left behind by the spirit, the soul falls into unrestrained rapture, while the spirit separated from the soul becomes inhuman and turns man into a machine. In so far as man aspires to be a global citizen, he is like a ship torn from its moorings, because a love for the universal can only take place within the framework of a community of 'a country, a city, a village, a family'.[17] Klages built upon this same ideological and motivational complex, and the echoes of the Nazi's blood-and-soil ideology are unmistakable, as is the clear strain of anti-Semitism that can be seen in both Arndt's and Klages' writings.

According to conservative romanticism, the alienation of man from his/her symbiotic embeddedness in nature and his/her national community is caused by a process that Sigmund Freud would later call 'progress in spirituality' and would highlight as the major achievement of Jewish monotheism.[18] And indeed the Bible, like Kant, describes this step not as a way out of self-imposed immaturity, but rather as an escape from slavery and oppression, as an exodus from Egypt. This original exodus was then repeated in the rationalism, secularism and cosmopolitanism of the Enlightenment – and this is the step that the conservative Catholic romanticists protested against, using the concept of *alienation*. Later, the national and fascist movements of the twentieth century would appropriate this romantic reaction for their own purposes. We thus find a neo-romanticism emerging in Germany before and after the First World War, which began as a reaction to modernization, mechanization and internationalization, and which was fortified and politicized after the war with fascist motives.

Starting in 1922, Thomas Mann began to stand up to this trend in his writing and lectures with an idea of the 'unity of human spirit' and a new form of humanism – especially in his four-part novel, *Joseph and His Brothers*. This confrontation is even more significant given that he had sounded a neo-romanticist horn in his *Reflections of a Non-Political Man* (1918), which portrayed an antithesis between culture, depth and poetry, on the one hand, and civilization, superficiality and literature, on the other. Among Mann's antipodes was Oswald Spengler, who distinguished eight different cultural cycles (*Kulturzyklen*) and attributed a unique 'soul' (*Seelentum*) to each of them. At first Thomas Mann was excited by Spengler's *The Decline of the West*, and wrote in his journal that Spengler's work might 'mark an epoch in my life'.[19] With his later republican turn, however, Mann distanced himself from Spengler because he saw an anti-humanist particularism in his theory of cultural groups.

For Spengler, Mann wrote, 'cultures are strictly closed forms of life, each steadfastly bound on their own stylistic laws of thinking, looking, feeling, experiencing, and each one cannot understand a word of what the others say and mean'.[20] To perhaps summarize this controversy, we might say that particularism denies intercultural commonalities and makes difference an absolute; in this sense, it represents a form of anti-humanism.

Another form of humanism based on the idea of equality through commonality is represented by Karl Jaspers' theory of the 'Axial Age' (*Achsenzeit*), which claimed that between 800 and 200 BCE, new ways of thinking developed independent of one another in different places around the world, and that modern man is a direct descendant of these developments. To the extent that all people today share in the intellectual and spiritual heritage of the Axial Age, Jaspers' theory implies a humanism based on unity. And although the term Axial Age comes from Jaspers, his theory also stems from the late eighteenth century, the same era as Lessing and Mendelssohn. The first to formulate such a theory was the orientalist Abraham Hyacinthe Anquetil-Duperron (1731–1805), who discovered the Zend-Avesta, and who spoke of a '*grande révolution du genre humain*' that took place from China to ancient Greece in the middle of the first millennium BCE.[21] Jaspers himself referred to the classical philologist Ernst von Lasaulx (1805–1861),[22] the Sinologist Victor von Strauss (1809–1899)[23] and the cultural sociologist Alfred Weber (1868–1958)[24] as his theoretical predecessors. Like Jaspers, Eric Voegelin also adopted the concept of a world-historical shift from Alfred Weber after studying under Weber in 1929.[25] But Voegelin explicitly rejected Jaspers' term Axial Age (which he translated as 'axis-time'), and instead referred to the Sinologist Jean-Pierre Abel-Rémusat (1788–1832).[26] In its more general, eighteenth-century form, this theory claimed that some time in the middle of the first millennium BCE, a historical shift took place across the globe. This period saw the first establishment of major religions such as biblical monotheism, Zoroastrianism, Buddhism and Jainism, as well as the first philosophical and theoretical writings, from the pre-Socratics to Aristotle in the west, and from Kautilya, Panini and other Indian theoreticians to Confucius, Lao Tse, Mengste and other Chinese philosophers in the east.[27] It is thus no coincidence that the first proponents of such a theory were Indologists, Iranologists, Sinologists and classical philologists, and decidedly not theologians; given the later dating of biblical monotheism and its association with other religions as merely a symptom of a more general human-historical shift, the theory found little theological support in the west.

Jaspers introduced the term Axial Age into this long-established theory, and expanded it by adding a hermeneutic dimension. For him, this age not only represented an important shift in history, it actually created 'man, as we know him today', that is, the intellectual world as we know it.[28] For Jaspers, the Axial Age was the time that 'gave birth to everything which, since then, man has been able to be',[29] and marks the first point in time that our present understanding can go back to because '[t]he source of understanding is our own present, the here and now, our sole reality'.[30] The basis of Jaspers' Axial Age theory was an awareness of the fact that he himself was living in a period of axial human-historical change, which he made clear in the very first sentence of his work: 'By virtue of the extent and depth to which it has transformed human life, our age is of the most incisive significance. It requires the whole history of mankind to furnish us with standards by which to measure the meaning of what is happening at the present time.'[31]

Thus, for Jaspers, the Axial Age represented a veritable mutation where '[t]he whole of humanity took a forward leap',[32] and where a new species was created, *homo sapiens axialis*, which we belong to today. The mark of this mutation was an enormous expansion of the human world into the infinite – both outwards, in the direction of transcendence (in the form of metaphysics and monotheism), and inwards, towards the soul, subjectivity and inner life (in the form of mysticism, spirituality, gnosis and other manifestations of what Paul called the 'inner man').[33] The most important principles of this breakthrough can be summarized as universalization and differentiation. On the one hand, universalization regards the postulation of absolute truths that are always valid for all men, while differentiation refers to categorical distinctions such as time and eternity, being and appearance, spirit or form and material, God and the world, being and becoming, or the given and the true. These principles are also associated with phenomena such as reflexivity, second order thinking, theories and the capacity for abstraction.

For Jaspers and his successors, the Axial Age thus represented an irreversible evolutionary step. While some residues of pre-axial people and cultures remained (in the same way that there are still cultures without writing), the development of human history has primarily followed a marked path that has pulled most peoples along with it.[34] Additionally, once man had undergone this change, he could never revert to an earlier level of development; just as Cro-Magnon man replaced the Neanderthal, over time, post-axial man prevails over pre-axial man.

Still, even more recent attempts to develop a new humanism – such as those proposed by Thomas Mann and Karl Jaspers to counteract the fascist and nationalist particularism of their time – have been based on an idea of unity and commonality, and are thus based on the Platonic model. In the age of globalization, however, such approaches get bogged down. The problem lies in the fact that the Platonic model has an innately Eurocentric perspective – even if concepts such as Thomas Mann's 'Unity of Human Spirit' or Jaspers' idea of a new form of man created during a universal Axial Age sought to overcome it.

In his essay titled 'Chances for a Global Humanism in the Clash of Culture', the Sinologist Helwig Schmidt-Glintzer calls for a humanism that is based not on unity but rather on difference – and we could place Anil Bhatti's concept of similarity within such a framework as well. According to Schmidt-Glintzer, neither *a priori* nor metaphysical unity will lead to a solution to the clash of cultures; instead, we must rely on a 'dialogic consensus'. Such a principle would look for commonalities, not in our origin, in a metaphysical or theological idea, or in the nature of man, but rather in a common goal for continually newer and farther-reaching attempts at coming to an agreement – not about 'man', but about certain fundamental and central values and goals that collectively could be called 'human rights'. If the clash of cultures is to be peacefully settled, finding such an agreement cannot merely remain a reasonable hope: it is an absolute necessity. The foundations of this consensus must be developed based on the traditions of various cultures around the globe: every culture has its own specific 'lessons for coexistence'[35] that can be used to distil the principles of a thriving coexistence and expanded to be useful at a global level. 'Dialogic consensus' thus views the search for commonality as a project instead of as a prerequisite starting point. And, as Anil Bhatti has discussed, this is where Wittgenstein's model of *family resemblances* can make a contribution; at its core, dialogic consensus seeks to use 'neighbourly intertwining' to create a global, load-bearing thread that binds people together.

It is clear, however, that 'neighbourly intertwining' is not exclusively about agreement – we need only look at Israel and Palestine, North and South Korea, India and Pakistan, or many other conflict regions around the world, to see that such connections are also about conflict and division. Indeed, in such cases it seems that a past of historical wounds and traumatic memories plays a more important role than a future of common goals. This is the problem of the past: it can bring people together, but it can also divide them from one another. As the Israeli author Amos Oz once put it:

> If I had any say in the peace negotiations – no matter whether in Wye, Oslo, or wherever – I would instruct the sound technicians to switch off the microphones as soon as any of the negotiating parties began to talk about the past. Because they are being paid to find solutions for the present and the future.[36]

In the same vein, Christian Meier has called attention to the ancient political adage that conflicts are resolved in the interest of a common future, not based on remembering, but rather through forgetting and remaining silent. Further, he made a reference to the Greek prohibition imposed on 'remembering the horrific' (*mē mnēsikakeîn*),[37] although we must add here that this principle was about de-emphasizing the terrible things that have been done to us and not those that we have done to others. But this is the exact same principle upon which we can establish a new culture of memory, one that Aleida Assmann has called a 'dialogic remembrance', in direct reference to Helwig Schmidt-Glintzer's principle of 'dialogic consensus'.[38]

Neither 'dialogic consensus' nor 'dialogic remembrance' deals with universals, with nature, or with rationality and humanity; instead, they are about a partial, local and felt closeness across borders. They are about similarity, about neighbourly intertwining that overcomes boundaries, but that acknowledges and respects those boundaries as well. In this sense, Anil Bhatti has recommended a policy of 'hermeneutic abstinence': 'More important than understanding the other and developing a dichotomizing hermeneutic of the relationship between oneself and the other, is the conscious development of a practice that allows us to get along with the other.'[39] As an example of such a practice, Bhatti points to Goethe's *West–Eastern Diwan*, which does not seek to appropriate the foreign – in this case, the work of the Persian–Islamic poet Shamsed-Din, also called Hafis – either with respect to commonalities or based on Goethe's own views; instead, the work seeks to 'start a conversation' with the foreign.[40] Goethe did this through paraphrasing adaptation, borrowing the voice of the Persian poet in order to say what he wanted to say. As Bhatti also stresses, Goethe did in fact emphasize differences, was not fond of Hinduism (with its many gods, some of them grotesque) and downright detested ancient Egypt. The Englishman Crabb Robinson once described a conversation with Goethe in 1804, in which Goethe said:

> I do hate the Egyptians and all that are connected with them. And then he added: And I am glad that I have something to hate, otherwise one is in danger of falling into the dull liberal habit of finding all things tolerable and good in their place, and that is the ruin of all good sentiments.[41]

The key word here is 'sentiment'. With his poetic adaptation Goethe followed his feelings, and not an idea of humanity or world literature that cannot be loved or hated, which exists only as a conception. His orientalized poetry emerged from a certain empathy, and empathy (in contrast to tolerance) is the force that holds the Wittgensteinian thread together. In this sense, we can see Goethe's *West–Eastern Diwan* as precisely the kind of practice that does not seek to appropriate the other through understanding, but rather to cooperate with it through poetry – or, like Edward Said and Daniel Barenboim's *West–Eastern Diwan Orchestra*, through music or even, like in the film *Football under Cover*, through the game of football.

Notes

1 Bhatti (2010).
2 Wittgenstein (1958): 32.
3 Ibid.
4 Cf. J. Assmann (2014).
5 Mendelssohn (1983): 89f.
6 Ibid.: 93.
7 Ibid.: 97.
8 Ibid.
9 The first three dialogues were published in 1778 as *Ernst und Falk: Gespräche für Freymäurer*; Adolph von Knigge apparently published the other two with Brönner in Frankfurt without Lessing's knowledge. The quotes included are from Maschler (1996).
10 Ibid.: 26 (abridged).
11 Erikson (1966).
12 Herder (1991): 132–41; translation taken from J. Assmann (2014): 138.
13 Ibid. (emphasis in original).
14 Herder (1968): 72.
15 Klages (1960).
16 Arndt (1940): 93.
17 Ibid.: 902f.
18 Freud (1939): 176–82.
19 Mann, (journal entry dated) 26.6.1919; also cf. 2.7.1919. On Thomas Mann and Oswald Spengler, cf. Besslich (2002).
20 Mann (2002a): 738. The first criticisms of Spengler can be found in Mann (2002b).
21 Cf. Metzler (1991); Metzler (2004): 565ff., 577ff. Incidentally, Jaspers himself made just as little reference to him as did most of his other predecessors.
22 Lasaulx (1952): 7–60.
23 Strauss *et al.* (1870); for an English translation of the Chinese original text, cf. Lafarque, trans. (1992).
24 Weber (1935). Weber's term is 'synchronistic world epoch'.
25 Henkel (1998): 16.
26 Cf. Voegelin (1974): 3–6. Voegelin rejects the term 'axis-time' because, as a proponent of diffusionism, he believes that there was no historical connection (i.e. no contact) between processes that took place in China and India, and those in the west.
27 On China, cf. Roetz (1992).
28 Jaspers (1958): 25.
29 Ibid.
30 Ibid.: 10.
31 Ibid.: xiii.
32 Ibid.: 4. Eric Voegelin talks about a 'leap in being'; cf. Voegelin (1956), passim.
33 Cf. Assmann and Sundermeier, eds (1993).
34 A. Assmann (1988).

[35] This was the preferred title of a book by Ekkehard Krippendorff, Helwig Schmidt-Glintzer and myself, which ended up being published in 2006 under the less fortunate title, *Ma'at Konfuzius Goethe: Drei Lehren für das richtige Leben*, Frankfurt am Main: Insel.

[36] Oz (1998): 83; translation taken from J. Assmann (2005).

[37] Meier (2010).

[38] A. Assmann (2012); A. Assmann (2007).

[39] Bhatti (2010): 263.

[40] Comments made on 11 January 2011 in a discussion about the actor Frank Lettenewitsch in Hofhalde in Constance, as part of a lecture series on the *West–Eastern Diwan*.

[41] Quoted from Hendrik Birus, in Goethe (2010): Commentary 922 for 'Vier Elemente'.

References

Arndt, Ernst Moritz (1940), *Germanien und Europa*, Stuttgart: Kohlhammer.

Assmann, Aleida (1988), 'Jaspers' Achsenzeit, oder: Schwierigkeiten mit der Zentralperspektive in der Geschichte', in Dietrich Harth, ed., *Karl Jaspers: Denken zwischen Wissenschaft, Politik und Philosophie*, Stuttgart: Metzler.

——— (2007), 'Die Last der Vergangenheit', *Zeithistorische Forschungen / Studies in Contemporary History*, 4 (3); available at http://www.zeithistorische-forschungen.de/site/40208791/default.aspx, accessed on 1 April 2017.

——— (2012), *Auf dem Weg zu einer europäischen Gedächtniskultur*, Wien: Picus.

Assmann, Jan (2005), *Religion and Cultural Memory*, Stanford: Stanford University Press.

——— (2014), *Religio Duplex: How the Enlightenment Reinvented Egyptian Religion*, Cambridge: Polity Press.

Assmann, Jan and Theo Sundermeier, eds (1993), *Die Erfindung des inneren Menschen: Studien zur religiösen Anthropologie*, Gütersloh: Gütersloher Verlagshaus.

Besslich, Barbara (2002), *Faszination des Verfalls: Thomas Mann und Oswald Spengler*, Berlin: Akademie Verlag.

Bhatti, Anil (2010), 'Heterogenität, Homogenität, Ähnlichkeit', in Andrea Allerkamp and Gérard Raulet, eds, *Kulturwissenschaften in Europa – eine grenzüberschreitende Disziplin?*, Münster: Westfälisches Dampfboot: 250–66.

Erikson, Erik H. (1966), 'Ontogeny of Ritualization in Man', in *Philosophical Transactions of the Royal Society of London*, 251 B, London: The Royal Society Publishing: 337–49.

Freud, Sigmund (1939), *Moses and Monotheism*, Letchworth: Hogarth Press.

Goethe, Johann Wolfgang von (2010), *West-Östlicher Divan*, new and fully revised edition, edited by Hendrik Birus, Frankfurt am Main: Insel.

Henkel, Michael (1998), *Eric Voegelin zur Einführung*, Hamburg: Junius.

Herder, Johann Gottfried von (1968), 'Gespräch über eine unsichtbar-sichtbare Gesellschaft', in Gotthold Ephraim Lessing, *Ernst und Falk: Mit den Fortsetzungen Johann Gottfried Herders und Friedrich Schlegels*, edited by Ion Contiades, Frankfurt am Main: Insel.

——— (1991), 'Briefe zur Beförderung der Humanität', in *Werke in zehn Bänden*, edited by Martin Bollacher, Second Anthology, 26th Letter, Vol. 7, Frankfurt am Main.

Jaspers, Karl (1958), *The Origin and Goal of History*, New Haven and London: Yale University Press.

Klages, Ludwig (1960), *Der Geist als Widersacher der Seele*, Bonn: Bouvier.

Krippendorff, Ekkehard, Helwig Schmidt-Glintzer and Jan Assmann (2006), *Ma'at Konfuzius Goethe: Drei Lehren für das richtige Leben*, Frankfurt am Main: Insel.

Lafarque, Michael, trans. (1992), *Lao-Tse: The Tao of the Tao Te Ching*, with commentary by Michael Lafarque, New York: SUNY Press.

Lasaulx, Ernst von (1952), *Neuer Versuch einer alten, auf die Wahrheit der Tatsachen gegründeten Philosophie der Geschichte*, München: Verlag für Geschichte und Politik.

Mann, Thomas (2002a), 'Über die Lehre Spenglers', in *Große kommentierte Frankfurter Ausgabe*, edited by Hermann Kurzke, Vol. 15, No. 1: *Essays II, 1914–1926*, Frankfurt am Main: Fischer: 735–44.

——— (2002b), 'Briefe aus Deutschland [1]', in *Große Komentierte Frankfurter Ausgabe*, edited by Hermann Kurzke, Vol. 15, No. 1: *Essays* II, 1914–26, Frankfurt am Main: Fischer: 566–75.

Maschler, Chaninah (1996), 'Lessing's *Ernst and Falk, Dialogues for Freemasons*: A Translation with Notes', *Interpretation: A Journal of Political Philosophy*, 1 (1), New York: Queens College Press.

Meier, Christian (2010), *Das Gebot zu vergessen und die Unabweisbarkeit des Erinnerns: Vom öffentlichen Umgang mit schlimmer Vergangenheit*, München: Siedler Verlag.

Metzler, Dieter (1991), 'A.H. Anquetil-Duperron (1731–1805) und das Konzept der Achsenzeit', *Achaemenid History*, Vol. 7, Leiden: Netherlands Institute for the Near East: 123–33.

——— (2004), *Kleine Schriften zur Geschichte und Religion der Antike und deren Nachleben*, Münster: Ugarit.

Mendelssohn, Moses (1983), *Jerusalem: Or on Religious Power and Judaism*, translated by Alex Altman, Waltham, MA: Brandeis University Press.

Oz, Amos (1998), 'Israelis und Araber: Der Heilungsprozeß', in *Trialog der Kulturen im Zeitalter der Globalisierung*, Sinclair-Haus-Gespräche, 11, Gespräch, 5–8 December, Bad Homburg vor der Höhe: Herbert-Quandt-Stiftung: 82–89.

Roetz, Heiner (1992), *Die chinesische Ethik der Achsenzeit*, Frankfurt am Main: Suhrkamp.

Strauss, Victor von *et al.* (1870), *Lao-Tsè's Tao tè King*, aus dem Chinesischen ins Deutsche über- setzt, eingeleitet und commentirt von Victor von Strauss und Torney, Leipzig (Neuausgabe mit Bearbeitung und Einleitung von Willi Y. Tonn, Zürich 1959, Kommentar S. 169–417).

Voegelin, Eric (1956), *Order and History I: Israel and Revelation*, Baton Rouge: University of Missouri Press.

——— (1974), *The Ecumenic Age: Order and History*, Vol. IV, Baton Rouge: University of Missouri Press.

Weber, Alfred (1935), *Kulturgeschichte als Kultursoziologie*, Leiden: Sijthoff.

Wittgenstein, Ludwig (1958), *Philosophical Investigations*, Oxford: Blackwell.

Work of Similarities / Work on Similarities

In the work of Sigmund Freud and Walter Benjamin

Ulrike Kistner

This article proposes to reinstate the role of similarities in perception, cognition, symbolization and historical-critical analysis. This involves not simply the replacement of a culturalistically conceived notion of difference by a culturalistically conceived notion of similarity, nor a simple reinstatement of the mimetic capacity within cultural semiosis. The task this article sets itself is to elaborate the role of similarities in relation to the critical humanities through inflecting the work *of* similarities by the work *on* similarities, which underlies the unique notion of 'interpretation' first formulated in Sigmund Freud's *Interpretation of Dreams* and analogously taken up in Walter Benjamin's attempt to reconstitute experience in the context of cognition.

The mimetic capacity – the capacity to produce similarities, Walter Benjamin avers, has a history, in both the phylogenetic and the ontogenetic sense.[1] Phylogenetically, the role of similarities as signatures of the visible tends to be relegated to non- or pre-rational forms of quasi-propositions, to the earliest forms of human thought, to magical forms of performativity and conferral, to myths, fables and stories (pre-dating narrative and linear writing). It tends to be associated with a pre-lapsarian state[2] ruptured by the eating of the fruit from the tree of knowledge, inaugurating a passage from myth through cults and religion to science, as recounted by Marcel Mauss's commentary on Frazer's *The Golden Bough* (1890–1915):

> Magic . . . [is] the earliest form of human thought. It must have once existed in its pure state; mankind, originally, thought only in magical terms. . . . Religion grew up out of the failures and mistakes of magic. Originally man unhesitatingly expressed his ideas and their associations in concrete form. . . . [T]he human mind, following on from religion, moved off in the direction of science. Once man became capable of noting the errors of religion he returned to a straightforward application of

the principle of causality. But from this time onwards it is a matter of experimental causality and not magical causality.[3]

Definitive for magic incantation, conjuration, ritual enactment and practice is sympathy (which includes its antonym, antipathy); it provides 'the route along which magic powers pass',[4] comprising the principles of similarity, contiguity, opposites, as well as synecdoche. The 'law of similarity' is formulated in the following terms: 'those in contact are and remain the same, like produces like [and cures like], opposites work on opposites, opposite drives away opposite';[5] one element of an assemblage may represent the whole – in wish, thought and deed. The idea of efficacious likeness – similarity – relates individual things to one another, providing a conduit for magical influences.[6]

Ontogenetically, similarities are referred to primary processes characteristic of the unconscious system, with free-flowing psychical energy governed by the pleasure principle, sliding from one idea to another, where ideas are linked by associations based on homonyms and verbal similarities.[7] In the way in which similarities operate in dreams, they access material from childhood.[8] Freud endorses his predecessors' views of dreams as 'the return of the mind in dreams to an embryonic point of view', or 'an archaic world of vast emotions and imperfect thoughts'.[9] Processes of the unconscious mind are called 'primary' according to their relative importance as well as their chronological priority: 'the primary processes are present in the mental apparatus from the first, while it is only during the course of life that the secondary processes unfold, and come to inhibit and overlay the primary ones';[10] secondary processes appear belatedly.

Epistemically, magic became a way of coming to know and of transmitting knowledge when resemblance/similarity came to organize the signs of things formally and systematically. Resemblance, similarity, similitude, contiguity, analogy, sympathy and its antonym antipathy were systematically related to knowledge in the form of the Renaissance episteme assigned to the mid-sixteenth to early seventeenth century. Drawing on Foucault's figures of knowledge for this order,[11] we can highlight the following principles for the organization of knowledge:

- Resemblance (visible proximity giving effect to the assimilation of signs of things)
- Similarity, similitude (of properties)
- Contiguity (things placed in space in relation to each other and communicating with each other)
- Analogy (vertical relations of resemblances corresponding with each other horizontally)

- Sympathy (drawing properties of things / things together horizontally – even the most distant things – bringing them into contact with one another and assimilating them with each other in the process)
- Antipathy (isolating things from each other, enclosing them and preventing their assimilation).

Through resemblance, marked at every turn by signs, the relationship between signature and sign and the relationships of forms became visible, their signatures became legible, meaning became explicable, texts became interpretable, and knowledge became possible and operable. Unearthing them from invisibility meant covering the face of the world 'with blazons, with characters, with ciphers and obscure words – with "hieroglyphics"'.[12] Through a slight displacement, two or several things, forms or properties linked through resemblance are prevented from total assimilation and overlap (which would render them identical to one another).

The meaning to be discovered in reading signs, and making them speak in and through signatures and similitudes, is not a representational one. It consists, rather, in the search for the intrinsic properties of letters, syllables and words; and in their combination in syntax, likewise on the basis of the properties of words, and the communion of these properties 'as of the noun with the noun or with the verb, of the adverb with all the words to which it is adjoined, of the conjunction in the order of things conjoined'.[13]

Interpretation was referred to the Ancients, who had already set it down for posterity to gather together, to read and to understand through learning their language, figuring out the etymology of words and their combinations through their respective properties, without distinction between the names of things and the properties of things, which were set in a mutually transparent relation,[14] producing infinite exegesis and commentary. Words and things, the read and the seen, the expressible and the visible, were interwoven to the point of indistinction. In interpretation and commentary,

> one speaks upon the basis of a writing that is part of the fabric of the world; one speaks about it to infinity, and each of its signs becomes in turn written matter for further discourse; but each of these stages of discourse is addressed to that primal written word whose return it simultaneously promises and postpones.[15]

Commentary and interpretation are themselves governed by the principle of similarity: 'The commentary resembles endlessly that which it is commenting upon and which it can never express.'[16]

From the point of view of the modern episteme, the form of knowledge based on resemblance/similarity/similitude as an organizing principle is considered primary, raw and 'structurally weak', being made up 'of an unstable mixture of rational knowledge, notions derived from magical practices, and a whole cultural heritage whose power and authority had been vastly increased by the rediscovery of Greek and Roman authors', and commanding, in equal proportions, 'fidelity to the Ancients, a taste for the supernatural' and an emergent sovereign rationality.[17]

However, the idea of a linear passage circumscribing the apparent 'rise' and 'fall' of similarity, from magic through cult and religion to reasoning from causes – and organizing knowledge in scientific and narrative forms, from primary to secondary processes, from the similarity between *signatura* and *signatum* to the bar separating signifier and signified, is a theoretical fiction, which is critiqued even in its theorization. Resemblance, similitude and similarity, while forming, phylogenetically speaking, the most archaic substrate of the capacity to name, to draw together and to order, remain fundamental capacities presupposed even in the highest order of mental functions.[18] Not only do resemblance, similarity and similitude constantly flow into the form of rationality that is supposed to supersede them, but they find their way back – even in their changed role within a semantic–semiotic account of signification – to their 'raw being', posing a 'counter-discourse'.[19] This counter-discourse owes its (re)appearance to an anamnesis – a return, albeit in transmuted form – of lost similarity at the point of its sedimentation in a substrate contrary to its own making, namely, in semiotic–semantic signification[20] at the moment of its deciphering.[21] The act of reading contains both magical and profane dimensions. Gathering up the signatures of the visible, it relies on similarity; referring them to the legible, it transfers the signatures to the semiotic signs in which they are extinguished.[22] Yet, if the process of reading is to yield any insight at all, it has to disinter the sedimented signatures lost under the primacy of the sign, reconnecting with and renewing the archive of mimetic assimilations.[23]

It is in this sense that the relegation of magic, the mimetic capacity, and the principles of resemblance, similitude and similarity, to the mists of primary, archaic, pre-historic and pre-rational realms appears itself as a pre-critical myth consequential in its denial of coevalness at best, and consequential in fostering ideologemes of culturalist progressivism and evolutionism, if not racist supremacism, at worst. This is where, very broadly speaking, culturalistically conceived notions of difference would attain a paradigmatic character.

A reading of the signatures of the visible within, between and beneath the significations upon which we premise the evidential warrant of our senses, in contrast, would mean reinstating the mimetic capacity in relation to historical-critical analysis.[24] It is not, however, in the simple replacement of a culturalistically conceived notion of difference by a culturalistically conceived notion of similarity, nor in the simple reinstatement of the mimetic capacity within cultural semiosis, that the critical task lies, but in the elaboration of the relationship between the signatures of the visible inscribed in the mimetic capacity and words in semiotic–semantic signification. It is a complex relation that cannot be grasped in homological, binary-oppositional or even analogical terms. Its first systematic elaboration, I would contend, is to be found in Freud's *The Interpretation of Dreams*,[25] which simultaneously marks a form of knowledge that becomes path-breaking for critique within the human sciences in modernity.

In naming, conceptualizing, and working with and on the challenge of this relation of signs of different orders lies the provocation of Freud's *The Interpretation of Dreams* (1900). Even the title of this work indicates a reversion from considerations of 'representation' to the skill of making the signs speak, and to discover their meaning in unearthing, from a different order, the resemblances linking them.[26] To appreciate the new role of interpretation, we would need to look at its relation to an earlier form of scholarly pursuit.

Within the epistemic formation that once contained it, the skill of interpretation featured as a restorative task imposed by the memory of a grand design of similitude in a language originally given to men by God, destroyed at Babel and hence lost, as 'an absolutely certain and transparent sign for things, because it resembled them': 'The names of things were lodged in the things they designated, just as strength is written in the body of the lion, regality in the eye of the eagle, just as the influence of the planets is marked upon the brows of men: by the form of similitude.'[27]

The highest form of learning of that earlier knowledge formation, it simultaneously relates magic and divination to erudition in referring similitudes to signs, and deciphering and interpreting the signs of things – signs that cover the world from end to end, making it legible as a text: 'To know . . . [meant] to interpret: to find a way from the visible mark to that which is being said by it and which, without that mark, would lie like unspoken speech, dormant within things.'[28]

> Knowledge therefore consisted in relating one form of language to another form of language; in restoring the great, unbroken plain of words and things; in making everything speak. That is, in bringing into being, at a level above that of all marks, the secondary discourse of

> commentary. The function proper to knowledge is not seeing or demonstrating; it is interpreting.[29]

Interpretation laid successive forms of language upon one another, each referring to a more 'primal' one below itself, which it set itself the task of restoring,[30] presupposing, even if by way of infinite regress, an underlying originary text.

We recognize in this all the ingredients of the event in the order of knowledge that launched psychoanalysis as a unique form of inquiry into the human, instituting itself within, and thereby irreducibly instituting the domain of the psychic between the biological–physiological–material and the mental, between the expressed/expressible and the unexpressed/inexpressible, between science and interpretation. The work on similarities entailed in the peculiar interpretation of psychoanalysis is that anamnesis of lost similarities that makes its appearance in the symptom, and in the dream. The archaic character of the dream thought, Freud wishfully states, would be best understood through an archaeology of languages.[31]

Thus does the work *on* similarities circumscribe the work *of* similarities,[32] imposing limits on the limitless proliferation of signs and the mode of their reading while not extinguishing them under the reign of semiotic–semantic signification.

The Dream Work	**The Work of Interpretation**
Work *of* the Dream	Work *on* the Dream
(Work *of* Myth	Work *on* Myth)
Work *of* Similarities	Work *on* Similarities

What interpretation retains is the search for what the visible mark signals (without signifying it) and which, without that mark, would lie like unspoken speech, dormant within things.[33] The task that remains for interpretation is relating one form of language to another form of language – not to restore the great, unbroken plain of words and things but, on the contrary, to limit and de-limit the latter, to analyse its elements, and to reconstitute them in relation to each other in such a way that (ideally) their interactions and inter-relations can be understood, critically and talking-curatively.

In Freud's terms of the first topography of the psychic apparatus instantiated in *The Interpretation of Dreams* (1900) and elaborated in his later essay on 'The Unconscious' ('*Das Unbewusste*', 1915), the relation structured by similitude, between words and things, finds a double registration in separate and distinct yet related domains – domains separated by repression and related by the possibility of translation. Thing presentations appear within the unconscious system and word-and-thing presentations within the (pre)conscious system:

> [T]he conscious presentation comprises the presentation of the thing plus the presentation of the word belonging to it, while the unconscious presentation is the presentation of the thing alone. The system *Ucs.* contains the thing-cathexes of the objects . . . the system *Pcs.* comes about by this thing-presentation being hypercathected through being linked with the word-presentations corresponding to it. . . . [W]hat [repression] denies to the [rejected] presentation is translation into words which shall remain attached to the object. A presentation which is not put into words, or a psychical act which is not hyper-cathected, remains thereafter in the *Ucs.* in a state of repression.[34]

Sigmund Freud: 'The Unconscious' (1915)

System Ucs – Primary Process	*System Pcs/Cs – Secondary Process*
Unconscious idea	Consciously held idea
Thing presentation ∿∿∿∿∿∿∿∿	Thing presentation *and*
	Word presentation[35]

What is associated with object presentations can only become conscious through a relation with word presentations.[36] But repression works against this transposition from thing presentations in the unconscious system to thing presentations allied with word presentations in the (pre)conscious system, pushing thing presentations back into the unconscious, whence the dream treats words as objects. This is where the work *on* dreams, the interpretation of dreams, finds the latent dream thought and sets about tracing the process by which it is registered in the manifest dream content, to investigate the relations between the manifest content of dreams and the latent dream thoughts. But most importantly, the work *on* dreams would go in search of the syntactic forms and relations between latent dream thoughts[37] structured by connections appearing in the guise of simultaneity or contiguity, with causal relations appearing as temporal sequences and similarity indicated through condensation of several elements into a single common element.[38] Processes of *transposition* effected in the *dream work* – the work *of* dreams – from word-and-thing presentations in the form of a pictographic script in the (pre)conscious system to thing presentations in the unconscious system, and the latter's *re-transposition* into syllables and words and elements of syntax in the *interpretation of dreams* – the work *on* dreams – as well as in metapsychology and critique more generally, are confronted by resistances of displacement (replacement of one element by another; or replacement of the verbal form of a single element by another verbal form; or exchange of an abstract expression for a pictorial, concrete one[39]) and repression – which pervade the function of language. Interpretation has to address the question as to how the unconsciously held wish destabilizes the word, and is itself destabilized by language in turn,[40] in a mutually illuminating fashion.

Similarly to Freud's double articulation of thing presentations – one of them residing mutely in the unconscious system and in different form in relation to word presentations, in the (pre)conscious system – Walter Benjamin (more or less at the same time) diagrammatically presents a picture of the doubly conflictual relationship between the spoken and speakable with the unspeakable and unspoken: 'Within all linguistic formation a conflict is waged between what is expressed and expressible and what is inexpressible and unexpressed.'[41] The complex relationship that Benjamin construes contains a double opposition – the (un)expressed vs. the (in)expressible on the one hand, and the expressed/expressible vs. the unexpressed/inexpressible on the other – which cannot be set in an analogical relation; hence the chiasmatic statement of the two pairs of opposites.

Walter Benjamin: '*Über Sprache überhaupt und über die Sprache des Menschen*' (1916) (On Language as such and on the Language of Man)
Conflict between
Expressed and *Expressible* with the
Inexpressible and *Unexpressed*

Contrary to idealist understandings of the role of language, Benjamin postulates an inverse proportionality between the expressible/expressed of language in fixed, incontrovertible expression, and the mind ('*geistiges Wesen*'): it is the inexpressible that harbours the principles of mental functioning;[42] (yet the nameless, mute language of things – of which the materiality of the language of poetry, art and sculpture constitutes a specific kind[43] – can attain this functioning only on condition of a complex relation to what Benjamin calls 'the name language of man' ('*die Namensprache des Menschen*').[44]

With respect to the location of experience in relation to knowledge, likewise, Benjamin re-enacts the Freudian duplication in the registration of 'thing-presentations', again at more or less the same time (1917) as Freud theorizes his first topography in his programmatic statement on 'The Unconscious' (1915). While taking his cue from a historical-critical reading of Kant's *Critique of Pure Reason*, with its rigorous distinction between '*Erfahrung*' and '*Erkenntnis*',[45] Benjamin postulates a relation of immediate experience and experience in the context of knowledge – closely resembling the relation drawn by Freud between words and things differentially positioned across the topographical model of the psychic agencies.

Freud on *Ucs–Pcs* and (Benjamin's) Kant on Experience–Knowledge

Freud:	
System Ucs – Primary Process	*System Pcs/Cs – Secondary Process*
Unconscious idea	Consciously held idea
Thing presentation	Thing presentation *and* Word presentation
(Benjamin's) Kant:	
Immediate experience	Experience in the context of knowledge Knowledge of experience
('*Unmittelbare Erfahrung*')	('*Erfahrung im Erkenntniszusammenhang*')

In contrast to Kant, whose evacuation of 'experience' in the context of knowledge he explains philosophically-historically but similarly to the move indicated in Freud's schema of the relation between thing presentations in the unconscious and thing presentations (allied to word presentations) in the (pre)conscious, Benjamin sets about reconstituting the relationship between 'immediate experience' and 'knowledge of experience'. He is prepared to venture a step further to posit continuity between immediate experience and experience that is the object of knowledge, even as it is differentially articulated between the different registers of experience and knowledge.[46] The correspondence between knowledge and experience becomes Benjamin's postulate for the coming philosophy: 'to create, on the grounds of the Kantian system, a concept of knowledge to which the concept of experience corresponds, of which the knowledge is the teachings (*Lehre*)'.[47]

The obstinate insistence on an unaltered notion of experience across different epistemic orders and psychic–topographic divisions and locations, I would argue, becomes explicable if we look at what is transported with it: in Benjamin's terms, 'lived similarities' ('*gelebte Ähnlichkeiten*').[48] These facilitate a translation in both directions indicated in Benjamin's postulate: from a concept of knowledge to experience, and from experience to a concept of knowledge. In the passage from primary to secondary processes is indicated a reverse direction of translation that is the work of the interpretation of dreams on the work of dreams, of the work *on* similarities (on the work *of* similarities) that is the field of psychoanalysis, art and philosophical critique. It is especially in that reverse direction of translation – that from the work *on* similarities to the work *of* similarities – that this translation encounters shifts and distortions. The 'displaced similarities' ('*entstellte Ähnlichkeiten*') demand a deciphering on the basis of tectonic shifts in the relationship between knowledge and experience, between primary and secondary processes, which would allow us to critically and transformatively inflect deformed experience.

Notes

1 Benjamin ([1933] 1977, 1991): 204.

2 Indeed, Benjamin notes, the *lapsus* is an event inaugurating the human word that ruptures magic-divine naming and knowing, stepping out of the internal practice of naming, in order for it to reappear in magical guise from the outside, as it were: 'the Fall marks the birth of the *human word*, in which name no longer lives intact, and which has stepped out of name language, the language of knowledge, from what we may call its own immanent magic, in order to become expressly, as it were externally, magic.' Benjamin ([1916] 2002): 71.

3 Mauss ([1950] 1972): 13.

4 Ibid.: 102.

5 Ibid.: 64, 68.

6 See Agamben (2009): 52.

7 Freud ([1900] 1975): 755.

8 Ibid.

9 See Havelock Ellis (1899): 721, quoted in Freud ([1900] 1975): 749.

10 Freud ([1900] 1975): 763.

11 Foucault ([1966] 1970): 17–30.

12 Ibid.: 27.

13 P. Ramus' *Grammaire* (1572), cited in Foucault ([1966] 1970): 35.

14 Foucault ([1966] 1970): 33, 35, 36.

15 Ibid.: 41.

16 Ibid.

17 Ibid.: 32.

18 See Benjamin ([1933] 1977, 1991): 204.

19 Foucault ([1966] 1970): 44.

20 Benjamin ([1933] 1992: 162) terms as 'semiotic' what Emile Benveniste casts as 'semantic' (as opposed to 'semiotic') – viz. the sense generated in a syntactic combinatory: 'This aspect of language as script . . . does not develop in isolation from its other, semiotic aspect. Rather, the mimetic element in language can, like a flame, manifest itself only through a kind of bearer. This bearer is the semiotic element. Thus the coherence of words or sentences is the bearer through which, like a flash, similarity appears.'

21 Benjamin ([1933] 1989, 1991).

22 Ibid.: 796.

23 Benjamin explains ([1933] 1979: 66): 'Thus even profane reading, if it is not to forsake understanding altogether, shares this with magical reading: that it is subject to a necessary speed, or rather a critical moment, which the reader must

not forget at any cost unless he wishes to go away empty-handed.' It is with the concern 'not to emerge from the reading process empty-handed' that Benjamin ([1917] 1985, 1991: 35) examines Kant's precautions against a metaphysic that makes transcendental use of the categories, and against the exercise of metaphysics of deducing the world from the principles of cognition, thus yielding speculative knowledge. Freud likewise cautions against the simple replacement of thing presentations of the unconscious system with word presentations of the (pre)conscious system, without connecting them with the thing presentations allied with word presentations in the (pre)conscious system. Drawing a simple connection of thing presentations with word presentations in an attempt at restoring the lost object, and doing so in the service of abstract thought, Freud avers, more likely characterizes 'the schizophrenic's mode of thought': 'When we think in abstractions there is a danger that we may neglect the relations of words to unconscious thing-presentations, and it must be confessed that the expression and content of our philosophizing then begins to acquire an unwelcome resemblance to the mode of operation of schizophrenics. We may, on the other hand, attempt a characterization of the schizophrenic's mode of thought by saying that he treats concrete things as though they were abstract.' Freud ([1915] 1985): 210.

[24] In Benjamin's words: 'The history of the dream remains to be written, and opening up a perspective on this subject would mean decisively overcoming the superstitious belief in natural necessity by means of historical illumination' (Benjamin [1926] 2008: 236).

[25] Freud ([1900] 1978).

[26] See Foucault ([1966] 1970): 29. While the work *of* similarities is in the service of repression, preventing a presentation of the drive from reaching the conscious system, the work *on* similarities in interpretation constitutes a reverse move, to undo the disguise.

[27] Ibid.: 36.

[28] Ibid.: 32.

[29] Ibid.: 40.

[30] Ibid: 41.

[31] Freud ([1910] 1970, 1994): 234.

[32] The notion of 'work' here would need to be specified – see note 26.

[33] Foucault ([1966] 1970): 32.

[34] Freud ([1915] 1985): 207.

[35] It is interesting to note that Kant undertakes the same move with his division of 'experience' between 'immediate experience' and 'experience in the context of knowledge/cognition', thus rupturing the pre-critical unity of knowledge and experience. It is this move that Benjamin picks up – see elaborations below.

[36] Freud ([1915] 1985): 207–08.

[37] Freud ([1900] 1978): 381, 412.

[38] Ibid.: 422–31, 454.

[39] Ibid.: 454–55.

[40] Ricoeur ([1965] 1974): 18.

[41] Benjamin ([1916] 2002): 66.

[42] Benjamin ([1916] 1977, 1991): 146.

[43] Benjamin explains the process of translation effected by the materiality of works of art, internal to the language of things: 'There is a language of sculpture, of painting, of poetry. Just as the language of poetry is partly, if not solely, founded on the name language of man, it is very conceivable that the language of sculpture or painting is founded on certain kinds of thing languages, that in them we

find a translation of the language of things into an infinitely higher language, which may still be of the same sphere. We are concerned here with nameless, non-acoustic languages, languages issuing from matter; here we should recall the material community of things in their communication.' Benjamin ([1916] 2002): 73.

[44] Benjamin ([1916] 1977, 1991): 155.

[45] This is how Benjamin reads Kant's demotion of 'experience': Impelled by his critiques of both transcendental and speculative idealism, and of 'enthusiasm', Kant rejects the conflation of two notions of 'experience' – that of immediate experience, and the concept of experience in relation to knowledge/cognition – which he wants to distinguish, firstly, by drawing a dividing line between them, and secondly, by asserting a qualitative difference between immediate experience and experience in the context of knowledge/cognition, where the former has been submitted to and transformed by symbolization (Benjamin [1917] 1985, 1991: 36). 'The distinction that must be made is between the immediate and natural concept of experience and the concept of experience in the context of knowledge. In other words, the confusion arose from conflating the concepts of "experience" and "knowledge of experience". For the concept of knowledge, experience is not anything new and extraneous to it, but only itself in a different form; experience as the object of knowledge is the unified and continuous manifold of knowledge. Paradoxical though it sounds, experience does not occur as such in the knowledge of experience, simply because this is knowledge of experience and hence a context of knowledge. Experience, however, is the symbol of this context of knowledge and therefore belongs in a completely different order of things from knowledge itself.' Benjamin ([1917] 2002): 95.

[46] Benjamin ([1917] 1985, 1991): 37.

[47] See Benjamin ([1918] 2002): 108. Benjamin's postulate, rendered in full (in German): '*Auf Grund des Kantischen Systems einen Erkenntnisbegriff zu schaffen dem der Begriff einer Erfahrung korrespondiert von der die Erkenntnis Lehre ist.*' (Benjamin [1918] 1977, 1991: 168)

[48] Benjamin (1985, 1991): 88.

References

Agamben, Giorgio (2009), *The Signature of All Things: On Method*, translated by Luca D'Isanto with Kevin Attell, New York: Zone Books.

Benjamin, Walter ([1916] 1977, 1991), 'Über Sprache überhaupt und über die Sprache des Menschen', in *Aufsätze, Essays, Vorträge: Gesammelte Schriften Bd. II.I*, edited by Rolf Tiedemann and Hermann Schweppenhäuser, Frankfurt am Main: Suhrkamp: 140–57.

Benjamin, Walter ([1916] 2002), 'On Language as such and on the Language of Man', translated by Edmund Jephcott, in *Selected Writings*, Vol. 1: *1913–1926*, edited by Marcus Bullock and Michael W. Jennings, Cambridge, MA and London: The Belknap Press of Harvard University Press: 62–74.

Benjamin, Walter ([1917] 1985, 1991), 'Über die Wahrnehmung', in *Fragmente, Autobiographische Schriften: Gesammelte Schriften, Bd. VI*, edited by Rolf Tiedemann and Hermann Schweppenhäuser, Frankfurt am Main: Suhrkamp: 33–38.

Benjamin, Walter ([1917] 2002), 'On Perception', translated by Rodney Livingstone, in *Selected Writings*, Vol. 1: *1913–1926*, edited by Marcus Bullock and Michael W. Jennings, Cambridge, MA and London: The Belknap Press of Harvard University Press: 93–96.

Benjamin, Walter ([1918] 1977, 1991), 'Über das Programm der kommenden Philosophie', in *Aufsätze, Essays, Vorträge: Gesammelte Schriften, Bd. II.1*, edited by Rolf Tiedemann and Hermann Schweppenhäuser, Frankfurt am Main: Suhrkamp: 157–71.

Benjamin, Walter ([1918] 2002), 'On the Program of the Coming Philosophy', translated by Mark Ritter, in *Selected Writings*, Vol. 1: *1913–1926*, edited by Marcus Bullock and Michael W. Jennings, Cambridge, MA and London: The Belknap Press of Harvard University Press: 100–10.

Benjamin, Walter ([1926] 2008), 'Dream Kitsch', in *The Work of Art in the Age of Its Technological Reproducibility*, translated by Edmund Jephcott *et al.*, edited by Michael W. Jennings *et al.*, Cambridge, MA and London: The Belknap Press of Harvard University Press: 236–39.

Benjamin, Walter ([1933] 1979), 'Doctrine of the Similar', translated by Kurt Tarnowski, *New German Critique*, no. 17, Spring: 65–69.

Benjamin, Walter ([1933] 1977, 1991), 'Lehre vom Ähnlichen', in *Aufsätze, Essays, Vorträge: Gesammelte Schriften Bd. II.I*, edited by Rolf Tiedemann and Hermann Schweppenhäuser, Frankfurt am Main: Suhrkamp: 204–10.

Benjamin, Walter ([1933] 1977, 1991), 'Über das mimetische Vermögen', in *Aufsätze, Essays, Vorträge: Gesammelte Schriften Bd. II.*I, edited by Rolf Tiedemann and Hermann Schweppenhäuser, Frankfurt am Main: Suhrkamp: 210–13.

Benjamin, Walter ([1933] 1989, 1991), 'Notizen zur Überarbeitung von Die Lehre vom Ähnlichen', in *Nachträge: Gesammelte Schriften Bd. VII.2*, edited by Rolf Tiedemann and Hermann Schweppenhäuser, Frankfurt am Main: Suhrkamp: 794–96.

Benjamin, Walter ([1933] 1992), 'On the Mimetic Faculty', in *One Way Street and Other Writings*, translated by Edmund Jephcott and Kingsley Shorter, London and New York: Verso: 160–63.

Benjamin, Walter (1985, 1991), 'Zur Erfahrung', in *Fragmente, Autobiographische Schriften: Gesammelte Schriften, Bd. VI*, edited by Rolf Tiedemann and Hermann Schweppenhäuser, Frankfurt am Main: Suhrkamp: 88–89.

Foucault, Michel ([1966] 1970), *The Order of Things: An Archaeology of the Human Sciences*, London: Tavistock.

Freud, Sigmund ([1910] 1970, 1994), 'Über den Gegensinn der Urworte', in *Psychologische Schriften (Fischer Studienausgabe, Bd. IV)*, Frankfurt am Main: S. Fischer: 229–34.

Freud, Sigmund ([1900] 1978), *The Interpretation of Dreams*, translated and edited by James Strachey, Harmondsworth: Penguin.

Freud, Sigmund ([1915] 1985), 'The Unconscious', in *On Metapsychology: The Theory of Psychoanalysis*, translated by James Strachey, edited by Angela Richards, Harmondsworth: Penguin: 167–222.

Mauss, Marcel ([1950] 1972), *A General Theory of Magic*, translated by Robert Brain, London and Boston: Routledge & Kegan Paul.

Ricoeur, Paul ([1965] 1974), *Die Interpretation: Ein Versuch über Freud*, translated by Eva Moldenhauer, Frankfurt am Main: Suhrkamp.

Similarity–Divergence–Convergence

For a historiography of relational processes

Jürgen Osterhammel

Paradigm Shift

'Similarity' has been declared the new 'paradigm in cultural theory'.[1] This is important because it appears that we are at the beginning of a new *turn*, and *turns* cannot be decreed from above.[2] This new paradigm has been proposed by daring theoretical strategists and provided with an initial push based on their reputations, but it must also generate enthusiasm among a wider range of scholars and the unavoidable systemic need for external funding. Because it represents the horizon of what is explorable and conceivable, a 'paradigm' spreads as an academic movement that opens up new intellectual and material resources over the course of its development. A *very* successful 'paradigm' creates new inclusions and exclusions. Those who resist conversion suddenly find themselves associated with the 'old way of thinking'. This is precisely what happened to social historians during the *cultural turn* of the late 1980s who rapidly went from being the victorious *avant-garde* to the equivalent of the last pagans of the Roman west in the fifth century.

We are not quite there yet with the current turn towards similarity. It must still be argumentatively established, and once its initial theoretical charisma has persuaded an inner circle of partisans, it must still convince a wider field of well-meaning sceptics who are waiting for the initial flashes of inspiration to be developed into a more robust theoretical architecture. As early as 1969, Niklas Luhmann perfectly characterized this critical phase in the acceptance of a new theory:

> One cannot simply jump into the saddle according to rules that apply after the destruction of esteemed theories by merely imitating their architecture. Those who work with foreign theories take on a subordinate role, and understandably, want to know whether it is worth it, where it will lead to, what sort of group they are joining, and who they are making enemies with.[3]

Another important factor in the 'practice of theory' (Luhmann) is the theory's disciplinary origin, and the extent to which this original discipline seeks to engage neighbouring fields in a discussion that is (at least at the beginning) open to debating some of the fundamental premises of the new paradigm in a way that is not predetermined from the outset.

The new *turn* towards similarity has been announced by a group of scholars who come primarily from (German) literary studies. Because literary studies have distinguished themselves as the most important driving force within cultural studies since the 1990s (overtaking anthropology), this polarity reversal from 'difference' to 'similarity' thus represents a claim to bring about a change in direction for cultural studies *as a whole*. Given the significant consequences that such a strategic course correction would have – including its potential effects on the organization and financing of research, and the future opportunities for an entire cohort of junior researchers – the debate surrounding it should be careful and remain dispassionate. Above all, this debate must examine whether the theoretical foundation offered by the new paradigm is sufficient and convincing, and how other disciplinary perspectives might react. In the light of ever-increasing calls for innovation in the social sciences, and the necessity to convert new ideas as quickly as possible into collaborative initiatives and externally funded programmes in an extremely competitive research environment, it may seem that there is little time for such leisurely assessments. But until such a discussion is at least tentatively concluded, it would be premature to apply a theoretical sketch that is clearly intended to be provisional to specific cases; in other words, to simply begin feeding new thematic material into the well-oiled machinery of producing project proposals and scholarly anthologies.

The following remarks have been written out of concern for exactly this kind of theoretical rashness. They also seek to point out that there are disciplines within the social sciences whose broad theoretical orientations are not necessarily limited to *culture* theory. These remarks come from a historian of international and global relations (including their cultural aspects) who has long been familiar with the problems of post-colonialism, but who does not himself work *within* a culture-theoretical frame of reference or language game – while openly professing an instrumentalist and eclectic relationship to *theory* in the singular and theories in the plural. Within the context of current international trends, this relationship might seem less anachronistic now than it did just a few years ago, during the height of admiration for grand hegemonic theories.

The Poverty of Theory in Historical Studies

The inescapable demand within historical studies for theories has generally been accepted in the post-historical understanding of the field,[4] but the extent to which it has become a guiding aspect of research has varied from historian to historian. This poverty can be found at least at three levels. *First*, it can be seen in methodological reflections on the possibilities of and limits to historical understanding, on the chances of making plausible, correct and maybe even true statements, and on the forms and strategies of argumentation and narrative construction. *Second*, different historians utilize theories from different theoretical fields: the history of ideas requires theories of semantics; economic history uses theories that deal with the accumulation of capital or consumer behaviour; social history needs theories of stratification, social change and the collective construction of identity; etc. *Third*, historical studies always work within the *zeitgeist* of their respective present. Even if they do not necessarily capitulate to the dominant spirit of the times, they still absorb it and are influenced by it. While it is clear that the challenges posed by postmodernity have rarely led to an explicit and consistent postmodern historiography, postmodernism has certainly influenced the thinking of most historians. Unwavering certainty in the stability of modern progress, for instance, has been in decline for decades. Those from outside of historical studies who suggest the existence of a naïve conceptual realism, or a lack of recognition regarding the constructed nature of historical objects, have mistaken the consensus self-image of the field.

The proposed shift of attention to 'similarity' has consequences for all three levels mentioned above. (1) From a methodological perspective, similarity is associated with a plea for attenuated concepts, even including the risk of the complete dissolution of precise terminology and the relativization of traditional forms of logical argumentation. As implied above, this is also associated with the revival of the old question regarding the amount of theory necessary for social sciences (and history in particular), and whether a *maximum* of theorizing might even sabotage the quest for knowledge in social science research. (2) As applied to different theoretical fields, similarity focuses our interest on concepts of mediation, transition and integration. This is connected to a way of thinking that we might call 'analytical gradualism', and which can be applied to many fields: a way of thinking that deals less with categories of Foucauldian abrupt *coupure* and more with continuously adjustable finetuning. (3) With regard to its connection to the *zeitgeist*, similarity is more opaque: the end of the Cold War (now a quarter-century ago) led to the dismantling of certain confrontational constellations, but also had little effect on other patterns of conflict and was unable to prevent the intensification of yet further differences. The world we live in today is not marked by weaker oppositions than it was in 1990. An academic shift towards 'similarity' thus only mirrors observable global developments to the extent that certain phenomena – which we can subsume under the comfortably broadly defined label of 'globalization' – imply an increasing global convergence of lifestyles and mentalities. Seen from a regional and social perspective, however, these developments are distributed very unevenly, and together, they do not add up to a converging overall trend towards global harmony and homogeneity.

Dichotomous Thinking

In general terms, the similarity paradigm by no means represents a sensational turn for the science of history. Despite its openness to theoretical developments of all kinds, history has never been a discipline that is *primarily* guided by theory. Thus, when it comes to changing hegemonic trends and paradigms, history has rarely been forced to undertake a fundamental reorientation. In other words, historians will not be surprised by the turn towards similarity because they never lost their trust in the concept of similarity in the first place.

Simple reasons for this can be found in the history of science. Other than the fundamental operations of Aristotelian logic, it is clear that the rough binarism that functions as the quasi-fundamental operating system in the *humanities* dates back to the beginnings of structural linguistics in the age of Ferdinand de Saussure, and spread to other social sciences through the linguistic reception of French ethnological structuralism. A certain tendency towards dichotomies was inherent in early and mid-career Foucauldian thought, and reappeared in a simplified and much more rhetorically effective way in Edward W. Said's 1978 juxtaposition of Orient and Occident. In this latter context, dichotomous thought has become an incredibly powerful and orthodoxy-forming standard description of *othering*.[5] This also hearkens back to dramatic interpretations of decolonialization, particularly those by Frantz Fanon (introduced to European intellectual discourse primarily by Jean Paul Sartre), who asserted a deep cleavage between colonializing perpetrators and colonialized victims, and left no space for a third grey zone of diffuse and unambiguous situations.[6]

Late postcolonialism, on the other hand, softened Edward Said's politically charged dichotomous categories of friend vs. foe by introducing concepts of 'hybridity' (Homi Bhabha) or intermediary 'contact zones' (Mary Louise Pratt) without directly questioning the guiding fundamental opposition between identity and alterity. Inasmuch as 'similarity' was incorporated into such polar and polarized thought, it took place within a framework of binary coding whose fundamental structure was never questioned.

For the practical work of historians, such a model has always been considered too coarse. The vast majority of historians have never warmed to the dichotomous mindsets found in both structuralism and poststructuralism; even Niklas Luhmann's considerations of binary coding (and his application of such coding to different social systems) found only limited acceptance in historical analytical practice.[7] The question of primacy between difference and similarity, between heterogeneity and homogeneity, has thus never been posed in historical practice, so that a theoretical U-turn finds no basis in the working practice of historical research and interpretation. There is another simple reason for this: even if the science of history often deals with supra-individual structures – social hierarchies, international orders, discourses, etc. – it operates with a form of methodological individualism that it can never entirely shake, and thus always returns to the consciousness and actions of individual people. As tools, dichotomous models are too coarse to help understand the action-logics of real people (or, incidentally, to morally evaluate such actions). In essence, they presume a mono-motivational anthropology and in turn a mono-causal methodology that does not get you very far when it comes to historical analysis.

For this reason, the similarity paradigm is even pre-theoretically plausible from the perspective of practising historians. It bestows theoretical dignity on the intuitive assumption of a fundamental level of anthropological trust that makes cooperation and communicative understanding possible. Thus the similarity paradigm legitimizes (if such legitimation is even necessary) what historians have always presumed to be the *model of man* when they based their work on the interaction – if not to say dialectic – between similarity and difference. When it comes to historians, the similarity paradigm is preaching to the choir.

We could express this in another way: the low-voltage theoretical transformation that expresses the modesty behind the suggested paradigm shift – seen in a favourable preference for Gabriel Tarde's old principle of imitation which itself cannot do justice to the more rigorous standards of modern theoretical architecture – comports with historians' sensibilities. Of course, each historian must grapple separately with the individual elements of the overall package offered by the new paradigm. There is no argumentative reason for a reorientation to 'similarity' to include weakening the demand for terminological clarity and semantic discrimination. Those who look for similarity must avoid falling back on the one-dimensional descriptive language of classical historicism – or that of the historical novel that arose with such classicism. The similarity paradigm comes along with a kind of theoretically unfounded conservativism that can only be explained as a libertarian resentment towards the apparent compulsory nature of carefully defined terms. It was not long ago that literary studies used exactly this kind of instrumental terminology (originally found in the field of rhetoric) to dissect texts. In turn, the systematic social sciences (including Niklas Luhmann, the great master of distinctions) saw terminological precision as the *sui generis* goal of knowledge. Within the discipline of history, even the development of conceptual history did not lead to a theoretically founded weakening of terminology; indeed, Reinhart Koselleck insisted on maintaining terminological distinctions until the very end. The only exception to the rule was a largely theoretically unassuming descriptivism that emerged as a reaction to some of the definitional excesses of 'historical social science' (*Historische Sozialwissenschaft*) around 1980, in the guise of '*Alltagsgeschichte*' or 'experiential history'.

Even conceptually alert forms of historiography – whether Marxist, Weberian or Luhmannist – have rarely lost contact with the language of educated readers outside academia.[8] As the *writing* of history, historiography cannot help but use both the emic and etic dimensions of linguistic expression, work with metaphors and metonymies, and borrow terms from other fields, simplify them and adapt them to specific use cases – in other words, 'roughen' them up to a certain extent. The programmatic criticism of 'the modern demands for a term to be exact',[9] the turn 'against fundamentalist efforts to divide the world into strict dichotomies' and the endorsement of a 'relational terminology',[10] all match perfectly with common international historiographical practice today. But regardless of whether they show an affinity for macro- or micro-historical approaches, historians have not yet seen a reason to jeopardize the fundamental basis for a scientific view of the world,[11] namely, an intersubjective terminology that constantly evolves within the interplay between consensus and criticism.

Comparison

The science of history demands a habitualized contextual sensitivity; the echoing call for 'contextualization' found in other disciplines is simply a matter of course. History very rarely deals with completely identical phenomena, and it does not intend to violently create such identity. Even more interesting than the simple sorting of cases into different conceptual classes are the documented examples of pronounced variations of such classes. To name one such universal historical example: it is necessary to have at least a working definition of the concept of 'empire' in order to be able to identify 'empires' throughout history, and particularly to evaluate borderline cases (such as, is the USA an empire?). Normally historical investigations regarding this topic would regard the further refinement of such a definition of empire as secondary. More important would be to compare the unique characteristics of different empires with one another and, in this way, to generate a certain typology of empires. Even if they often stop short of explicit typologies (which are often seen to be too coarse), in principle historians think typologically and are attuned to contrasting considerations of mid-level abstractions between the individual case and the macro-type or the historical regularity. The science of history is a science of subtle differences or, to put it more specifically, of the calibration of differences across the course of time. Those historians that are considered canonical owe their reputations not least to their special talent for making elastic distinctions, a talent that many of their readers might not even recognize. It would be worthwhile to study all of the great historiographers, from Thucydides and Sima Qian to Eric Hobsbawm, Natalie Z. Davis and Peter Brown, from the perspective of their talent for making linguistic-conceptual distinctions. In contrast to the polarization that the similarity paradigm seeks to remove from its cultural-theoretical throne, making distinctions implies a constant dealing with similarity. The work of historians almost always moves within the wide realm *between* the identity of phenomena and their incommensurable differences – and thus in a zone of endlessly shaded similarities.

Occasionally, the habit of thinking in comparisons leads comparison to become a method. All historical studies are in some ways comparative, but only occasionally do they explicitly integrate comparative experimental designs. In order to make the logical operation of comparison useful, differences between similar things must be consciously exaggerated and must be made undeniable; otherwise there would be no *tertium comparationis* and no comparison could be made at all. The strict discipline of comparative methods requires the establishment of clear-cut units of comparison according to a methodological set of rules that has remained largely unchanged since John Stuart Mill's *A System of Logic* (1843).[12] Still, only the variable-focused social sciences strictly follow Mill's guidelines; historiography plays with meanings and narratives and is thus less strict and freer in its representations. A comparison using formalized criteria could never be represented in a readable form.

There is thus generally not much to say about the comparative method in historiography. Normally it is a hermeneutically relaxed process, and it only becomes a methodically controlled instrument when it is used to *explain*. Why was there a revolution in *France* in 1789 even though there had been a much higher level of social protests in England in the years prior? Why did anti-Semitism become so virulent in Germany (and not, for instance, in Russia, as many expected just before 1900)? As scientifically cool and exact that explanations of such historical phenomena often (must) appear, they are also usually riddled with contrafactual speculation, with visions or retroactive prognoses of what would be expected and what 'actually' happened: 'actually', the political revolution of the late eighteenth century should have taken place in England; 'actually', the conditions for a further radicalization of anti-Semitism were more favourable in Russia than anywhere else. 'Actually', the industrial revolution should have begun on the Lower Yangtze river in China and not in the English Midlands. Why didn't it? This was the question posed by the American historian Kenneth Pomeranz in a book that has become perhaps one of the most widely discussed comparative works of the last decade.[13]

This 'actually' contains a significant amount of similarity: nobody would ever get the idea that the industrial revolution began in Greenland or in Central Africa. It is only because two or more cases (or classes of cases) share a critical mass of common characteristics and preconditions that the differences between them become significant. To put it another way, the commonalities make a difference. Small variations between otherwise significantly similar situations can have large effects, and can even lead to the destruction of the similarities themselves. A slight shift backward in time, for instance, can lead to insurmountable structural consequences – even within the sciences: those who are even one day faster with the publication (or submission) of an article in *Nature*, or with registering a patent, may be more likely to gain fame and even fortune. Another example would be the First World War. In 1913 the great powers in Europe were relatively similar both structurally and ideologically. The war developed in what one could call a system of competitive similarity. The onset of war was not random or contingent, but it was also in no way an inevitable result of unavoidable conflict between completely differently conceived social and political systems – as war propaganda on all sides (and the later Sonderweg thesis) claimed. It was instead a European family feud based on family resemblances, one which led, after the war, to the breakdown of the family and ultimately to a reduction of similarity. The Europe of 1923, which for the first time in history had both a Bolshevik and a fascist state on the continent, was more heterogeneous in every way than in 1913.

This allows us to draw a general conclusion: historians are primarily interested in changes. Regardless of whether similarity intrinsically exists between things or is simply ascribed to them, it changes over time – sometimes slowly and sometimes very rapidly. Similarity is a *gradual*, shaded dimension that fills the white space between complete identity and non-identity with many different gradients. Similarity is a dimension that can rarely be precisely *measured*, but must almost always be *estimated*. Assessing similarity requires a good eye. And if we see this in the context of change over time, we realize that there is no sharp distinction between a pre-modern, static world of magical correspondences and inert hierarchies, and a completely different 'modernity'. Instead we find a permanent dynamic of becoming more or less similar, of convergence and divergence, a dynamic of long waves and rapid upheavals, as well as the categories of proximity and distance. Thus, to put it simplistically (and from the perspective of a Christian European intellectual), Christianity and Islam were *culturally* more similar to one another in 1200 or in 1800 than in 900, 1500 or 2000. The entire history of the Jewish minorities in Europe – a history of coexistence, assimilation, anti-Semitism and genocide – is also a history of shifting attributions of similarity and foreignness. Such attributions operate using the versatile semantics of depth and surface, of authenticity and non-authenticity. In truth, as Shakespeare had his Shylock proclaim, under the surface of a different culture we Jews are people just like the Christians, and we even share the same thirst for revenge: 'if we are like you in the rest, we will resemble you in that.'[14] The Enlightenment philosophers emphasized this 'actual' similarity: despite their foreign appearance Jews were people too. On the other side, beginning in roughly 1860, French, German and Austrian anti-Semites began to claim that the similarities between assimilated Jews and Christian civil society were a ruse that hid the 'true' nature of Jewish dissimilarity.

Within the context of rationality-based science, the judgment of similarities relies on standards that cannot be derived directly from the logic of comparative methods but rather must be introduced from somewhere else. How could we, for instance, classify both the historical and contemporary similarities between the United States and Western Europe? Is Heinrich August Winkler right when he emphasizes the homogeneity of the so-called west based on centuries of shared common values?[15] Or should we rather agree with Shmuel N. Eisenstadt who criticized the idea of a homogenous west in his comments on *multiple modernities*, and instead postulated a unique North American model of civilization that is distinctly different from the Western European model?[16] Who is closer to and who is farther from today's enlightened Western European: a liberal Muslim or a Trumpist Republican?

These reflections have already gone significantly beyond the realm of a *lege artis* macro-history. And they still have not touched on a keyword that may have already occurred even to non-historians in this context: namely, *l'histoire croisée*. Behind this name, however, hides a theory that no outsider could expect even if they have read Michael Werner and Bénédicte Zimmermann's programmatic 2006 essay on the topic.[17] The enlightening effects of Werner and Zimmerman's concept (briefly: the connection of transnationality, reflexivity and contextualization) can really only fully unfold for those who have seen the primacy of national history as self-evident and who now seek to think outside of their own national histories. When this occurs, it quickly becomes clear that national histories very often overlap with one another.

In principle, they do this in two types of historical situations: the horizontal sharing of relatively stable border regions with a high degree of similarities (such as in the Lake Constance region), and the vertical, hierarchical foreign domination seen in colonialism and naturally in countless other instances of inner European history. If we expand the concept of overlapping or interwoven histories further, two other case-types emerge: the transfer of ideas and institutions across political borders, and the unprecedented case of broad European integration and the creation of a supranational legal system and quasi-government over the last fifty years.

The concept of interwoven or, even better, incomprehensibly entangled histories has always had a certain provocativeness for inflexible national historians, but its practical application suffers from its inability to create differentiation. It can handle simple and peaceful conditions, and it is no coincidence that scholarly and literary transfers between France and Germany or the inner European circulation of welfare state models are commonly cited examples of successful application of such an entangled approach to history. But the concept is less helpful when dealing with violent entanglements. To say that European national histories were *entangled* during great periods of war (such as in the 1630s, in the period of the Napoleonic empire or during the two world wars) would be an expression of embarrassing banality. In such situations history should seek to untangle, and differences must be recognized – such as those between French control over the kingdom of Westphalia and the Rhine alliance states, and German control of Ukraine and Belarus during the Second World War: both are examples of *entanglement* but both had entirely different consequences!

Similarity without Proximity

Some of the greatest discoveries of the early modern period in Europe were in finding similarities with farflung parts of the world or, to put it somewhat less neutrally, with 'foreign' cultures. We quickly come across such discoveries when studying travel diaries of the seventeenth and eighteenth centuries. In 1724, the Jesuit priest Joseph-François Lafitau published *Mœurs des sauvages amériquains comparées aux mœurs des premiers temps*, in which he claimed that the Native Americans of the Canadian forests were closely related to the ancient Greeks. It is clear that Lafitau used such imagery as a way to make these 'naked savages' more sympathetic to his European public, but he was also by all means making an anthropological statement as well, and voicing an objection to too-steep cultural hierarchization. Even more explicit are the reports of missionaries – again, mostly Jesuits and merchants – from Japan and China. Starting in the middle of the sixteenth century on the other side of the world, one finds other societies and civilizations that were at least on par with (or even superior to) the 'west' with regard to living standards and cultural refinement. The authors of such reports thus had no qualms about making comparisons between Europe and Asia: comparability was not a problem. Neither the term 'savages' nor the less degrading term 'barbarians' was used to describe these societies. Their religious differences were seen less as a principal flaw than as a practical challenge of missionary work, and provided a rich field of observation for the ethnographic curiosity of the epoch.

The similarity felt by observers on the ground and their 'philosophical' readers in Europe was *so* great that it appeared to be possible to learn directly from the others – something Leibniz sought to organize. Critics of middle European absolutism, for instance, cited the example of the Chinese emperor who was restrained by laws. At least until the middle of the seventeenth century, India was dominated by a religious tolerance that some Europeans saw as an exemplary model; the religious liberality of the Mughal emperor Akbar was often applauded. From the humanist Giovanni Botero and his *Relationi universali* (1596) to the English statesman Lord Brougham in the 1840s, the political systems in Asia were quite naturally compared to those in Europe on the basis of perceived fundamental similarities.

But this trend began to shift in the early nineteenth century. In his studies of August Wilhelm Schlegel, Anil Bhatti convincingly demonstrates the emergence of what he calls a 'hard' orientalism in Germany: a judgmental hierarchization of peoples that can be seen in the transition from Wilhelm von Humboldt and the Schlegel brothers to Hegel's *Lectures on the Philosophy of History*.[18] For a long time, the relative openness towards similarities and equivalences outside of European civilization was little noticed. Eventually, however, it was confronted by the dilemma that is Orientalism. Edward Said, for instance, assumed *a priori* that Europeans could not help but distance themselves from Asian civilizations, to objectify, alterize and exoticize them; in short, to deny similarity. Said was able to plausibly illustrate his point using several nineteenth-century authors, but was careful not to project his thesis farther back into the eighteenth century. Some of his supporters, however, were less cautious. If there was no caricaturing alterization to be found in a given text of the early modern period or the nineteenth century, then its authors were accused of a naïve or even malicious Eurocentrism, because they were incapable or unwilling to give the alien its due right to *be foreign*. In other words, those who found similarities must have been simpletons. Historical authors with a grasp of similarity were thus caught in a trap between arrogance and autism, until a post-postcolonial perspective allowed them to be appreciated. In extreme cases, the entire Enlightenment has been seen as suspect, accused of either constructing alterity or denying it.

The search for assumptions of similarity in European texts thus depends on overcoming Said's paradigm. While we should not completely throw out certain gains made by deconstructivist and unmasking textual analysis, we need to allow for a more genuine recognition of similarities in the history of ideas. In the later chapters of his own famous book – often largely disregarded by his own supporters – Said himself acknowledged the possibility for empathy and the ability to understand others, citing the example of the French scholar of Islam, Louis Massignon.[19] Still, Said was unable to provide even minimal conditions for such empathy, and saw no connection between individual cases and what he saw as his more generalizable theory of the occident's ineluctable, power-based blindness.

Divergences and Convergences

In the ideal case, similarities should be as empirically definable as possible, and at best, even be measureable. The psychology of perception provides relatively exact methods for recording perceptions of similarity. In art history, stylistic criticism and material analysis can sometimes allow a given work to be attributed to a specific artist. Musicology deals with standardized audio materials that contain countless familial relationships (related tonality). But history does not have it so easy. When it comes to broad interpretative contexts, similarities are most easily seen when the data-set allows for quantification. One example of this is the ability to compare economic systems with one another according to their structures and their overall performance. But in almost all other cases, the estimation and measurement of similarity (as a mixture of proximity and distance) require complex considerations that are not easily objectified. The fact that two things *are* similar is perhaps relatively easy to determine. The difficulty arises when it comes to making a judgment about the *type* and *degree* of similarity. How similar or dissimilar were the societies of Germany and the United States in 1930 and in 2000 (respectively)? How similar or dissimilar are Christianity and Islam? Such questions can only be rationally discussed if we allow for a high degree of leeway in defining how similarity should be judged.

Although it is almost always more difficult to analyse processes than to describe static conditions (or conditions that have been defined statically), it should paradoxically be easier to recognize diachronic tendencies as synchronic distances. Similarity is most obvious – can most easily be understood in terms of size categories – when it changes over time. The two basic forms of such change are convergence and divergence. Such a processual perspective brings into view changes that are also both politically and cultural-sociologically interesting. Convergence – that is, the process of becoming more similar – is associated with political hopes for reconciliation and peace, and with cultural-sociological prognoses of syncretism, synthesis, and the unification of norms, values, experiences and patterns of consumption as a sign of a transculturally active globalism.

Such considerations open a broad subject area that becomes even more interesting in light of the fact that convergences and divergences do not necessarily follow long-term path dependencies; indeed, both politics and culture can rapidly shift. In such cases, historical retrospection may reveal the illusory nature of a given collapsed convergence, or might see the potential for convergence behind superficial divergences. Convergences and divergences can also overlap in different areas of reality. Thus, the convergent development of European supranationality does not necessarily correspond to the same amount of convergence or unification when it comes to the economies, political orders, cultures or mental attitudes of peoples within the borders of the European Union. During the Cold War, hopes for the development of an industrial society on both sides of the iron curtain embodied by a western 'theory of convergence' were realized only to a very limited extent. The economies and societies in both camps of the east–west confrontation developed divergently, while the convergences set in motion by the CSCE (Commission on Security and Cooperation in Europe) process were mostly limited to the political level. The end of the Cold War was less an automatic effect of social evolution than the result of political contingencies and decisions.[20]

Convergences and divergences can be explored within very different temporal frameworks. This is why opinions vary broadly in the current discussion about 'the Great Divergence' between Europe and Asia – the gap of economic development that is only today beginning to close.[21] At one end of the spectrum is the view that the decisive bifurcation[22] took place thousands of years ago (Jared Diamond). At the other end is the argument that the wealthiest areas of both China and Europe were materially on par with one another even after the industrial revolution of the late eighteenth century in England, and that it was not till the nineteenth century that such developmental gaps emerged (Kent Deng). Questions such as these will never be unequivocally answered using empirical methods. Each of the prominently supported positions will naturally be evaluated based on the quality of its empirical foundations, but ultimately, multifactoral arguments exist in opposition to one another and must be evaluated using criteria of plausibility.

The search for tendencies toward convergence and divergence, of coming closer or distancing, of similarization and dissimilarization, of integration and alienation, is not the realm of science alone. Over the course of history, individuals and groups have continually placed themselves in changing relationships with others. Comparison is a cognitive operation of self-positioning.[23] Entire societies, and at the very least large groups of elites, are obsessively concerned with their similarities to certain benchmarks. Since the middle of the nineteenth century, for instance, all of the great countries in Asia, from the Ottoman empire to Japan, debated how one could become more similar to the west without losing one's own 'substance' (taken literally from the Chinese *ti*). Other than a small circle of extremely uncompromising 'westernizers' and a few stubborn traditionalists, most leaders of these countries have sought to find a politically and culturally responsible optimum of dissimilar similarity.[24] Even today, Russian intellectuals question the positioning of their country between Europe and Asia.[25] The relationship between Europe and the United States of America has always been characterized by the ambiguities of distant proximity and proximate distance. The expansion of the European Union, and the differences between the North and the South in Europe that have become more pronounced since the beginning of the twenty-first century, make this topic both historically and contemporarily more important today. 'Similarity' is a spotlight that allows us to recognize the way in which countless historical processes are related to one another. Such processes deal with the cultural construction of dynamic spacing; that is, with the awareness of convergence and divergence, and occasionally even their describable and measurable reality.

Notes

1 Bhatti *et al.* (2011). For more background, see also Bhatti (2005); Bhatti (2011).

2 For more on the function of 'turns' from a scientific-sociological perspective, cf. Conrad (2006); for more on the greatest global 'turn' of the late twentieth century, cf. Cusset (2003).

3 Luhmann (1970): 263f.

4 The starting point for any such discussion remains Koselleck ([1972] 2000).

[5] Cf. Said (1978).
[6] Fanon (1963). On self-interpretations in anti-colonial liberation movements, cf. Jansen and Osterhammel (2017): 156–70.
[7] A particularly clear explanation of 'binary coding' can be found in Luhmann (1992): 194ff.
[8] For more on this connection to the public as an essential feature of historical studies, cf. especially Noiriel (2005): 43–45, and many other parts of this collection of essays.
[9] Bhatti *et al.* (2011): 236.
[10] Ibid.: 245.
[11] Which has been accepted as legitimate since the 'Crisis of Historicism' around 1900.
[12] A more recent clear explanation of these guidelines can be found in Lorenz (1997): 231–84; also cf. Haupt (2001), Mahoney and Rueschemeyer (2003).
[13] Pomeranz (2000); a good overview of the debate is provided by O'Brien (2010).
[14] William Shakespeare, *The Merchant of Venice*, III.1; Shakespeare (2001): 60–61.
[15] Cf. Winkler (2009–15).
[16] Cf. Eisenstadt (2000), especially the chapter on the United States of America: 46–109.
[17] After the previous French work, the definitive version of the concept: Werner and Zimmermann (2006).
[18] Bhatti (2010).
[19] Said (1978): 264–74.
[20] On the balance of research and debate on the east–west convergence, cf. Inkeles (1998).
[21] Cf. Kramper (2009).
[22] An important concept for historical theory that could be made more fertile among other things on the basis of a variety of statements made by Niklas Luhmann: it indicates 'selection' and 'path differentiation', but not necessarily 'polarization'. From an entirely different direction, cf. Schramm (2004).
[23] Cf. the further observations made in Heintz (2010).
[24] Mishra (2012) provides a panoramic overview of these debates.
[25] Marlène Laruelle (2008) has written brilliantly on this topic.

References

Bhatti, Anil (2005), 'Aspekte gesellschaftlicher Diversität und Homogenisierung im postkolonialen Kontext: Anmerkungen aus Indien', in Wolfgang Müller-Funk and Birgit Wagner, eds, *Eigene und andere Fremde: 'Postkoloniale' Konflikte im europäischen Kontext*, Wien: Turia und Kant: 31–47.

——— (2010), 'August Wilhelm Schlegels Indien Experiment: Kulturtransfer und Wissenschaft', in York-Gothart Mix and Jochen Strobel, eds, *Der Europäer, A.W. Schlegel: Romantischer Kulturtransfer – romantische Wissenswelten*, Berlin and New York: De Gruyter: 237–53.

——— (2011), 'Kulturelle Ähnlichkeit bedeutet nicht, daß unsere Hemden gleich sind: Ähnlichkeit und Differenz in Kultur und Kulturtheorie', interview with Anil Bhatti conducted by Bernhard Kleeberg and Andreas Langenohl, *Zeitschrift für Kulturphilosophie*, Vol. 5: 343–56.

Bhatti, Anil *et al.* (2011), 'Ähnlichkeit Ein kulturtheoretisches Paradigma', *Internationales Archiv für Sozialgeschichte der deutschen Literatur*, 36 (1): 233–47.

Conrad, Christoph (2006), 'Die Dynamik der Wenden: Von der neuen Sozialgeschichte zum cultural turn', in Dieter Langewiesche, Paul Nolte and Jürgen Osterhammel, eds, *Wege der Gesellschaftsgeschichte*, Vol. 22, Göttingen: Vandenhoeck and Ruprecht: 133–60.

Cusset, François (2003), *French Theory: Foucault, Derrida, Deleuze & Cie et les mutations de la vie intellectuelle aux États-Unis*, Paris: La Découverte.

Eisenstadt, Shmuel N. (2000), *Die Vielfalt der Moderne*, edited and translated by Brigitte Schluchter, Weilerswist: Velbrück Wissenschaft.

Fanon, Frantz (1963), *The Wretched of the Earth*, New York: Grove Press.

Haupt, Heinz-Gerhard (2001), 'Comparative History', in Neil J. Smelser and Paul B. Baltes, eds, *International Encyclopedia of the Social and Behavioral Sciences*, Vol. 4, Amsterdam: Pergamon: 2397–403.

Heintz, Bettina (2010), 'Numerische Differenz Überlegungen zu einer Soziologie des (quantitativen) Vergleichs', *Zeitschrift für Soziologie*, Vol. 39: 1621–81.

Inkeles, Alex (1998), *One World Emerging? Convergence and Divergence in Industrial Societies*, Boulder, CO: Westview Press.

Jansen, Jan C. and Jürgen Osterhammel (2017), *Decolonization: A Short History*, Princeton, NJ: Princeton University Press.

Koselleck, Reinhart ([1972] 2000), 'Über die Theoriebedürftigkeit der Geschichtswissenschaft', in *Zeitschichten: Studien zur Historik*, Frankfurt am Main: Suhrkamp: 298–316.

Kramper, Peter (2009), 'Warum Europa? Konturen einer globalgeschichtlichen Forschungskontroverse', *Neue Politische Literatur*, Vol. 54: 9–46.

Laruelle, Marlène (2008), *Russian Eurasianism: An Ideology of Empire*, Washington D.C.: Woodrow Wilson Center Press with Johns Hopkins University Press.

Lorenz, Chris (1997), *Konstruktion der Vergangenheit: Eine Einführung in die Geschichtstheorie*, Köln, Wien und Weimar: Böhlau Verlag.

Luhmann, Niklas (1970), 'Die Praxis der Theorie', in *Soziologische Aufklärung: Aufsätze zur Theorie sozialer Systeme*, Vol. 1, Opladen: Westdeutscher Verlag.

——— (1992), *Die Wissenschaft der Gesellschaft*, Frankfurt am Main: Suhrkamp.

Mahoney, James and Dietrich Rueschemeyer (2003), 'Comparative Historical Analysis: Achievements and Agendas', in James Mahoney and Dietrich Rueschemeyer, eds, *Comparative Historical Analysis in the Social Sciences*, Cambridge: Cambridge University Press: 3–38.

Mishra, Pankaj (2012), *From the Ruins of Empire: The Revolt against the West and the Remaking of Asia*, London: Allen Lane.

Noiriel, Gérard (2005), *Sur la 'crise' de l'histoire*, Paris: Gallimard.

O'Brien, Patrick K. (2010), 'Ten Years of Debate on the Origins of the Great Divergence', Review no. 1008, *Reviews in History*, available at http://www.history.ac.uk/reviews/review/1008

Pomeranz, Kenneth (2000), *The Great Divergence: China, Europe, and the Making of the Modern World Economy*, Princeton, NJ: Princeton University Press.

Said, Edward W. (1978), *Orientalism*, London: Routledge and Kegan Paul.

Schramm, Gottfried (2004), *Fünf Wegscheiden der Weltgeschichte*, Göttingen: Vandenhoeck and Ruprecht.

Shakespeare, William (2001), *The Merchant of Venice*, London: Methuen.

Werner, Michael and Bénédicte Zimmermann (2006), 'Beyond Comparison: *Histoire croisée* and the Challenge of Reflexivity', *History and Theory*, Vol. 45: 30–50.

Winkler, Heinrich August (2009–15), *Geschichte des Westens*, 4 vols, Munich: C.H. Beck.

Resemblance

Functions and fields of a controversial concept[1]

Klaus Sachs-Hombach

Introduction

There is little doubt that in many contexts, resemblance is a criterion that we use to judge circumstances and objects without really thinking about what it means at a fundamental level. At the same time, attempts to find a precise definition of resemblance quickly demonstrate that terminological clarity is elusive. The fundamental problem of possible definitions of resemblance is that general formulations seem trivial, and more informative formulations seem like ad-hoc rules that are only plausible for extremely concrete contexts. To provide an example, one possible general definition might read: an object A resembles an object B if both objects share at least one property. The problem here is that any object can be considered similar to any other object, because we will *always* be able to find at least one shared property. In contrast, a more concrete definition of resemblance might state: an object A resembles an object B if both objects appear the same. This definition is informative and certainly is not trivial, but is only plausible or valid for an extremely limited domain.

One fundamental criticism of the concept of resemblance has become particularly prominent within the field of picture theory, where it is often used to contrast pictures with linguistic signs. In his influential and important work, *Languages of Art*, Nelson Goodman criticized the theory of resemblance, as it is called, for being theoretically unproductive.[2] This marginalized the concept of resemblance theory for understanding pictures despite the fact that it had long been common and unproblematic – indeed we can trace its roots to Platonic philosophy. According to Goodman, the problems with the concept of resemblance for picture theory do not lie in the fact that pictures have nothing to do with resemblance, nor that the theory of resemblance is always wrong or generally meaningless. Rather, critics of resemblance theory claim that it is unproductive regarding decisive philosophical questions of conceptual analysis: that a concept of resemblance provides neither sufficient nor necessary conditions for answering the question of what makes a picture a picture, or answering questions of how to determine a picture's concrete referent. According to such criticism, resemblance theory only identifies a problem but offers no solution.[3] In this sense, Nelson Goodman's contribution was to free picture theory from its reliance on the concept of resemblance. Nevertheless the criterion of resemblance may have functions within the theory of pictures apart from its prominent historical application with respect to representational theory. The following considerations follow the idea that there are multiple areas and functions for resemblance judgements which ought to be first conceptually differentiated from one another and then investigated for their reciprocal connections to one another. This is especially necessary for the relationship between representational conceptions of resemblance and those based on theories of culture, which, to me, is a relationship between semantic and epistemic references. The resemblance-oriented view of cultures suggested by Anil Bhatti assumes that there are common properties in the characterization of cultures, much in the same way that prototype theory has suggested for other fields.

In order to illustrate my remarks, I will start by describing three areas (or functions) of resemblance. First, within the field of representation theory, relations of resemblance have an important semantic function in determining the meaning of a picture. At a more fundamental level, relations of resemblance can be understood as a general ontological relationship between physical (or abstract) objects; this is the sense in which we might say that identical twins are similar to one another. Resemblance is also epistemologically important for questions of classification, i.e. questions regarding the relationship between *type* and *token*. This is how the concept of resemblance has been used in prototype theory: in contrast to the penguin, for instance, the sparrow clearly belongs to the category of 'bird', because it obviously embodies the important properties of birds – i.e. it is very similar to our prototype of 'bird'.

In what follows I begin with a discussion of resemblance within the field of representation theory, because the connection between picture and resemblance has already been extensively discussed elsewhere.[4] My remarks here draw on preliminary work that has already been published in a different form elsewhere,[5] and will show how the uniquely complex concept of representational resemblance includes the other meanings of resemblance as well. This becomes especially clear as the discussion turns towards the concepts of relevance and typicality, without which we cannot satisfactorily explain resemblance. With these two concepts, however, we are able to better understand the interplay between the semantic, ontological and epistemological functions of resemblance. I then further specify why and in what form the concept of resemblance can be understood as an 'internalized' resemblance (at least in the context of representation theory). Finally, I describe the connections between the different functions of resemblance and end my remarks with a brief note on the concept of family resemblance.

Picture and Resemblance

Goodman presented his criticism of resemblance theory within the framework of a more general theory of signs. According to Goodman's theory, it is a mistake to try and distinguish between the pictorial and non-pictorial forms of representation by describing the semantic relationship between them, because graphic and linguistic signs are semantically identical with one another.[6] As a result, the relationship between a picture and that which is depicted is not 'more natural' than that between linguistic signs and the objects they refer to. Thus, resemblance can be seen as a contingent property of pictorial representation that is only significant according to appropriate conventions. According to Goodman, this is why pictures do not imitate; instead – like linguistic signs – they classify.[7]

Despite Goodman's extensive criticism, resemblance theory has not lost all of its supporters. On the one hand, it is clear that resemblance is not an appropriate candidate for finding an answer to the general question of what makes a picture a picture. On the other, however, the concept of resemblance *can* represent a valuable criterion when it comes to the concrete question of the distinguishability between pictorial and linguistic signs as well as the question of how pictures represent – provided that we can more strictly define what 'resemblance' refers to and which functions it has. To do just this, I will begin by defining a picture as follows: '(B1) A sign is considered a picture if we use its form (in particular the relational positions of its elements with one another) as a criterion to determine its meaning. This means that we attribute the form that we recognize in the sign to that which is being represented.'

According to this definition, resemblance is used as a sort of rule of interpretation, as a semantic criterion. Resemblance in itself does not, of course, imply the status of 'picture'. The semantic function of resemblance only determines meaning after a sign has been recognized as such and a meaning has been ascribed in relation to an object. Accordingly, the meaning of a picture is (at least somewhat) dependent on an evaluation of resemblance. Formulated somewhat more technically and with explicit reference to the concept of resemblance, this can be formulated as follows: '(B2) An object G_1 is a picture of G_2 in so far as G_1 is considered a sign that is assumed to be interpreted depending on its resemblance to G_2.'

This clause clearly determines the function of resemblance as one of interpretive guidance, but it is still unclear exactly what 'resemblance' means. Based on its normal use in language, the following seems to be an appropriate general formulation to define a *qualified resemblance*: '(R1) Objects resemble one another if they share typical properties based on relevant property dimensions.'

Here, property dimensions include elements such as form, weight and colour, while a concrete property might then be a specific kind of curvature that is typical for certain objects, such as balls. If we are not talking about the relationship between two arbitrary objects but rather about the relationship between a sign and that which is signified, we can reformulate this definition with the following necessary restrictions: '(S2) A sign resembles another object if the sign vehicle and the referent share typical properties based on relevant property dimensions for the representational relationship.'

Among other advantages, one strength of this definition is that it illustrates why, under certain circumstances, it is possible or even probable for us to mistake a visual representation for that which is being represented. We often mistake twins for one another, for instance, and an illusionistic representation is an example of how such mistakes can also occur regarding visual representations. My definition of resemblance implies that such mistakes can be made in so far as the relationship between sign vehicle and the referent is like a relationship between two physical objects. On the other hand (and unlike with twins), such mistakes should be relatively improbable, because in the case of representation resemblance is limited to representationally relevant properties. Saying that the visual representation of an object resembles the object itself does not by any means imply that the picture resembles the object in all aspects (such as being made of the same material, for instance), but only in those aspects that are important for representation. As theoretically expected, the borderline case of illusionistic representation thus only occurs in very special circumstances.

Relevant and Typical Properties

In the definition of resemblance suggested above, I have left the terms 'relevant' and 'typical' undefined. Regarding representational relationships, the term 'relevant' can be refined by emphasizing that it refers to visual properties, in particular to the visual quality of form.[8] 'Relevant' should therefore be seen as a variable that can and should be specified according to the context in which it is used. If the topic is 'cultures', for example, then the dimension of colour would not be relevant for an explication of resemblance; instead, we would look to the culturally relevant social dimension which might find its concrete expression in certain rituals of interaction. We could then describe cultures as similar (despite the different appearances of members of each culture, etc.) if they have the same social manners or the same family structures. As a central concept of communication theory and hermeneutics, the term 'relevance' can be traced back to the intentionalist semantics of Paul Grice, who conceived of communication as an inferential process in which the sender's intended meaning must be inferred by the receivers.[9] Particularly in the case of uncoded signs – such as spontaneous gestures, deictic action or even visual communication – using a theory of relevance to describe processes of understanding can be helpful.[10]

For our current context, the cognitive implications of relevance are most important. According to the model inspired by cognitive science and developed by Sperber and Wilson, the goal of every cognitive activity is the maximization of relevance. Resemblance judgments are thus merely a special form of processing information: they are the result of data taken from different sources with differing accessibility and according to specific considerations of relevance. In this case the information to be processed comes from perception as well as from long- and short-term memory. This order of elements also indicates the relative level of accessibility: the farther one moves away from the direct working memory of the deductive apparatus and towards long-term memories, the greater is the cognitive effort required to process the assumptions at hand. The lesser the effort required to process and judge how new information fits with pre-existing information, the more relevant it is.

Even this brief look at the theory of relevance illustrates how introducing the category of relevance to resemblance judgements makes such judgements extremely dependent on cognitive, and thus subjective, processing standards. The inferential processes involved are based on an individual's own conceptual foundation, which is based on individually (and naturally also culturally) shaped logical, lexical and encyclopaedic entries. Thus the qualities considered to be relevant for a judgement of resemblance may differ significantly from person to person.

The expression 'typical' also addresses a general and quite complex problem. The question of which and how many qualities two objects must share to be considered similar is in no way confined to representational resemblance; it applies to the comparison of any two objects whatsoever. This question is difficult to answer because resemblance is a gradual relationship with fluid boundaries. There are obviously clear cases (such as the resemblance between twins) in which the impression of resemblance is simply generated by an abundance of common properties. In many other cases certain properties of an object stand out more than others and are thus considered 'typical' properties that carry more weight in making resemblance judgements. Having a long trunk, for instance, is considered a typical property for elephants. We would thus consider other animals with long snouts to resemble elephants even if they only shared this single property. In individual cases what counts as typical can usually be immediately recognized, but may also often be difficult to clearly articulate. Thus the determination of the specific considerations of typicality in a given case requires psychological (and therefore empirical) study – especially when it comes to judging the resemblance between a representation and its referent. This also explains why it is often easy for a person to differentiate between the depiction of a dog and the depiction of a wolf, while it can be extremely difficult for that same person to draw pictures with the corresponding properties.

In the realm of pictures, the concept of typicality overlaps somewhat with the concept of relevance because the typical properties of an object lie within representationally relevant property dimensions, and are thus considered iconically relevant properties. In this respect the determination of an object's typical properties always involves aspects of relevance. For the classificatory concept of resemblance, not only is the number of iconically relevant properties important, but also the degree of their iconic relevance and the accessibility of their respective prototype.[11] This last aspect in particular can vary widely between individuals and cultures, and can thus directly influence the perceived degree of iconic relevance for individual properties. For properties that are only weakly iconically relevant, context has a strong influence on the prototype that is activated. Accordingly, as a criterion for the classification of objects, protoypicality is not merely the result of the sum of shared properties; instead, individual properties are weighted and determined to be more or less suitable for categorization. What makes a given property relevant for a prototype is not only its frequency, but rather a combination of frequency and distinctiveness.[12] In this sense a property is particularly important in determining typicality if it is shared by as many specimens in the category as possible, and by as few specimens outside of the category as possible. 'Having feathers', for instance, is a property that is shared by specimens of the category 'bird', and is not found in any specimens of other categories of animals.

Internalized Resemblance

These clarifications of both 'relevance' and 'typicality' allow us to conclude that judgments of resemblance are made based on specific cognitive resources, and thus contain necessarily subjective aspects. In order to deal with this, I suggest shifting to a concept of internalized resemblance as proposed for picture theory by Christopher Peacocke.[13] He distinguishes between representational content and sensational content. The representational content of a perception includes all of the properties that correspond to a part of the world as such, while 'sensational content' refers to properties that depend on the particular perception of that part. If an object is viewed from different perspectives, for instance, we have to consider one representational content but different sensational contents. Most notably, distortions of perspective depending on an observer's position are not properties of the perceived object. Instead, they are properties that we must attribute to the mechanisms of perception. Sometimes complex mechanisms are required for determining the corresponding representational content. From a certain perspective, for example, a wheel might appear to be elliptical. Objectively speaking, a circle and an ellipse have quite different relevant properties, but the perception of circular objects and the perception of an elliptical representation of circular objects may provide us with identical sensational content due to the laws of optics and perception. In such cases it may even be possible to mistake the representation for the actual object being portrayed.

It is important to emphasize here that Peacocke's expression, 'sensational content', does not simply refer to private experience in a more arbitrary sense, as there is always a clear correlative relationship between sensational content and the perceived object. Peacocke determines this relationship with what he calls the 'visual field': an imaginary plane between the observer and the object similar to a perpendicular cut through the visual cone, as has been described in detail by classical perspective theory since Alberti. The gestalt properties of the visual field – i.e. the sensational content – can be determined by geometric principles, depending on the observer's perspective. The representational content of an object can then be inferred from this sensational content.

The differentiation of perception contents also enables us to differentiate between an objective resemblance and a subjective (or internalized) resemblance. The latter of these is of primary interest for a theory of representation. A visual representation resembles an object subjectively if (and only if) it generates a form within the visual field that might also be created by the object itself from a certain perspective. This form of resemblance is thus based on the respective shapes found within the visual field. The concept of internalized resemblance allows us to understand how judgements of resemblance can be made with recourse to subjective perspectives without discounting the connection of the object to the factual situation.

Based on these considerations, the concept of resemblance as it applies to a theory of representation can be further refined as follows: '(S3) A sign resembles an object if, based on relevant property dimensions, the sensational content of the perception of the signifier shares typical properties with the sensational content of the perception of the object from a certain perspective.'

Conclusion: Areas and Functions of Resemblance

Until now I have exclusively discussed resemblance within the context of picture theory, that is, as a representational relationship. In doing so I have shown that resemblance is a complex phenomenon that consists of many different aspects and functions. In addition to representational resemblance, other important types of resemblance include both ontological resemblance and classificatory resemblance. Both of these types of resemblance are implied by representational contexts, but can also exist independent of such contexts. To conclude, I would like to briefly explain the connections between these different aspects and functions of resemblance.

To begin with, ontological resemblance is an elementary relationship between physical (or abstract) objects. In this sense, identical twins are very similar to one another. To the extent that a picture possesses a (physical) picture-carrier – a medium – and (in the case of representational pictures) depicts a further (physical) object, representational resemblance presupposes ontological resemblance. The same also goes for the classificatory function of resemblance, because the recognition of specific picture-contents implies that we recognize them as concrete elements (*token*) of a more general category (*type*). As the discussion of typicality above illustrates, such recognition is generally more successful, the more typical the selected properties are for the overarching category. In this way, the classificatory function of resemblance also depends on ontological resemblance. Thus, both classificatory and ontological forms of resemblance are contained within the representational concept of resemblance, even if they both manifest themselves independently of representation. It is clear that ontological resemblance is the most elementary form regardless of how 'resemblance' is defined, because the classificatory function of resemblance utilizes ontological resemblance itself as a possible category of classification. Ontological, classificatory and representational concepts of resemblance can thus build on each other, and allow for more complex functions when appropriately combined.

I consider the classificatory function of resemblance to be especially important. To recognize something as something else implies that we understand a concrete object as an element of a category. This classification of things as belonging to a category is an interpretation that is often crucial for judgements of resemblance. This is certainly the case when we refer to prototypes, because prototypes provide us with a perceptual pattern that a concrete object can be compared with. The more similar the concrete object is to the pattern, the more rapidly and unequivocally we can assign it to the relevant category. We might recognize a certain object as a ladybug because we perceive the visual properties (colour, spots, etc.) that we associate as typical for ladybugs. In this sense classification is a fundamental process that underlies all human action. But we are only aware of that fact in those special cases where we have limited perceptual access to the object, or when the corresponding concept is particularly vague in our mind. This also makes it clear why there are multiple types of resemblance combined in representational resemblance: the perception of pictures involves using existing similarities between objects – for instance, the ontological resemblance between the outline of a boulder and the contours of an animal – to representationally expand the classificatory function. Such classification might initially be wrong if we mistake the boulder for an animal. Once we have determined that it is not an animal, however, and recognize that the shape of the boulder looks like an animal, we can use this (primarily visual) resemblance to evoke the idea of the said animal in the future by using the boulder as a visual sign. The ability to perceive pictures – to use a formulation from Wollheim:[14] the ability to see something *in* something – occurs the moment we understand that we can use a mistaken classification (as it were) as a representation. Recognizing the shape of an animal in the outline of a boulder requires that we judge both shapes to resemble each other enough that we can use the boulder's shape for activating the classification for the animal's shape. Still, we need to remain conscious that it is in fact a boulder and not an animal, so that the act of classification takes place in an 'as-if' manner, i.e. as a symbolic act.

The situation described above also clarifies the broader context of the concept of resemblance. As a classificatory concept resemblance is closely connected to prototypes, which, above all, facilitate an effective orientation in the world. This fact is important for perception in general but applies especially to pictures, which can support such orientation through their ability to emphasize typical visual properties. Still, to a certain extent, this form of perceptual orientation based on resemblance is inaccurate. The more exact variation of orientation, which we usually find in the natural sciences, comes from the attempt to develop definitions for terminological concepts. Definitions provide identity criteria that (if sufficient) serve to unambiguously identify objects, but the testing process for such definitions is often laborious. Classification using prototypes, on the other hand, allows for an effective and usually rapid identification of objects, but remains susceptible to errors. There is thus a tension between resemblance-based perceptual procedures and terminological definitional procedures. Within the living environment the concept of resemblance plays the more important role because such contexts are more about effectiveness and less about precision. In contrast, definitions are much more appropriate as scientific instruments because the difficulties associated with their use in daily life do not apply in the scientific contexts.

The concept of family resemblance, which I would like to address briefly in closing, can be seen in this context as an attempt to augment the usual scientific definitional procedures with alternatives from the ordinary life-forms of orientation. Appropriately, the concept of family resemblance has had its largest impact on prototype theory. Wittgenstein illustrated his idea of family resemblance using the concept 'game', which refers to a heterogeneous field of phenomena for which we are not able to formulate a clear definition based on necessary and sufficient conditions.[15] This does not mean that we cannot formulate definitions for subsections of the heterogeneous overarching field; we might generate, for example, a clear definition of what constitutes a board game. The concept of family resemblance should thus not be misunderstood as a complete alternative to traditional definitions. Nor does it imply that the search for clear definitions is fundamentally flawed or inappropriate. In the sense of a 'linguistic turn' towards ordinary language use, the concept of a 'game' invokes a definitional procedure clearly distinct from scientific definitional processes, while at the same time retaining its own form of valid internal 'logic'. Resemblance – representing the decisive criterion in the concept of family resemblance – is thus an extremely effective criterion for circumventing the juxtaposition of identity and difference in ordinary life.

Notes

1 Philosophical discussions in the English language on a theory of similarity often use the term 'resemblance' to refer to the phenomenon. In this essay, I thus use the term 'resemblance' as a direct synonym for 'similarity', and do not intend to imply any difference of meaning.

2 See the extensive illustration of the problems associated with similarity theory in Scholz ([1991] 2004).

3 Cf., for example, Black (1972): 122: 'The objection to saying that some paintings resemble their subjects is not that they don't, but rather that so little is said when only this has been said.'

4 Cf. Scholz ([1991] 2004).

5 Cf. Sachs-Hombach ([2003] 2014): Chapter 5.

6 The semantic relationship of visual and linguistic signs is the same; e.g., either ambiguous or non-disjointed. Because of this, a theoretically sound distinction

can only be made based on syntactic differences (Goodman and Elgin 1988: 131): '[W]hat distinguishes pictorial symbols lies not in resemblance or any other relationship to anything they may refer to, but in their syntactical relationship to each other.' But this is exactly what similarity theory challenges by assuming that images are characterized by a special type of semantic relationship.

[7] Cf. Goodman ([1968] 1976): 31: 'representing is a matter of classifying objects rather than of imitating them'.

[8] When it comes to representational relationships, the decision of which concrete characteristic dimension is 'relevant' depends on the type of image being considered. Different aspects will be seen as representationally relevant for different types of images. When dealing with black-and-white photography, for instance, the colour dimension is clearly not (representationally) relevant (i.e. we should not assume that the objects in the photo are also black-and-white), while the thickness of individual lines in a diagram is also not necessarily relevant.

[9] Cf. Sperber and Wilson ([1986] 1995).

[10] Cf. Blanke (2003): 153ff.

[11] Cf. ibid.: 96.

[12] Cf. Rosch (1978).

[13] Cf. Peacocke (1987); for a criticism of Peacocke's view, see Lopes (1996).

[14] Wollheim ([1980] 2015): 142.

[15] Cf. Wittgenstein ([1953] 1986).

References

Black, Max (1972), 'How Do Pictures Represent?', in Ernst H. Gombrich, Julian Hochberg and Max Black, eds, *Art, Perception, and Reality*, Baltimore, MD: John Hopkins University Press: 95–130.

Blanke, Börries (2003), *Vom Bild zum Sinn: Das ikonische Zeichen zwischen strukturalistischer Semiotik und analytischer Philosophie* (Reihe Bildwissenschaft, Bd. 4), Wiesbaden: Deutscher Universitätsverlag.

Goodman, Nelson ([1968] 1976), *Languages of Art: An Approach to a Theory of Symbols*, Indianapolis, IN: Hackett Publishing Company.

Goodman, Nelson and Catherine Elgin (1988), *Reconceptions in Philosophy and Other Arts and Sciences*, London: Routledge.

Lopes, Dominic (1996), *Understanding Pictures*, Oxford: Clarendon Press.

Peacocke, Christopher (1987), 'Depiction', *Philosophical Review*, Vol. 96: 383–410.

Rosch, Eleanor (1978), 'Principles of Categorization', in Eleanor Rosch and Barbara B. Lloyd, eds, *Cognition and Categorization*, Hillsdale, NJ: Erlbaum: 27–48.

Sachs-Hombach, Klaus ([2003] 2014), *Das Bild als kommunikatives Medium: Elemente einer allgemeinen Bildwissenschaft*, Köln: Halem.

Scholz, Oliver R. ([1991] 2004), *Bild, Darstellung, Zeichen: Philosophische Theorien bildlicher Darstellung*, third edition, Frankfurt am Main: Klostermann.

Sperber, Dan and Deirdre Wilson ([1986] 1995), *Relevance: Communication and Cognition*, Oxford: Blackwell.

Wittgenstein, Ludwig ([1953] 1986), *Philosophical Investigations*, translated by G.E.M. Mascombe, Oxford: Blackwell.

Wollheim, Richard ([1980] 2015), *Art and Its Objects*, Cambridge: Cambridge University Press.

Similarity as a Concept within Difference Theory

A reformulation of modernization theory

Andreas Langenohl

Introduction: Similarity as a Radical Concept within *Theory*

This is the place for a 'thinking about similarity' that casts a critical eye on favoured preferences for the polarity between identity and difference, and challenges unambiguousness, authenticity and purism. In contrast, thinking about similarity emphasizes the importance of tentativeness, the transitory, the unclear, fluid boundaries, nuances, minimal deviations, fuzziness and vagueness, and describes these concepts using flexible, polyvalent language. Instead of the principle of 'either–or', thinking about similarity emphasizes a principle of 'this . . . as well as that', and contradictions are seen as stimulating instead of discouraging.[1]

According to a recent programmatic work,[2] the current scholarly interest in the category of similarity can be attributed to its capacity to go beyond the epistemology of identity and difference that characterized the twentieth century: 'the function that "similarity" can serve next to the concepts of identity and difference must be explained'.[3] The theoretical proposition of this essay is that the category of similarity is helpful in radicalizing considerations of *difference* theory.

This assessment serves as the starting point of the argument presented in this essay. Above all, similarity represents an alternative to the reciprocal gesture of confirmation between identity and difference that consists of a radicalization of difference and an abandonment of identity. In this respect similarity does not dismiss the concept of difference but, rather, re-establishes it conceptually beyond its opposition to identity.

As a sociologist, I would first like to try out this argument as it applies to my own field. For sociologists similarity is particularly important conceptually because it allows us to identify the different ways in which the concept of 'difference' has been used in sociological research, and at the same time holds the promise of a rigorous advancement of the foundations of sociology as based on theories of difference. In other words, this essay asserts that the heuristic value of similarity is primarily based on its capacity to radically reconceptualize difference and thus to provide a new perspective on sociological theory.

In order to present this argument in detail and simultaneously develop the concept of similarity for sociological theory, I dedicate the next few pages of this essay to describing differentiation theory in sociology. This theory represents the most prominent branch of sociology based on a theory of difference. An important reason for this is that differentiation theory was a critical element in the theory of modernization, upon which sociology was founded. Still, it can be shown that differentiation theory is not a rigorously conceptualized expression of a theory of difference, at least inasmuch as its conceptual framework is based on a theory of identity. In this respect, differentiation theory only allows for difference at the cost of accepting a concept of identity.

This is different for sociological approaches that deal with theories of association. Such approaches make it possible to conceptualize difference without identity, and work with categories that imply 'similarity'. This is particularly prominent in Gabriel Tarde's theory of imitation, in which imitation – as a fundamental social process – can give rise to assimilation as well as differences. But approaches based on theories of association are not only found in Tarde and Bruno Latour (who helped rediscover Tarde's work), but also in the work of Georg Simmel and in situationist sociology. All such approaches conceptualize social processes in categories of difference without relying on the existence of an identity that precedes difference or has been created by differentiation.

However, as I argue further, attempts to (re)integrate the theories of association – and thus the concept of similarity – back into sociology (and in particular those of Bruno Latour) have been afflicted by the problem that their methodological approaches have been micro-sociological. They have thus only been able to describe society at the situative level, and have failed to take into account or have been unable to integrate important insights from macro-sociology (including differentiation theory). This naturally applies first and foremost to the meaning of the concept of 'modern society', which theories of association have been remarkably allergic to.

If the concept of similarity is to be made useful for sociology, there is no alternative but to somehow connect it with modernization while at the same time recognizing the criticisms of modernity and modernization that come from theories of association. I then go on to argue that similarity does in fact provide a conceptual category that allows us to describe the differences and variety of modern sociability while still accounting for the typical impulse towards totality found in processes of modernization. I close my conceptual proposals by providing an example of how processes of modernization can be reformulated using the concepts of similarization and dissimilarization. Finally, the concluding section of the essay summarizes the results of my considerations here.

Sociological Unease with the Category of Similarity: The Identity-based Theoretical Foundation of Differentiation Theory

The theory of difference does not represent a uniform theoretical paradigm. Instead, various theories of difference have been formative – not only in sociology but in the broader field of the social sciences. At the same time, difference theory has effects on many different levels of conceptualization. The best example of this comes from the theory of signs. Ferdinand de Saussure introduced the concept of difference into the theory of language in order to explain how linguistic signs gained their meaning: namely, through reciprocal differentiation of their phonological content. This concept of difference was then adopted by Claude Lévi-Strauss and applied to symbolic systems more generally, thus shifting from the category of language to a more general theory of signs (such as that of Greimas). As such this new, expanded concept of difference became applicable to a broad range of social sciences, from linguistics to anthropology to psychoanalysis. Finally, Jacques Derrida, Gilles Deleuze and François Lyotard expanded the palette of scholarly fields with an affinity for difference even further to include philosophy, culture theory and theory of literature, and stretched the concept of difference, which had until then been used in a structuralist manner, to include both diachronic and open-ended constellations.

Within sociology, however, since the nineteenth century, a different theory of difference has developed (usually referred to as 'modernization theory'), based on the idea of sociology as a science of *society*. In contrast to the concept of difference found in the theory of signs, whose distinctive feature is its presence in a wide variety of different social science disciplines, modernization theory constitutes sociology as its own independent discipline with its own independent object of study. For this reason, modernization theory is extremely difficult to apply to other disciplines in the humanities and social sciences.

To put it very broadly, modernization theory claims that societies go through generalizable patterns of development that are irreversible, inasmuch as they change the structural conditions for further processes of transformation.[4] Modernization theory thus presents itself as a social-scientific variation of macro-historiography; indeed, the birth of sociology as a science of society has been defined as the transition 'from history to modernity'.[5] Within modernization theory, considerations of difference are based on the theorem of societal differentiation described by Hans van der Loo and Willem van Reijen as one of four macro-processes (alongside rationalization, domestication and individualization) that modernizing societies undergo.[6]

It is important to note here that the theorem of differentiation is not equal to the other macro-theorems; it is conceptually an antecedent of and fundamentally important for modernization theory as a whole. This is best seen using an example from one of the most recent updates of modernization theory. The so-called 'multiple modernities' paradigm attaches a high degree of importance to culturally variable and culturally contingent semantics, and to the corresponding structural forms of modernity, in order to account for the variability of modern societies.[7] Of the four theorems of modernization described by van der Loo and van Reijen, this new paradigm retains only the theorem of differentiation.[8] According to the multiple modernities theory, despite all their cultural differences, modern societies share process logics that lead to increasing specification and reciprocal differentiation of institutional complexes.

This latter point can also be seen as a brief outline of how modernization theory understands differentiation: it is the transformation of societal institutions towards increased specialization to precisely defined tasks (sometimes called 'functions'). This transformation leads them to develop increasingly uniform internal process logics and, simultaneously, to increasingly differentiate themselves from one another. Sociological theories have come up with a range of different names for such specialized institutional complexes: they are 'organs' and 'bodies' for Émile Durkheim;[9] 'legal spheres' for Max Weber;[10] 'subsystems' for Talcott Parsons;[11] 'functional systems' for Niklas Luhmann;[12] 'action contexts' for Jürgen Habermas;[13] and 'fields' for Pierre Bourdieu.[14] The precise social-theoretical importance of the differentiation theorem has also been a subject of dispute, especially with regard to the question of whether the theorem should be historically substantiated and specified (as done by Max Weber), or if it should instead be considered from a functionalistic perspective and separated entirely from historiographic considerations (as Durkheim, Parsons and Luhmann suggested). Untouched by such debates is what I would like to call the *identity-based theoretical foundation of the differentiation theorem*. By this I mean that differentiation is considered a divergence *from* something: as the development of process patterns, operational criteria and categories of communication that are internally uniform and organized according to their own internal logic. Differentiation thus always involves the disambiguation of social processes, the crystallization and intensification of social logics, and the distancing and decoupling of such logics from one another. There is no significant difference on this point among the theoreticians named above.[15]

The identity-based foundation of these differentiation theories is diametrically opposed to a conceptualization of difference based on similarity. The following arguments illustrate why this is the case. First, as Anil Bhatti has stated, similarity connotes the blurring of differences and boundaries between entities. But modernization theory has no alternative but to designate such processes as 'dedifferentiation'. As Shmuel Eisenstadt has asserted, this would mean nothing less than a 'breakdown of modernization' and the decline of societies into chaos.[16] Second, the differentiation theorem prominently marginalizes the concept of similarity altogether: namely, in Émile Durkheim's work, where he defines the characteristic 'mechanical solidarity' of premodern societies as based on 'similarities' while the 'organic solidarity' that marks modern societies is based on 'the division of labour', that is, on structural differentiation.[17] Third – and I will return to this argument later – the differentiation theorem is normally accompanied by the diagnosis of a problem: namely, that as differentiation increases, normative resources decrease, thus endangering societal cohesion.[18] Differentiation is thus not only an identity-forming divergence *from* something, it is the tendency towards *over*-differentiation: it is 'as if planes were to take off all over the place before the runway at their target airport is finished'.[19]

The differentiation theorem normally approaches this problem by introducing a theorem of cultural abstraction according to which the differences in semantics, policies and normative principles are bridged by increasingly abstract value generalizations. For Durkheim, this meant the recognition of mutual dependence that arises from the division of labour; for Parsons, it led to generalized values such as 'rationality', 'agency' and other concepts that can be used in a variety of specific situations; for Habermas, it meant an extremely demanding balancing act between communicative and instrumental rationality; and for Luhmann, it required the meta-insight of the constructedness of all observational positions. The necessity for abstraction implied by the differentiation theorem blocks thinking in terms of similarity because the latter is characterized by a concept of lateral convergence – as Bhatti puts it, 'through networks of relationships and boundary crossing connections' – instead of abstractive upscaling.[20] In other words, similarity is about associations that are *set against* abstraction.

Similarity: Difference without Identity

As will be shown here, affirmative references to the concept of similarity are primarily found in sociological theories that can be described as based on theories of *association*. This means that such theories conceptualize sociality less as 'society' and more as 'sociality'. To put it another way, 'society' is nothing more than the sum of processes of 'sociation' (as Simmel puts it); that is, the initiation of social relationships with other people.[21] Approaches based on association – and this is critical for their incompatibility with identity-based approaches – fundamentally claim that entities are constituted by others and not through self-generation, inherent emergence or the differentiation of one entity through dissociation from others. This is seen in Gabriel Tarde's concept of imitation which presupposes the existence of role models to be imitated. Georg Simmel followed this same fundamental idea when he attributed the genesis of individualized persons not to the emergence of an identity, but rather to their affiliation with different 'social circles'.[22] In the case of Erving Goffman, the constitution of entities by others can be found in his arguments regarding the cooperation of roles in the maintenance of *image*. As he puts it, because individuals have an interest in being judged positively by others, they are dependent on the cooperation of others in order to generate and maintain a positive *image*.[23] Similar rules go for ethnomethodology, as dramatically illustrated by 'breaching experiments'.[24] Above all, Bruno Latour[25] and Michel Callon[26] have shown the most explicit interest in the constitution of entities by other entities. According to Latour, entities are constructed solely by their connections or 'articulations' to various other entities. He expands this concept to an ontology that claims to overcome the dichotomy between realism and constructivism: the more constructed entities are, the more they are articulated as the confluence of other entities, the more real they become.[27]

This idea undercuts any concept of the substantiality of a social entity or a social process because every entity and process is continually constitutively connected to others. It is not about the constitution of identity through differentiation but rather, conversely, about the constitution of entities through continual contacts, associations, amalgamations and fusions. As stated earlier, this has been formulated most clearly in actor network theory, but it is also almost as tangible as early as Georg Simmel and, above all, Gabriele Tarde.[28] Tarde's concept of imitation also comes the closest to a concept of similarity and demonstrates the potential of similarity to consider differences between social entities without recourse to the auxiliary construct of identity. In Tarde's theory, imitation is responsible for the generation of both similarities and dissimilarities (which he calls 'innovations'). If different streams of imitation meet together at a given point, each stream becomes increasingly similar to the other.[29] At the same time, the combination of such similarization processes can generate something completely new through processes of recombination. Conceptually speaking, difference thus no longer requires the precursor of identity (as it does in differentiation theory). Instead it arises as the result of processes of similarization. Imitation and difference represent two sides of the same process without requiring conceptual recourse to identity.

Finally, Tarde's theory also clearly establishes that a concept of difference based on association theory is processual. It is thus more consistent to speak of processes of *similarization* and *dissimilarization*.[30] These terms hold the promise of a radicalized, process-based variation of difference theory that does not rely on the concept of identity.

Similarization and Dissimilarization beyond Micro-logic

It is important to note that until now this promise has been subject to an important limitation. The heuristic of similarization and dissimilarization can easily be applied to the level of concrete social and cultural (and material) processes. This is because the category of similarity is closely associated with a micro-analytical epistemology, and is not amenable to a 'metaphysical' upscaling of social ontology like the concept of identity (for instance, so that one can speak of a 'collective identity').[31] Explicit examples of this can be found in the literature based on association theory. Latour calls for a 'flat' ontology of process patterns, and rejects any attempts to look behind phenomena and their genesis through processes of association.[32] Anil Bhatti (who we can thank for a conception of similarity founded on intellectual history) refers first and foremost to scenes of 'direct' contact prior to any form of abstraction when he states that 'similarities first become evident through practical experience'.[33] Simmel saw society as a continually provisional (and social-scientifically abstracted) consequence of processes of 'sociation' in which concrete individuals enter into interactive relationships with other concrete individuals. And Tarde clearly refuted the idea that the heuristic of society is something that exists at a different level of being than individuals and their relationships: '[H]owever intimate, profound and harmonious a given social group may be, we will never see springing forth *ex abrupto* from among its members, to their surprise, a *collective ego* which is real and not only metaphorical.'[34]

The strategy to conceptualize society as nothing more than situatively describable and observable social and material processes – and the dismissal of any concept of higher-level structures or processes – can be helpful in illustrating the constructed character of macro-concepts such as 'social structure', 'collective identity' or 'culture'. Sometimes this strategy slides into normative categories and ethically celebrates situative practices as such, to the point that Latour's maxim of following the objects is not only understood as an epistemic strategy, but also becomes an ethical demand.[35] At the same time, however, such a conception cannot provide any clue about the dynamics at analytical levels that exist only as theoretical models. To put it another way: by criticizing non-observable social and societal phenomena as nothing but metaphors, metaphysics and erroneous ontologies, the theory of association denies itself the possibility to use such imaginary phenomena for *heuristic* purposes.[36] With this in mind, Ute Tellman criticized Latour for failing to integrate valuable insights provided by the sociological differentiation theorem because he was unable to analytically reconstruct different process logics, and was thus forced to continually restart his analysis from scratch.[37] If this is indeed the case, then any cumulative ideal of knowledge is a lost cause.

The question that emerges from such criticism is how the concepts of similarization and dissimilarization can be made heuristically useful for sociology without, on the one hand, sacrificing the insights gained by macro-models of describable differences between social, cultural and material practices – without throwing the baby out with the bathwater, so to speak – while still retaining the fundamental criticism of identity implied by similarity. This question is posed most virulently when it comes to describing the highest possible level of modelling macro-processes – namely, '(modern) society'. While association-theoretical criticism of sociological 'metaphysics' is most prominent regarding the concept of 'society', the associative analysis of just such an imaginary heuristic could prove particularly useful – exactly *because* modern society itself is for the most part considered (by both social sciences and 'society' itself) as an imaginary construct that nevertheless has serious real-world implications. To a certain extent associative analysis is about social reality, and the real-world consequences of imagination and model-building.

This brings us back to the problem of social abstraction. As discussed above, sociological differentiation theory generally postulates a dilemma by which processes of differentiation lead to declining normative cohesion in a society. They seek to answer this problem with a theorem that cultural points of reference can (at least potentially) be generalized across a society. From this perspective, cultural (normative, symbolic, semantic) abstraction seems to be a symptom of modern society. Any conception of similarity that insists on retaining its micro-logical theoretical tone would necessarily be blind to such abstractions. The question is thus whether such processes of abstraction, which at first glance seem to be incompatible with similarity, can instead become precisely the stage upon which the category of similarity can be expanded beyond its original micro-logical realm. If this is possible, then the category of similarity can be extended to be a useful analytical heuristic of *modern* society and thus – only superficially, paradoxically – take a turn towards modernization theory. The task is thus to expand the associative impulse of similarization and dissimilarization from the micro-level to the level of social and cultural abstractions that have real-world effects on culture and society.

Similarity and Modernization Theory

The theorem of abstraction postulated by differentiation theory is not the only factor that encourages us to find a way to utilize the category of similarity to analyse modern societies with reference to social and cultural abstractions. Most importantly, we can say that a mark of modern societies is that processes of abstraction unleash *totalizing social tendencies*. Conversely, this is exactly why a theory of modernity – or, more specifically, a modernization theory – is epistemologically necessary; without it we cannot take such totalizing tendencies into account. Harry Harootunian, for instance, has argued (following Karl Marx) that the totalizing tendencies of modern societies can be seen in the radical synchronization of practices with the temporality of a capitalist, commodified economy.[38] For Thomas Lamarre, the consequence of such synchronization is that 'it is a question of how critiques of modernity (or modernization or both) must operate with (and within) an underlying totality – in particular, some kind of totalizing prefiguration that implies limits to the subject, epistemologically, ontologically or historically'.[39]

But we could also sound out such totalization using other means, such as the concept of the *social imaginary*,[40] according to which the meaning of many practices in modern society is dependent on the implication of an abstract commonality while the practices themselves simultaneously create such commonality through their implementation. This is more evidence of the real-world effects that 'abstract' social concepts can have.[41] There are many such *social imaginaries* in modern societies that guide social actions but remain unobservable, from 'nation' to 'public sphere' (described as 'rational abstraction' by Gayatri Spivak[42]) to 'market'.[43] These tendencies towards totalization represent a problem for both classical and contemporary theories of modern society, and even for criticism of such theories. The classical differentiation theorem of modernization theory, for instance, cannot account for totalization tendencies because it assumes a pluralization of patterns of agency based on diverse internal logics. This is why current theories of modernity that cast off a concept of modernization and replace it with a concept of modernity (seen most prominently in the multiple modernities paradigm), while at the same time retaining the differentiation theorem, run the risk of ignoring totalization tendencies as a central characteristic of modern sociality.[44]

At the same time, such totalization tendencies can also not be fully accounted for by radical challenges to the concept of modernity. Postcolonial criticism, which is dedicated to describing the cultural reconstruction of modern self-constitution by colonial others and thus seeks to demonstrate that the modernist demand for universalism is a fiction, cannot do justice to tendencies of totalization because totalization and universalism are two separate things. While universalism refers to the claim that articulated premises can have universal validity (which can relatively easily be refuted), totalization refers to processes that attempt to universally – but always in certain constellations – apply modern societal characteristics *prior to any articulated claims*, and to the fact that such attempts themselves have consequences. In light of the multifaceted resistance to such attempts, emphasized by postcolonial studies in particular, totalization always remains a tendency, never living up to the demands of universalism. Still, this does not preclude totalization as an extremely consequential social impulse towards uniformity, if only inasmuch as it generates resistance to such impulses. I would like to develop this argument even further and show how precisely the totalization tendencies of modernization demand a reformulation of modernization theory based on a theory of similarity, and thus on a radical theory of difference. In doing so I will demonstrate how the category of similarity can be conceptually situated within the sociological theory of modern societies.

The epistemological description of modern totalization tendencies

The totalization tendencies of modernization have naturally not gone completely unnoticed by sociological theory, despite the dominance of the differentiation theorem. Such tendencies are particularly noticeable in Max Weber's project on comparative religion, which attempted to map the specific features of those cultural constellations that he saw as causally underlying a model of capitalism, which then developed unseen totalization tendencies. This case also clearly illustrates the difference between universalism and totalization. From the perspective of universalism, the realization of capitalism appears to be the result of an internal, universal logic of social processes – and this is how Weber was often understood in the twentieth century, particularly by the '*take-off*' prophets of modernization. The perspective of totalization, on the other hand, sees the capitalization of the world as a series of attempts to generalize extremely particular social process logics (namely, those of capitalism) – attempts that did not join together in a universal convergence but rather led to significantly different results in different places.

The totalizing tendencies of modernization are most clearly seen, however, if we shift views away from the west as the standard model of modernization and towards epistemological decentralization.[45] Such a perspective is by all means compatible with a Weberian approach; we just have to accentuate the line of questioning somewhat differently. While Weber posed the question of why the birth of capitalism took place in the historical 'west', the interesting question here would be formulated differently: what insights into modern totalization processes can we gain from the resistance to such totalization that has formed in historically non-western contexts (for instance, in [post-]colonial and [post-]state-socialist contexts)? Such a reformulation means nothing more than handling the historical course of modernization in the west as an exception and not the rule. Doing so clearly demonstrates the difference between totalization tendencies, which are always faced with and generate resistance, and claims of universalization.

In my view, the reason that this difference between totalization (as a social impulse) and universalization (as a cultural claim) has been at best implicitly recognized is that modernization has been able to invoke a wide consensus opinion, the substance of which has yet to be refuted: namely, that despite all of the criticisms of modernity, the political shape of modern sociality lies in the historical west.[46] Eisenstadt provides a good example of this: in situations where social and political macro-crises in modern societies cannot be overlooked, they have been classified as 'breakdowns of modernization', and not as crises of modernization or modernity in and of itself. The countless sociological diagnoses of the twentieth century that have cast doubt on the effects of modernization still offer an intrinsic criticism of modernization as an unfulfilled promise of modernity.[47] They have depicted the degeneration of political activism, cultural sophistication, social solidarity, or individual authenticity and autonomy in modernity – but these are all abstractions that themselves are deeply entwined in the project of modernity.[48]

Such implicit criticisms of modernization which measure their real effects based on the promises of modernity lose their resonance in situations where modernization cannot be considered intrinsic because it is not entwined with a universal-historical telos. This can be seen, for instance, in the former European colonies and in the alternative project of modernization found in communism. These historical cases have also exhibited consequences of modernization, but the criticism of such consequences has stood within the context of political and institutional upheavals (decolonization and the end of state socialism). Such upheavals showed that a criticism of modernity could not remain intrinsic because it affected the parameters of the *political* condition of society. It was exactly these political and social upheavals, and the crises of modernization they entailed, that made the identification with modernity impossible to imagine.[49] To put it another way: in the west, the crisis of modernity was normally interpreted in comparison to the culturally normative contrast image of the *promise* of modernity, but on the periphery, the imaginary identity of modernity itself began to falter.

This is why, outside of the historical west – and here I come to the epistemological consequences of this decentralized modern constellation – 'difference' has taken on a different meaning than in metropolitan sociology. As illustrated above, while the latter based its diagnoses of crisis on an expansion and escalation of the *differentiation* theorem, post-colonial and post-communist discourse is dominated by different idioms of difference – namely, those that formulate radical alternatives to modernity by confronting the universalist claims of (western) modernity with alterity. Assertions of difference thus become epistemological weapons against modernization, inasmuch as it proclaims that there is only one all-encompassing identity of social, economic, political and cultural processes in modern societies.[50]

This epistemological decentralization of modernity can serve as the starting point for a reconceptualization of macro-level processes based on a theory of similarity (that is, a radical theory of difference) that makes it possible to analyse the totalization tendencies of modernity as processes of similarization and dissimilarization. My suggestion is that, in contrast to the historical west, the effects of modernization on the peripheries did *not* result in societal differentiation (despite claims by works on multiple modernities which tend to consider differentiation as a core sociological component of modernization and to shift all other differences to the theoretical level of culture). Indeed, the effects of modernization in the historical west could only be modelled as societal differentiation because the western political and social *idée directrice* – modern statehood, and political and social inclusion – had never been challenged by a direct criticism of modernity itself. In reality, the impacts of totalization tendencies outside of historically western societies have appeared as tendencies towards similarization and dissimilarization within climates of political and social turmoil and conflict, which themselves have been partially triggered by the totalization of modern processual patterns.[51] A concept of similarity extended to the realm of macro-sociology holds the promise of recognizing 'multiple modernities', not as a manifestation of conflict between deep cultural elements and societal processes of differentiation (which would require a description of their *identity* according to a deep cultural hermeneutic), but rather as constellations of lateral and horizontal conflicts which flare up around the drive towards uniformity that constitute modernization processes, and which take the form of similarization and dissimilarization.

To be clear, unlike in the multiple modernities paradigm, this is not about merely expanding sociological differentiation theory with a conception of 'cultural difference' that is similarly based on a concept of identity. Instead, it is about considering similarization and dissimilarization as addressing modern totalization tendencies regardless of whether they are found in cultural, political, social or economic spheres. Any investigation along these lines should seek to empirically contour the conflict dynamics of modern totalization processes, and not the epistemological rejection of the demand for universalism found in historical western modernization. Similarity would thereby represent a methodological mode to describe social and cultural processes that come into conflict with the totalization tendencies of modernity. Such processes might be found, for instance, in the fields of political community, judicial generalizations or the marketplace. Such an approach would lay bare the divide between the self-expectation of a universal and thus identity-based modernity (which has been, and continues to be, so thoroughly refuted on the periphery), and the social and cultural dynamics engendered by – and which seek to provide an answer to – the drive towards totalization.

Example: human rights

This should in no way imply, however, that just because such social and cultural dynamics are most visible on the peripheries of historically western modernization, they only occur on the periphery. On the contrary, the category of similarity – and its extrapolated concepts of similarization and dissimilarization – can serve to pose fundamental questions of identity-theoretical conceptions of modernization more generally (whether in the form of differentiation theories or theories of oppositional difference). Similarity and its counterparts can thus help to *epistemologically and symmetrically* localize processes of confronting the totalizing project of modernity both inside and outside of the historical west. In what follows I would like to briefly discuss how this can work using the example of human rights.

Over the last few decades, human rights have taken centre stage in debates about claims of cultural difference and demands for universalism.

They are paradigmatic of a conflict-filled debate surrounding the universal applicability of a specific type of rights. Especially in post-colonial and (post-)socialist contexts, we find arguments regarding the western-cultural specificity of human rights, and thus arguments that such rights are not or are only partially applicable to non-western contexts. In the 'west', such arguments are criticized as inappropriate cultural relativism. In turn such criticism is often met by accusations that the 'west' seeks to impose its own culturally specific normative system on others. Political philosophy has spent considerable energy trying to find a balance between these two irreconcilable positions, or to overcome them with some higher synthesis.

What unifies the 'cultural relativist' and 'universalist' positions is that they both assume a concurrence between legal norms (human rights as defined by various charters) and legal institutions (the laws designed to guarantee human rights). But, as Cornelia Vismann has shown, in the case of human rights no such common identity exists.[52] The concept of human rights is better understood as 'crossed-out text' that formulates legal norms whose primary aspiration is the criticism of *all* legal institutions, and which thus have no potential to ever be fully implemented even by positive legal institutions – not for empirical reasons but rather for epistemological ones. This is because human rights formulate norms whose 'universalist claim' (which I will soon show to be actually a tendency towards totalization) arises from the fact that they can never be fully realized in social practices and societal order, which change over time. Human rights are thus genuinely *modern* norms, in the sense that they represent a standardization project whose effects are not seen in the project's ultimate (and presumably impossible) completion, but rather in the constant new attempts made to meet its standards.

From this perspective we can just as little approximate perfect human rights as we can completely renounce them – unless, that is, we abandon the idea that legal norms can be applied against existing practices and orders.[53] In truth, human rights represent a point of reference and crystallization for similarization and dissimilarization processes that should be looked for symmetrically (in epistemological terms) both inside and outside of the historical west. Similarization processes might manifest themselves in the controlled process of reviewing laws and legal institutions for their compatibility with human rights (such as in the form of the European Court of Human Rights), or in public protests against governmental and legal practices which the protesters claim to be in violation of human rights (such as in present-day Russia). Dissimilarization processes regarding human rights, on the other hand, are to be found not only in the clearly unconstitutional state and police practices denounced by such protesters. They can also be seen in the establishment of spaces of social 'remote controls'[54] outside of the political borders of the European Union, which are designed to prevent travellers from undertaking the trip to Europe *prior* to their arrival and which, to the extent that such controls are necessarily *incomplete*, lead travellers to risk their lives travelling by sea to Europe.[55] This illustrates the extent to which the similarization and dissimilarization of social processes regarding the abstract principle of human rights can be established in highly specific and identifiable practices.

The unattainability of complete self-realization of modernity in the area of human rights thus provokes practices of similarization and dissimilarization in both the historical west and elsewhere that should be symmetrically (in epistemological terms) conceptualized, and seen as gradual and locally specific heuristics – and not as cultural *matches* or *mis-matches* of legal norms and legal orders.[56] It is therefore crucial to consistently maintain a strategy that strictly avoids conceiving of human rights as self-evident – something that cannot be the case due to the empirical interminability of the totalization of the abstraction, 'human rights'. Instead, we must view the 'essence' of human rights in their constitutive but gradual and locally pronounced differences from positive systems of legal order.

Summary and Prospects

'Human rights' are rational abstractions, and as ideals, they will never be totally attainable. Still, the attempt to totalize these abstractions causes existing social practices to position themselves either by getting closer to or by distancing themselves from the abstraction. In other words, social practices constitute differences despite the absence of positivistically conceived entities or identities. Human rights practices are thus not anchored in culture, as a culturalistic reading of modernization theory would have it. Instead, such practices represent specific and different ways in which a given culture positions itself with regard to 'human rights' as a totalizing tendency in modern society.

The brief example provided here should illustrate the value that a reformulation of sociological modernization theory using a category of similarity could provide. There is no question that the classical differentiation theorem has shaped the field of sociology in disciplinary terms, but it has also generated problems: with the unanswerable question of how diagnoses of social-structural differentiation can be reconciled with diagnoses of the enforcement of hegemonic tendencies; in the accusation that the theorem is Eurocentric or western-centric and thus looks down on non-western societies as latecomers; and finally, with respect to the indisputable plurality of modern societies. The multiple modernities theorem attempts to solve the latter issue, but also tends to overvalue the category of 'culture' as a causal variable while at the same time reducing it to a residual category. In order to avoid such problems, I suggest conceptualizing modernization processes as totalization tendencies that lead to processes of similarization and dissimilarization towards or away from this totalization. These totalization tendencies are not to be mistaken for movements towards universalization or particularization.

A crucial point regarding this situation that I want to emphasize in conclusion is that the dynamics of similarization and dissimilarization regarding totalization tendencies are not inherently connected with 'culture'. Instead, culture is one of many factors that drive (dis)similarization. In the case of border regimes on the periphery of the European Union, for instance, dissimilarization tendencies regarding human rights are not driven by cultural differences (even if, in light of the common association of human rights with European values, such differences would certainly be interesting objects of investigation). Instead, in very concrete terms, the practices of these border regimes make the protection of human rights impossible. If a culturalistic perspective is to remain profitable, it will be above all for *empirical* reasons: for instance, in examining ways in which 'culture' is used to *cause* similarization or dissimilarization. With regard to the debates between 'cultural relativism' and 'universalism' alluded to above, we might formulate the hypothesis that culture represents an effective instrument of dissimilarization when it conceives of difference as opposition. Universalists and cultural relativists, conversely, define themselves around the idiom of culture and as the opposite ends of a spectrum. And culture will remain such an instrument of division as long as it operates with a concept of difference based on a theory of identity. Just as this essay demonstrates how the category of similarity can be applied to the macro-abstraction of 'society', the work that remains is to apply the category of similarity to the abstraction of 'culture'.

I would like to thank Nicole Falkenhayner and Doris Schweitzer for their extremely helpful comments on an earlier version of this essay.

Notes

1 Bhatti (2014): 161f.
2 Bhatti *et al.* (2011): 236.
3 Ibid.
4 Cf. van der Loo and van Reijen (1997).
5 Cf. Turner (1993).
6 Cf. van der Loo and vanReijen (1997).
7 Cf. Eisenstadt, Riedel and Sachsenmaier (2002).

[8] Eisenstadt (2002): 28.
[9] Durkheim (1992): 237, 244.
[10] Weber (1978): 707.
[11] Parsons (1961): 36.
[12] Luhmann (2003).
[13] Habermas (1987): 202, 219.
[14] Bourdieu and Wacquant (1992).
[15] When it comes to the entry point to identity theory and its commonalities with the various forms of differentiation theories, however, differences do exist, and can be sorted into functionalist or non-functionalist, or more or less constructivist versions.
[16] Eisenstadt (1973): 47.
[17] Durkheim (1992): 118, 162.
[18] Durkheim was also concerned with this question as it applied to the problem of decreasing mechanical solidarity (cf. Émile Durkheim 1957). Talcott Parsons also picked up on this problem diagnosis but attempted to solve it not by increasing the importance of profession-specific ethics, but rather by abstracting referential values and then applying them to specific professional relationships (cf. Wenzel 2005). Habermas, on the other hand, specified the problem in such a way that the lack of normative references in the two functionally differentiated subsystems of the economy and political administration becomes problematic, because the consequences of their actions take place quasi behind people's backs (cf. Habermas 1987: 183).
[19] Offe (1986): 111.
[20] Bhatti (2014): 162.
[21] Cf. Simmel (2009).
[22] Simmel (1977): 58. This distinguishes Simmel's concept of differentiation from that of Durkheim, Weber or Parsons.
[23] Cf. Goffman (1971). Goffman's work with the category of identity should not cover up the fact that he did not actually approach the modelling of the social using a theory of identity. For Goffman, identity in its social dimension ('social identity') was primarily an attributive phenomenon that conceptually relied on the anteriority of the other.
[24] Cf. Garfinkel (1967).
[25] Cf. Latour (1986).
[26] Cf. Callon (1986).
[27] Latour (1999).
[28] Cf. Tarde (1903).
[29] Here Tarde occasionally speaks of the 'brain' or the 'mind' as the intersection of different currents of imitation, thus signalling his impartiality towards psychological approaches that were significantly different from Durkheim's sociological rigour (cf. ibid.: 74f).
[30] This also allows us to avoid being limited by Tarde's metaphor of imitation as the transfer of movement impulses, which originated from the physical phase of sociology.
[31] See also the criticism in Niethammer (2000).
[32] Cf. Latour (1996).
[33] Bhatti (2014): 162.
[34] Tarde (2012): 64.
[35] Andrew Pickering's concept of the 'dances of agency' provides a similar impulse: 'Instead of continually struggling to impose this dualist telos on nature, might it be possible to go with the flow – to organize our lives in ways that thematize and

take advantage of open-ended performative dances of agency instead of seeking to extinguish and efface them?' (Pickering 2009: 198).

36 For Tarde and Latour, this denial is not only present but is thematic: according to Latour, only material things are able to overcome situative boundaries or to stabilize situations over time through their mere presence (see Latour 1996). In Goffman and Garfinkel we find a concentration and systemization of situative processes, which has led their approach to be described as micro-sociology and whose relationship to macro-structures is at the very least considered to be difficult. Simmel's approach is the only one that allows meta-situative structures to be conceptually integrated into analyses of societies, such as in the analysis of changing patterns of interaction within urban contexts, or in the analysis of socialization along 'functional chains' in the circulation of money. It would be worth independently studying the extent to which Simmel utilized such meta-situative contexts metaphorically, in the sense of as heuristics, without granting them the same ontological dignity as concrete processes of socialization.

37 Cf. Tellmann (2014).

38 Cf. Harootunian (2004).

39 Lamarre (2004): 34.

40 Cf. Taylor (2002); Gaonkar (2002).

41 Cf. Langenohl (2010a).

42 Spivak (1993): 237.

43 Cf. Lee and LiPuma (2002).

44 Cf. Langenohl (2010b).

45 Cf. Chakrabarty (2000); Connell (2007); Bhambra (2007).

46 Tellingly, theoreticians who consider political and societal collapses as part of (or a result of) processes of modernization (the most prominent example being the Frankfurt school of an *Enlightenment Dialectic* and recently Zygmunt Bauman) also reject classical theories of modernization, or interpret them in a radically different way, such as understanding 'individualization' as 'atomization' and 'rationalization' as subjectless control.

47 This motif was most prominently suported by Jürgen Habermas (cf. Habermas 1992; for a critique, see Langenohl 2006).

48 Examples would include the temporal diagnoses of David Riesman (*The Lonely Crowd*), Robert D. Putnam (*Bowling Alone*) or Richard Sennett (*The Fall of Public Man*), as well as cultural criticisms made on multiple occasions since the nineteenth century (also cf. Bollenbeck 2007).

49 Cf. Langenohl (2007).

50 As critics of 'postcolonial' categories such as hybridity and of 'essentialist' claims of difference in post-communist intellectual and social-scientific discourse have shown (cf. ibid.), this still leaves room for alternatives that are often, ironically, found *within* a paradigm of society that uses the logic of identity. In other words, while such criticisms of modernization seek to dispute its universalist claims, they do so with the help of instruments that themselves have little feel for the totalizing tendencies of modernization processes.

51 The examples provided by Anil Bhatti have at least an implicit political virulence, for instance, when it comes to regulating the handling of multilingualism and multi-confessionality.

52 Cf. Vismann (1998). See also Bachmann-Medick (2012): 350.

53 This caveat is at the core of Hannah Arendt's scepticism of a concept of human rights: they are so dependent on the existence of a political community that even grant individuals legal rights (Arendt 1979: 267–304).

54 Bigo and Guild (2010): 257.

[55] The total abjuring of human rights also naturally breaks down here based on the fact that European border practices have been criticized in very prominent ways, indeed in the *name of* human rights.

[56] Cf. Bachmann-Medick (2012): 347–50.

References

Arendt, Hannah (1979), *The Origins of Totalitarianism*, San Diego, New York, London: Harcourt.

Bachmann-Medick, Doris (2012), 'Menschenrechte als Übersetzungsproblem', in *Geschichte und Gesellschaft: Zeitschrift für historische Sozialwissenschaft,* 38 (2): 331–59.

Bhambra, Gurminder K. (2007), *Rethinking Modernity: Postcolonialism and the Sociological Imagination*, Basingstoke, New York: Palgrave Macmillan.

Bhatti, Anil (2014), 'Ähnlichkeit', in Özkan Ezli and Gisela Staupe, eds, *Das neue Deutschland: Von Migration und Vielfalt*, Konstanz: Konstanz University Press: 161–63.

Bhatti, Anil *et al.* (2011), 'Ähnlichkeit: Ein kulturtheoretisches Paradigma', *Internationales Archiv für Sozialgeschichte der deutschen Literatur*, 36 (1): 233–47.

Bigo, Didier and Elspeth Guild (2010), 'The Transformation of European Border Controls', in Bernard Ryan and Valsamis Mitsilegas, eds, *Extraterritorial Immigration Control: Legal Challenges*, Leiden, Boston: Martinus Nijhoff: 257–78.

Bollenbeck, Georg (2007), *Eine Geschichte der Kulturkritik: Von Rousseau bis Günther Anders*, München: Beck.

Bourdieu, Pierre and Loïc Wacquant (1992), *An Invitation to Reflexive Sociology*, Cambridge, Malden: Polity Press.

Callon, Michel (1986), 'Some Elements of a Sociology of Translation: Domestication of the Scallops and the Fishermen of St Brieuc Bay', in John Law, ed., *Power, Action and Belief: A New Sociology of Knowledge?* Sociological Review Monograph 32, London: Routledge and Kegan Paul: 196–233.

Chakrabarty, Dipesh (2000), *Provincializing Europe: Postcolonial Thought and Historical Difference*, Princeton, NJ: Princeton University Press.

Connell, Raewyn (2007), *Southern Theory: The Global Dynamics of Knowledge in Social Science*, Cambridge, Malden: Polity Press.

Durkheim, Émile (1957), *Professional Ethics and Civic Morals*, translated by Cornelia Brookfield, London: Routledge and Kegan Paul.

——— (1992), *Über soziale Arbeitsteilung: Studie über die Organisation höherer Gesellschaften*, Frankfurt am Main: Suhrkamp.

Eisenstadt, Shmuel N. (1973), *Tradition, Change, and Modernity*, New York: Wiley.

——— (2002), 'Some Observations on Multiple Modernities', in Shmuel N. Eisenstadt, Jens Riedel and Dominic Sachsenmaier, eds, *Reflections on Multiple Modernities: European, Chinese and Other Interpretations*, Leiden: Brill: 27–41.

Eisenstadt, Shmuel N., Jens Riedel and Dominic Sachsenmaier (2002), 'The Context of the Multiple Modernities Paradigm', in Shmuel N. Eisenstadt, Jens Riedel and Dominic Sachsenmaier, eds, *Reflections on Multiple Modernities: European, Chinese and Other Interpretations*, Leiden: Brill: 1–23.

Gaonkar, Dilip Parameshwar (2002), 'Toward New Imaginaries: An Introduction', *Public Culture*, 14 (1): 1–19.

Garfinkel, Harold ([1962] 1967), 'Common Sense Knowledge of Social Structures: The Documentary Method of Interpretation in Lay and Professional Fact Finding', in *Studies in Ethnomethodology*, Englewood Cliffs: Prentice Hall: 76–115.

Goffman, Erving (1971), *Relations in Public: Microstudies of the Public Order*, New York: Basic Books.

Habermas, Jürgen (1987), *The Theory of Communicative Action*, Vol. 2: *Lifeworld and System: A Critique of Functionalist Reason*, translated by Thomas Mc Carthy, Boston, MA: Beacon Press; German edition: *Theorie des kommunikativen Handelns, Bd. 2: Zur Kritik der funktionalistischen Vernunft*, Frankfurt am Main: Suhrkamp, 1981.

——— (1992), *Die Moderne – ein unvollendetes Projekt: Philosophisch-politische Aufsätze 1977–1992*, Frankfurt am Main: Suhrkamp.

Harootunian, Harry (2004), 'Ghostly Comparisons', in Thomas Lamarre and Kang Nae-hui, eds, *Impacts of Modernities* (*Traces* series: *A Multilingual Series of Cultural Theory and Translation*, Vol. 3), Hong Kong: Hong Kong University Press: 39–52.

Lamarre, Thomas (2004), 'Introduction: Impacts of Modernities', in Thomas Lamarre and Kang Nae-hui, eds, *Impacts of Modernities* (*Traces* series: *A Multilingual Series of Cultural Theory and Translation*, Vol. 3), Hong Kong: Hong Kong University Press: 1–35.

Langenohl, Andreas (2006), 'Öffentlichkeit und politisch-kulturelle Differenz in Europa: Jenseits von Kulturalismus und Anti-Kulturalismus', in Kathrin Ruhl *et al.*, eds, *Demokratisches Regieren und politische Kultur: Post-staatlich, post-parlamentarisch, post-patriarchal?*, Münster: Lit: 177–97.

——— (2007), *Tradition und Gesellschaftskritik: Eine Rekonstruktion der Modernisierungstheorie*, Frankfurt am Main, New York: Campus.

——— (2010a), 'Imaginäre Grenzen. Zur Entstehung impliziter Kollektivcodierungen in EU-Europa', *Berliner Journal für Soziologie*, Vol. 1: 45–63.

——— (2010b), 'Modernization, Modernity, and Tradition: Sociological Theory's Promissory Notes', in John N. Kim and Richard Calichman, eds, *Rethinking Cultural Difference: Around the Work of Naoki Sakai*, London: Routledge: 192–210.

Latour, Bruno (1986), 'The Powers of Associations', in John Law, ed., *Power, Action and Belief: A New Sociology of Knowledge?*, London, Boston: Routledge and Kegan Paul: 264–80.

——— (1996), 'On Interobjectivity', *Mind, Culture, and Activity*, 3 (4): 228–45.

——— (1999), *Pandora's Hope: Essays on the Reality of Science Studies*, Cambridge, MA: Harvard University Press.

Lee, Benjamin and Edward LiPuma (2002), 'Cultures of Circulation: The Imaginations of Modernity', *Public Culture*, 14 (1): 191–213.

Luhmann, Niklas (2003), *Social Structure and Semantics*, Stanford: Stanford University Press.

Niethammer, Lutz (2000), *Kollektive Identität: Heimliche Quellen einer unheimlichen Konjunktur*, Reinbek bei Hamburg: Rowohlt.

Offe, Claus (1986), 'Die Utopie der Null-Option: Modernität und Modernisierung als politische Gütekriterien', in Johannes Berger, ed., *Die Moderne – Kontinuitäten und Zäsuren* (= Soziale Welt, Sb. 4), Göttingen: Otto Schwartz: 97–117.

Parsons, Talcott (1961), 'An Outline of the Social System', in Parsons *et al.*, eds, *Theories of Society*, New York: Simon and Schuster, The Free Press: 30–79.

Pickering, Andrew (2009), 'The Politics of Theory', *Journal of Cultural Economy*, 2 (1–2): 197–212.

Simmel, George (1977), *The Problems of the Philosophy of History: an epistemological essay*, translated and edited by Guy Oakes, Detroit: Free Press.

——— (2009), *Sociology: Inquiries into the Construction of Social Forms*, translated and edited by Anthony J. Blasi, Anton K. Jacobs and Mathew Kanjirathinkal, Boston: Brill.

Spivak, Gayatri Chakravorty (1993), 'Reading the Satanic Verses', in *Outside in the Teaching Machine*, New York and London: Routledge: 217–41.

Tarde, Gabriel (1903), *The Laws of Imitation*, New York: Henry Holt; available at archive.org

——— (2012), *Monadology and Sociology*, translated by Theo Lorenc, Melbourne: re.press.

Taylor, Charles (2002), 'Modern Social Imaginaries', *Public Culture*, (14) 1: 91–124.

Tellmann, Ute (2014), 'Die Welt als Labor – Über eine folgenreiche Gründungsszene der ANT', in Sina Farzin and Henning Laux, eds, *Gründungsszenen soziologischer Theorie*, Wiesbaden: Springer VS: 25–40.

Turner, Bryan S. (1993), *Max Weber: From History to Modernity*, London and New York: Routledge.

van der Loo, Hans and Willem van Reijen (1997), *Modernisierung: Projekt und Paradox*, München: dtv.

Vismann, Cornelia (1998), 'Menschenrechte: Instanz des Sprechens – Instrument der Politik', in Brunkhorst and Hauke, eds, *Demokratischer Experimentalismus*, Frankfurt am Main: Suhrkamp: 279–304.

Weber, Max (1978), *Economy and Society: An Outline of Interpretive Sociology*, edited by Guenther Roth and Claus Wittich, Berkeley, CA: University of California Press.

Wenzel, Harald (2005), 'Profession und Organisation: Dimensionen der Wissensgesellschaft bei Talcott Parsons', in Thomas Klatetzki and Veronika Tacke, eds, *Organisation und Profession*, Wiesbaden: VS: 45–71.

The Locale of Comparison and Transnationality

Towards comparative humanities

Naoki Sakai

Similarity is equivocally connected with comparison. Similarity is necessarily concerned either with a judgment that is issued after an act of comparison or with anticipation that invokes a judgment of comparison. It is given in the form of an assertion or prediction that one item can be judged to have a certain relationship – similarity or dissimilarity – with a different item or items as a result of comparison. In discussing similarity, therefore, we cannot evade a preliminary inquiry into the notion of comparison, upon which is premised the alternative judgment of being either similar or dissimilar.

Similarity can be predicated upon a wide spectrum of objects in many different disciplines of knowledge. However, I cannot discuss the problems of similarity in general within the scope of my inquiry here, which is limited to the problem of similarity in the humanities or human sciences.

At the outset, let me separate out the two moments in the act of comparison in what I understand as 'comparative humanities'. These two moments – we may characterize one as logical and the other as political – can always be discerned when we are engaged in a judgment about similarity, a judgment that is dependent upon the procedure of comparison in the humanities. The first is the postulation of the class of *genus* among compared items, of some common element by which items are compared. Comparison is performed between or among unified objects preliminarily identified as two *species*; at the same time, comparison is constitutive of the logical dimension of *genus* where *species difference* (*diaphora*) is discovered, measured or judged. Attributed to the class of *species* are particular cultures, languages, economic systems, political ideologies, literatures and so forth; each of these is postulated both as a unified entity and as a particular (*species*) example of the general class (*genus*).

When we submit even such items as culture and political ideology to comparison, they are regarded as unified units. Thus we compare the English language with the Chinese language, for instance, because these two particular languages belong to the category of language – more specifically, *langue* in the vocabulary of Ferdinand de Saussure – in general. As long as English is assumed to be a systematicity, it can be regarded as an individual,[1] unified, indivisible entity; but we are far from certain that the item to be compared – English or Chinese in this case – exists at the level of the immediately empirical, in the way that classical logic has sometimes attributed the property of empirical existence to the concept of the individual. As one of many particular languages, English is a particular *species* of the general *genus* of language.

However, it must be added that a particular language should be able to be conceived of as an indivisible unity precisely because we want to regard it as an individual. The individual is after all an *individuum*, an entity that cannot be further divided. Very often comparison is conducted on the presumption that this basic operation of logical and formal reason is still valid and sustainable, and that the individuality of a particular language is indisputable. The discipline of Comparative Literature, for instance, has long been legitimated on the basis of this logical economy of *species* and *genus*, of particular national literatures and the general literature with which universal humanity – which used to be no other than the European humanity – is endowed. It goes without saying that our faith in this logical economy has been challenged many times; today, it is generally agreed that it is a matter of poor intellectual taste to confess one's faith in this logical economy.

In reference to this topic of similarity, the conceptual economy of *genus* and *species* of classical logic seems, in my view, to be vastly inadequate to comprehend the politics of similarity and difference, particularly in view of Wittgenstein's argument about family resemblances. The differential perception of similarity and dissimilarity is not organized according to the classification of *genus* and *species*, of generality and particularity.[2] How we attribute a racial feature to a person in an everyday social encounter, for instance, is not primarily dictated by the classical logic embedded in the system of classification in natural history, zoology or physical anthropology. On the contrary, the belief that humankind can be coherently and systematically classified into sub-classes of races justifies the normative attribution of racial identity to a person. What underlies this is the very belief that similarities and dissimilarities are already organized by the logical economy of *species* and *genus* in nature. What is important to note in apprehending the differential perception of similarity and dissimilarity is that the conceptual economy of *genus* and *species* constitutes an apparatus of the normative attribution appealed to in organizing the diversity of perceived manifolds. Let us return to the famous no. 66 of *Philosophical Investigations I*.

> Consider for example the proceedings that we call 'games.' I mean board-games, card-games, ball-games, Olympic games, and so on. What is common to them all? Don't say: 'These *must* be something common, or they would not be called "games"' – but *look and see* whether there is anything common to all. – For if you look at them you will not see something that is common to *all*, but similarities, relationships, and a whole series of them at that. To repeat: don't think, but look! – Look for example at board-games, with their multifarious relationships. Now pass to card-games; here you find many correspondences with the first group, but many common features drop out, and others appear. When we pass next to ball-games, much that is common is retained, but much is lost. – Are they all 'amusing'? Compare chess with noughts and crosses. Or is there always winning and losing, or competition between players? Think of patience. In ball games there is winning and losing; but when a child throws his ball at the wall and catches it again, this feature has disappeared. Look at the parts played by skill and luck; and at the difference between skill in chess and skill in tennis. Think now of games like ring-a-ring-a-roses; here is the element of amusement, but how many other characteristic features have disappeared! And we can go through the many, many other groups of games in the same way; can see how similarities crop up and disappear.
>
> And the result of this examination is: we see a complicated network of similarities overlapping and criss-crossing: sometimes overall similarities, sometimes similarities of detail.[3]

So as to find similarities among various games – board games, card games, Olympic games and so on – do we have to apply the classificatory scheme of *species* and *genus* to them? In order for the *species* of card games or Olympic games to be included in the *genus* of games, do they have to share something in common? For instance, another organization of similarities and dissimilarities in the classification of human beings is known as racism. It is not difficult to see a procedure of classification similar to that of games apply to races as sub-sets of humankind. Must differences in physiological or behavioural appearances among people be classified according to the logical economy of *species* and *genus*, precisely since every one of these different people shares humanity in common?

Although normally or normatively, and in the world in which this normalcy has been almost universally accepted, the classification based upon *genus* and *species* is not distinguished from the descriptive or constituting claims about racial identity, people do not receive the classification of races in the immediate perception of persons they encounter; the perceived similarity and dissimilarity are not given according to the order systematized in terms of *genus* and *species*. Instead, the operation of racial classification, without which it would be simply impossible to attribute a racial identity to a person, is a retrospective imposition upon our primordial exposure to the world. The recognition of similarity comes before the identification of a particularity in terms of the economy of *genus* and *species*, of generality and particularity. Therefore, in the Wittgensteinian manner of speech, we must see but not think. It seems to me that in the first instance, racial classification is a matter of thinking rather than looking.

In exploring what is entailed in the politics of similarity, therefore, I want to discern a stage prior to the conceptual articulation in terms of *genus* and *species*, a stage where the classical logic is only one of the alternative strategies. In short, I want to acknowledge a space for genealogical analysis in the topic of similarity. This of course leads to the other moment in the act of comparison.

This second moment is the occasion or locale where we are obliged to compare. Comparison takes place because determination of *species difference* is needed. But for the sake of discerning a certain political complexity involved in the notion of the determination of species difference, let me ponder over what is often referred to as *cultural difference* – over two distinct approaches to *cultural difference*.

In the presence of a person who appears to be speaking, I can understand neither what she wants nor what she is meaning to do. Consequently, I am at a loss. At such a locale, naturally and in due course, some explanation as to why I or we are at a loss is demanded. Reasoning may well provide a schematic explanation about some generalized experience of incommensurability and about the situation marked by *cultural difference*: supposedly, what she speaks is the Chinese language whereas what I speak is English. Both belong to the general class of languages but we cannot make ourselves understood to one another because the Chinese language is *different* from English.

Let me pause here momentarily since I do not think that the difference at stake in this instance can in due course be subsumed under the concept of *species difference*. What is at stake here is some *difference*, but it is not reduced to the conception of difference between Chinese as a particular language and English as another particular language, of difference that conforms to the economy of *species* and *genus*.

It is worthwhile to emphasize the fact that it is believed that the determination of *species difference* is offered as a solution to the initial problem of our being at a loss, in response to the perplexity we come across in such a locale. Presumably, language difference is a kind of *species difference* whose purport is to offer a clue as to why we are at a loss in a locale of incomprehension, perplexity or helplessness. As I have argued elsewhere, however, the determination of *species difference* only leads us to 'confusionism'.[4] And it is important to note that confusionism of this kind is almost always present in the term *cultural difference*.

Thus the language difference is supposed to cause a situation where we need to know why we are at a loss with one another. Language difference, which is already preliminarily determined as *species difference*, is a serious matter when we do not understand one another, when we cannot be confident in our directives for the immediate future; it is usually assumed that our sociability is grounded on some primordial communality, on our capacity to be immediately and instantaneously in a common sharing. Language difference is therefore understood to cause our inability to share, to result in the absence of this communality. Commonly we presume that normalcy consists of this unwarranted assumption that people do understand each other, unless the presumed common sharing is disrupted by some abnormality – we do not express doubt about either the comprehensibility of our expressive behaviours or our ability to apprehend the actions and expressions of others. Hence it is supposed that the need for comparison occurs only on occasions when we are forced to become aware of *different* people, *different* beings in our presence. The encounter with cultural difference or discontinuity is interpreted as an encounter with one type or another of *species difference*.

The term 'difference' becomes marked precisely because of this experience of 'nonsense', 'being at a loss' or 'being unable to make sense of the occasion'; in short, of 'being deprived of the world'. The determination of *species difference* becomes something urgent, and even desperately important, precisely because we are in the presence of others in *discontinuity*. Most often we talk of this encounter with discontinuity in terms of the foreign, but it is significant that initially the foreign does not connote the outside or the external in a strictly spatial sense. Instead, it is an *outside* of a given and familiar register, an outside indicative of the nonsensical that evades the spatial alternative of either inside or outside.

It is an 'outside' but it cannot be accommodated in the spatial register of our thought. It is important to note that the foreign acquires the status of the external or the outsider only through the assumption that we are inside the common element – language, culture or nationality – represented as an 'inside', spatially delimited by borders. Only when the 'being in common' is represented by a spatial figure of enclosure does the foreign gain the trope of the external to or outside of the domain, or domesticity or familiarity.[5] And discontinuity is something that is fundamentally incommensurate with the logic of location in a spatial economy. For at this stage, discontinuity cannot be represented as a relationship within a smooth continuous space. And, most importantly, it is imperative to keep in mind that if we are at a loss, it is not because some person or people are *different* – in the sense of *species difference* – from me or us. On the contrary, it is because we are at a loss or unable to make sense in the first place, that we attempt to determine this encounter with *difference* within the logical economy of *species* and *genus*.

At stake in this presentation is whether or not we are allowed to conceptualize *cultural difference* in the sense of 'nonsense' or 'being at a loss' in terms of *species difference*, in terms of the difference categorized in the economy of *species* and *genus* within classical logic. Are we to overlook the very difference between the difference in the sense of 'nonsense' or 'being at a loss', and the species difference already regulated by the logical economy of *species* and *genus*?

Allow me to consider another situation where we need to know how we are different from one another, why certain people are not subjugated to the imperatives or commands I normally obey or yield to, or why some of us are free from a set of proscriptions and others are not. Thus, we compare ourselves to find where we are situated vis-à-vis one another in a practical sense, along the direction of what we must do. Comparison is indispensable precisely because we want to know how we are related to one another, who should lead among us, who should follow, who should work for whom among us, and so on. It is through the act of comparison that we comprehend the configuration of our subject positions in which we apprehend who we are in terms of socially determinate relations: gender, commodity exchange, race, social class, nationality, civilization, kinship, religion, culture, professional qualifications, pedagogic hierarchy, gift-giving, academic expertise and so forth. When we cannot locate ourselves in the configuration of subject positions, we are also at a loss or do not know how to act in accordance with others in a situation. On such occasions we sense that something is *different*, and that we ought to behave in such a different manner from the ways in which we are normally and normatively expected to. Yet it is important to note that this sense of *difference* cannot be simply reduced to difference in the paradigm of the same and the different, of the homologous and the heteronomous. Indeed, this also is of crucial importance to how we understand two different approaches to *cultural difference*.

In the context of our discussion of *cultural difference*, I would like to introduce this conceptual ambiguity of the individual into my understanding of the locale of comparison, of a place where we are articulated to one another in ways that elsewhere I have called 'heterolingual'.[6]

Transnationality and Internationality

Following this preliminary guideline, let me state at the start that nationality has been one of the most predominant topics under the name of which, if not explicitly, the process of comparison in knowledge production has been addressed in the humanities. Normatively, nationality signifies some communal premise and shared emotive bond that supposedly guarantees sympathetic communion among the members of the national community. It is often the case that the term 'nationality' suggests the existence of some common ground, thanks to which 'we', the members of the nation, are supposed to be similar to one another. Yet the assumed similarity among the members of the nation, of national culture or of the national society of sympathy cannot be manifested unless their dissimilarity to other nation, other ethnicity or other culture is highlighted. As a matter of fact, the homogeneity implied by nationality is most often an inverted image of a nation's relationship to other nations.

In discussing the topic of nationality, therefore, transnationality and internationality must be conceptually distinguished from one another. Of course, neither transnationality nor internationality is intelligible without reference to the operation of comparison. Nationality is a form of aesthetic investment necessarily associated with the imagination of community, of being together with a certain people – and this collectivity of people is imagined as a totality, the contours of which are delineated by a spatial shape analogous to geographic territory. In due course, nationality presents itself most often in terms of a figure, schema, design or image, resultant from the determination of either transnational or international *species difference*. What is at issue in transnationality as well as internationality is to compare, to distinguish, to divide and to draw a border, thereby marking its inside (compatriot) from the outside (foreigner).

In this context, it is noteworthy that the significance of the problematic of 'bordering', is increasing in knowledge production today.[7] This problematic has to be specifically marked as not one of 'border' but of 'border-ing', because what is at issue is a lot more than the old problem of boundary, discrimination and classification. At the same time that it recognizes the presence of borders, discriminatory regimes and the paradigms of classification, this problematic sheds light on the processes of drawing a border, of specifying the element of comparison, of instituting the terms of distinction in discrimination, and of introducing a *continuous* space[8] of the social, against the horizon of which a divide is inscribed. I find it particularly significant that Sandro Mezzadra and Brett Neilson first introduced this term 'border-ing' in what they termed 'the multiplication of labour'.[9]

By introducing the concept of the multiplication of labour, Mezzadra and Neilson challenged the conventional categorization of labour and the familiar notion of the international division of labour. They questioned 'the orthodoxy that categorizes the global spectrum of labour according to international divisions or stable configurations such as the three worlds model or those elaborated around a binary such as centre/periphery or North/South'. What has to be taken into consideration is the dynamic and constantly transforming relationship between labour and power.

The world is not becoming borderless today. On the contrary, borders are constantly redrawn and multiplied; the boundaries of national territories, ethnic cultures and civilizations are not the only dominant ones; there are many borders being newly inscribed. Hence the analytic of bordering requires us to examine simultaneously both the presence of border and its drawing or inscription.

Within the scope of this essay, I want to draw attention to the problematic of bordering, firstly to elucidate the differentiation of transnationality from nationality. Most importantly, I want to reverse the order of apprehension in which transnationality is comprehended on the basis of nationality, on the presumption that nationality is primary while transnationality is somewhat secondary. Consequently, the transnational is assumed to be derivative of the national. This widely accepted pattern of reasoning derives from the thought habit characteristic of modernity,[10] according to which the adjectival 'transnational' is attributed to an incident or situation uncontainable within one nationality: the transnational indicates something that cannot be restricted within the schema or figure of nationality.

What must be highlighted first of all is the implicit presumption that underlies the concept of nationality: it cannot make sense unless it is postulated against the horizon of internationality. And we must keep in mind that internationality is utterly incomprehensible unless we take for granted a manner of comparing and categorizing the units of the world to be compared – the unities of the nation-states, each of which is represented by a single state sovereignty. Essentially, internationality is a historically particular regime of comparison that operates in the logical economy of *species* and *genus*.

For the very reason of the politics of comparison, nationality does not make sense unless in conjunction with internationality. Nationality becomes conceivable only when the scene of juxtaposing nations is institutionalized within some scheme of government, traditionally designated as 'territorial state sovereignty'. Of course, it is with respect to this paradigmatic affinity of nationality and internationality in our vision of the modern world that a disclaimer must be issued once again: just as the sense of difference concerning the experience of 'being at a loss' must not be equated to *species difference*, so too, transnationality must not be confused with internationality.

In due course, therefore, distinguishing transnationality from internationality becomes the central issue in the politics of comparison. It follows that our first move is to delineate the semantics of transnationality as distinct from internationality in order to assert the priority of transnationality over nationality.

One of the distinguishing characteristics of the modern world can be found in its internationality; the modernity of the modern world has manifested itself in the formation of the international world. Today, unfortunately, transnationality is all too often understood within the schema of the international world. Here 'schema' means a certain image or figure in terms of which our sense of nationality is apprehended. The schema of nationality is embedded within the larger schema of internationality, and, needless to say, the very relationship between national and international schemata is understood to be one of *species* and *genus*. But it is important to note that in some regions, such as East Asia, the international world did not prevail until the late nineteenth century. This was also the case in Africa, the Middle East, Southeast Asia and the Pacific (granted, I am using very problematic names for geopolitical regions on the globe). I suspect that this was the case in Northern and Eastern Europe as well, even though the international world had supposedly been established in Western Europe, a long time ago.

In East Asia the international world was entirely new; it took more than a century before East Asian states surrendered the old tribute system and yielded to the new inter-state diplomacy dictated by international law. So in this case – which also applies to many other regions of the globe – the international world signalled the arrival of colonial modernity. And it is in the very process of introducing the international world that the binary of the West and the Rest began to serve as the framework in which the world's colonial hierarchy was globally actualized and institutionalized.

Of course, the international world is not a phenomenon exclusive to the twentieth century. The dividing of the world into two contrasting areas, the West and the Rest, has been a widely accepted institutionalized practice in academia for a few centuries (sometimes going as far back as the year 1492, which has played a symbolically important role in historical narratives).[11]

Some argue that this dichotomy may be traced back to the seventeenth century, when the system of international laws was inaugurated with the Treaty of Westphalia in 1648.[12] This peace treaty, subsequent to the Thirty Year War, preliminarily established the division of the two geopolitical areas in the world. The first of them would deserve a proper characterization as 'the international world', in which four principles were to be observed through the reciprocal respect of the diplomatic protocol called a 'treaty' among the sovereign states of the international world: (i) the territorial sovereignty of the national state and its self-determination; (ii) legal equality among national states; (iii) the reign of international laws among the states; and (iv) the non-intervention of one state in the domestic affairs of another. By the way, the term 'national state' is not without problems. By national state, I imply neither the nation-state nor the state based upon popular sovereignty. In the seventeenth century, when the Treaty of Westphalia was first introduced, there was no state that derived its legitimacy from the new and peculiar communality called 'the nation'. The national state, therefore, does not mean the sovereign nation-state, which was not actualized until the eighteenth century.

The second of these areas of the world was a geopolitical one excluded from the first, in which these four principles – including the reign of international laws – had no binding force. The first area where the system of international law was observed would be called 'Europe', while the second would be excluded from 'the international world' and would become literally 'the Rest of the world', meaning the world minus Europe, with its states and inhabitants remaining in an eternal state of exception; in other words, it was subjected to arbitrary uses of colonial violence.

In East Asia, Japan's colonization of Korea, for instance, was sanctioned according to the protocols of the international world. The Japanese government followed the terms of international law in every step of its colonizing manoeuvres so as to secure the international approval of the legitimacy of its colonizing policies. Many parts of the globe were also colonized according to the schema of the international world. By the beginning of the twentieth century, the majority of the second area – the Rest of the world – had been transformed into colonies that were administered by a few imperialist powers of Europe. Then, gradually, 'the West' began to replace Europe. An increasing number of intellectuals began to use the term 'the West'. It was only towards the beginning of the twentieth century that this geographic designation of 'the West' gained currency. Even though the basic dynamism of the hierarchical bifurcation of the world remained unchanged, it was no longer Europe but 'the West' that dominated the Rest of the world by means of economic, military, administrative and cultural strategies which are summarily called 'modern colonialism'.

It may thus appear that the world was bifurcated geographically into the West in which the colonizing states had originated, on the one hand, and the territorial regions of the Rest that were inhabited by the colonized but governed by the colonizers, on the other. Taking into consideration the hegemonic nature of the West, one would not be surprised that the distinction of the West from the Rest appeared to be further reinforced by the racist distinction of white and non-white. Nevertheless, the West is at best a pseudo-geographic index, no more than a marker indicating a configuration of dramaturgical positionalities pretending to be a geographic indicator, because, in the final analysis, the West refers to much more than a geographic direction.[13]

In the twentieth century, the international world had to expand to cover the entire surface of the earth as a result of three developments: (i) colonial competition among the imperialist states; (ii) the emergence of the United States and Japan as modern imperial powers; and, most importantly, (iii) the increasingly widespread anti-colonial struggles for national self-determination in the Rest or the non-West. In this historical characterization of the West, one can single out two paramount factors distinguishing it from the Rest of the world: the legacy of colonialisms on the one hand, and the comparative operation based upon the logical economy of *species* and *genus* on the other.

For a colony to gain independence, the colonized had to establish their own national sovereignty and gain recognition from other sovereign states. In other words, the process of decolonization for a colonized nation meant entering the ranks of nation-states in the international world. As the number of nations recognized in the international world increased, the presumptions of nationality and internationality were accepted as naturally given. As the schematic nature of the international world was somewhat forgotten, both nationality and internationality were dehistoricized and reified, as though the institutions symbolically marking the border of the national community – national territory, national language, national culture, national history and so forth – had been both genetically inherited and innately existent for many centuries. It is no surprise that the vast majority of comparative studies in the humanities and social sciences – comparative literature, comparative law, comparative sociology and so-called area studies – fall into the general genre of comparative nationality today.

It is at this juncture that the concept of transnationality must be invigorated. It must be rejuvenated in order to undermine the apparent naturalness of nationality and internationality, as well as to disclose the very historicity of our presumptions about nationality, national community, national language, national culture and ethnicity, which more often than not are associated with 'the feeling of nationality'. Here, the classical notion of *nationality* in British liberalism is of decisive importance so as to historicize the schematism of the international world.

By 'nationality', British thinkers of the nineteenth century meant a new form of communal solidarity that united a portion of humanity to the exclusion of all others. This united portion of humans is called 'nation', and is consolidated through shared sympathies. In this sense, this community finds its own *raison d'être* in an aesthetic investment, an organization of emotive communality. These common sympathies exist exclusively among the insiders (compatriots) and must not be shared by the outsiders (foreigners); they make these insiders cooperate with each other more willingly than with other people, and desire to be governed by a government made up of themselves or their representatives. John Stuart Mill, for instance, called this common sympathy 'the feeling of nationality'; it may be generated by various causes such as the identity of race and descent, language and religion. Shared geographic residence may well be a cause. But, Mill argued, the most important factor is the identity of political antecedents; the possession of a national history; communally shared recollections, collective pride and humiliation, pleasure and regret. Through national history this new community can believe that every one of its members is connected with the same incidents in the common past.[14]

In East Asia, it was arguably Fukuzawa Yukichi (1835–1901) who first introduced this British discussion on the nation and nationality systematically and comprehensively. Today, he is remembered as one of the leading Enlightenment intellectuals who advocated for the creation of a modern nation in Japan, and who translated the English term *nationality* into *kokutai* (national body) a few years after the Meiji Restoration (1868). Later the word *kokutai* was used as a fetish to express the sovereignty of the Japanese emperor, and the word *nationality* or *national body* acquired almost a sacrosanct and proscriptive nature in the Japanese empire in the early twentieth century. In his *Outline of the Theory of Civilization,* however, Fukuzawa included Mill's explications of nationality and the *feeling of nationality (kokutai no jô)* almost verbatim in his exposition of *kokutai.*[15] For him, the project of creating the feeling of nationality among the inhabitants of the Japanese archipelago was an absolutely indispensable part of the construction of a nation-state. First of all, what had to be acknowledged was the absence of the feeling of nationality among the masses that inhabited the islands of Japan under the reign of the feudal governments; there was no nation of Japan, no Japanese as a nation. Therefore, the task of creating an unprecedented type of community called 'nation' must be found in the manufacture of the feeling of nationality.

Thus, for Fukuzawa, to modernize Japan was first and foremost to create the institutional conditions for the feeling of nationality. But for this sentiment, he argued, people would never form a national community; neither as individuals nor as a collectivity would the Japanese be able to become independent without the feeling of nationality.

In the late nineteenth and early twentieth centuries, almost without exception, nationalist intellectuals in East Asia and elsewhere in the Rest believed that the introduction of nationality was an absolutely necessary condition, without which peoples in the Rest of the modern world could not deal with the very actuality of colonial modernity into which they were inadvertently placed. They understood that only by turning local masses into a *people* with nationality could they incite them to reject their predicament of colonial subjugation and humiliation. Of course, it was imperative to institute the systems of industrial capitalism in their own countries and to educate the population so as to make it capable of scientific rationality. The fate of the nation could not be divorced from the project of modernization. Modernization necessitated the introduction into a society of industrial production skills, national education, a system of national transportation, a national currency printed and regulated by the national bank, a modern military built with national conscription, and a spirit of scientific rationality guiding modern technology and industrial production. But any of these institutions necessary for nation-building would be redundant if not accompanied by the feeling of nationality to bind people together as a nation, as a community with a shared destiny. Nationalist intellectuals firmly believed that people under colonial domination would never be able to deal with the actuality of colonial modernity unless they formed a political community called 'nation', a new political camaraderie shaped in the pattern of a 'fraternity' independent of previous familial, clannish, creedal or tribal affiliations. They were convinced that unless the indigenous population first formed a nation, they would never liberate themselves from the shackles of colonial subjugation.

A disclaimer must be issued here. As a guiding outline or trope I introduced the modern binary of the West and the Rest of the world, yet it is imperative to keep in mind that it is no more than a trope, a figurative expression. This binary gives us a synoptic vision of the modern world as a hegemonic configuration, but this vision can hardly sustain coherence in many concrete historical contexts. The task of modernization that many Asian intellectuals had to confront from the late nineteenth century onwards was equally urgent for those intellectuals living in the geographic areas that might well be included in Europe or the West. The very boundary between the West and the Rest is so arbitrarily drawn that there are innumerable cases where certain regions of today's European Union may well be located outside the West. Some social strata of the United States which have enjoyed the reputation of being the hub of the West's modernity since the end of the Second World War, for instance, manifest the same characteristic of pre-modernity typically attributed to the Rest. Certain aspects of everyday life in some regions in East Asia, for example, are indisputably more 'Western' than in some sectors of 'white' population in the United States.

Depending upon the context of comparison, the very distinction between the West and the Rest shifts constantly and articulates itself differently. Here it is important to remind ourselves of the theoretical significance of 'the multiplication of labour' introduced by Mezzadra and Neilson. In some instances, the dichotomy of the West and the Rest may appear to be solidly instituted. In others, it may well seem arbitrary and contingent. It is almost impossible to find a lucid coherence to connect many different manifestations of this dichotomy. The West and the Rest are undoubtedly both historical and mythical constructs. However, although I would never claim that the West is unreal or illusionary under any circumstance, I would also never dare to talk about it as a kind of trans-historical continuity or an essentialist category of tradition such as 'the Western Civilization since Greek Antiquity'. We must remind ourselves time and time again that the binary opposition of West and Rest does not consist of two separate entities, the West and the Rest of the world, but that it is an operation of bifurcation, a bipolar articulation of difference, or a co-figurative schematization that sustains the appearance of separation between the West and the Rest.

Translation and Bordering

As is obvious by now, the problematic guiding my inquiry in this essay is quite different from the nationalist concern shared by many Asian intellectuals in the twentieth and twenty-first centuries. I am committed to an interrogation of how to emancipate our imagination from the regime of the nation-state, not through a negation of this regime itself, but rather, by problematizing the methodological nationalisms that permeate knowledge production in the humanities, particularly in the academic discipline of Area Studies, and thereby to posit an alternative apprehension of the transnational community. In suspending the nationalist conviction, I refuse to view nationality as a given; rather, I reverse the order of priority while never underestimating the nationalist rhetoric mobilized in our struggles with colonial modernity. Simply put, my starting point is that nationality is a restricted and distorted derivative of transnationality. In other words, nationality is always secondary to transnationality. And my guiding question is how the transnational, the primary modality of sociality, is delimited, regulated and restricted by the rules of the international world. It is in this context that I must confront the issue of *border-ing*. In order to problematize the priority of nationality and the international world, we must first study the tropics of the border.

It goes without saying that the border cannot exist naturally; physical markers such as rivers, mountain ranges, walls and even lines on the ground become borders only when made to represent a certain pattern of social action. In this respect a border is always man-made and assumes human sociality. Only when people react to one another does a border come into being. Even if a border separates, discriminates or distances one group from another, people must be in some kind of social relation for that border to serve as a marker or representation of separation, discrimination or distance. A border is a trope serving to paradoxically and irrevocably represent primordial sociality. Only where people agree to 'border' can we talk about a border as an institution. Thus, 'bordering' always precedes a border. To apprehend a border is to study how it is inscribed, erased, redrawn or reproduced.

Prior to this bordering, it is impossible to conceptualize the national border. Thus, the national territory is indeterminate prior to 'bordering'. Similarly, it is impossible to determine a national language prior to it. What we conventionally call 'language' is not a unity; it is not given as an individual entity within an interior already distinct from its exterior before bordering. A language is distinguished from another language only after it is rendered representable as an enclosure that is clearly marked by its border. It may be a system but it is never a systematicity; it does not consist of a finite set of fixed rules; even a grammatical mistake makes sense and becomes an effective expression in language. In every use of it, or in what de Saussure called '*language*', it is modified and reproduced. In short, language is manifold. Therefore it is impossible to talk about language as if it were primordially an identifiable unity. It follows that a reference to 'bordering' is necessary to comprehend how the individuality of a particular national or ethnic language, the very indivisible unity of a language presumed in the figure of national (ethnic) language, came to prevail. In other words, it is not to the language but rather at the level of its *representation* that its identity and unity are attributable. Unless the operation of comparison, by means of which *species difference* between languages is postulated, measured and judged, is presumed, the individuality of one particular language as distinct from another would be impossible. The individual unity of language is possible only after it is compared at the level of *representation*. This is to say that it is a retrospective projection in the register of *re*-presentation: in the register of a repeated or second-time presentation.

Only at the level of representation, therefore, can one language be compared with another as an instance of one particularity as opposed to another within the economy of *species* and *genus*. When we are at a loss, when we come across a situation of incommensurability, when we face non-sense *before translation*, we are in the presence of *cultural difference* that does not conform to the logical economy of internationality.

So what corresponds to this 'bordering' as far as language is concerned? Of course, it is translation. What I want to put forth here is that in the context of schematism, translation comes prior to the determination of language unities that supposedly translation is understood to bridge. For that reason, against a commonsensical prejudice or pre-judgment, it must be insisted that there is translation before the postulation of a national or ethnic language. Translation must occur before the attribution of identity to language, just as there is transnationality before nationality. In short, as far as the representation of languages is concerned, translation precedes the determination of *species difference*. Only after translation are individual languages available for comparison. In other words, it is in translation that we are able to talk about similarity and dissimilarity of languages. And let us not forget that *there is no reason why similarity and dissimilarity thus encountered must necessarily be restricted by the economy of genus and species*.

At this juncture, we can see one reason why it is necessary to touch on the act of bordering prior to a focus on comparison. Of course, the process of comparison cannot be initiated unless the items to be compared are postulated as comparable. In other words, in the occasion of *discontinuity*, in which one is at a loss, unable to comprehend what is going on and faces non-sense, one cannot even start to compare. Yet it is this occasion of discontinuity which demands that one should translate. In this particular context of our discussion, what opens the place of comparison is nothing but translation. Before one compares, one must translate. Only after translation comes the schematism of *species* and *genus*, of nationality and internationality.

I do not know whether a focus on 'bordering' has gathered momentum across different disciplines in the humanities at this point. But this much can be asserted: bordering and translation are both problematics projected by the same theoretical perspective. Just as bordering is not solely about the demarcation of land, translation is not merely about language (in the sense of *langue*). Hence, this essay pursues a preliminary investigation into the discussion of translation beyond the conventional domain of the linguistic. Yet the first issue that must be tackled is how to comprehend language from the viewpoint of translation, or, in other words, how to reverse the conventional comprehension of translation that depends on the trope of translation as a bridging or communication between two separate languages or *langues*. However, precisely because my approach is discursive analysis that does not confine itself to the domain of the linguistic, or that is conducted irrespective of the rules, protocols and assumptions of linguistics in general as discourse, it involves questions of figuration, schematism, mapping, cartographic representation and the postulation of strategic positions, among others. In the conventional understanding of translation – elsewhere I have characterized it as 'the schematism of co-figuration'[16] – the separation of two languages or the border between them is already presupposed. This view of translation always presumes the unity of one language (as in *langue*) and that of another, since their separation is taken for granted or already given; the contour of language is never understood as something to be drawn or inscribed since it is supposed to be given in language itself. In other words, the conventional view of translation does not know 'bordering'.

It is in this order of reasoning regulated by 'the modern regime of translation' that I detect one of the delimitations imposed by the presumptions of nationality and the international world. In the dominant image of the international world, nationality is supposed to be postulated prior to the process of transnational transaction. Nationality must come before transnationality precisely because internationality cannot be conceptualized within the system of international law unless nationality is postulated prior to transnationality. In a strict analogy to this international configuration of the modern world, the modern regime of translation holds that national language must be assumed to exist prior to the process of translation since translation is preordained to be represented as bridging the gap between two separate languages. For this reason, the international world cannot but be predetermined as the juxtaposition of distinct nationalities that are external to one another. Thus, from the outset, the economy of the international world excludes the potentiality of 'heterolingual address'.[17]

Translation almost always involves a different language, or at least a difference in or of language. But we must ask the same question again, although from a slightly different perspective this time. What difference or differentiation is at issue here? How does it demand that we broaden our comprehension of translation? From the beginning, we have to guard against the static view of translation in which difference is substantialized; we should not yield to the reification of national or ethnic languages in translation, for this would deny translation its potentiality to deterritorialize. Hence it is important to introduce the difference in and of language, so that we can comprehend translation, not in terms of the communication model of equivalence and exchange, but rather as a form of political labour to create a continuity at the elusive point of discontinuity in the social. Then, what view of comparison can we acquire?

It is said that the world accommodates only one humanity but a plurality of languages. It is generally upheld that precisely because of this plurality, we are never able to evade translation. Consequently, our conception of translation is almost always premised on a specific way of conceiving the plurality of languages. Not surprisingly, we are often obliged to resort to the story of Babel when we try to think through the issues of the unity of humanity and the necessity of translation. However, from a trans-historical perspective, can we take the 'oneness in plurality' for granted? Can we conceive of discourses in which the thought of language is not captured in the formula of 'many in one'? Is there any other way to construe the inevitability of translation? Are we able to conceive of language in an alternative way?

How do we recognize the identity of each language, or, how do we justify presuming that languages can be categorized in terms of one and many? Is language a countable among the nominals, like an apple or an orange and unlike water? To render water countable, for example, we must appeal to a unit of measurement such as a glass or a bucketful. Do we not need to introduce such 'measure words' as a cup (of tea), a glass (of juice) or a loaf (of bread)? Is it not possible to think of language in terms of grammars in which the distinction between the singular and the plural is irrelevant?

What is at stake here – and this is something that I have repeatedly drawn attention to – is the unity of language, a certain *positivity of discourse* or historical *a priori* in terms of which we understand a different language or difference in language. To put it slightly differently, it is to understand how we allow ourselves to tell one language from another, to represent language as if it were a unity.

My answer to this question, which I posed some twenty years ago, is that the unity of language is like Kant's *regulative idea*.[18] It organizes knowledge but is not empirically verifiable. The regulative idea does not concern itself with the possibility of experience; it does not partake of the constitutive faculty; it is no more than a rule by which a search in the series of empirical data is prescribed. It guarantees a not empirically verifiable truth but, on the contrary, 'forbidding [the search for truth] to bring it [-self] to a close by treating anything at which it may arrive as absolutely unconditioned'.[19] Therefore, the regulative idea gives only an *object in idea*; it only means 'a *schema* for which no object, not even a hypothetical one, is directly given'.[20] The unity of language cannot be given in experience because it is nothing but a regulative idea that enables us to comprehend related data about languages 'in an indirect manner, in their systematic unity, by means of their relation to this idea'.[21] It is not possible to know whether a particular language exists as a unity or not. But by subscribing to the idea of the unity of language, we can organize knowledge about languages in a systematic and scientific manner.

To the extent that the unity of national language ultimately serves as a *schema* for *nationality* and offers a sense of national integration, the idea of the unity of language opens up a discourse on not only the naturalized origin of an ethnic community, but also on the entire imaginary associated with national language and culture. It is essential to note that Kant also qualifies the regulative idea as a *schema*, that is, an image, design, outline or figure, not exclusively in the order of idea but also in the order of the sensory, not only in the realm of spontaneity but also in that of receptivity. It is perhaps necessary to assert again that the unity of national language is never given at the level of primordial receptivity but rather at the level of representation. Therefore, this unity is in the order of image, figure or *schema*: it comes into being in re-presentation. And this figurative representation of national language allows us to discuss the communal experience of the common national or ethnic language. A language may be pure, authentic, hybridized, polluted or corrupt, yet regardless of a particular assessment of it, the very possibility of praising, authenticating, complaining about or deploring it is offered by the unity of that language as a regulative idea. However, we all know that the institution of the nation-state is a relatively recent invention. It assumes the presence of a territorial national state sovereignty in the international world, so that it could not have existed before its earlier form of territorial state sovereignty.[22] Thus we are led to suspect that the idea of the unity of language as the *schema* for ethnic and national communality must also be a recent invention whose historicity must be unambiguously marked.

How should we understand the formula of many in one, the plurality of languages in one humanity, when the unity of language has to be understood as a regulative idea or *schema* for an object in idea? For Kant, a regulative idea is explicated with regard to the production of scientific knowledge; it ensures that the empirical inquiry of some scientific discipline will never reach any absolute truth and is therefore endless. Every scientific truth changes as more empirical data accumulate.

Similarity beyond the Schematism of Co-figuration

From the postulation that the unity of national language is a regulative idea, it follows that this unity of national language enables us to organize various empirical data in a systematic manner, so that we may be able to continue to seek knowledge about the language. At the same time, it does not offer an object in experience but rather an *objective* in praxis, toward which we aspire to regulate our uses of language. The principle is not only epistemic, but also strategic and practical. Hence it works in a double register: on the one hand, it determines epistemologically what is included or excluded in the database of a language, what is linguistic or extralinguistic, and what is proper to a particular language or not; on the other hand, it indicates and projects what we must seek as our proper language, what we must avoid as heterogeneous to our language and reject as improper for it. The unity of a national language as a schema guides us as to what is just or unjust for our language, and what is in accord or discord with the propriety of the language.

Of course, *translation* is a term with much broader connotations than the transferral of meaning from one national or ethnic language into another, but in this essay I am specifically concerned with the delimitation of translation according to the *modern regime of translation* by which the idea of the national language is put into practice. I suggest that in this regime of translation, it is represented through a *schema of co-figuration*: only when translation is rendered representable thanks to the schematism of co-figuration, does the putative unity of a national language as a regulative idea ensue.

This schema allows us to *imagine* or *represent* what goes on in translation, to give ourselves an *image* or *representation* of translation. Once imagined, translation is no longer a movement in potentiality. Its image or representation always postulates or projects two figures, which are necessarily accompanied by a spatial division in terms of border. In so far as the representation or image of translation rather than the act of representation is concerned, we are already implicated in the *tropes* and images of translation. As long as we represent translation to ourselves in the *modern regime of translation*, it is impossible to evade the *tropics of translation*. Primarily, border is a matter of tropics as far as translation is concerned because the unity of a national or ethnic language as a schema is already accompanied by another for the unity of a different language; this unity of a language is possible only in the element of many in one; and for there to be many, one unity must be distinguishable from another. In the representation of translation, therefore, one language has to be clearly and visibly distinguished from another. Consequently, the unity of a language requires the postulation of a border or gap that separates one language from another in the tropics of translation.

Translation takes various processes and forms, to the extent that it is political work to overcome points of incommensurability. It is nothing but a testimony to the universality of sociability. It need not be confined to the modern regime of translation; it may well lie outside this particular regime to which the majority of us are accustomed today.

Returning to the question of the relation between translation and discontinuity, I have outlined how our commonsensical notion of translation is delimited by the schematism of the international world (i.e. our representation of the world according to the logical economy of *species* and *genus* at the levels of nationality and internationality), and, conversely, how the modern figure of the world as international (i.e. the world consisting of basic units of nations) is prescribed by our representation of translation as a communicative and international transfer of a message between a pair of ethnolinguistic unities.

The measure by which we are able to assess a language as a unity – here again I am not talking about phonetic systems, morphological units or syntactic rules of a language, but rather about the whole of a language as a *langue* – is given to us only at the locale where the limit of a language is marked, at the border where we come across a non-sense that forces us to do something in order to make sense of it. This occasion of making sense out of non-sense, of doing something socially – acting toward foreigners, soliciting their response, seeking their confirmation and so forth – is generally called translation, provided that we momentarily suspend the conventional distinction between translation and interpretation.

Let us keep in mind, therefore, that the unity of a language is always represented in relation to another unity; it is never given in and of itself but rather in relation to an other. Internationality is implicit in the very notion of *a* language (as in *langue*) already when we represent to ourselves the whole or totality of a language as a unity.

One can hardly evade dialogic duality when determining the unity of a language; language as a unity almost always conjures up the co-presence of another language. Yet, and I cannot stress this point too strongly, the locale of comparison can never be identified cartographically with a national border on the geographic surface of the earth. The representation of translation in terms of the trope of border is nothing but an effect of the tropics of translation, precisely because translation is preliminarily an act of drawing a border, of *bordering*, before it can be represented or imagined as a crossing of a border or a bridging of a gap allegedly existent between languages. The act of translation occurs in the place prior to the location where a border is drawn; translation as a performance of bordering takes place before the reterritorialization of location in the geopolitical order of internationality. Thus, the locale of translation designates a place prior to the one cartographically assigned to it within the international world; the locale of translation is *dislocated*, outside the system of geographic locations in the international world.

One possible consequence we can draw from the discussion above is that the locale of translation is potentially able to dislocate the system of allocation by which a language is located in the economy of nationality and internationality: in other words, to dislocate the putative coherence of the *modern regime of translation*. The locale of translation opens up the place of comparison, but it cannot be located within the configuration already prescribed by the schemata of *species* and *genus*. It is not located within the international world. On the contrary, it makes the location possible – in the sense of identifying an object within already existing coordinate grids – of nationality and internationality; it facilitates the place of comparison while pointing to a place without location.

By transnationality, I want to designate not the systematic of location configured by the logical economy of *species* and *genus*, but rather the locale of translation that opens up the place of comparison. While internationality operates within the logical economy of *species* and *genus*, transnationality undermines and reconfigures the schemata of nationality and internationality. It is in this sense that translation deterritorializes. And this deterritorializing potential of translation has been compulsorily reterritorialized by the schematism of co-figuration. Hence, transnationality indicates to us the locus of the foreign, something irreducible to the logical economy of *species* and *genus*. If I may use a paradoxical expression, translation takes place at the locale of dislocation; it dislocates the very distinction of inside and outside. It is the foreign that does not necessarily come from the outside of the national border; it is the foreign inherent in us all, regardless of whether within or outside of the nation. The conceptual topos of the foreign, where translation is in demand, can be found not in internationality but rather in transnationality, precisely because translation is prior to the determination of *species difference*.

Finally, we can return to the initial discussion of *cultural difference* once again. Now it is comprehensible why it is of decisive importance to discern two distinct approaches to *cultural difference*. The conventional notion of *cultural difference*, according to which the experience of discontinuity and non-sense is appropriated in the scheme of internationality, projects into our experience of *cultural difference* the very logic of *species* and *genus*, and postulates the presence of the foreigner, foreign language and foreign culture as an outside of nationality, spatially external to what John Stuart Mill called 'a society of sympathy', outside of a somewhat essentialized realm of homogeneous national culture and language. But in our experience of *cultural difference*, the logic of inside as opposed to outside which always determines the foreign as an intrusion of the outside is not imminent. Cultural difference need not be regulated by the economy of *species* and *genus*. For before the translation, cultural difference cannot be reduced to the species difference between one *species* and another in the generality of *genus*. Too often has multiculturalism been captured by the rhetoric of internationality and the logic of specific difference.

In this essay, I have tried to rescue the project of Comparative Humanities from the dominant mode of comparative nationality in such a way as to allow for configurations of similarities outside the economy of the internationality of race, ethnicity, culture, civilization and nationality. Yet this effort is far from exhaustive; here I can only intimate how we can possibly conceive of the project of Comparative Humanities in a different direction with a different thrust from the schematism of co-figuration.

Notes

1 The presumption of regarding an ethnic/national language as individual is dubious, to say the least. In our examples, what is designated by 'the Chinese language' is far from clear. Does it connote an ensemble of languages that are used in the People's Republic of China? Does it connote a family of languages that are affiliated with one another through some common phonetic, syntactical or semantic features? Or does it imply the set of grammatical rules that the state of the People's Republic of China imposes upon its population as the standard language? It is doubtful that the individuality of this individual constitutes the priority of the empirical with which the individual has traditionally been endowed.

2 Wittgenstein (1968): 31e–35e.

3 Ibid.: 31e–32e.

4 See Sakai (1997): 1–17.

5 In regard to the concepts of 'being in common', communication and communion, I owe much to Jean-Luc Nancy's essay, 'La communauté désoeuvrée' (1983). Also important is Nancy's essay, 'De l'être-en-commun' (2004).

6 For the term 'heterolingual,' see Sakai (1997): 1–17.

7 Mezzadra and Neilson (2013). I learned the term 'bordering' from Sandro Mezzadra and Brett Neilson's 'Border as Method, or, The Multiplication of Labour', a paper presented at the International Conference on 'Italian as second language – citizenship, language, and translation', in Rimini, on 4 February 2008. It is now available online: see European Institute for Progressive Cultural Policies, *transversal*, http://eipcp.net/transversal/0608/mezzadraneilson/en

[8] The problem of *discontinuity* must be highlighted precisely because politics is a set of actions by which to create *continuity*. It is important to stress that to divide is not to introduce discontinuity. On the contrary, it is possible to divide only when the space in which a divide is introduced is already continuous. The presence of a border is a sign of continuity rather than discontinuity.

[9] See note 7 above.

[10] Historically, this thought habit owes much to what Carl Schmitt referred to as *Jus Publicum Europaeum* or the system of Eurocentric International Law. The international world initially outlined in the Treaty of Westphalia is conceptually dependent upon the concept of territorial state sovereignty, according to Schmitt. I adopt his argument as far as the historical formation of the modern international world is concerned. See Schmitt (2006); German edition, 1950.

[11] The idiom 'The West and the Rest' has been used by a number of historians of modern colonialism. Arguably the most important is Stuart Hall's article entitled 'The West and the Rest: Discourse and Power'; see Hall (1996): 184–228.

[12] See Schmitt (2006); German edition, 1950.

[13] The west is a social imaginary which serves in multiple registers. Hence it is almost impossible to find a small number of contexts in which its connotation is determined. In a forthcoming book, *Dislocation of the West*, I explore the range of uses this term serves and historicize them.

[14] Mill (1972): 391.

[15] Fukuzawa (1973).

[16] Sakai (1997): 1–17, 41–71.

[17] Ibid.: 1–17.

[18] Sakai (1992): 326.

[19] Kant (1929): 450 (A 509; B 537); German edition, 1981.

[20] Ibid.: 550 (A 670, B 698); emphasis added.

[21] Ibid.: 550.

[22] Interestingly enough, Schmitt (2006) does not discuss the historical specificity of the nation-state and the territorial *national* state sovereignty. See note 8 above.

References

Fukuzawa, Yukichi (1973), *An Outline of a Theory of Civilization*, translated by David Dilworth and G. Cameron Hurst, Tokyo: Sophia University Press; Japanese edition: *Bunmei ron no gairyaku*, Tokyo: Iwanami Shoten, 1937.

Hall, Stuart (1996), 'The West and the Rest: Discourse and Power', in Stuart Hall, David Held, Don Hubert and Kenneth Thompson, eds, *Modernity: An Introduction to Modern Societies*, London: Wiley-Blackwell: 184–228.

Kant, Immanuel (1929), *Critique of Pure Reason*, translated by Norman Kemp Smith, New York: St. Martin's Press; German edition: *Kritik der reinen Vernunft*, Hamburg: Felix Meiner Verlag, 1981.

Mezzadra, Sandro and Brett Neilson (2013), *Border as Method, or the Multiplication of Labour*, Durham: Duke University Press.

Mill, John Stuart ([1861] 1972), *Utilitarianism: Liberty, Considerations on representative government*, London: Dent.

Nancy, Jean-Luc (1983), 'La communauté désoeuvrée', *Aléa*, No. 4: 11–49.

——— (2004), 'De l'être-en-commun', in *La communauté désoeuvrée*, Paris: Christian Bourgois Editeur: 199–234.

Sakai, Naoki (1992), *Voices of the Past: The Status of Language in Eighteenth Century Japanese Discourse*, Ithaca and London: Cornell University Press.

——— (1997), *Translation and Subjectivity: On 'Japan' and Cultural Nationalism*, Minneapolis: University of Minnesota Press.

Schmitt, Carl (2006), *The Nomos of the Earth in the International Law of the Jus Publicum Europaeum,* translated by G.L. Ulmen, New York: Telos Press Publishing; German edition: *Der Nomos der Erde im Völkerrecht des Jus Publicum Europaeum*, Berlin: Duncker and Humblot, 1950.

Wittgenstein, Ludwig (1968), *Philosophical Investigations*, translated by G.E.M. Anscombe, Oxford: Basil Blackwell.

Beyond Difference and Complete Identity

Bringing in similarities

Gurpreet Mahajan

Why do we need the category of 'similarity' in the social sciences? Does the lens of 'similarity' offer a viable framework for the study of different societies? Will a reference to similarities eclipse differences between societies and cultures? Can we speak of similarity without foregrounding assimilation, complete identity or sameness? This essay reflects on these questions in an effort to address some of the anxieties raised by the paradigm of similarities. Taking the example of multiculturalism – a theory that privileges difference – it argues that it is necessary to accord epistemic priority to similarity without negating the presence of difference, for deepening democracy as well as for sustaining cross-cultural conversations. Instead of positing an either/or situation where we must choose between the categories of similarity or difference, it suggests that notions of similarity must be present even when we recognize differences that exist between communities and cultures. It is only by bringing in the idea of similarities that we can move beyond tolerance to meaningful coexistence and respect. Similar and yet different is not only a viable conception, it is the condition of our historical existence and offers the only reasonable basis for sustaining cross-cultural conversations.[1]

The social sciences today are facing an epistemological challenge as the dominant frameworks of analysis, centred around the category of either identity (complete sameness) or difference, are clearly inadequate for understanding or representing the contemporary world. These optics fail to capture the nature of historical being, as well as the relationship between self and other, in a meaningful way. In paradigms that privilege sameness, Europe and its experience become the norm. Whether it is the trajectory of capital (as it moves from the centre to the rest of the globe) or the conception of what is rational, the normative ideal is defined by Western Europe. The rest of the world is judged and ordered hierarchically depending upon its ability to replicate that ideal.

The project of colonialism was guided by this pursuit of sameness.

Looking at the world through this lens, it saw the colonies as 'uncivilized' and 'stagnant' societies that required external intervention and energy to revitalize them and send them on the right course. Subsequently, even after the societies were decolonized, theories of modernization and functionalism continued to operate with this orientation. Drawing upon the experience of Western Europe, they associated progress with an individual-centred, achievement-oriented society that had a democratic political culture. Non-western societies were placed far behind in the continuum and identified as traditional societies bound by ascriptive ties, a communitarian outlook and a collectivist approach. In other words, the non-west was marked by a lack of all that was valued in the modern world – namely, science, reason, individual liberty and strong democratic political institutions. The goal was to overcome the difference and arrive at that identity which Western Europe was said to possess; and it was hoped that processes of industrialization and rational technical organization of society would provide the push necessary for making the transition from a traditional to a modern society.

Frameworks of difference were a response to this Eurocentric discourse. They put the spotlight on the experience of those who stood in the margins previously. The focus on difference revealed, on the one hand, the manner in which the non-west was constructed to serve the interest of empires, and on the other, it gave room to the subaltern to speak and offer principles, ideas and modes of organization which did not frequently conform to the Enlightenment reasoning that structured the modern west. In all of this, the post-colonial stood up for itself and against what was offered by Europe as the universal. Indeed, this framework suggested that the post-colonial can, and must, constitute itself in its own terms. The difference here knocked down the constructed universal and offered in its place, concrete alternatives.

The necessity to dislodge the centrality accorded to Europe's experience and thinking propelled these alternatives. It is not surprising that the political project of decolonizing the mind and overthrowing the 'imperialism of categories' returned the gaze inwards – that is, upon itself. Historically, perspectives that underlined the difference from the dominant west played an important role, but they left untheorized the nature of the self that constituted their discourse. Nevertheless, such theorization gave a positive weightage to the distance between Western Europe and the decolonized world; it valued the difference that the latter represented, and pluralized the social and political imaginary. This was an important departure but it too confronted a formidable challenge.

Could the self in the decolonized world be identified merely in terms of its difference? Had this self categorically rejected all that was symbolized by the modern west? Besides, the singular emphasis on difference meant that one had to not only reject the categories that made their appearance first in Europe, but also privilege that which was indigenous. How could one displace the authority of tradition while simultaneously also challenging the hegemony of the west? These are the questions that the paradigm of difference engendered and they loom large over social sciences in post-colonial societies today, compelling one to interrogate and move away from frameworks that speak only of identity (complete sameness) or absolute difference.

It is against this backdrop that the paradigm of 'similarity' (*ähnlichkeit*) opens up a possibility that one needs to consider seriously; since the pursuit of sameness or difference by itself yields little space for a real conversation between the self and the other, it makes the task of searching for an alternative even more urgent. If the former (the pursuit of sameness) tries to erase difference and sees (or would like to see) its own image everywhere, the latter (the paradigm of difference) turns its back on the 'other' – the erstwhile centre. Neither position allows one to initiate, let alone sustain, a meaningful conversation. Worse still, both these paradigms create binaries that ossify the self and the other, bestowing a fixed, pre-given identity to each. This forecloses the space for a conversation or a dialogue in which due consideration is given to both the self and the other: something that is necessary for addressing the dilemmas confronting people the world over (in Europe and post-colonial societies) today.

To apprehend the nature of our historical being in the contemporary world, we need a framework that acknowledges difference but allows space for defining one's destiny in terms of ideas that characterize our cultural and historical world. Frameworks that stress 'sameness' have a tendency to impose a universal, while 'difference' often privileges the indigenous in the guise of accommodating particularity. One has to avoid both these ways of thinking and look instead for frameworks of analysis that allow for intercultural conversation, and recognize that the self is constituted both by its cultural inheritances and the ideas that define our modern historical time. To the extent that the idea of 'similarities' allows for this possibility, it deserves to receive epistemic priority over existing paradigms of complete identity or absolute difference.

Let me take the example of multiculturalism to illustrate both the limits of the paradigms of sameness and difference, and the desirability of working with a framework that speaks of identity and difference – namely, similarity (ä*hnlichkeit*).

As a political theory, multiculturalism surfaced as a response to liberalism; specifically, its effort to conceive the population as a homogeneous lot: that is, as citizens whose substantive differences – related to kinship, ethnicity, religion – are bracketed out. Liberalism was not unaware of the presence of difference in society, but it wanted to render those differences insignificant in the public political domain. That is, socially ascribed identities (as markers of difference) were to be irrelevant when it came to distribution of rights or treatment before the law. Instead, as citizens, persons were *to be treated alike* irrespective of their caste, community, language or gender. In this sense, liberalism prioritized sameness: the same rights for all persons as citizens.

This privileging of sameness was, for a while at least, an enabling principle. It had the potential of including all persons in the political domain. Against existing structures where birth, religion, gender, race and caste, in the case of India, were the basis of distributing offices, functions and privileges, the idea that all persons as citizens should be given the same opportunities and rights performed an important transformative role. Indeed, successive social movements – such as women's movements, civil rights movements – invoked the ideal of identical treatment to question prevailing social norms and laws, and demanded identical rights and equal liberty for all citizens.

Difference entered into the liberal discourse, but only as reflected at the level of the individual: that is, in terms of different preferences, beliefs, tastes, dispositions and opinions. Individual expression of these differences was important to the liberals, and they aimed to create a society that is open and hospitable to the presence of such differences. For this reason, they considered a procedural state – one that was not committed to any one conception of a good life – to be an essential condition of a liberal democratic polity.

Thus, in the liberal framework, difference was identified with individual liberty and freedom to choose, and it neglected differences embodied and present in the form of collectives. In a framework where individual expression of differences was valued the most, there was little normative need for taking the 'other' seriously or engaging with the difference that it embodied. One required tolerance for such an 'other' rather than active engagement or dialogue with it. So long as the procedure of decision-making was laid out and followed, each one could express his or her view; but beyond that, they were expected to accept the decision taken through due process.

Theories of difference went beyond the 'self', and placed the 'other' in the frame more centrally and visibly. While post-colonial thought brought in the difference articulated by the experience of the colonies and decentred Europe, multiculturalism focused on the cultural differences that were already present in most European societies in the contemporary world. It showed that the laws and state practices of many liberal democracies reflected the cultural orientation of the majority community. Even laws that appeared to be neutral and indifferent to all cultures tended to disadvantage the minority communities. For instance, the Sabbath laws that existed in many parts of the United States and Western Europe appeared to be neutral as they applied equally to all. However, on closer scrutiny, it was evident that this seemingly neutral practice was in line with the Christian ethic, and tended to disadvantage members of other communities such as Jews and Muslims. While practising Christians could go to church and offer prayers on Sunday, Muslims did not get a similar opportunity – that is, to have time off to offer prayers on Friday afternoon. Jews too were disadvantaged as they observed Saturday as the day of rest. Under the existing laws, they could not open their trade and business establishments on Sunday. Similarly, the choice of a national language – for example, English in Canada – disadvantaged internal minorities. Adopting English as the medium of instruction in state schools meant that children of the French-speaking population would not be taught in their mother tongue even at an early age. This placed a heavier burden on them at all stages of life: they had to work harder to excel in school, to compete for jobs and prestigious positions in society. In other words, many state policies tended to reflect and be of advantage to the majority cultural community by placing the minorities at a disadvantage.[2]

In bringing difference into the public domain, theorists of multiculturalism pointed to this structural inadequacy and argued that individuals inhabit two worlds: public/political and cultural. They have dual membership: they are members of a political community and at the same time members of different cultural communities. As such the population (the citizens) is culturally heterogeneous, and the claims they make as members of different communities also have to be recognized and accommodated in the public domain. Theorists such as Will Kymlicka[3] argued that even if liberalism wants to be true to its own ideal of equal treatment, it has to acknowledge and accommodate the claims of minority cultural communities.

Multiculturalists put forward a different idea of equality. Instead of equating it with sameness, they argued that identical treatment might actually discriminate against minority groups. What we need to do is to ensure that different groups are treated as equals, and this might at times require that some groups be treated differently. Just as treating women as equal members might require a different set of rules and regulations – such as maternity leave, crèches in the workplace – in order to have equal opportunity to work and be part of the marketplace,[4] similarly, members of minority cultures may require different treatment in some spheres so as to ensure that they are not disadvantaged in the public arena. They may, for instance, require primary school education in their mother tongue (rather than the official language of the state), or relaxation of dress codes in places of work, or separate prayer rooms in public places, so that they can enjoy the same opportunities and the possibility of pursuing what they desire or consider important for themselves.[5]

Multiculturalism made a plea for accommodating differences in the public domain, sometimes through informal measures of making exceptions and/or extending similar opportunities and privileges to members of different communities, but at times it asks for formal laws/measures in the form of special rights for minority communities to govern themselves within the larger framework of a federal polity.[6]

To destabilize the prevalent norms, multiculturalism looked at existing laws and structures from the position of the 'other'. However, its emphasis on difference and its attempt to associate the 'other' with difference created a rather ossified picture of the 'other'. On the one hand it retained the binaries that structured nineteenth-century colonial discourse. The only significant difference was that colonialism weighed the qualities of the 'other' negatively while multiculturalism assessed these in positive terms. But in both cases, the self and the other were marked by a stark difference.

In the colonial world-view, reason, and scientific, technological and material progress, were seen as attributes of the west while the 'other' (the non-west/the colonies) was marked by relative absence of these qualities; the latter lacked the capacity to govern itself, and needed protection, guidance and direction from the colonizer. In multicultural discourse, too, protection was desired for minority cultures that were primarily non-western cultures. The latter, it was argued, were under pressure from Enlightenment modernity on the one side, and processes engendered by industrialization and global capital on the other. Thus, even though the difference that minority cultures embodied was valued and accommodated, the binary of west and non-west persisted.[7]

Representation of the 'other' in terms of difference also justified the existing practices of a community and identified them as essential aspects of a community culture. Whether polygamy or female circumcision, these differences were seen as markers of cultural identity. The fact that many of these practices have been revived under certain circumstances or that they are contested internally was shelved to the back.[8] Instead, such practices came to be viewed as markers of difference (radical difference) that separated the culture of minority communities from that of the majority.

A part of the multicultural argument was that minority cultures were under threat from external pressures, that they could not survive and required protection. Without the latter it was likely that they would disappear, or at least not be able to continue with their distinct way of life. The case for protecting cultures rested on the value accorded to cultural diversity in a society. The latter was seen as being an essential condition of critical self-reflection,[9] or, at times, a condition for nurturing choices – something that was deeply valued within liberalism. If we accept, with Kymlicka, that people do not choose *de novo,* we would recognize that the presence of concrete differences or ways of life was important, as they provide individuals with tangible alternatives from which they may choose.[10]

However, the goal of protecting cultures (even for the sake of protecting cultural diversity) actually restricts individual choices. If the French culture has to survive in Quebec, then the Francophone population must send its children to French-medium schools. This is an essential condition for protecting that culture. Although the assumption here is that protecting one's culture is desired by the concerned population, the need to ensure the survival of cultural diversity meant that these individuals were called upon to willingly accept or live by the cultural norms of that community. Accommodating differences to ensure that diversity continues to flourish left the individual with little choice; indeed, the individual was firmly placed within the community and was expected to act in a manner that would protect the interests of the community.

Another consequence of this reasoning was that cultures were now identified as incommensurable wholes with little possibility of cross-cultural communication. The emphasis on difference implied that those situated in the culture of the majority were likely to misunderstand the 'other'. The difference that the 'other' represented could not be translated and made comprehensible to outsiders. One had to leave each culture (and its practices) to its members to manage, and assess the latter in terms of their world-view. Since decision-making bodies within the community were often controlled by men, often orthodox clerics, this further implied that traditional perspectives received a fresh lease of life as they became sites for enunciating the cultural norm.

Absolutizing difference, as was noted earlier on, was beset with these problems. It rendered tradition legitimate, or at least provided space for accepting the authority of tradition or the orthodoxy of existing practices in defining the 'other'. While the majority (constituted through liberal practices) made room for individuals to define themselves, it was the voice of community leadership and community institutions that was accommodated and expected to represent individuals in other minority communities. If liberalism eclipsed the community, multiculturalism silenced the individual. Both perspectives – the former emphasizing sameness in the form of the citizen and the latter stressing difference – remain inadequate.

One has therefore to break out of this double bind: of either imposing sameness on all to bracket out group difference or absolutizing differences in a way that leaves the individual within the community vulnerable. Even to be attentive to the concerns raised by the multiculturalists and other theorists of the difference perspective, one has to consciously set aside the singular emphasis on difference and look for alternative ways of representing the 'other'. In the search for such a paradigm, one needs to recognize that while individuals are members of a cultural world, they are simultaneously also part of a larger historical world. As such they are exposed to ideas and values that characterize the latter. To an extent all cultures –majority and minority cultures – are faced with the challenge of accommodating the values that are central to the modern imagination and bring their practices in line with the latter. As a result, even when minority cultures reflect difference, their identity is continuously being defined and rearticulated from within. In other words, members of minority communities too interrogate the practices existing in their communities; exposed to the values of our historical time, they also attempt to question and resignify prevalent practices. One has therefore to be cautious in endorsing policies that unequivocally privilege and protect existing cultural practices in the name of difference.

Even at the risk of repeating oneself, the point that must be underlined here is that representing the 'other' only in terms of its difference (that is, absolutizing difference) has to be avoided, and so also the policies aimed at protecting cultural differences. Both yield disastrous consequences. To put it another way, one must begin with the understanding that the 'other' cannot be defined merely in terms of the absence of the norms that define the liberal self. Difference is, in actuality, much more mediated. It is present, and must be searched for, in a different way: namely, by seeking out and identifying the form in which different values, including those of equality and freedom (values essential to the modern historical imaginary), are structured and placed alongside other values that may have little space on the liberal horizon. Only when we begin with such a historical and mediated conception of self and other do we open ourselves to the possibility of a mutually enriching conversation and respectful coexistence.

Minority cultures and communities living in Western Europe, for instance, need to recognize that the values cherished by the liberal worldview have an appeal to many of their citizens across different cultural communities. They cannot be bracketed aside as external influences. Living in a historical world, one has of necessity to look beyond cultural boundaries, and find ways of accommodating values that have a much wider appeal and presence. An internal dialogue within the community is perhaps one way to take on board that which appears to push one outside the security of a given cultural boundary. At the other end, the dominant culture (even if it is only liberalism rather than a religious-cultural tradition) has to accept that space for individuals need not eclipse the presence of communities and community membership. For one, some degree of respect for one's culture is a condition for free expression of one's views and a willingness to reconsider what is handed down to us through tradition. Hence, even what liberals regard to be desirable cannot be pursued by itself – that is, by eliding the presence of community identities.

To take an example: in contemporary democracies we would have to begin with the understanding that all persons, by virtue of being a part of the human species, possess some intrinsic value or dignity, and treat this Kantian view as a shared premise across different cultures. But an acceptance of this idea as a kind of (of what might be called a) 'historical universal' does not close the door to the presence of difference. In fact, differences would come in through various readings of what constitutes dignity and assessments of social cultural practices that are perceived to be affirming or denying human dignity. Similarly, even if a more specific norm, like gender equality, is identified with the modern world-view, differences would still be present in terms of practices that are considered as signs of that value. In other words, differences would come into play as that value is realized and institutionalized in different ways – and as different sorts of justifications are provided for it in different cultures and communities.

Even more importantly, since the modern is not reducible to just one value or principle, some may privilege liberty of the individual while others may favour order and security; a few may lean more towards equality of treatment while others seek group equality. Differences, therefore, cannot be eclipsed, and diverse forms of cultural reasoning and experiences are bound to throw up a diversity of world-views. At the same time, the presence of difference and the focus on difference must not blind us to the affinities in underlying concerns and agendas. It is the acknowledgment of this difference along with sameness that throws up the possibility of cross-cultural conversations and meaningful interaction between cultures and communities.

To the extent that the paradigm of 'similarity' allows one to retain notions of sameness and difference simultaneously, it offers a viable and better starting point for engaging with the self and the other. When similarities are taken out of the equation, the balance of power between the west and non-west remains undisturbed; that is, it remains tilted in favour of the west. The west emerges as a powerhouse, able to change, grow and develop, while the non-west remains caught in its own time-preserved traditions, somewhat fixed in orientation and likely to fade away when confronted with change. In a sustained conversation, this equation and perception of the 'other' itself has to change: the 'other' has to be historicized instead of understood in terms of timeless practices and traditions that have persisted and remained, supposedly, unaltered. At present, only the west is placed in history with qualities of forgetfulness and innovation, while the non-west remains fixed in time.

To conclude, social science and analysis must start with the recognition that the universal cannot be defined only in and through the experience of Western Europe; equally, one must also realize that recognition of difference can create space for tolerance. But dialogue and meaningful conversation require something more: respect for the other, emanating from an effort to consider the other as an equal. As paradigms predicated on complete sameness or difference flounder and fail to ensure this, the framework of 'similarity' has to be privileged, albeit contingently and remembering that it pins on neither sameness nor difference. It is eventually this hermeneutic of seeing the self and the other as similar yet different that allows one to go beyond mere curiosity about the other while avoiding bounded existence and ghettoization. It alone opens the possibility of dialogue between equals – an element that can nurture democratic space.

Notes

1 In the essay 'Similarity/Ähnlichkeit: A Cultural-Theoretical Paradigm', Bhatti, Kimmich, Koschorke, Schlögl and Wertheimer have drawn our attention to the cultural and political implications of privileging the category of difference absolutely (Bhatti *et al.* 2011). On the positive side, they have explained the potential of the paradigm of similarity for 'dissolving or supplementing' established binaries, such as those of 'homogeneity and heterogeneity, identity and alterity'. I hope that this paper builds on that argument by suggesting that frameworks that sensitize us to the errors of assimilation may sometimes legitimize existing structures of inequality and oppression when they are articulated in the language of difference. It is only by granting priority, in relative terms, to the idea of similarity that one can initiate a dialogue which prompts critical reflection that allows the self to move beyond a received and given way of life.

2 See Parekh (1994; 2000), Carens (2000) and Taylor (1994).

3 Kymlicka (1995): 86–90.

4 Phillips (1992).

5 Bouchard and Taylor (2008).

6 Kymlicka (1995) and Levy (1997).

7 Tamir (1997).

8 Pollitt (1997).

[9] Parekh (1994): 208.
[10] Kymlicka (1991): 164–66.

References

Bhatti, Anil *et al.* (2011), 'Ähnlichkeit: Ein kulturtheoretisches Paradigma', *Internationales Archiv für Sozialgeschichte der deutschen Literatur*, 36 (1): 233–47.

Bouchard, Gerard and Charles Taylor (2008), *Building the Future: A Time for Reconciliation*, Quebec: Consultation Commission on Accommodation Practices Related to Cultural Differences, Government of Quebec.

Carens, Joseph (2000), *Culture, Community and Citizenship: A Contextual Exploration of Justice as Evenhandedness*, Oxford: Oxford University Press.

Kymlicka, Will (1991), *Liberalism, Community and Culture*, Oxford: Oxford University Press.

——— (1995), *Multicultural Citizenship*, Oxford: Oxford University Press.

Levy, Jacob T. (1997), 'Classifying Cultural Rights', in Ian Shapiro and Will Kymlicka, eds, *Ethnicity and Group Rights*, NOMOS XXXIX, New York: New York University Press.

Parekh, Bhikhu (1994), 'Cultural Diversity and Liberal Democracy', in David Beetham, ed., *Defining and Measuring Democracy*, London: Sage.

——— (2000), *Rethinking Multiculturalism: Cultural Diversity and Political Theory*, Cambridge, MA: Harvard University Press.

Phillips, Anne (1992), 'Feminism, Equality and Difference', in Linda McDowell and Rosemary Pringle, eds, *Defining Women, Social Institutions and Gender Divisions*, Cambridge: Polity Press and The Open University.

Pollitt, Katha (1997), 'Whose Culture', *Boston Review*, October–November.

Tamir, Yae (1997), 'Who Do You Trust', *Boston Review*, October–November.

Taylor, Charles (1994), 'The Politics of Recognition', in Amy Gutmann, ed., *Multiculturalism and the Politics of Recognition*, Princeton, NJ: Princeton University Press.

Similarity, Assimilation, Integration

In between hybridity and grafting

Uwe Wirth

In his 1914 essay, 'Racial Assimilation in Secondary Groups', Robert Park discussed the ambiguity of the term 'assimilation', noting that it could have two different meanings: 'according to earlier usage it meant "to compare" or "to make like". According to later usage it signifies "to take up and incorporate".'[1] This tension between 'to make like' and 'to incorporate' harbours eminently political implications, because both the adoption of foreign languages and lifestyles as well as the integration of groups of individuals into larger groups represent decisive steps on the path to the 'formation of modern nationalities'.[2] But even at the beginning of the twentieth century, Park questioned the notion of homogeneity within nations when he noted that even 'the' modern Italian, Frenchman or German is a 'composite of the broken fragments of several different racial groups'.[3] Thus, upon closer inspection, the supposed homogeneity of a given nation proves to be the result of a process that is anything but 'natural'; instead, it is a process in which unity is created by connecting heterogeneous fragments, and through 'interaction and imitation'.[4]

Meanwhile, moments of incorporation, imitation and composition, each trigger specific and fundamental changes in the elements involved: namely, they change their identity. This can also be seen in the definition of assimilation provided by Haim Hillel Ben-Sasson in his *Encyclopedia Judaica*, where it is defined as a socio-cultural process 'in which the sense and consciousness of association with one national and cultural group changes to identification with another such group, so that the merged individual or group may partially or totally lose its original national identity'.[5]

Against the backdrop of Park's sceptical consideration of national identity, there are three questions that can be posed regarding this definition. First, what does 'original national identity' mean in the context of the lifestyles mentioned above? It would have to include language, but also dietary habits and specific forms of dressing.

The second question deals with the idea of the *merged individual*. In this context, *to merge* means 'to incorporate', 'to unfold', 'to melt' or 'to fuse' – and thus refers to a semantics that broadly outlines what we today call 'hybrid'. Especially in postcolonial studies, hybridity has become a central concept by which relationships between different cultures – but also relationships within a given culture – can be described as an ambivalent process of hybridization: as contact between bodies, languages and world-views from a wide variety of backgrounds whose mixture leads to something new, something 'third'. As García Canclini wrote in his book, *Culturas Hibridas*, the classic concepts used to describe such fusion dynamics are creolization, syncretism and *mestizaje*. The last of these terms is personified by Malinche, the indigenous translator for the Spanish conqueror Cortés who also bore him a child – and thus became the first mother of the so-called mestiza. Particularly from a political perspective, she remains a highly problematic figure.[6]

The concept of hybridization is also used in other ways within the field of postcolonial studies. On the one hand (as seen in work by Homi Bhabha), it can be used to describe colonial constellations in which those being colonized blend their own culture with that of the colonizers as part of a strategy of subversion. In such situations, this blending represents nothing but a feigned assimilation, a *colonial mimicry*.[7] On the other hand, the concept of hybridization can also refer to a *crossing of cultures*, in which the crossing is not only understood in a biological sense but also as a literal crossing of paths. In this sense, migrants and intellectuals embody hybridity: 'they move cosmopolitically between cultures'.[8]

The third question follows to a certain extent from the first two, and deals with the relationship between processes of assimilation and translation: to what extent do processes of translation depend on a 'making similar', a 'resembling': an assimilation of the foreign language to one's own? To what extent can translation be described as 'to make similar'? Is it possible that translation also entails moments of incorporation? This line of questioning extends beyond the purely linguistic problems of translation and touches on what can be called *cultural translation*. This concept has also been significantly shaped by Homi Bhabha, who bases his considerations on Walter Benjamin's essay, 'The Task of the Translator'. Bhabha understands cultural translation as a process in which there is no longer a static own language and no original self from which the process of translation originates:

> [I]n that sense, there is no 'in itself' and 'for itself' within cultures because they are always subject to intrinsic forms of translation. This

> theory of culture is close to a theory of language, as part of a process of translations – using that word . . . not in a strict linguistic sense of translation as in a 'book translated from French into English', but as a motif or trope as Benjamin suggests for the activity of displacement within the linguistic sign.[9]

For Bhabha, translation thus becomes a 'way of imitating . . . an original', in which the predominance of the original dissolves through the possibility for it to be copied and transformed, thus becoming a sort of original 'that is never finished or complete in itself'.[10] This implies a concept of the original that does not appear as a homogenous, static unit, but rather as something unfinished, as something still in motion. This conception of a composite, non-homogenous and incomplete original has an effect on our understanding of both assimilation processes as well as processes of cultural translation. The original is no longer considered an unchangeable archetype around which processes of adjustment and translation orient themselves; instead, the original itself becomes an object that changes during the translation process – an original in motion.

This idea that the original itself undergoes a change during the process of translation – that translation leads its own life and no longer orients itself according to the principle of equivalence or fidelity to the original – picks up from the central argument of Benjamin's thoughts on the act of translation, namely, that 'no translation would be possible if in its ultimate essence it strove for likeness to the original. For in its afterlife – which could not be called that if it were not a transformation and a renewal of something living – the original undergoes change.'[11] In this passage, Benjamin clearly rejects the idea of an assimilating 'making similar' of the translation with the original. Instead, translation is described as a vibrant process that has the capacity to change the original over the course of translation.

Within this context, we must also pose the question of how such a concept of translation can be applied to the different definitions of hybridity described above. Doing so leads to a striking realization: namely, the extent to which the historical semantics of translation theories have been based on biological and organological metaphors. Above all we find the image of 'transplanting' languages, which we also see in Benjamin's work when he writes, 'thus translation, ironically, transplants the original'.[12] Here, Benjamin joins a tradition in the history of translation theory that sees transplantational relocation as a form of *translation*, a tradition that engages in *cultural translation*. In what follows, I would like to attempt to illustrate the implications of this engagement as it pertains to the concepts of similarity, assimilation and integration. In doing so, I will also show why the concept of *hybridity* alone is not sufficient to do justice to the complexity inherent in processes of cultural translation. Indeed, my thesis is that we need a second concept as well: namely, *grafting*.[13]

I shall begin by showing why I believe this concept is relevant to the problem area of translation, and also briefly explain what grafting might mean in this context. In his treatise titled *On the Different Methods of Translation*, Friedrich Schleiermacher compares the act of translation to an exotic horticultural intervention when he writes that the 'diverse transplantation of foreign plants have made our soil richer and more fertile'.[14] The decisive question is, of course, what actually happens in this translational transplantation. Schleiermacher describes the method of translation as a 'composure of language that is not grown freely, but is rather bent over towards a foreign similarity'.[15] With the formulation 'foreign similarity', he makes reference to a form of translation that 'followed the phrases of the original writing' as closely as possible, thus giving readers the feeling that 'they have something foreign in front of them'.[16] Schleiermacher's theory thus represents an example of what has been called an *alienating translation*. Anne Bohnenkamp has suggested that this kind of translation should be classified as a 'phenotypically hybrid translation' that seeks to:

> mix elements of the original text and the original language in such a way that the mixture remains recognizably a mixture – that is, a heterogeneity of parts. The antithesis *naturalizing–alienating* would thereby be replaced by a model that makes not only the differences but also the similarities of different translation processes obvious.[17]

This reformulation is focused above all on the linguistic surface of the translation, because it is obvious that from a *genotypic* perspective, translations are always 'hybrid'. We see this point clearly in Schleiermacher's essay as well when he writes, 'who would not rather have children that represent the fatherly lineage purely, rather than as *Blendling*?'[18] Here, he explicitly introduces the concept of hybridity into his theory of translation – but also a curious discourse of purity. With reference to the Greek expression '*hibrida*', *Grimm's Dictionary* defines a *Blendling* as a 'bastard and hermaphrodite in which the pure, natural type is blurred and mixed, from humans, animals, and plants'.[19]

Interestingly enough, Schleiermacher utilizes a different metaphorical register as soon as the foreign similarity of two languages becomes overlaid with the cultural differences between two styles of thought; instead of questions of impurity, he shifts to questions of compatibility. In *Hermeneutics and Criticism*, he states that the 'Christian spirit' in the

New Testament 'emerges from a mixture of languages in which Hebraic is the root within which the new is originally conceived, while the Greek is grafted on to it'.[20] Here, the agricultural technique of grafting is used as a metaphor in which *transfer* into a new syntactic context becomes a mental and linguistic *translation* into a different cultural context. Indeed, strictly speaking, grafting becomes a metaphor for an incorporating process of adoption in which the foreign is naturalized but not completely assimilated, in which the self and the foreign are connected but not intermixed. At the same time, we can also read Schleiermacher's two-sided description of translation as an indication that recourse to a model of hybridity alone is not sufficient. Indeed, the situation surrounding translation seems to be characterized by interferences and interactions between a model of grafting and a model of hybridity.

In this sense, the model of grafting assumes an interesting position in the interplay between 'making similar' and incorporation. While the crucial point of hybridization is a crossbreeding of different types, grafting explicitly avoids genetic *blending*.[21] Instead, two different parts are *connected* to become one functional organic unit, and each connected part remains a genetically distinct entity even when the two begin to grow together. Here, one of the two parts is defined as the 'rootstock': 'the host plant that is rooted in the soil and provides nourishment for the other growth, the dependent top section, which is called the scion'.[22] Apparently, the grafted scion functions as a sort of friendly parasite[23] that grows together with its rootstock through *incorporation*. Horticulturally speaking, this requires both sides to be accurately cut with special tools so that the damaged cambium of the stock comes into direct contact with the damaged cambium of the scion. Afterwards, both parts are bound together and sealed with grafting wax. The result is a fragile entity of *heterogeneous*, artificially joined, non-assimilated parts that are still organically integrated with one another. Still, such grafting requires a minimal level of 'compatibility', which is referred to in biological terms as 'vegetative affinity' or 'collateral affinity'.[24]

In this respect, grafting connects aspects of similarity and incorporation by integrating separate parts to one another without assimilation. And here we can see the aspects of a model of grafting that could be of considerable importance to the cultural sciences. On the one hand, grafting can be used to describe ambivalent processes of cultural integration and translation in which foreignness and the differences between translations remain visible. On the other, grafting can also be used to describe political constellations that are characterized by dominant conditions. It is in this latter sense that Max Weber described 'grafted social orders',[25] and described the relationship between European and Chinese culture as the merely superficial grafting of a foreign mind-set.[26] Around seventy years later, Robert Young used similar language in his book *Colonial Desire: Hybridity in Theory, Culture, and Race*, when describing the political and conceptual implications of using organic metaphors to describe forms of social organization. Both concepts – *hybridity* and *grafting* – are of central interest, he states, because both describe a phenomenon 'of forcing incompatible entities to grow together (or not)'.[27]

This relationship between a model of hybridity and a model of grafting can also be applied to the problem area of cultural translation. As we saw in the passage from Bhabha quoted above, translation in this context becomes a trope for the 'activity of displacement within the linguistic sign'.[28] The concept of *displacement* appears here as a concept of transplantation that has been purged of its biological roots, but remains compatible with both a model of hybridity and a model of grafting. Grafting also appears in Derrida's writing as a metaphor for the 'essential iterability' of all signs; he writes in his essay, 'Signature Event Context', that:

> a written syntagma can always be detached from the chain in which it is inserted or given without causing it to lose all possibility of functioning, if not all possibility of 'communicating', precisely. One can perhaps come to recognize other possibilities by inscribing it or grafting it on to other chains.[29]

Here, grafting represents the possibility of a 'force of rupture' in external (historical, spatial, social) contexts, but also within internal, linguistic-syntagmatic contexts. While Austin's speech-act theory, for instance, is based on the assumption that the process of citation results in the loss of illocutionary power in what is said, and that citation is a 'parasitic' form of language use, Derrida's conception turns grafting as a *greffe citationnelle* into a figure of movement and circulation that fosters the circulation of communicative power through an act of displacement. Against this backdrop, Bhabha's term *displacement* denotes two different things. First, it can refer to the internal sign structure of expressions and from there be projected to the external dynamics of sign usage as a quotational trope. Second, *displacement* can refer to a dynamic in which people are torn from their ancestral living conditions and forced to migrate. In this case, it becomes a trope of migration.

As we see in Schleiermacher's work, grafting is thus a model that makes it possible to conceive of *transplantation* to other syntactic contexts as a mental and linguistic *translation* to other cultural contexts. In other words, grafting becomes a central aspect in the concept of *cultural translation*. This context, however, also illustrates the precarious political implications that a model of grafting brings with it: it transports the traces of being uprooted as a *sign of cultural difference* to other, foreign contexts – and thus becomes a model to justify the *integration*, or rather the *incorporation*, of peoples and signs. But even though grafting is an operation that integrates without complete assimilation, the concept of grafting also implies something violent. This goes especially for the idea of cutting as an act of fitting in: while grafting does not imply full assimilation, in the sense that different parts retain their heterogeneity, it does involve a moment of 'making similar' in order to make integration as incorporation possible. Further, the model of grafting implies a certain form of *cultural dominance*. Within the context of colonial constellations, it expresses a form of superior power: it assigns to those colonized, the role of a wild stock that requires refinement through the quasi-horticultural intervention of the colonists. In this vein, Amar Acheraïou writes in his book, *Rethinking Postcolonialism*, that 'grafting was a crucial component of the Western civilizing mission. It contained in germ the idea of transplanting the European spirit on to the stagnant natives in order to regenerate them.'[30]

Against the backdrop of what I have written above, I would like to pose the question of what it means when Schleiermacher describes the act of translation as a 'transplantation of foreign plants' that 'have made our soil richer and more fertile'.[31] Interestingly enough, he did not introduce this motif of reciprocal influence between foreign plants and native ground in the sense of a concept of *terroire*, in which the ground influences the plant through the roots. Instead, his conception is reversed: the ground is influenced by the plant. This is an opposing model to the concept of originality made prominent by the European genius-aesthetic as proposed by Edward Young. In his 1759 work, *Conjectures on Composition*, Young makes the assumption that the original is rooted in the fertile ground of a natural genius: 'an Original may be said to be of a vegetable nature; it rises spontaneously from the vital root of Genius'.[32] In contrast, the imitator appears as a 'transplanter of Laurels, which sometimes die on removal, always languish in a foreign soil'.[33] In other words, the process of copying and imitation is described here as transplantation to new ground, which leads the transplanted plant to become weaker.

There is a third possibility to reformulate the problematic relationship between assimilation and transplantation, namely, with recourse to a concept of originality that uses botanical metaphors without paying homage to the idea of a homogenous primitive nature as found in Young's writings. Such a concept can be found in Herder's *Fragments on Recent German Literature* (1768), where he first writes, following Young, that 'every book is a bed of flowers and growths; every language an immeasurable garden of plants and trees'.[34] Shortly after this, however, Herder provides a totally different kind of linguistically critical summary when he – in contrast to Schleiermacher – strikes rather xenophobic tones while remaining in the garden paradigm:

> Which revolutions has the German language undergone, partially within its own nature and partially through the admixture of foreign languages and ways of thinking, in order to change its mind while its body remained the same? How full is the language with foreign colonies that have taken on German dress, German citizenship, and German habits? How many foreign branches have been grafted onto the tree-trunk of our literature – where it is not degenerated, but rather changed and often refined?[35]

The question here, of course, is what Herder means by the formulation 'foreign colonies'. I would like to suggest that this expression refers to the so-called *Antiqua–Fraktur dispute*. In my view, it is an allusion to the typographical convention of printing all foreign words in *Antiqua*, while German text was printed in *Fraktur*. According to this convention, the difference between *Antiqua* and *Fraktur* becomes a cipher for ostentatious non-assimilation: foreign words remain foreign within a field of the native *Fraktur* script.[36] At the same time, foreign words also represent an externalized 'foreign similarity' that forms the basis of Schleiermacher's concept of an alienating translation.

But if foreign words are colonies that are marked *as foreign words* by a different typographical form (*Antiqua*), then don't German words written in *Fraktur* take on the systematic position of an indigenous people? And when Herder claims that foreign colonies have taken on 'German dress, German citizenship, and German customs', the formulation 'German citizenship' obviously plays with the possibility of a naturalizing form of translation. The naturalization of a foreign word, the translational adoption of a 'foreign similarity', appears here as a form of *colonial mimicry* within the framework of written culture: both as assimilation of the *typographical dress-code* and as linguistic assimilation of foreign words with regard to 'German' grammar. In this respect, Herder's metaphorical reference to foreign colonies points to the sensitive political problem of linguistic incorporation that remarkably parallels the so-called 'integration debate' seen in Germany today.

What I find most noteworthy about Herder's writing, however, is that despite the somewhat lachrymose tone with which he first characterizes the German language as an entity that has been grafted together, he also recognizes that the 'original, peculiar' nature of the *national language* is a result of exactly this historical grafting. As he puts it: 'it is like it is after its branches have been trimmed and transplanted, with all of its grafted foreign twigs, but still standing as a self-grown tree-trunk, injured but not dismembered by bare hands'.[37] To the extent that around 1800 (but also for the remainder of the nineteenth century), language as 'national language' constituted the definitive point of reference for what was described above as 'original national identity',[38] Herder describes in this passage a conception of national language in which originality and grafted-togetherness interfere with one another. The national language that has been grown on native soil proves to be a pieced-together entity, namely, a grafted-together language tree that is remarkably unstable and incomplete – and remains 'never finished or complete in itself'.[39] National language thus becomes an *original in motion*, a *mutable mobile* (as one might say with reference to a term coined by Bruno Latour[40]) that becomes *an original* as soon as it is grafted together with linguistic branches from other cultures.

Notes

1 Park (1914): 606.
2 Ibid.
3 Ibid.
4 Ibid.
5 Ben-Sasson *et al.* (2007): 605.
6 Cf. Canclini (2005): xxxii.
7 Cf. Bhabha (1994): 75f.
8 Bachmann-Medick (2006): 200.
9 Bhabha (1990): 210.
10 Ibid.
11 Benjamin ([1921] 2007): 73.
12 Ibid.: 75.
13 Cf. Wirth (2011) .
14 Schleiermacher ([1813] 1973): 69; my translation.
15 Ibid.: 55.
16 Ibid.: 54.
17 Bohnenkamp (2004): 20; my translation.
18 Schleiermacher ([1813] 1973): 54; my translation.
19 'Blendling' in Grimm and Grimm (??). Also cf. Giuriato (2011).
20 Schleiermacher ([1833] 1977): 90; my translation.
21 Cf. Mudge *et al.* (2009).
22 Allen (1978): 60.
23 Cf. Serres (1982): 130.
24 Cf. Hertwig ([1906] 1923): 505ff.
25 Weber ([1918] 1988): 516; my translation.
26 Cf. Weber ([1920] 1986): 440; my translation.
27 Young (1995): 4.
28 Bhabha (1990): 210.
29 Derrida ([1972] 1988): 9.

30 Acheraïou (2008): 33.
31 Schleiermacher ([1813] 1973): 69; my translation.
32 Young (1759): 12.
33 Ibid.: 10.
34 Herder ([1768] 1985): 552.
35 Ibid.: 567.
36 Cf. Wehde (2000): 216ff.
37 Herder ([1768] 1985): 571; my translation.
38 Ben-Sasson *et al.* (2007): 605.
39 Bhabha (1990): 210.
40 Cf. Latour (1986): 6.

References

Acheraïou, Amar (2008), *Rethinking Postcolonialism: Colonialist Discourse in Modern Literatures and the Legacy of Classical Writers*, New York: Macmillan.

Allen, Oliver (1978), *Pruning and Grafting: The Time-Life Encyclopedia of Gardening*, New York: Burdett.

Bachmann-Medick, Doris (2006), *Cultural turns: Neuorientierungen in den Kulturwissenschaften*, Reinbek bei Hamburg: Rowohlt.

Benjamin, Walter ([1921] 2007), 'The Task of the Translator', in *Illuminations*, edited by Hannah Arendt, translated by Harry Zohn, New York: Schocken Books: 69–82.

Ben-Sasson, Haim *et al.* (2007), 'Assimilation', in *Encyclopedia Judaica*, edited by V. Fred Skolnik and Michael Berenbaum, Farmington Hill: Macmillan: 605–13.

Bhabha, Homi (1990), 'The Third Space: Interview with Homi Bhabha', in Jonathan Rutherford, ed., *Identity: Community, Culture, Difference*, London: Lawrence and Wishart.

——— (1994), *The Location of Culture*, London and New York: Routledge.

Bohnenkamp, Anne (2004), 'Hybrid statt verfremdend? Überlegungen zu einem Topos der Übersetzungstheorie', in Peter Colliander, Doris Hansen and Ingeborg Zint-Dyhr, eds, *Linguistische Aspekte der Übersetzungswissenschaft*, Tübingen: Stauffenberg Verlag.

Canclini, Néstor García (2005), *Hybrid cultures: Strategies for entering and leaving modernity*, Minneapolis and London: University of Minnesota Press.

Derrida, Jacques ([1972] 1988), 'Signature Event Context', in *Limited Inc*, Evanston, IL: Northwestern University Press: 1–23.

Giuriato, Davide (2011), '"Blendlinge": Zur Theorie der Übersetzung bei Friedrich Schleiermacher', in Uwe Wirth, ed., *Impfen, Pfropfen, Transplantieren*, Berlin: Kadmos: 121–34.

Grimm, Jacob and Wilhelm Grimm (??), *Deutsches Wörterbuch*, Leipzig, 16 Bde in 32 Teilbänden, Leipzig 1854–1961, Quellenverzeichnis Leipzig 1971; available at http://www.woerterbuchnetz.de/DWB?lemma=blendling.

Herder, Johann Gottfried von ([1768] 1985), 'Über die neuere deutsche Literatur', in Herder and Ulrich Gaier, eds, *Werke in zehn Bänden: Band 1 Frühe Schriften 1764–1772*, Frankfurt am Main: DKV: 541–650.

Hertwig, Oskar ([1906] 1923), *Allgemeine Biologie*, Jena: Fischer; available at https://archive.org/details/allgemeinebiolo00hert.

Latour, Bruno (1986), 'Visualization and Cognition: Drawing Things Together', *Knowledge and Society: Studies in the Sociology of Culture and Present,* Vol. 6: 1–40.

Mudge, Ken *et al.* (2009), 'A History of Grafting', *Horticultural Reviews*, Vol. 35: 437–93.

Park, Robert (1914), 'Racial Assimilation in Secondary Groups with Particular Reference to the Negro', *American Journal of Sociology*, 19 (5): 606–23.

Schleiermacher, Friedrich ([1833] 1977), *Hermeneutik und Kritik*, Frankfurt am Main: Suhrkamp.
——— ([1813] 1973), 'Ueber die verschiedenen Methoden des Ueber-setzens', in Hans Joachim Störig, ed., *Das Problem des Übersetzens*, Darmstadt: Wissenschaftliche Buchgesellschaft: 38–69.
Serres, Michel (1982), *The Parasite*, Baltimore, MD and London: John Hopkins Press.
Weber, Max ([1920] 1986), 'Die Wirtschaftsethik der Weltreligionen', in *Gesammelte Aufsätze zur Religionssoziologie*, Tübingen: Mohr Siebeck Verlag: 238–442.
——— ([1918] 1988), 'Der Sozialismus', in *Gesammelte Aufsätze zur Soziologie und Sozialpolitik*, Tübingen: Mohr Siebeck Verlag: 492–517.
Wehde, Susanne (2000), *Typographische Kultur: Eine zeichentheoretische Studie zur Typographie und ihrer Entwicklung*, Tübingen: Niemeyer.
Wirth, Uwe (2011), 'Gepfropfte Theorie: Eine "greffologische" Kritik von Hybriditätskonzepten als Beschreibung von intermedialen und interkulturellen Beziehungen', in Mario Grizelj and Oliver Jahraus, eds, *Theorie Theorie: Wider die Methodenmüdigkeit in den Geisteswissenschaften*, München: Wilhelm Fink Verlag: 151–66.
Young, Edward (1759), *Conjectures on Original Composition*, London: A. Millar and R. and J. Dodsley.
Young, Robert J.C. (1995), *Colonial Desire: Hybridity in theory, culture and race*, London and New York: Routledge.

CASE STUDIES

Similarity as Performance

A new approach to identity construction and empathy regimes

Aleida Assmann

Resemblance does not make things so much alike as difference makes them unlike.

– Michel de Montaigne

Those who only seek what divides people will never recognize commonalities. Those who only think in terms of cultural or religious differences will never discover political or human similarities.

– Carolin Emcke[1]

Similarity: Category Formation and Tilting Images

The identification of similarities is deeply rooted in the evolution of the human mind. This individual mental equipment includes the constructive ability to form categories. Even an 18-month-old child with a limited vocabulary operates within a wide-ranging category system based on observed similarities. For example, an electric toy car and a wok could both be assigned to the 'Gaugauwa' (vacuum cleaner) category; dogs, cats and also birds might fall under the 'Wauwau' category, to which new discoveries such as Christmas angels and chocolate Santas could also be assigned. Long before language dissects and orders the world, the human mind forges an organizational system of categories on the basis of similar features, with significant room for creative extension. The poet and theorist Paul Valéry describes this mental activity as the task of moving from disorder to order: 'The existence of similar things is the foundation for everything. If no features were ever repeated, we could never identify anything. The son unlike the father, each man perpetually dissimilar even to himself, every moment incomparable to any other – that indeed would be chaos.'[2]

This thinking underscores the constructive nature of the human mind, which continuously produces relationships of similarity by ignoring certain differences in order to arrive at relevant categories and to organize meaningful systems. This applies generally to a variety of levels. There is, for instance, a discourse that considers similarity to be a pre-modern, epistemic form of world experience (our distinction between 'allopathy' and 'homeopathy' is a legacy of this period); this theory was popularized by Michel Foucault in his intellectual-historical study, *The Order of Things*.[3] Another literary discourse focuses on the identification and establishment of similarities as a fundamental aesthetic principle, in contrast to scientific reasoning. However, no neat dividing line should be drawn between the exact sciences, on the one hand, and the notoriously vague humanities, on the other. Rather, the similarity theories of modern authors such as Novalis, Charles Baudelaire, Paul Valéry and Walter Benjamin, which resolve the dichotomy between subject and object in various ways, are today being positively reappraised.[4] Indeed, these modern thinkers were interested in forms of similarity that are not once and for all defined in fixed categories or characteristics but instead suddenly appear in surprising constellations and new configurations. Their theories include the dimension of time, emphasizing historical variability and the modern experience of transience as important preconditions for the perception of similarity. According to Walter Benjamin, for example, similarity is always transitory in appearance: '[I]ts creation just as its perception by humans is in many and the most important cases, revealed in a flash and disappears as quickly.'[5]

As this discursive work on the concept can be summarized, similarity is created in the eye of the beholder, and is therefore contingent, ephemeral, unpredictable and perhaps even intangible. It has been disconnected from substances and migrated into situations. My contribution to the collective project of forging a new access to the concept of similarity will pick up some of these elements and develop them further by stressing the performative dimension. In order to give the concept more shape, a few more elements have to be added to the general definition.

Similarity is always framed by deviation and surrounded by differences. It cannot be addressed outside of this dialectic; as in the optical interaction between figure and ground, in which one can focus either on the foreground or on the background but never on both at once, similarities are always perceived by bracketing differences, as differences in turn become manifest through the bracketing of similarities. Similarities and differences come into being in a fluid field of visual phenomena, constructed by different perspectives involving the selection of relevant characteristics that can be sorted in different ways. 'Thinking in similarities', Waldemar Fromm asserts, 'means not being able to perceive a fundamental opposition between self and other.'[6] The question of similarity as it is debated here moves the focus from qualities or substances to forms of perception.

I want to contend that this perception always occurs in the context of a situation in which criteria of relevance, decision-making, and a shifting between knowledge and ignorance play a vital role. In any situation, divergent and even opposing perspectives are principally possible. These choices, however, are reduced through the power of habitualized social narratives and cultural values. Individuals are driven by these preconceptions, but they are also, under specific circumstances, capable of overriding this collective framework. By ignoring and bracketing certain elements new aspects can be discovered that change the configuration of relevant stimuli, which means that a new picture of the situation emerges, and a different reaction and relation with the world becomes possible.

An Example of Similarity and Difference: Geopolitical Identity Construction

Let me introduce an example that shows how our realities and identities can be changed by the shuffling and shifting of relevant criteria. In the preface to her book *The Archive and the Repertoire*, Diana Taylor vividly describes the impact of external parameters on her identity and the changes that it effected at various stages in her life. When growing up in northern Mexico as a child, she had the impression that there was only one big America in one hemisphere. When she moved to the United States to study, she learned that 'America' was synonymous with the USA and that this America/USA was situated in the north of the hemisphere, whereas Mexico (although it is also in the northern hemisphere) was differentiated as 'Latin America' and assigned to the south. With the help of an atlas she later discovered that there were three different Americas: one in the north, one in the south and one in the middle.[7] Through this example she realized how ambiguous geographical descriptions can be. The concept of America means different things to different groups; the boundary between self and other – and between commonalities and that which divides them – may be drawn with different effects in a number of ways. Those who emphasize language as the decisive characteristic will discover a common thread linking the USA and a large part of Canada, but will separate these two Americas from any parts in which Romance languages are spoken. However, there are fundamental differences between the USA and English-speaking Canada in terms of their national–cultural self-identities. In light of their divergent histories, geographies and art, the two countries perceive each other as emphatically dissimilar and different.

By means of such strategies of distancing and separation, permanent and highly consequential borders are drawn that define similarities and differences in a given situation. When these borders are cemented and fixed in the form of constitutions, history textbooks and literature, these borders have the power to define the fate and identities of individuals and groups. For the people who inhabit these regions, these geopolitical boundaries obviously have a decisive impact. As they are a part of the cultural and political truth, they create structures and realities, and it would be naïve to think that it would be easy to defy them because they are only cultural or political 'constructs'. It would be equally naïve, however, to believe that these boundaries must determine our world-views forever and in all situations. People cannot and do not want to free themselves entirely of such classifications and affiliations, but that does not mean they are merely the objects of previous boundary decisions. When it comes to expressing their self-image, they remain (as is often forgotten), to some extent, the subjects of their own definitions and choices in concrete and contingent situations. 'I require', Diana Taylor writes, 'an identity as an American in the hemispheric sense. That means: I have lived comfortably and perhaps also uncomfortably in various overlapping worlds.'[8] As Taylor attests here, established barriers and boundaries can always be 'renegotiated' anew, to make use of the current jargon. This term, which stems from the language of diplomacy, jurisprudence and trade, is generally applied as though needing no further explanation. We seldom reflect on the framework negotiations, inquiring into the conditions that enable dialogic transactions.

The requirements, however, for the negotiations that we refer to here may be described very clearly. They can be reduced to a simple rule that is generally applicable in any situation: this rule is a shift of perspective. Through this reorientation of the gaze, one can suddenly discover similarities where one had previously only perceived differences. The practice of re-perspectivizing is reminiscent of the optical puzzle of tilting images. As long as one shape is in focus the inverse form remains invisible; as soon as the hidden figure is revealed, however, the dominant figure disappears. This example describes the most radical case of re-perspectivizing, which is based on an either–or decision. In everyday situations, when one discovers new similarities where only differences were seen before, it is usually the effect of a less comprehensive change of perspective. One is suddenly in a position to detect certain aspects of a thing, a person or a situation that had been excluded from one's habitual field of view. These elements may then inform a half-conscious form of knowledge that suddenly gains contours and new relevance. It is this fundamental possibility of re-perspectivizing, together with the situation-dependent discovery of similarities, that set our cognitive maps and orientation in motion. Strictly speaking, the term 'negotiation' is not applicable here since re-perspectivizing has nothing to do with a social interaction in which two sides reach an agreement through discursive or pragmatic means. Quite the contrary, in this case the impulse comes only from one side, due to a cognitive or emotional change in the situation. Like Diana Taylor, all humans live comfortably or uncomfortably in various overlapping worlds; as a result apparently fixed boundaries are in fact permeable and allow new vistas of ignored, denied or simply forgotten connected spaces. Whether people can discover and recognize similarities with their counterparts that are negated and hidden by the prevailing social, religious or political norms depends in each case on the creative imagination, the empathetic powers and the intellectual independence of the actors.

Although the concept of similarity addressed here is actually very easy to define, it is nonetheless constantly obscured by misunderstandings. The similarity I have in mind is performative in origin and always tied to a concrete situation. Consequently, one cannot approach this concept through general classification principles, established associations or other historical descriptions. The question of specific 'epistemologies of similarity', as analysed by Foucault, cannot lead to the performative act of creating similarity in a specific interaction. We are dealing here not with a fixed category of knowledge but instead with contingent subjective, emotional or ethical resources and decisions. Nor should this performative similarity be confused with the expansive gesture of appropriation and subjugation described by ethnologists as 'nostrification'. What is being discussed here is the recognition of similarity in a person, action or object that had been deemed strange, and is suddenly perceived to show traits of familiarity or similarity. In the interaction between humans, the decisive factor is the recognition of a common humanity in spite of divisive markers of difference. The unpredictable recognition of this momentary and ad-hoc similarity in the midst of manifest difference accounts for the ethical nature and form of perception. It neither overrides nor erases the evident differences in any way but enables new forms of communication, overcoming existing obstacles. In this way it expands the perspective beyond social frames and identity boundaries created by culture, religion and ethnic groups. The discovery of such unforeseen similarities pragmatically or playfully suspends the pressure on difference, facilitating spontaneous actions, paradoxical interventions and unlikely alliances that interrupt rigid patterns of identities and differences.

One question is crucial for the methodology of this similarity paradigm: Who detects the similarities that undermine the boundaries and contours of predetermined identity constructions? The answer is: The perception is not that of a distanced observer who provides an objective description. The similarity discussed here is exclusively performative, subjective and situational, perceived in concrete social interaction and implemented in an action or reaction. The performative and situational framework is therefore just as important as the transgressive nature of the perception of similarity that ignores cultural boundaries and ingrained truths.

The Rash Loss of Similarities in the Construction of Enemy Stereotypes

This performative form of similarity involves the creation of a surprising, new – in part even paradoxical – connection that ignores culturally determined and socially internalized categories. It is not based on previous equivalences, analogies or otherwise essentialist definitions; rather, it arises from acts of bridge-building between self and others across the abyss of difference, whereby the difference is somewhat mitigated but in no way eliminated. As the term similarity lies outside the semantic field of identity-and-difference, it may serve to undermine the iron logic of identity politics that enforces identity via difference, thus undermining rigid hetero-stereotypes. While the term identity tends to stabilize difference, the term similarity, if used as a mode of perception and a cultural strategy, tends to bracket and unsettle difference by ignoring its exclusionary force.

In this view, difference and similarity are not objectively determined categories but correlated flexible positions that shift constantly, depending on specific situations and intentions according to which they are continuously reconstructed and transformed. The important advantage of the concept of similarity as discussed in this essay is that it opens a door out of the trap of identity politics as played out in the contradictory relation between self and other. It does not eliminate difference but defies it. Through re-perspectivizing, it neutralizes the poisonous essence of difference that creates and maintains essentialized friend–foe relationships.

In the fields of religion and politics, we have many examples of how human relationships consistently regress to this malignant core of difference. For instance, following the invasion of Crimea by Russian troops and the annexation of Ukrainian territory, a new term of debasement circulated: *Putinversteher* ('Putin understander'). Already the act of seeing things from the perspective of the other was resisted and detested. When suspending the cognitive tools of empathy and a 'theory of mind', the field of interaction reorganizes itself in strong oppositions; the link of understanding is broken up when there is no longer anything that one has in common with the political opponent. Carl Schmitt developed his concept of the 'providential enemy' to describe the absolute boundary between friend and foe in the context of the religious wars of the seventeenth century, but this concept was also later applied to support the murderous system of 'redemptive anti-Semitism' in which the survival of the Aryan race was portrayed as dependent on the annihilation of the Jewish race. Such a conceptual framework leaves only the radical decisions of either–or, as there is no room for both groups to coexist. In the cases of the IS militia and Boko Haram – groups that use civil war to prey on ailing and failing states to destroy religious minorities, and to kill or kidnap vulnerable men, women and children – we are again confronting this hard core of the friend–foe difference, this time not within the fantasy of a pure force but as a real and repeated experience of traumatized victims. This confrontation indeed over-rides any form of empathy based on similarity between oneself and the other. When exposed to internet videos depicting horrific acts of rage and violence, western audiences are paralysed and resort to a demonizing rhetoric that refuses to recognize the others as members of the human race. Just as people have the opportunity to identify their fellow-humans as equals, they can deny them this status.

Armed conflicts would not be possible if one recognized the other as a neighbour and partner, rather than as an enemy to be killed. All wars make use of this possibility to flip the switch of empathy. The soldiers on the frontlines of the First World War, however, also demonstrated that one can shake off this inflexible friend–foe pattern for short spells. They organized and abided by temporary cease-fires, interspersing into the daily business of warfare, joint Christmas parties and football games. This example indicates that the perception scheme of absolute difference could be briefly suspended and, through the recognition of similarity, a space – however transitory – created for interaction.

War is the ultimate example of a situation ruled by radically altered emotions and values that trigger an exclusively strategic way of thinking. This leads to a 'frame change' that drastically modifies the relationship between self and other. It is not just the war, however, but also the mood that precedes it which is characterized by a precipitous reduction of similarities. Wolfgang Kemp comments on this mental frame in his book on the relationship between the British and the Germans in the inter-war period:

> Generally speaking, increased interest in the other is a bad sign. This interest was never greater than during the First World War, during Hitler's dictatorship, and in the immediate post-war period. The images of the other that were constructed during these times are mostly of the sort of which one must be ashamed afterwards.[9]

Similarity and Empathy

In her books on history and the use of emotions, Martha Nussbaum has re-read canonical western texts on the subject. She shows that in the theories of compassion developed by Aristotle and Rousseau, the concept of similarity plays an important role. Compassion, both thinkers agreed, requires the insight that 'one recognizes a potential for vulnerability in oneself similar to that of the sufferer'.[10] This recognition of similarity supports the belief that the same suffering could afflict the observer. This shared feeling of affective concern is based on the ability to see similarities between oneself and others.

When this is the case, the reverse is also true – that is, the requirement of similarity significantly restricts the group of potential empathy candidates. Nussbaum confirms that in real life the potential for a universal flow of empathy is limited by various social barriers, be it 'class, religion, ethnicity, gender, sexual orientation, which prove to be averse to the imagination, and this inability to imagine impedes emotions'.[11] If empathy depends on a foundation of culturally predetermined similarities, then its field of action is severely constrained from all sides.

Humans are bound to interrupt the flow of empathy as soon as they are confronted with a sign of dissimilarity. The flipping of the empathy switch generally happens unconsciously. This emotional control works automatically below the level of consciousness. It is a matter of emotional conditioning that is culturally produced and habitualized, for example, through narratives. A narrative is far more than the thematic construction of a narration; it can be defined as 'a fundamental form of organizing human experience and knowledge'.[12] Narratives also create meaning through the shaping of emotions, by neatly dividing fictional characters into those that are deemed worthy of empathy and those that are not.

In Hollywood films, for example, there are surprisingly robust rules for this decisive emotional distinction. If a slight shadow is cast on a fictional character, the bond of similarity is abruptly broken and he (literally) becomes fair game. Such a character in a film may be shot down, fall on bad times, contract a serious illness or fall off a cliff; the viewer will not be moved to shed a single tear. For participation in a narrative, the supportive feelings of empathy for a figure stimulating compassion and identification on the part of the viewer is just as important as the blocking of empathy when confronted with negative figures. In the words of Judith Butler, such characters are not 'grievable'; that is, they are not candidates for investing compassion, pain or grief.[13]

In such narratives, empathy works as a reflex that responds to a script, and is unconsciously turned on and off. This logic does not depend on the individual decisions of viewers but rather on internalized rules of genres. In their cultural socialization viewers have profoundly internalized this knowledge, and can therefore react 'correctly' and collectively to the plot of a given story. The logic that drives this dynamics is the distinction between 'similar and dissimilar'. Whoever is perceived as similar to us deserves our sympathy and our compassion; whoever appears as dissimilar (or even alien) deserves the withdrawal of compassion and punishment within the system of 'fictional justice'. Fictional justice is a variant of the concept of *poetic justice*, a term coined by the neo-classicist Thomas Rhymer at the end of the seventeenth century. Rhymer's normative poetics accepted only tragic tales in which evil was punished and good was rewarded. His rules were not followed in great literature that produced more complex plots and characters. Today's narratives of popular mass-culture, however, have exchanged Rhymer's moral rule of poetic justice with fictional justice and the simple empathy rule based on a regime of similarity.

In fact empathy is always selective. People have empathy for groups with whom they have learned to identify and for whom they have compassion. If, however, a group has been consistently presented over time as radically dissimilar, with the help of traditions, stereotypes and a form of propaganda which emphasizes differences that separate the group from the rest of humanity, pro-social feelings are numbed and empathy is blocked. National Socialist propaganda portrayed Jews in alienating images not only as enemies, but also as a racial threat, which increased the difference to the extreme generating emotions such as danger and disgust as a reliable self-protective reflex. In the National Socialist state, schoolchildren in the first grade were already indoctrinated with slogans like 'The Jews are our curse!' written in large letters on the blackboard. Such slogans created enemy stereotypes that utterly excluded any similarities between the self and the other. In the 1930s and 1940s, this indoctrination resulted in a comprehensive blocking of empathy as Jewish citizens disappeared from schools, universities, orchestras, firms and neighbourhoods. 'The Jews were simply different, separate', a witness reconstructed his feelings as a boy of ten at the *Kristallnacht* of 1938: 'At that time I was a *Pimpfenführer* [youth leader], and a *Pimpfenführer* had nothing to do with the Jews. The next morning, I distributed the drums to the members of my group – these worlds were kept totally separate.'[14]

It is not so simple, however, to create an absolutely fixed habitus, since the question of similarity and difference can be unsettled and recalibrated from one situation to the next. Propaganda films manipulate negative feelings and have the power to block empathy. The prime example is the film *Jud Süß*, directed by Veit Harlan (1940), which even today must not be shown publicly in Germany due to its still contagious powers of seduction. But the media in general can also have the opposite effect if they highlight similarities and reduce existing thresholds of difference. In her book on memory and empathy in public and global media, Alison Landsberg shows that the mass media today offer new opportunities for creating an emotional impact on a global audience.[15] They have a unique power to transport human experiences and historical knowledge across the boundaries of nation, race, religion and other constraints of collective identity. In an essay on 'Memory, Empathy and the Politics of Identification', Landsberg took up and extended the question posed by Nussbaum on the relationship between similarity and empathy. She analysed certain films with regard to their potential to elicit the empathy of viewers beyond the prescribed and fixed boundaries of similarity and difference. Indeed, in our global age of media, films have the power to construct and present narratives in such a way that they can stimulate audiences intellectually and emotionally to empathize with persons and groups that are radically different from themselves. Here Landsberg makes an important distinction between 'sympathy' and 'empathy'. Whereas sympathy 'presupposes similarity and thus a pre-existing affinity between two people wherein one shares the feelings of the other', empathy entails a much more complex emotional orientation that ignores differences without dissolving them. Empathy maintains the distinction between self and other, and introduces two elements that are not active in sympathy: reflection and distance. 'Empathy unlike sympathy', Landsberg writes,

> requires mental, cognitive activity, it entails an intellectual engagement with the plight of the other; when one talks about empathy one is not talking simply about emotion, but about contemplation as well. Contemplation and distance, two elements central to empathy, are not present in sympathy. Empathy takes work and is much harder to achieve than sympathy. In part, empathy is about developing compassion not for our family or friends or community, but for others who have no relation to us, who resemble us not all, whose circumstances lie far outside of our own experiences.[16]

If seen in this light, cinema in the globalized mass-culture could become an important school for empathy and an effective tool for ethical thinking. Critical attention focused on audience reactions and a differentiated analysis of the shifting dynamics of identification in the cinema can provide us with important insights into the complex interaction between artistic structures and emotional processes. Referring to the film *The Pianist*

(2002), directed by Roman Polanski, Landsberg describes the complex case of a cinematic identification that is not built on sameness or similarity, but on distance and difference between spectator and protagonist. Through the use of surreal symbols in his cinematic language, Polanski signals the impossibility of an identification that is based on sympathy. This is precisely the purpose of the film: 'to force us to stay with Wladyslaw, to recognize his humanity, no matter how altered and unrecognizable it has become'.[17] Landsberg hopes that

> film practices and strategies might be deployed to serve a pedagogical function, to teach viewers how to identify with the other especially in the face of difference, to encourage spectators to take on traumatic prosthetic memories that might lead to the development of empathy, and that might open the door to more radical democratic engagements and movements in the future.[18]

Similarity in Dissimilarity: Shylock's Lesson in Empathy

Landsberg's approach to empathy as 'similarity across difference' will be illustrated here by another example – probably the most striking, the most difficult and best known example of the problem of empathy in western cultural memory. I am referring to the first scene in the third act of Shakespeare's *Merchant of Venice*, in which Shylock, the Jewish moneylender, takes the audience on an emotional rollercoaster. From the start the play makes it clear that Shylock stands for 'the Jews', a people who over centuries have been despised, abused and excluded by their Christian neighbours. Shylock's humanity is not only denied by calling him 'dog', he is also singled out by the Christian community as the providential foe (in the sense of Carl Schmitt) and referred to as the 'devil'.

Shylock expresses a strong appeal for compassion directed at two minor characters on stage, but the force of his words directly targets the heart of each audience member in theatres of various eras, people who either themselves harbour anti-Jewish feelings or who are well-acquainted with the discriminatory practices he describes. In other words, through legends and stereotypes passed down over centuries, the audience perhaps knows far more about this character than about any other figure in Shakespeare's dramas, and this additional worldly knowledge inevitably interferes with their perception of the action in the play.

From the outset it is clear that Shakespeare has constructed a prototype of the stranger, presented as an eccentric and a lone wolf in every way. The scene I am referring to here is introduced with a discussion of similarity and dissimilarity. Shylock has just had to cope with the loss of his daughter Jessica, who left his house with a Christian lover while stealing gold and jewellery on the way like a common thief. His laments over this profound shock do not directly resound on stage; rather, they are mediated by the mocking voice of a secondary character, Solanio, who re-enacts the personal tragedy of Shylock as a farce (Act II, Scene 8). In sharp contrast to their response to the misfortune of Shylock, which amuses Solanio and his associate Salerio enormously, the two muster deep compassion for the bad luck of Antonio, who has suffered the loss of ships on the high seas.

In Act III, Scene 1, Shylock speaks with Solanio and Salerio about his recent tribulations, and argues for at least a minimum level of compassion: 'My own flesh and blood to rebel!' As this appeal has no effect, Shylock must intensify it: 'I say, my daughter is my flesh and blood.' The two react only with further mockery. While Shylock insists on his identity with his daughter, Solanio and Salerio insist on their difference, as his daughter has moved from the Jewish world to the Christian camp. They make it clear that the moneylender no longer has any connection to his daughter and that he has been left behind as a solitary stranger. Where once there was kinship, now absolute difference prevails: 'There is more difference between thy flesh and hers than between jet and ivory; more between your bloods than there is between red wine and rhenish' (Act III, Scene 1: 33–35). It should be noted that in the same play, a dark-skinned suitor named Morocco claims that his blood is just as red as that of the palest Nordic people (Act II, Scene 1: 4–7). These pleas, however, have no chance of being heard – either by the other characters on stage or by the audience in the theatre. The solace-seeking Shylock only hears that there is no longer any similarity between him and his daughter. Through her flight to and acceptance by Christian society the ties of kinship have been cut, and she is no longer of his own flesh and blood.

At this point in the action of the play, the two catastrophes collide: Shylock's loss of his daughter and Antonio's loss of his ships. It does not take long for Shylock to realize this surprising coincidence, which he quickly turns to his own strategic use. This inspiration infuses him with a new theatrical energy that he discharges in a series of threats. He has just lost his own flesh and blood, but his contract with Antonio offers him compensation for which he grimly prepares. 'If he forfeit,' Salerio asks, appalled, 'thou wilt not take his flesh: what's that good for?' Shylock's answer initiates the famous passage that is the topic of interest here. It starts with Shylock's cynical response that he can use the flesh as bait for fish. But then he speaks clearly: it will nourish his vengeance; a vengeance not only for the insults and injuries he has borne, but one that will pay for all the humiliations endured by the Jews in their long history of suffering. These afflictions are not tied to individuals but rather to the 'category' of Jews. After Shylock's threatening announcement of taking revenge, Shakespeare puts the following astonishing words in the mouth of this ultimate stranger:

> Hath not a Jew eyes? Hath not a Jew hands, organs, dimensions, senses, affections, passions? Fed with the same food, hurt with the same weapons, subject to the same diseases, healed by the same means, warmed and cooled by the same winter and summer, as a Christian is? If you prick us, do we not bleed? If you tickle us, do we not laugh? If you poison us, do we not die? (Act III, Scene 1: 52–60)

At the point of extreme confrontation and alienation where all bridges of possible communication have been broken Shakespeare incorporates into Shylock this astounding plea for similarity, in which the prototypical juxtaposition of enemy groups, of 'us' and 'them' (historically meaning Jews and Christians, and later Jews and Aryans), is momentarily transcended. In this scene Shylock is completely isolated. From this existential loneliness comes his appeal for similarity, presenting himself not as 'the Jew' but as a representative of the human race. Through repeated reference to the physical sensations of the body, he reclaims his membership in the common family of humanity. At this level he transforms himself into an absolutely passive and vulnerable being that no longer desires, plans or bargains, but exclusively reacts, feels and suffers. Humanity is here reduced to the body, the senses and mortality; these are the common denominators that bind the human family together below all artificial distinctions and divisions. If we bracket off culture, religion, status, age, profession, nationality and other classifications, what remains is the liminal existence of mere humanity.

Shylock's six rhetorical questions are all oriented towards inevitable consent; one cannot help but repeat 'yes' six times. This confirmation of a common humanity revealed by his insistent questions under the façade of persistent enmity is overwhelming and designed to impact the viewers in the theatre who he is also indirectly addressing.

But no catharsis or change of affect is achieved at this point, no breakthrough of emotions; all we feel is a brief swell of empathy. Even this, however, is immediately quelled and turned upside down by Shakespeare's dramaturgy of emotions – this is what I mean by 'emotional rollercoaster'. The last question – 'If you poison us, do we not die?' – is immediately followed by: 'And if you wrong us, shall we not revenge? If we are like you in the rest, we will resemble you in that.' With these words Shylock instantly shifts from one extreme image – Jews as exposed and vulnerable – to the menacing spectre of a vengeful race. The lines that follow seal the eternal enmity between the two religions.

This appeal to empathy is framed several times in Shakespeare's play: through the theme of 'flesh and blood', through the close parallels of Shylock and Antonio's catastrophes, through the motif of revenge, and through the collective Jewish history of suffering that is here transformed into a phantasmatic collective history of vengeance. Shylock's moving speech about a common humanity originating in neediness and vulnerability is embedded in a context of scorn, hate and revenge. The empathy he invokes must remain inconsequential, as it leads to a pronouncement of revenge and instead reaffirms eternal enmity. The uncanny nature of this scene stems from the fact that the same argument for similarity is raised both in support of empathy and bonding as in support of escalating the conflict and increasing difference.

Performing Similarity and Difference

As Shakespeare depicted in his play, the division of the world into two types of people, 'us' and 'them', is the source of anti-Semitism and racism, both of which are based on a premise of fundamental and insurmountable difference. While in the out-group the other is no longer acknowledged as a member of the same species, in the in-group the self is connected to the others by thick relations, supported by a selective empathy that excludes those who are not classified as different and alien from pro-social attention, respect and appreciation.

On 19 January 2007, the Turkish–Armenian writer and journalist Hrant Dink was the victim of a race-motivated murder in Istanbul. On the day of his funeral thousands of Turks joined the funeral procession carrying signs that proclaimed, 'We are all Hrant Dink!' and 'We are all Armenians!' There is a striking similarity in the design of these signs dedicated to Hrant Dink and the expressions of solidarity that flooded the streets following the attack on the editorial offices of the satirical magazine *Charlie Hebdo* in Paris on 7 January 2015. Both signs of mourning and empathy can be read as the signature of a new, cosmopolitan form of *citizenship* that is performed in the *cross-cultural theatre of the public* – in the metropolis of media-led society and its globalized internet.

Three weeks after the attack in Istanbul I participated in a conference sponsored by the Böll Foundation on the theme, 'From the Burden of the Past to Social Freedom and Democracy' – a meeting that Dink had helped organize. At that conference I asked the question: I wonder what it would have been like if, after *Kristallnacht* (the night of violence and pogroms harassing Jewish citizens in German cities in November 1938),

thousands of non-Jews had crowded the streets of those cities with placards reading, 'We are all Jews'? It is not unlikely that after such protest and murmur, Hitler's obsession with the so-called 'final solution' would have been difficult to realize. Instead, however, what prevailed in Germany was a frightened, embarrassed and above all indifferent silence. Today, such an act of solidarity no longer requires great civil courage but it does require empathy.

There was another possible cause for similar protests in connection with the ten National Socialist Underground (NSU) murders, which were perpetrated by a neo-Nazi gang against German immigrants over a period of ten years. These crimes, which had been attributed by the police to the victims themselves, were finally publicly exposed on 4 November 2011. One year later, demonstrations against racism took place in thirty German cities.

An 'alliance against the silence' has been formed to take on the problems of structural racism, using its energetic voice to make demands on the associated authorities. Civil society, as it turns out, is a precarious institution and an unstable asset. The project is never complete once and for all but rather must prove itself again and again, confirming its accomplishments and winning acceptance, not least through performative acts that reaffirm similarity with others that are labelled as strangers. As Volkhard Knigge stresses, the core of civil society is based on the stabilization of basic solidarity among its members. Due to the effects of racism, but also due to growing egotism and societal indifference in the wake of the financial crisis, this basic solidarity has crumbled. The vital signs of solidarity with the victims of the NSU murders were meagre and came late. Whereas the last victim (police officer Michèle Kiesewetter) was memorialized by a large crowd in Oberweisbach in April 2007 (more than a thousand people came to her funeral), society took little notice of the other dead and wounded. On 10 December 2010 there was a memorial march in Kassel with a demonstration by the relatives of the victims. 'What a pity that so few Germans are walking with us!' – noted a participant, glancing at passers-by who were eagerly engaged in Christmas shopping.[19]

The decade of the NSU murders and its late uncovering reveal a key weakness in our society: self-centredness and an indifference to those who are excluded from the group of significant and equal others with whom we enter into meaningful social relations. This becomes manifest in a lack of empathy that confirms the fundamental similarity between people, and is able to over-ride cultural and social differences. Empathy is the decisive prerequisite for acts of social recognition, emotional sympathy and political solidarity. When respect and trust are withdrawn, an environment of uncertainty, eroded self-worth, isolation and fear develops among the devalued.

It needs to be emphasized that empathy is not a sentimental expression of emotion but rather begins with education, information and the acquisition of concrete knowledge. It depends on a concrete experience that has the power to turn abstract and anonymous information into a relevant and meaningful relationship with people who have received names, faces and are acknowledged with their stories. It was striking how, in the NSU affair, the media focused on the perpetrators and their accomplices, and how brief and scarce the reporting on the victims was; most journalists reduced them to the compact phrase of '10 dead'. The more one knows about a person, the more likely one is to overcome predetermined classification barriers and recognize the other as similar to oneself. In Schloss Bellevue, on 18 February 2013, President Gauck addressed the surviving relatives of the NSU victims with the words: 'You have all seen how an entire life can change overnight. You needed comfort and support. Instead, you found yourselves suspected, humiliated, and ultimately left alone.'[20]

The photographer Helena Schätzle, sociologist Lisa Kellermann and activist Antonia Heyn chose the murder of the final Turkish NSU victim in Kassel, Halit Yozgat, as the starting point for their exhibition project *Augenzu* (eyes closed), which they displayed in Kassel at the 'Documenta 13' art festival in 2012. Their theme was not specifically the ninth victim but rather an attempt 'to make latent and everyday racism visible and discussible, and to let people who are never or hardly ever shown in media reports have their say'.[21] The exhibition assembled cityscapes as potential settings and scenes of crimes of everyday racism along with statements about experiences of discrimination that were collected in interviews and compiled into an audio-collage. The exhibition was displayed in other cities as well, where new local elements were added. According to the organizers the focus of the project was narrating and listening, 'as narration can be considered a form of reflection and processing for the narrator, while listening can function as a place of empathy and solidarity'. As a statement from the group asserts: 'They will always attack Halit Yozgat as a Turk, not as a "Kasseler" [a person from Kassel]. This is what remains unacknowledged and hurts so deeply – a Kasseler was murdered, not a Turk.'[22] In the denial of similarity and the overemphasis of difference, we recognize racism as a form of 'group-related animosity' (*gruppenbezogene Menschenfeindlichkeit*). In light of the 'Pegida' demonstrations in December 2014, Carolin Emcke wrote that 'group-related animosity does not become correct just because many people express it'. She contends that it involves 'a type of exhibitionism of a pervasive cold-heartedness, proudly and shamelessly displayed, that prefers to hide its intellectual avarice and emotional impotence'.[23]

By collecting and analysing these performative acts of re-perspectivizing in their historical contexts and concrete situations, I have attempted to conceptually retool the notion of 'similarity'. To this end I have extracted it from its existing discourse and have, to a certain extent, redefined it. As I have tried to show, this revised concept is urgently needed in connection with questions of identity (re)construction and empathy dynamics. By discovering unexpected similarity and through public performative affirmation of it, the personal pronouns 'I' or 'we' can suddenly can take on new meanings. Standardized dichotomies such as 'self' and 'other', or 'identity' and 'difference', are thereby replaced by the concept of 'similarity', as a more flexible and open instrument for readjusting social, political and cultural relations. After the long and exhaustive domination of the discourse and concept of difference, more detailed and conceptual work on the concept of similarity lies before us, and it is to be hoped that the programmatic impulse of this volume can generate interest and encourage additional investigation of this important tool of thought. In following this track, we would have to determine more precisely how the concept of similarity as presented here relates to other concepts, such as 'equality', which represents an abstract and generalized political demand, or 'commonality', which refers to an empirical overlap between shared experiences. The performative concept of 'similarity' is presented here in the sense of a momentary intuition, a subjective insight and an ethical act. If connected to a humanistic social discourse and a political agenda, there is hope that it can be further developed into a culture of empathy that leads to more lived connectivity in a hyperconnected world.

Notes

1 Emcke (2014): 3.
2 Valéry (1989): 121.
3 Cf. Foucault (1974).
4 Cf. Funk, Mattenklott and Pauen (2001): 26.
5 Benjamin ([1933] 2005): 722.
6 Fromm (2001): 36.
7 Cf. Taylor (2003).
8 Cf. ibid., 'Introduction', n.p.
9 Kemp (2010): 24.
10 Nussbaum (2001): 317.
11 Ibid.
12 Neumann and Nünning (2008): 8.
13 Cf. Butler (2009).
14 Cited in the documentary film, *Anfang aus dem Ende: Die Generation der Flakhelfer*, directed by Aleida Assmann (Assmann Filmproduktion, Germany, 2013).
15 Cf. Landsberg (2004).
16 Landsberg (2009): 223.
17 Ibid.: 227.
18 Ibid.: 228.
19 Cited in a film by WDR that was broadcast on 20 April 2012.
20 Cited in *FAZ*, No. 42, 19 February 2013.
21 The citations here come from a short project description, and I thank the artists for supplying the documents.
22 Citation from the exhibition: Helena Schätzle, Lisa Kellermann and Antonia Heyn, *Augenzu*, Fotomotel Kassel, June–September 2012.
23 Emcke (2014): 3.

References

Benjamin, Walter ([1933] 2005), 'On the Mimetic Faculty', in *Walter Benjamin: Selected Writings*, edited by Michael W. Jennings, Howard Eiland and Gary Smith, Vol. 2, Part 2: 1931–1934, Cambridge, MA and London: Harvard University Press: 719–22.

Butler, Judith (2009), *Frames of War: When is Life Grievable?*, New York: Verso.

Emcke, Carolin (2014), 'Von draußen betrachtet', *Süddeutsche Zeitung*, 27–28 December.

Foucault, Michel (1974), *The Order of Things: An Archeology of the Human Sciences*, New York: Vintage.

Fromm, Waldemar (2001), 'Die Sympathie des Zeichens mit dem Bezeichneten: Ähnlichkeit in Literatur und Sprachästhetik um 1800', in Gerald Funk, Gert Mattenklott and Michael Pauen, eds, *Ästhetik des Ähnlichen: Zur Poetik und Kunstphilosophie der Moderne*, Frankfurt am Main: Fischer: 35–68.

Funk, Gerald, Gert Mattenklott and Michael Pauen (2001), 'Einleitung: Symbole und Signaturen: Charakteristik und Geschichte des Ähnlichkeitsdenkens', in Gerald Funk, Gert Mattenklott and Michael Pauen, eds, *Ästhetik des Ähnlichen: Zur Poetik und Kunstphilosophie der Moderne*, Frankfurt am Main: Fischer: 7–34.

Kemp, Wolfgang (2010), *Foreign Affairs: Die Abenteuer einiger Engländer in Deutschland 1900–1947*, München: Hanser.

Landsberg, Alison (2004), *Prosthetic Memory: The Transformation of American Remembrance in the Age of Mass Culture*, New York: Columbia University Press.

——— (2009), 'Memory, Empathy, and the Politics of Identification', *International Journal of Politics, Culture, and Society*, 22 (2): 221–29.

Neumann, Birgit and Ansgar Nünning (2008), *An Introduction to the Study of Narrative Fiction*, Stuttgart: Klett.

Nussbaum, Martha (2001), *Upheavals of Thought: The Intelligence of Emotions*, Princeton, NJ: Princeton University Press.

Taylor, Diana (2003), *The Archive and the Repertoire: Performing Cultural Memory in the Americas*, Durham, NC and London: Duke University Press.

Valéry, Paul (1989), *Cahiers/Hefte*, Vol. III, edited and with an introduction and comments by Hartmut Köhler and Jürgen Schmidt-Radefeldt, Frankfurt am Main: Fischer.

Places of Similarity

Literary negotiations in bourgeois realism[1]

Dorothee Kimmich

Introduction

Thinking in categories of 'similarity' is by no means an absolutely new idea, and it is clearly not a concept without pre-existing connotations. Still, this tradition has yet to be fully accounted for in current discussions surrounding concepts of culture, interculturality or transculturality. 'Similarity' is thus not introduced here as a new paradigm but rather as an innovative concept for further research. To begin with, I will draw on a few arguments from Bruno Latour, and then expand my reflections based on authors from classical modernism including Sigmund Freud, Georg Simmel and Aby Warburg. Finally, I will incorporate literary examples from works that I consider to be foundational texts of bourgeois modernism: novellas by Gottfried Kellner and Adalbert Stifter.

Bruno Latour's scientific and historically based revision of modernity makes it clear that scientific paradigms alone are not sufficient to explain modern thinking, even if most self-descriptions of modernity suggest that this is the case. 'We have never been modern' is a title that has become something like a slogan.[2] Latour's thesis – that modernity never really established itself, and that the differentiation between modern and pre-modern cultures was nothing but a delusion of modernity – is based on his analysis of the main heuristic 'divisions' described by modern science. The distinctions between nature and society, subject and object, human and machine lead to a number of false conclusions, a direct consequence of which is the mis-diagnosis of an end to history and the end of metaphysics.

In contrast, Latour has described modernization as a significantly more complex process of the differentiation of discourses. Surprisingly enough, this differentiation works not only according to a model of difference, but also using a model of similarity. This is especially true for the relationship between people and objects.[3] With his concept of 'hybrid' things Latour provides a significant philosophical impulse for a new approach towards the question of living things in modernity. For him, modernity is not exclusively the consequence and result of scientific evolution; quite the contrary, scientific epistemology is but *one* aspect of modernity. Beyond that he considers other epistemological constellations to be conceivable (including epistemologies of similarity) that have long been latent but never completely obsolete. To a certain extent this connects Latour's reflections with Michel Foucault's characterization of similarity as a pre-modern epistemology. Still, Latour's observations and theses go beyond Foucault's.[4]

It is clear that Latour has sought to present a revised 'order of things' and to 'rehabilitate' similarity with the help of contemporary observations. Modern cultural theories (and cultural anthropology in particular) have developed approaches that avoid describing the relationship between modernity, imagination and magic, nature and culture, people and things as dichotomies. Instead, such approaches seek to suitably describe the complexities of the relationships between these phenomena.

The Magic of Modernity

Latour was not the first theoretician to think along these lines. If we concentrate on early modern thinkers up to 1930, we find similar theories regarding the anthropological study of magic practices. For one important example we can look at the prominent function that magic, animism and the so-called 'omnipotence of thoughts' had in Sigmund Freud's theory of culture. In *Totem and Taboo*,[5] for instance, Freud reminds his readers that the practical desire to control the world is understood by some as 'magic' and by others as the foundation of culture or of mechanization. 'I should prefer', he noted critically, 'to regard them [sorcery and magic] as technique.'[6] In making such comparisons, Freud referred to existing ethnological research, and in particular cited the work of James G. Frazer, who described the empowerment of the world and nature as the performance of 'similar gestures', as 'imitative' or even 'homeopathic' magic.[7] This meant that magic functioned according to the principle of *Similia similibus curant.*[8] As a result he reduced magic to laws of the association of ideas and specifically to the fundamental rules of combination: similarity – and thus analogy, and contact – and thus contiguity.

Aby Warburg followed a very similar approach to the cultural comparison and reconciliation of modern concepts in his book on the 'Serpent Ritual', which can also be described as a form of 'homeopathic magic': 'This synchrony [*Nebeneinander*] of fantastic magic and sober purposiveness appears as the symptom of a cleavage; for the Indian is not schizoid but, rather, a liberating experience of the boundless communicability between man and environment.'[9]

Warburg's comments that the ritual represents a form of 'danced causality'[10] emphasize the similarity between modern technical and pre-modern magical practices in the same way as Freud – who did not fundamentally differentiate between magic and technology in the field of cultural analysis. Freud also connected magic with the principles of association; for him there was a magic of imitation as well as a magic of contact, participation or contiguity. The manner in which magic was transmitted did not take place according to a principle of causality but rather by association. According to Freud it was striking that 'the two principles of association – similarity and contiguity – are both included in the more comprehensive concept of "contact". Association by contiguity is contact in the literal sense; association by similarity is contact in the metaphorical sense.'[11]

Reading this passage today provides us with a specific, methodologically distinct connotation of Freudian teachings about association, than that which emerged from his contemporary surroundings. Within the field of linguistics, association through (a) similarity or (b) participation is represented by the function of metaphor. The fact that Freud did not have a theory of metaphor at his disposal may also be the reason why his considerations in *Totem and Taboo* regarding the connection between association, similarity, contiguity and art are somewhat too simple and not very convincing. What is lacking is a complex theory of metaphors, or even a 'Theory of Non-Conceptuality' ('*Unbegrifflichkeit*'), as proposed by Hans Blumenberg.[12] Blumenberg's theory is not about the illustrative emphasis of provisionally vague forms of speech, but rather about the genuine and untranslatable epistemological function of metaphoric speech. Here more research is needed: the theory of non-conceptuality seems to be an answer to a proposition made by early culture theory that pointed to a specific continuity between the first and a newer form of modernity. The concept of 'similarity' plays a central role in such discussions on many levels.

Freud, Frazer and Warburg – like Franz Kafka, Alfred Polgar, Maurice Merleau-Ponty, Francis Ponge, Latour and Blumenberg – were obviously not naïve devotees of magical practices, nor did they believe in ghosts or promote homeopathic medicine. But they did emphasize the insecurity and fragility of modern explanations of the world. Causality, natural laws, technology and the use of tools seemed to offer only a superficial security, and caution (or better, prudence) called for such developments to be supported by other practices – including thinking in categories of similarity. This would also allow one to assert – as Latour has – that modernity and non-modernity are not categorically distinct from one another, but rather are more or less different and more or less similar.

All of these authors were thus interested in identifying relevant traces of pre-modernism in modernity. In other words, they were interested in the Latourian question of how modern we actually are. To put it yet another way, these authors were concerned with the radical question of whether we even *should be* as modern as we claim to be, and whether the line between 'modern' and 'non-modern' might not be more fluid than we assume. Similarity plays an important role in such considerations in two ways: there is more similarity between 'modern' and 'non-modern' than previously assumed, and this similarity is found in exactly the sense of what we can call 'thinking in similarities'. This is why the works of these authors always included a critical examination of their own cultures alongside their descriptions of foreign cultural conditions. The implicit questioning behind such examinations applied to the practical, scientific and even ethical potential of the modern interpretation of the world.

Let us briefly summarize: the authors named above all reflect on similarity and its connections to fundamental questions regarding the modern interpretation of the world. Within such reflections, similarity is initially considered to be a criterion of pre-modern thinking and magical practices. Upon closer inspection, however, it becomes clear that their actual interest was much more focused on the remnants of such thinking and such practices within the modernist and the modern *episteme*. We can conclude that these authors had the impression that modernity – and above all, an interpretation of the world based on causality – does not cover all phenomena, among them the centrally important relationship between man and his things. In the works named above, we find indications that thinking in similarities is associated with a certain kind of knowledge that we can describe today with Blumenberg's theory of non-conceptuality and the metaphorical. This is a knowledge that seems to be simultaneously precise and diffuse, foreign and familiar, traditional and contemporary, and immediate but non-conceptual.

This characterization demonstrates that thinking about similarities has a certain function or is suitable for specific communicative situations. My estimation is that it is a concept or way of thinking that is intended to be used in situations in which understanding (or better, 'hermeneutic' understanding) breaks down; that it enables communication in situations where communication cannot usually take place. To put it another way: I think that considerations of similarity are not about describing how others – the foreign, the non-modern, the 'primitives' – think, but rather how one would have to think and act in order to communicate with the other – with the neurotic, the insane, or even with things, the 'wild' and with children. The specific potential of thinking in similarities can be seen in areas that deal with the foreign – the historically, culturally, biographically, sexually or normatively foreign.

In the No Man's Land of Similarities

This leads us to the question of how the communicative practice of similarities can structure and influence our handling of the foreign. To answer this question, I fall back on and link together two works by Georg Simmel. The insights gleaned from this synthesis will allow me to show how similarity is modelled in literature while simultaneously functioning as aesthetic self-commentary, using examples by Gottfried Keller and Adalbert Stifter.

Both Simmel's 'On the Spatial Projections of Social Forms' (1903)[13] and his 'Excursus on the Stranger' (1908)[14] deal with space and the foreign. According to him the foreign is that which 'comes today and stays tomorrow';[15] that is, that which becomes a part of the community. The tension-filled unity of proximity and remoteness generated by such processes determines the relationship between the foreign and the non-foreign. This relationship is a 'form of interaction'.[16] In Simmel's case, the foreigners were mostly traders, and they were often Jews. Foreigners are not typical 'land owners' and do not have a fixed location in space. Particularly important for Simmel was the objectivity that foreigners could develop regarding their relationships with non-foreigners: 'Objectivity can also be called freedom: The objective person is bound by no commitments that could prejudice the grasp, the understanding, and the evaluation of data.'[17] In this sense, foreignness – which parallels Siegfried Kracauer's concept of 'extraterritoriality' – is assigned an existential status that includes both moral and scientifically ethical aspects. To a certain extent it transforms the foreign from a pariah to a 'hero'.

In the final section of his essay, 'On the Spatial Projections of Social Forms', Simmel develops the idea that this status of foreignness is not merely reserved for migrants, but rather shapes a space in which *everyone* is foreign, thereby shifting the economy of proximity and remoteness. Initially, Simmel's considerations deal concretely with no man's lands, geographic buffer zones that are created in order to protect a country's territory. In addition to creating protection through separation, such areas also represent zones of neutrality and objectivity in which meetings take place that could not happen anywhere else:

> An unforeseeable number of examples show us areas where commerce, meetings, and material contacts of the kind possible between opposed

> parties, so that the conflict does not come to words, without having to give up the conflict, so that one in fact goes out from the border that otherwise separates us from the opponent, but without crossing over into it, but rather remains beyond this separation.[18]

Significant here is the formulation that one can temporarily remain beyond the division between 'self' (in the sense of inherent or innate) and 'foreign' (in the sense of alien or other), and that doing so allows for the suspension of certain conflicts, disputes and hostilities. This creates the conditions for a temporary 'contact' that does not require understanding. Such contact can obviously take place when trading with outsiders, but Simmel also sees other spaces – both in the concrete sense of specific buildings as well as in a figurative sense – where contact can occur: in social spheres, in churches, in art and in science. Universities, for instance, are thus not only places for research, but also Simmelian 'no man's lands': places for the social negotiation of differences and similarities between groups and individuals who might be hostile to one another in everyday, extramural life.

Still, it would be premature to call this space 'beyond division', this societal no man's land, a 'heterotopia'. Simmel defined his concept much more narrowly and precisely than did Foucault. This space is also not one in which the Habermassian idea of domination-free discourse can finally be realized. Simmel's concept is much more modest: it is not about principles, but rather about the partial and temporary suspension of principles. It is specifically *not* about understanding one another but about communicating with one another. It is thus, in my opinion, more of an anti-hermeneutic concept than a hermeneutic one: the foreign remains the foreign. It is not about the interpretation, recognition or comprehension and understanding of the other, but much more about the alignment of interests, the preservation of distance, about civility, negotiation, and the partial, pragmatic completion of specific goals. As Simmel put it, it is about the practical exploitation of the neutrality of the space.[19] As a result, it would be self-defeating to work with criteria of 'self' and 'foreign'; instead, those in spaces 'beyond division' must learn to think in similarities rather than in identities and differences.

In the following section, I will use literary examples to further illustrate and flesh out questions regarding the function of no man's lands. In doing so I by no means seek to deny the fact that Simmel seemed to be sceptical and somewhat defensive of his own observations. For this reason, it may be helpful to extend Simmel's approach with the help of Gabriel Tarde's theory of imitation. Tarde's theory is not just a model of conflict avoidance, but rather a concept that can be used to describe social and cultural progress according to terms described by a 'theory of the practice of similarities'. In the second chapter ('Social Resemblances and Imitation') of his *The Laws of Imitation* (1885) Tarde develops a sociology based on the measurability and descriptiveness of imitation, variation and difference.[20] Imitation and variation lead to the gradual breakdown of differences, or, more specifically, to cultural and social similarities. At the same time, many of Tarde's observations on cultural evolution deal with spatial concepts of proximity and distance, and thus parallel Simmel's spatial theory in this respect as well.

Bourgeois No Man's Lands

Two canonical works of realism will serve as literary examples: Gottfried Keller's *Romeo und Julia auf dem Dorfe* (*Romeo and Juliet of the Village*, 1856)[21] and Adalbert Stifter's *Katzensilber* (*Muscovite*, 1853).[22] Both novellas deal with commonplace catastrophes. Keller's story is about the downfall of two families that are both wealthy and friendly with one another initially, but are destroyed by bitter hostility, insanity, alcoholism, financial ruin and, in the end, the deaths of their children. Stifter's work is somewhat more pleasant, and describes both a hailstorm and a conflagration in which nobody is hurt because a magical and maidenly saviour takes timely action and saves the potential victims.

A central theme of both texts is contact with the foreign or, more specifically, foreigners. Keller's story deals with the so-called 'black fiddler', a homeless musician who is unable to assert his rights over a piece of land because the town's citizens refuse to acknowledge his citizenship. For Stifter, the foreign is represented by the family-less and also clearly homeless 'brown girl' who is the saviour of the story, but who also represents a challenge to peace in the family.[23]

If we did not know better, we might think that Gottfried Keller wrote the beginning of his novella expressly in order to illustrate Gabriel Tarde's theories of imitation and similarity. The farmers Manz and Marti both plough their lands next to one another at the same time and in the same rhythm, they take their breaks together, and their children Vrenchen and Sali bring their meals together on the same cart. Social life seems to have a natural order. The only tiny variation that enters into this analogy comes at the moment when Manz uses his plough to work the piece of land between the two farmers, a no man's land that stands between their fields. To a certain extent this is merely a genuine depiction of cultivating fallow land, and, in principle, this is the sort of variation that breaks up uniformity to make way for progress. In this case, however, the act of cultivation also represents a crime of theft: as both farmers know, the land actually belongs to the black fiddler. The fiddler is a typical example of Georg Simmel's stranger who comes today and stays tomorrow: he is homeless and without rights, and is described as a gypsy or a Jew.[24] He lives in a world that is not completely foreign and is ultimately not that far away (namely, just outside the village) – a world analogous to that of the farmers and citizens (families live there but with unmarried partners, they have celebrations but with different music, etc.).

It seems that as long as the world of Manz and Marti contains this empty, desolate space, this no man's land (in which the children also play extremely Freudian doctor games and organize animistic rituals), the sensible balance between the foreign and the native is maintained despite all the injustice, the mutual contempt and social tensions between them. But the moment that 'culture', the plough, the furrow and the 'line' begin to appropriate the space and all of the knowledge and conduct within it,[25] both families begin a decline into madness, obsession and delusion, because they immediately start fighting over the piece of land.

It is clear that this plot is about the appropriation of space, about cultivation in the original sense of the word, about colonialization and the occupation of land. It addresses the question of how one should deal with foreigners who stay but do not settle down. The answer is that they require both a real and a symbolic space, and that this space should remain foreign and empty. It is precisely this no man's land that upholds the idea of potential communication, and it is the greed and brutality of the Swiss farmers (who consider their version of the world to be the only true one) that ultimately destroys both these 'margins' and themselves.

Like in almost all of his works, Stifter's story is also about the cultivation of space, the reclamation of space by nature and the question of how cultivated nature itself is.[26] On the first page of *Katzensilber*[27] we read a long-winded and detailed description of an estate in the mountains, of the construction of different greenhouses, the grafting of fruit trees, of terrace complexes and windscreens, etc. This is contrasted by the description of the wild mountain landscape surrounding the estate. Not only is it dangerous, it is above all the setting for the terrifying legends and tales that the grandmother tells her three grandchildren on their walks through the mountains. We are thus presented with two different versions of nature: that of the children's father and that of their grandmother.

One day while walking in the mountains they meet a 'nut brown' girl wearing boys' clothing who can't talk and who keeps her distance. The next forty pages describe the gradual process by which the child grows closer to the family: step by step, as it were, word by word and piece by piece of clothing, until in the end she lives with the family as an adopted child. Various members of the family react in similar but distinct ways – from the awestruck passivity of the grandmother to the rationally driven actions of the father. After initial failure, the mother successfully develops a practical way to deal with the girl by dressing her like the oldest daughter and treating her like just another of her children. In doing so the mother imitates the way the children act, but uses it for the purposes of education.

This process of assimilation is interrupted by two events. First, the girl saves the children and their grandmother from a hailstorm by constructing a shelter from tree branches, and then she saves their younger brother from a burning house. In both cases the grandmother is at fault: in the first, she does not turn back towards the estate early enough; in the second, she locks the door of the children's room because she is afraid of thieves. This shows how the grandmother's magical world-view is not to be relied upon. But the father's attempt to build a shelter in the forest after the storm also ends in disappointment: it quickly starts to bore the children. Similarly, there is a new danger: a fire that breaks out right in the middle of the estate just at the moment he is away. When faced with the contingency of natural phenomena, the rational measures taken by the cultivator of nature seem just as naïve as the grandmother's prayers. This is also made clear by the father's failed attempts to locate the nut brown girl's family or parents. Thus, when it comes to nature, both fully irrational and fully rational approaches represent extremes, and neither leads to success. And both make the mistake of not – at least to a certain extent – accepting nature as foreign. On the one hand, nature is demonized; on the other, it is minimized by technical cultivation. The story also illustrates a positive model of dealing with nature: namely, the playful assimilation of the children. The lengthy process of coming together, the practice of gradual and mutual familiarization, and the silent communication using gestures and especially food require a reciprocal respect that never goes beyond the boundaries of the possible: the children do not consider allowing the girl into the house or allowing her to spend the night, for instance, until the very end of the story. The story continually alludes to this feeling of distance and of abstinence, not only when it comes to questions of the girl's background and her family, but also particularly regarding the risk of getting too attached. The children become very devoted to the nut brown girl – perhaps because they foresee that she will not stay forever.

The conclusion of the story comes as a surprise. At the precise moment when the children become adults – or better, when the girls become young, sexually mature women – something happens: 'a call' rings out from the forest (an event that had been described earlier in one of the grandmother's stories),[28] the nut brown girl begins to cry (as had the woman in the grandmother's tale) and then she disappears. 'The stubborn landslide is dead, the high cliff is dead',[29] the girl cries and walks away, never to be seen again. She too is one of Simmel's foreigners who comes and stays – and might leave again. The 'wound' left by her departure becomes 'ever hotter' as the years pass.[30]

It is clear that this story describes contact with the foreign on multiple levels, and that the relationship between nature and culture represents but one sub-group of the dichotomy between 'self' and 'foreign'. It is important to note that the various types of differentiation are not presented as strict extremes, but are rather described as transitions, shades of grey, intermediate stages. Just as the story presents many other intermediate forms of dealing with nature between the extremes of the grandmother and the father, so too is the nut brown girl described in different passages as more foreign or more familiar, as more a boy or more a girl, as more wild or more belonging. The mother learns by imitating the children, the children learn by imitating the girl, and the girl even learns to read and write by imitating the other children. Imitation, similarity and variation thus represent a model of (relatively) stable development.

What remains taboo are elements such as past and future, beginning and end: the girl's original family remains unknown, and when she becomes old enough to marry, she is forced to disappear. She is barred from settling down, and she leaves longing in her wake. Contact with the foreign is described as a trip through no man's land, as the cautious crossing of thresholds and as the construction of transitional zones. As soon as these zones become fixed – for instance, through marriage – the verdict of division takes hold. Thus, in contrast to most interpretations, I would say that the estate as a whole, with all of its inhabitants and its surrounding areas, by all means represents a successful experiment as a no man's land – at least until the threat of marriage and irrevocable settledness emerges.

What remains is the following conclusion: reflections on similarity are embedded in the discourse of modernity, present in the writings of Latour, Warburg, Freud, Simmel and Frazer, and also found in bourgeois realist works. Considerations of similarity represent a central argument of modernist self-reflection, and are thus an important counterpoint to the dialectical model of the enlightenment.

Notes

1 An earlier version of this essay was published as 'Gefährliche Nachbarschaften: Bürgerliche Grenzwüsten bei Stifter und Keller'; see Kimmich (2012) .

2 Latour (1993).

3 Cf. Kimmich (2011).

[4] Cf. Foucault (1994): 46.
[5] Freud ([1913] 2001).
[6] Ibid.: 91.
[7] Ibid.: 81.
[8] Cf. Harmening (2005): 285.
[9] Warburg (1992): 10. The translation is taken from Steinberg (1997): 99.
[10] Ibid.: 54. Cf. Schüttpelz (2005).
[11] Freud ([1913] 1944): 99 ; emphasis in the German original.
[12] Blumenberg (2007).
[13] Simmel (1995). The translations quoted in my essay are taken from a revised version integrated into 'Excursus on the Stranger', in Simmel (2009).
[14] Simmel (2009).
[15] Ibid.: 601.
[16] Ibid.
[17] Ibid.: 602.
[18] Ibid.: 620; my emphasis – cf. the concept of contiguity.
[19] Cf. ibid.: 218.
[20] Tarde (1903): especially 46. Cf. Latour and Lépinay (2009): especially 17.
[21] Keller (1919). See also Fetscher (2010); Hahn *et al.*, eds (2007); Harnisch (1994); Holmes (1991); Honold (2004); Swales (1994); Titzmann (2002).
[22] Stifter (1982). See also Begemann (1995; 2007); Berger (1996); Blasberg (1998); Brüning (2005); Doppler (2007); Federmair (2005); Geulen (1992); Grätz (2006); Hillebrand (1971); Irmscher (1971); Hunfeld (2008); Lachinger, ed. (2004); Lachinger, ed. (2005); Laufhütte (2006); Öhlschläger (2009).
[23] Stifter (1982): 258.
[24] Cf. Uerlings (2007a; 2007b).
[25] Cf. Keller (1919): 212f.
[26] Cf. Plumpe (1984); Preisendanz (1966); Ragg-Kirkby (1999; 2000); Schiffermüller (2001); Sebald (1994).
[27] Cf. Uhde (2004); Halse (2008); Kugler (2007); Pintar (2005); Vogel (2008).
[28] Cf. Stifter (1982): 248.
[29] Ibid.: 313.
[30] Ibid.: 315.

References

Begemann, Christian (1995), *Die Welt der Zeichen: Stifter-Lektüren*, Stuttgart, Weimar: Metzler.

——— (2007), 'Adalbert Stifter und die Ordnung des Wirklichen', in *Realismus: Epoche–Werke–Autoren*, Darmstadt: WBG: 63–84.

Berger, Christian-Paul (1996), '. . . welch ein wundervoller Sternenhimmel in meinem Herzen . . .', in *Adalbert Stifters Bild vom Kosmos*, Wien: Böhlau.

Blasberg, Cornelia (1998), *Erschriebene Tradition: Adalbert Stifter oder das Erzählen im Zeichen ver- lorener Geschichten*, Freiburg: Rombach.

Blumenberg, Hans (2007), *Theorie der Unbegrifflichkeit*, Frankfurt am Main: Suhrkamp.

Brüning, Ludger (2005), *Wirklichkeit als literarisches Problem: Voraussetzungen und Formen des Erzählens bei Adalbert Stifter*, Münster: Telos.

Doppler, Alfred (2007), *Stifter und Stifterforschung im 21: Jahrhundert. Biographie–Wissenschaft–Poetik*, Tübingen: Niemeyer.

Federmair, Leopold (2005), *Adalbert Stifter und die Freuden der Bigotterie*, Salzburg, Wien: Müller.

Fetscher, Justus (2010), 'Neutralität: Eine sachliche Lektüre von Gottfried Keller's "Romeo und Julia auf dem Dorfe"', *Zeitschrift für Religions-und Geistesgeschichte*, 62 (2): 125–41.

Foucault, Michel (1994), *The Order of Things: An Archeology of the Human Sciences*, New York: Vintage.

Freud, Sigmund ([1913] 1944), *Totem und Tabu: Einige Übereinstimmungen im Seelenleben der Wilden und der Neurotiker*, in Ders., *Gesammelte Werke in Einzelbänden*, Bd. 9, hg. von Anna Freud, Edward Bibrig und Ernst Kris, Frankfurt am Main: Fischer.

Freud, Sigmund ([1913] 2001), *Totem and Taboo: Resemblances between the Mental Lives of Savages and Neurotics*, New York: Routledge.

Geulen, Eva (1992), *Worthörig wider Willen: Darstellungsproblematik und Sprachreflexion in der Prosa Adalbert Stifters*, München: Iudicium.

Grätz, Katharina (2006), *Musealer Historismus: Die Gegenwart des Vergangenen bei Stifter, Keller und Raabe*, Heidelberg: Winter.

Hahn, Hans-Joachim *et al.*, eds (2007), *Romeo und Julia auf dem Dorfe: Kritische Studien*, Bern: Lang.

Halse, Sven (2008), 'Begegnungen mit "dem großen Anderen": Fremderfahrung und kulturelle Identität in Stifter's "Bunten Steinen"', *Stifter-Jahrbuch*, 15: 9–22.

Harmening, Dieter (2005), *Wörterbuch des Aberglaubens*, Stuttgart: Reclam.

Harnisch, Antje (1994), *Keller, Fontane, Raabe: Geschlechter, Sexualität und Familie im bürgerlichen Realismus*, Frankfurt am Main: Lang.

Hillebrand, Bruno (1971), *Mensch und Raum im Roman: Studien zu Keller, Stifter, Fontane*, München: Winkler.

Holmes, Terence M. (1991), '"Romeo und Julia auf dem Dorfe": The Idyll of Possessive Individualism', in John L. Flood and Martin Swales, eds, *Gottfried Keller 1819–1890: London Symposium 1990*, Stuttgarter Arbeiten zur Germanistik, No. 256, Stuttgart: Heinz.

Honold, Alexander (2004), 'Vermittlung und Verwilderung: Gottfried Keller's "Romeo und Julia auf dem Dorfe"', *Deutsche Vierteljahrsschrift für Literaturwissenschaft und Geistesgeschichte*, 78 (3): 459–81.

Hunfeld, Barbara (2008), 'Zeichen als Dinge bei Stifter, Keller und Raabe: Ironisierung von Repräsentation als Selbstkritik des Realismus', in Sabine Schneider, ed., *Die Dinge und die Zeichen: Dimensionen des Realistischen in der Erzählliteratur des 19. Jahrhunderts*, Würzburg: Königshausen & Neumann.

Irmscher, Hans D. (1971), *Adalbert Stifter: Wirklichkeitserfahrung und gegenständliche Darstellung*, München: Fink.

Keller, Gottfried (1919), 'Romeo and Juliet of the Village', in *Seldwyla Folks: Three Singular Tales*, New York: Brentano's; available at www.archive.org, accessed 9 February 2017. German edition: 'Romeo und Julia auf dem Dorfe', in Ders., *Sämtliche Werke: Historisch-kritische Ausgabe*, Bd. 4: *Die Leute von Seldwyla*, Erster Band, hg. von Walter Morgenthaler, Basel u.a.: Stroemfeld u. Neue Zürcher Zeitung, [1856] 2000: 74–159.

Kimmich, Dorothee (2011), *Lebendige Dinge in der Moderne*, Konstanz: Konstanz University Press.

——— (2012), 'Gefährliche Nachbarschaften: Bürgerliche Grenzwüsten bei Stifter und Keller', in Sandra Evans and Schamma Schahadat, eds, *Nachbarschaft Räume Emotionen: Interdisziplinäre Beiträge zu einer sozialen Lebensform*, Bielefeld, transcript: 141–56.

Kugler, Stefani (2007), 'Katastrophale Ordnung: Natur und Kultur in Adalbert Stifter's Erzählung "Katzensilber"', in Kittstein and Kugler, eds, *Poetische Ordnungen*, Würzburg: Königshausen & Neuhausen.

Lachinger, Johann, ed. (2004), *Adalbert Stifter 2000: Grenzüberschreitungen*, Linz: Adalbert–Stifter–Institut des Landes Oberösterreich.

——, ed. (2005), *Sanfte Sensationen – Stifter 2005: Beiträge zum 200: Geburtstag Adalbert Stifters*, Linz: Stifter-Haus.

Latour, Bruno (1993), *We Have Never Been Modern*, Cambridge, MA: Harvard University Press.

Latour, Bruno and Vincent Lépinay (2009), *The Science of Passionate Interests*, Chicago: Prickly Paradigm Press; German edition: *Die Ökonomie als Wissenschaft der leidenschaftlichen Interessen*, Frankfurt am Main: Suhrkamp, 2010.

Laufhütte, Hartmut (2006), 'Harmoniemetaphern gegen das Chaos – Naturkonzepte und ihre Funktionalisierung bei Adalbert Stifter und Gottfried Keller', in Jattie Enklaar and Hans Ester, eds, *Geborgenheit und Gefährdung in der epischen und malerischen Welt Adalbert Stifters*, Würzburg: Königshausen & Neumann: 107–21.

Öhlschläger, Claudia (2009), '"Die Distanz bewohnen": Zur Ethik der Scham bei Adalbert Stifter', *Jahrbuch der Deutschen Schillergesellschaft*, Vol. 5: 226–42.

Pintar, Regina (2005), 'Die "Domestizierung" der Wildheit in Adalbert Stifters Erzählungen "Katzensilber" und "Der Waldbrunnen"', in Herwig Gottwald, Christian Schachenreiter and Werner Wintersteiner, eds, *Adalbert Stifter*, Innsbruck: Studien-Verlag.

Plumpe, Gerhard (1984), 'Zyklik als Anschauungsform historischer Zeit', in Jürgen Link and Wulf Wülfing, eds, *Bewegung und Stillstand in Metaphern und Mythen: Fallstudien zum Verhältnis von elementarem Wissen und Literatur im 19. Jahrhundert*, Stuttgart: Klett-Cotta: 201–22.

Preisendanz, Wolfgang (1966), 'Die Erzählfunktion der Naturdarstellung bei Stifter', *Wirkendes Wort*, 16: 407–18.

Ragg-Kirkby, Helena (1999), '"So ward die Wüste immer größer": Zones of Otherness in the Stories of Adalbert Stifter', *Forum for Modern Language Studies*, 35: 207–22.

—— (2000), '"Eine immerwährende Umwandlung der Ansichten": Narrators and Their Perspectives in the Works of Adalbert Stifter', *Modern Language Review*, Vol. 95: 127–43.

Schiffermüller, Isolde (2001), 'Die Provokation des Unzeitgemäßen: Adalbert Stifter in der sprachphilosophischen Diskussion der Moderne', in Maria Luisa Roli, ed., *Adalbert Stifter: Tra filologia e studi culturali*, Milano: CUEM.

Schüttpelz, Erhard (2005), *Die Moderne im Spiegel des Primitiven: Weltliteratur und Ethnologie 1870–1960*, München: Fink.

Sebald, Winfried G. (1994), *Die Beschreibung des Unglücks: Zur österreichischen Literatur von Stifter bis Handke*, Frankfurt am Main: Fischer.

Simmel, Georg (1995), 'Über räumliche Projektionen socialer Formen', in Rüdiger Kramme, Angelika Rammstedt and Otthein Rammstedt, eds, *Aufsätze und Abhandlungen 1901–1908*, Vol. I (Georg Simmel-Gesamtausgabe in 24 Bänden Bd. 7), Frankfurt am Main: Suhrkamp.

—— (2009), 'Excursus on the Stranger', in Anthony J. Blasi, Anton K. Jacobs and Mathew Kanjirathinkal, eds, *Sociology: Inquiries into the Construction of Social Forms*, Vol. 1, Leiden: Brill.

Steinberg, Michael P. (1997), 'Aby Warburg's Kreuzlingen Lecture: A Reading', in Aby Warburg and Michael P. Steinberg, *Images from the Region of the Pueblo Indians of North America*, Ithaca: Cornell University Press.

Stifter, Adalbert (1982), 'Katzensilber', in Helmut Bergner, ed., *Bunte Steine* (Journalfassungen),Werke und Briefe, Historiche-kritishe Gesamtausgabe, 2 (2), Stuttgart: Kohlhammer: 241–316.

Swales, Erika (1994), *The Poetics of Scepticism: Gottfried Keller and 'Die Leute von Seldwyla'*, Oxford: Berg Publishers.

Tarde, Gabriel (1903), *The Laws of Imitation*, New York: Holt and Company; available at archive.org, accessed 30 November 2016. French edition: *Les lois de l'imitation*, 1890.

Titzmann, Michael (2002), '"Natur" vs. "Kultur": Keller's "Romeo und Julia auf dem Dorfe" im Kontext der Konstituierung des frühen Realismus', in Michael Titzmann, ed., *Zwischen Goethezeit und Realismus: Wandel und Spezifik in der Phase des Biedermeier*, Studien und Texte zur Sozialgeschichte der Literatur, Vol. 92, Tübingen: Niemeyer: 441–80.

Uerlings, Herbert (2007a), '"Diesen sind wir entflohen, aber wie entfliehen wir uns selbst?": "Zigeuner", Heimat und Heimatlosigkeit in Keller's "Romeo und Julia auf dem Dorfe"', in Ulrich Kittstein and Stefani Kugler, eds, *Poetische Ordnungen: Zur Erzählprosa des deutschen Realismus*, Würzburg: Neumann & Königshausen: 157–85.

——— (2007b), 'Fremde Blicke: zur Repräsentation von "Zigeunern" in der Schweiz seit dem 19: Jahrhundert (Gottfried Keller, Carl Durheim, Mariella Mehr)', in George Guţu, Iulia-Karin Patrut and Herbert Uerlings, eds, *Fremde Arme – arme Fremde: 'Zigeuner' in Literaturen Mittel- und Osteuropas*, *GGR-Beiträge zur Germanistik*, Vol. 3/Inklusion, Exklusion, Vol. 3, Frankfurt am Main: Lang: 143–202.

Uhde, Milan (2004), 'Adalbert Stifter: Nachbarschaft, Zusammenhänge, Verfehlungen', in Johann Lachinger, ed., *Adalbert Stifter 2000 – 'Grenzüberschreitungen'*, Linz: Adalbert-Stifter-Institut des Landes Oberösterreich.

Vogel, Juliane (2008), 'Stifters Gitter: Poetologische Dimensionen einer Grenzfigur', in Sabine Schneider, ed., *Die Dinge und die Zeichen: Dimensionen des Realistischen in der Erzählliteratur des 19. Jahrhunderts*, Würzburg: Neumann & Königshausen.

Warburg, Aby (1992), *Schlangenritual: Ein Reisebericht*, Mit einem Nachwort von Ulrich Raulff, Berlin: Wagenbach.

Assimilation and *Circulation*

A nineteenth-century universalistic model of knowledge

Andreas Kilcher

Reading and Writing

In his *Notes for a Romantic Encyclopaedia* (the notorious *Das allgemeine Brouillon,* 1798/99 – a fragmentary outline for universal knowledge), Friedrich von Hardenberg developed a remarkable theory on reading and writing. Hardenberg, also known as 'Novalis', was the son of the manager of a salt mine and a student at the Bergakademie Freiberg. His model was significant at the time since it brought forth an innovative concept of knowledge that proved to be both intersubjective and dynamic, as reading and writing are two complementary operations of one and the same creative process. Deciphering the specific nature of the process was his primary aim, as he announced in his well-known outline: 'My book must contain the critical metaphysics of reviewing, of writing, of experimenting and observing, of reading, of speaking etc. Classification of all scientific operations.'[1]

Thus, reading *is* a scientific procedure that is both receptive and generative, and writing a process that is not only procreative but also inclined to receive and transform. Consequently, both reading and writing prove to be part of the same intellectual process of formation and transformation. With a terminology that oscillates between nature and culture, Novalis characterizes 'reading and working' ('*Lesen und Arbeiten*'), which to him are unique and '*truly acquired* occupations' ('*wahrhaft gelehrte Beschäftigung*'), as 'generative, and assimilative, of ideas' ('*Ideen produciren und Ideen assimiliren*').

The discourse about assimilation, which is partly literal and partly metaphorical, includes a physiological and an intellectual process of incorporation, of digestion (*Verdauung*) and burning (*Verbrennung*) – a multi-phase process in the course of which a new 'one's own' (*Eigenes*) is moulded out of matter that has been retrieved as a variant of a neo-Aristotelian hylomorphism.

'To devour is an assimilation process' ('*Alles Fressen ist ein*

Assimilationsprocess'), as Novalis claimed, and took care to illustrate further with the use of fire and water as examples. 'The flame is the voracious *kat exochin*' ('*Die Flamme ist das Gefräßige kat exochin*') and 'metals that oxidize water in turn also produce some' ('*Die Metalle, die Wasser zersetzen, componieren gewiss auch welches*'). To turn our discussion back from physics to the analogical 'metaphorical assimilation' ('*geistige Assimilation*'), we may claim that Novalis perceived reading and writing as involving a process of intellectual transformation as well as of digestion and assimilation. This analogy in part modifies the pre-modern method of perceiving reading as *ruminatio* (*Wiederkäuen*). In Novalis' view, reading and writing are combined in a single yet multi-shaped exchange process: 'The differently combined movements or operations of an author – reading – observing – everything is related to reflecting and writing.'[2] Reading and writing, mutually related intellectual techniques within assimilation, become, in other words, a *single* act of 'circulation'.

The circular interconnection of reading–writing – 'the art of reading [and] writing' ('*Kunst des Lesensand Schreibkunst*') – becomes the 'intertwining of production and knowledge'.[3] The process is rooted in the epistemic change that occurred around *c.* 1800. Indeed, during the Romantic Age one may observe a fundamental dynamization of knowledge in the very notion of knowledge: rational or empirical predefined objects yielded a collective objectification, i.e. a product with a historical index in society, language and culture. Static metaphysical constituents such as truth (*Wahrheit*), the world (*Welt*), reason (*Vernunft*), subject (*Subjekt*), origin (*Ursprung*), etc., which had managed eighteenth-century epistemes, gradually corroded.

The emergence of notions such as 'assimilation' and 'circulation' illustrate the multilayered dynamization of knowledge at the beginning of the nineteenth century, since they make reference to altered ideas of order and of the exchange (transfer) of knowledge. Destabilizing, relativizing and processual principles – like 'assimilation' and 'circulation' – emerged as new and versatile aspects of knowledge during the nineteenth century, in relation to three major defining features of the Enlightenment. The first, when Enlightenment devalued a non-original mimesis so as to aspire for originality and autonomy; the second, when Enlightenment considered man as the key actor of knowledge, i.e. knowledge as empirically experienceable or rationally justifiable; and third, the rise of notions such as 'assimilation' and 'circulation' which materialized when Enlightenment took as an exoteric basis both contingent signs and cultural systems of a non-motile and universal notion of reason.

Michel Foucault made the pre-moderns entirely responsible for the category of '*Ähnlichkeit*' or 'Similarity' in its more specific forms of analogy (*convenientia*) and sympathy (*aemulatio*). However, these very forms gained new meaning thanks to assimilation and transformation when, in 1800, knowledge shifted from static to dynamic parameters and thereon to forms of organization. This more general historical-epistemological tendency may be clearly exemplified by the dynamizing concept of *assimilatio* (or by the closely related concepts of similarity, analogy, imitation, repetition, transformation, etc.) as well as by the idea of the circulation of knowledge (generated by *assimilatio*'s notion of circulation) during the nineteenth century. These concepts illustrate that the areas of notions, concepts, figures and metaphors for dynamization are neither firmly established nor accurately defined; rather, they are in progress. In this respect, we might refer to a fluent language of circulation as it were, where mobility (as in compounds, analogies and transferences) is introduced performatively in language, or may also occur on the level of language. To that extent, not only should it be expected that its terminology spreads out to develop, but also that a *poiesis* of circulation arises.

This fundamental shift in the understanding of language and knowledge may be illustrated by two examples from the nineteenth century, however far apart they seem at first sight. Pursuing our preliminary reflections about reading and writing, we will first focus on Novalis' universal concept of science, and then turn to Gabriel Tarde and his *Les lois de l'imitation* (1890; *The Laws of Imitation*, 1903). In his treatise, Tarde delineates a general notional outline of society. Indeed, the intellectual contexts and theoretical profiles of the two works – one by Novalis and the other by Tarde, dating back to the early and late nineteenth century, respectively – are very different, especially with regard to the elaboration and arrangement of the subject. Nevertheless, after careful consideration on a more abstract level, the two prove to be comparable and hence mutually enlightening, namely, as dynamizing and universalizing models of knowledge. They share the notions of assimilation and circulation, which are fundamental means in both works to pursue the universalistic claim.

Novalis conceived circulation within the Romantic notion of complex and universal relation and analogy, according to which the most disparate things of the world and the most different areas of knowledge may be brought together in a comprehensive relationship. With Tarde, in turn, the figures of repetition, similarity and circulation become meaningful and gain their role within the liberalistic idea of a 'law of imitation' that is universally recognized, and that manages natural phenomena as well as the order and circulation of knowledge in society.

Inter-relations: Novalis

According to our preliminary observations, if reading and writing are not disjoined techniques to Novalis but belong to one and the same enclosing circulation, then it still remains to assert the legitimacy of circulation as a *scientific* procedure. In this view, the interest lies not in specific cultural procedures but rather on a fundamental aspect of a central epistemological draft – which may be shown *ex negativo* with Novalis' concept of reading and writing. His notion, in turn, also modifies the educational concept (*Bildungsbegriff*). Education is no longer last, as it was in the eighteenth century, in the humanism of the classics, the self-assertion of a responsible and thinking human being, or the unfolding (*Entfaltung*) and the development (*Entwicklung*) of the subject out of its own concealed, innate predisposition. Yet, if we make reference to Novalis' terminology and notions, Romantic education is rather an intersubjective exchange process, a co-philosophizing in dialogue, a merging, an inquiry by analogy, potentization, etc. An example is the educational programme that the teacher Jean Paul employs to teach Gustavus, his student, in Jean Paul Friedrich Richter's novel, *The Invisible Lodge* (*Die Unsichtbare Loge)* (1793):

> I accustomed my Gustavus to hear, to understand and thereby to invent for himself, analogies from different sciences, e.g. all things great or weighty move slowly; hence the Oriental Princes do not walk at all – nor the Dalai Lama; the Sun – the Sea-crab – wise Greeks (according to Winkelmann) walked slowly – so does the hour-hand – the ocean – the clouds in fair weather – move slowly. . . . It is indescribable what pliability of all ideas is thereby communicated to children's minds. Of course the various kinds of knowledge must be there first, which one would thus associate.[4]

As might be inferred from the above quotation, the Romantic theory of education asserts the transition towards a new way of thinking similarity, which employs assimilation as a procedure and strives after circulation as the effect of knowledge. Novalis drafted this model of education and knowledge in a vast number of corresponding concepts, notions and metaphors that bring forth the permeability of outside and inside, of the external, the foreign (reading) and the 'one's own'. At the very basis we discover the ground-breaking idea of a comprehensive 'sympathy of the universe' (*Sympathie des Weltalls*). Knowledge, therefore, is a complex network of inter-relations such as interconnection, interproduction, reciprocal representation and mutual saturation[5] – these comprise Novalis' idiosyncratic terminology of the appropriation and transformation process.

To Novalis, the combination of reading and writing in *one* single process of assimilation and transformation is not just one scientific operation among many others but, by and large, the leading process of his universal draft. Thereby, as opposed to Fichte, he conceived his project as an alternative (*Wissenschaftslehre*), an epistemology – the reductive, hierarchical, totalizing and static idealistic systematics of which is replaced by a non-hierarchical, non-linear, decentred knowledge order. The organization of knowledge touches upon various dynamizing processes, such as mixing, flow, combination, transformation and reciprocity. On a more general level of knowledge order, Novalis further introduces the notion of assimilation: 'A science gains through the devouring – through the assimilation of other sciences etc. Mathematics too, for example, gains through the devoured concept of the infinite.'[6]

The description of such dynamic inter-relationships (*Wechselverhältnisse*) among the sciences by the notion of assimilation as rooted in the life sciences is equally remarkable and needs further clarification; yet again, the very notion of life plays a crucial role in dynamization. A suggestion of the origin of Novalis' semantics of life and metabolism may be found in the essay 'Assimilatio' in Johann Heinrich Zedler's *Universal Lexicon of Sciences and Arts* (*Universal-Lexicon aller Wissenschaften und Künste* (*1731–1754*). Zedler's dissertation leads far back within the pre-modern period to Galenic humoral pathology, according to which the more similar a being is to the substance, the better the being may absorb it. Zedler defines the idea as follows:

> Assimilatio is an additive to, or the completion of, nourishment, if those who have a diet accordingly, are changed and those who are fed accordingly, are transformed in the very same nature (Galenus, de fac. Nat. I). In order for them to happen, adglutinatio, agglutination, or adaeratia, attachment must progress just like they lead the way to appositio, apposition (de fac. Nat. c. II).[7]

In 1800, Romantic life sciences as well as medicine – a fundamental component of Novalis' epistemology – integrated the pre-modern concept of assimilation. Christoph Wilhelm Hufeland, for instance, used assimilation as the basis for a form of '*Vitalismus*', by which nutrition gains a central place value. In his *System der practischen Heilkunde* (1800), Hufeland defines 'Assimilation' (a constituent of 'Nutrition') as an adaptation of substances within the absorbing body, which is accomplished 'gradually and by subsequent operations':[8]

> The being of assimilation consists of . . . a modifying mixture of the

> absorbed substance since only thereby it is possible to transform it. Assimilation has two conditions: 1) the assimilating requirement of the given substance. This has a double reference: a) to the chemical affinity with or analogy of the substance to the essence it should be transformed into . . . b) to the irritant force of the essence. The more it irritates the organs and forces (of necessary vital activities) to the act of assimilation, the easier and the more complete is assimilation. 2) The power of assimilation of the body, or the ability of the living body to give imparted substances the character of its individual organic nature.[9]

In his distinctly syncretistic (*synkretistischen*) draft of science, Novalis' life-scientific theorems and terms such as kinship (familial proximity), analogy, assimilation, transformation, mixture, etc., are not isolated cases. He transforms them figuratively to integrate them as constitutive elements of a dynamic model of knowledge that puts notions as well as entire sciences in relationships of exchange. This way, he infers them with a model function: namely, they are regarded as models of a processual organization of knowledge that is based on adaptation (*Assimilation*) and exchange (*Zirkulation*). Not only does this clarify the following thesis, that 'a science gains by devouring, by assimilating other sciences';[10] more significantly, Novalis reflects on and varies the principle of circulation through assimilation in manifold ways, and, more precisely, partly in theoretical and partly in metaphorical form. Analogous to the relation between reading and writing is the answer to how a system of one's own (*eigenes System*) is to be found, namely with the inclination (*Zueignung*) towards another:

> Theory of spiritual education. One studies foreign systems in order to find one's own system. A foreign system is the stimulus for one's own. I become conscious of my own philosophy, physics etc. – by becoming affected by a foreign one – provided of course I myself am sufficiently active. My philosophy or physics may now be in agreement or disagreement with the foreign one. In the first instance it exhibits homogeneity. . . . (Marriage of heterogeneous systems).[11]

Elsewhere again, Novalis attaches the idea of homogeneity (*Homogenëitaet*) to the circulation between the two notions (one's own/the foreign) by introducing the notion of assimilation once more:

> The question of the reasons and the laws of manifestation . . . is based on the affection for, the assimilation of the object. By explanation the object is no longer foreign. The spirit aspires to absorb the stimulus. That which is foreign stimulates the spirit. The transformation of the

> foreign in the one's own, natural affection is also a ceaseless dealing of the spirit. . . . Sciences dissolve in sciences.[12]

In contrast to Fichte, Novalis understands the sciences not as analytical structures of differences, but as both the unifying synthetic-analogical merging as well as the correlation of theories, terminologies, hypotheses, etc. In so doing, he does not formulate a local or specific thesis; rather, he posits the general dynamic, and, to some extent, the organic and vitalistic rationale of a new model of knowledge. Hence he sights 'a universal tendency of the assimilation of heterogeneity – the inter-transformation'.[13]

If the differential system of knowledge wears away analogies, similarities, inter-relations, combinations, etc., then, according to Novalis, we are left with composition and movement (*Bewegung*) alone. This additional central term of dynamization is echoed within a whole series of further notions and metaphors among which we may identify not only compounds such as movement-series, movement-mixtures and the discipline, the art of motion-transformation,[14] but also the analogies of 'vibration and *circulation*'. Broadly speaking, Novalis argues that with new variants and metaphors, the disposition of circulation, of reading and writing, as a scientific operation (*wissenschaftliche Operation*) is universal: it aims at an 'all-inclusive and universal eclecticism' ('*allumfassenden, universalen Eclecticism*'), at a conglomeration of 'ingenious associating disciplines' ('*genialen Verbindungslehren*'), thanks to the creation of even more heterogeneous inter-relations ('*Mischungsverhältnisse*').

Novalis posits 'mutual relationships – similarities – equalities – effects of the sciences'[15] as the real principles of a synthetic epistemology, as previously defined. Also, in this respect it becomes evident that the order and the inter-relations of knowledge are not guided by analytical operations such as differentiation, classification and systematization, but by synthetic procedures such as the assimilation and circulation of notions and images on the micro-level of knowledge and, owed to entire sciences, also on the macro-level of knowledge. The vanishing point of a similar circulation – that redefines boundaries – is the combinatory adaptation (*Anverwandlung*), respectively application (*Anwendung*) of all sciences and their application on everything: 'a science is accomplished 1. when it may be applied to everything, 2. when everything applies to it.'[16] This is – to put it differently – scientific organization as 'Vibration and *Circulation*'.

The growth of this logic of assimilation and circulation into a multitude of analogies and paradigms may be clarified by two examples that are indeed very different (wit and chemistry). Yet a closer look shows that wit and chemistry are strictly related. Wit (*Witz*) is the ingenious skill that brings together the heterogeneity of knowledge and thereby generates similarities (analogies), while chemistry (respectively alchemy) is the paradigm for the art to transform and to mix (*Mischungskunst*), which Novalis marks as leading. This becomes even clearer with the alternative notions Novalis holds in readiness to discuss Fichte: universal knowledge as 'a chemical scientific discipline' ('*eine chemische . . . W[issenschafts] L[ehre]*'). No matter whether it is rationalized as a mathematic art of combination, or aestheticized as a musical composition, or again, transformed as an (al)chemical combination, the guiding scientific operation of the 'art of mixing' ('*Mischungskunst*') is the interconnection among the heterogenic elements that reside in the compendium of knowledge: 'What inexhaustible quantity of materials for new individual combination is scattered around! Only someone who has discovered this secret – is in need of nothing else – except the decision to abnegate infinite diversity and its mere relish and to *begin* somewhere.'[17] Thus goes the maxim of the circulation of knowledge. Always in a new way, it tags along the 'analogical calculus'[18] that groups parts of knowledge in sections, and in this structure it leads from the foreign to the own just as from the known to the unknown: 'analogical analysis (the analysis, the art to find the familiar in the unknown)'.[19]

Wit (*der Witz*) – not as comic wit but as the technical procedure that is equivalently rhetoric and epistemological – follows precisely this type of analogical analysis. 'Wit is creative – it generates similarities.'[20] Wit, therefore, is not restricted to isolated analogies (such as the metaphor). It proves instead to be more a universal procedure of analogical combinations: in a potentially infinite progressive process of comparison, wit succeeds in integrating or similarizing that which is related just as that which is disparate. The universalizing and combinatory function of wit marks the crucial moment of a significant analogy: 'Wit as the principle of relations is likewise the *menstruum universale*. Wit's mixtures . . .'.[21] The discourse on the *menstruum universale* leads towards the alchemical interpretation of the assimilative art of mixture (*Mischungskunst*). The *menstruum*, a genuine alchemical *terminus technicus*, labels a means of mediation that may dissolve solid matter. In his *Curieusen und realen Natur-Kunst- Berg- Gewerck- und Handlungs-Lexicon* (1746) Johann Hübner defines *menstruum* as 'a juice that is a liquor or moisture opens up in a solid body, or is capable to draw virtue or power out of things'.[22] The *menstruum universale* is a universal solvent, and it has the mediating quality to integrate and connect *any* matter. Since Paracelsus, the most appropriate example for *menstruum universale* is the notorious solvent by George Starkey and Jean-Baptiste van Helmont, namely, the very substance that carries the humorous name Alkahest (a blend of alkali with alcohol, to Starkey a blend of fire with water, *ignis-aqua*). The solvent has the power to dissolve every other solid substance, including gold.

Novalis gives prominence to Alkahest in his novel, *The Novices of Sais* (*Die Lehrlinge zu Sais*); to the writer, the *menstruum universale* becomes a universal medium for the circulation of knowledge: thereby that which is shown with assimilation, was accomplished and set in 1800, primarily by natural phenomena, and became the paradigm for a new dynamized idea of the organization and circulation of knowledge. This may be emphasized with a short yet meaningful final case. Novalis himself makes his readers aware of its importance and it shows how the structure due to the *menstruum universale* is substantially analogous to the universal *medium* of circulation: (the theoretical) '*Fluidum*'. Franz Anton Mesmer, whom Novalis – among others – refers to, understood *Fluidum* as 'a widely spread and distinguished fluid which by its very nature has the ability to assimilate, communicate and reproduce every type of movement'.[23] Novalis has taken over the scientific hypothesis of circulation not only by acknowledging an 'absolutely elastic fluid' ('*absolut elastisches Fluidum*') that flows through the 'universe' ('*Weltall*'), but also by transferring the notion of a general 'fluidity' ('*Fluidität*') to the epistemological level of knowledge and language, when he acknowledges that it is the vowels in '*das elastische Fluidum*' that set the consonants in motion.

Among other things – with assimilation as the appropriation and the correlation of sciences, with wit as the *menstruum universale* of a universal mixture, with language as an '*elastischen Fluidum*' – a dynamic model of nature discloses in new variants. The model allows for the organization and allocation of knowledge to mutually prove an interminable process of new mixtures, similarities and effects of sciences. This way, with Novalis, the formal and functional possibilities of a universal concept of knowledge develop on the basis of the natural circulation phenomena. The concept rejects the encyclopaedia-based classification and rationalization of eighteenth-century sciences, as well as the totalizing system notion of idealism. Circulation – or the idiosyncratic terms motion, combination, mixture, change, comparison, etc. – all belong to Novalis' Romantic alternative model for an even more fragmentary and synthetic universalism. Novalis in turn programmatically evaluates their totality and complexity as 'Chaos' or 'Confusion' with an alchemical model of nature. Alternatively, he does the same as in '*Confusions System*', an alchemical notional wit-and-word-hybrid that is equal to the artfully coined 'Alkahest', as a chaotic abundance of circulating mixtures of world and knowledge constituents.

General Circulation: Tarde

It seems that the nineteenth-century history of science inhibits the relation between Novalis, the Romantic *Wissenspoet par excellance*, and the French lawyer, criminologist, sociologist and philosopher Gabriel Tarde. Novalis experimented with the sciences poetologically and within post-Enlightenment; Tarde developed a universal model of society by dealing with the dominant scientific paradigms of the nineteenth century such as Hegelianism, Darwinism, Positivism and Marxism. However, if Tarde's model of society by imitation should be set here in connection with Novalis' analogous-synthetic model of knowledge of inter-relations, as already mentioned in our initial reflections, it would mean far more than simply allowing heterogenous elements to follow each other. Therefore, it is neither a matter of suggesting a narrow genealogical correlation, nor an extensive systematic correlation. Both examples are mutually illuminating in their shared relation to a general model of knowledge of the nineteenth century, which abandons static as well as metaphysical constituents such as origin, identity, subjectivity, etc., for dynamic and procedural ideas of scientific organization and mediation.

Undoubtedly, there are other examples for the nineteenth century as well; however, the comparison between Novalis and Tarde is particularly illuminating since both envisage dynamization in relation to assimilation and to circulation. More specifically, they justify the circulation of knowledge with phenomena of assimilation, although the comparison may be traced quite differently. As a matter of fact, this connection becomes more evident with Tarde's concept of assimilation, which he outlines more sharply in his understanding of *imitation*. Whereas Novalis worked with an isolated notion of assimilation that took its origins from the natural sciences and was metaphorically transferred on to the organization of knowledge, Tarde amplified assimilation with the notion of *imitation* (similarity, repetition). He established it as a universal category of description and with it he described the fundamental phenomena of organic as well as inorganic nature and society. Tarde also established a corresponding distinctive concept of circulation upon this universalized notion of imitation; a concept that brings forth an idea of society that differs from Novalis' more specific model of knowledge.

Tarde's intellectual profile is in no way homogeneous. It dwells within the post-Romantic scientific discourse of the nineteenth century, discussing Hegel, Comte, Darwin, Spencer, Marx and Engels whenever the principle of imitation occupies centre stage of his universal and liberal theory of society. Especially the ideas of social organization that find their principle in Darwin play a crucial role for Tarde. Nevertheless he sets himself apart critically and in many ways from the preceding positions of the nineteenth century. As opposed to Comte, he does not focus on determination but rather on action; as opposed to Marxist determination, on individual parameters through economic relations (Hegel); against Spencer's biologistic social theory, he fosters imitation as technique for combination. Although Tarde makes reference especially to Spencer and despite his mention of the 'great struggle for existence that eradicates the less adapted',[24] his stance is far from Social Darwinian biologism. His interest lies not in Spencer's principle that pleads for the 'survival of the fittest' but rather opposite; he is more concerned with a varied and universal approximation, adaptation and agreement of individuals, societies and cultures.

According to Tarde, society is a dynamic structure of imitated ideas and actions. On the one hand invention and discovery, and on the other imitation become two complementary procedures. For the development of society imitation proves fundamental, as he argues in his work, *The Laws of Imitation* (*Les lois de l'imitation*, 1890), where the social finds its shortest definition, namely: 'society is imitation' ('*Gesellschaft ist Nachahmung*') or 'a social group is a group of individuals, who imitate each other for a period of time'.[25] The actual social performance is thereby an intelligence of imitation; it is guided by skills such as learning, acquisition, adaptation, or, according to Tarde's conception (that still needs explication): society 'assimilates by contagious imitation' ('*assimiler par contagion imitative*').[26] Thus Tarde regards imitation as a universal principle that may be identified in the biological sphere of life (e.g., as reproduction and inheritance), likewise in the physical and chemical appearance of nature (e.g., oscillation, radiation, waves) and in the societal sphere of the social (e.g., in education and science, but also in fashion). In all these areas Tarde observes the figure 'universal repetition' ('*universeller Wiederholung*' or '*répétition universelle*') of similarity; similitude (*des* '*Ähnlichen*'), whereby the French notion of similitude echoes the procedure of assimilation as 'make alike, make similar, similarize' ('*Ähnlichmachung*'). Tarde regards the alternative model, a mere causal mechanical world that 'embraces no similarity or repetition',[27] as 'a peculiar, yet in need as a clear hypothesis'.[28] In such a world there is one thing only that is impossible by all means, namely, science: 'Would any kind of science be possible? It would not be because, to reiterate, neither resemblances nor repetitions would be found there.'[29]

However, science knows no absolute emergence *ab initio*, no *arché*; science rather proposes an inevitable process of reproduction (*Reproduktion*): in the form of 'similitude and repetition of phenomena',[30] reproduction happens within heredity (in the organic field), fluctuation (in the field of physicalism) or, again, imitation (in the social field). In these three areas, Tarde monitors a multitude of forms of universal repetition, '*Formen der universellen Wiederholung*', that counter nature's necessity of causality with a flow of transformations, '*Strom von Veränderungen*', and likewise the static system, with the flexible universe of similarities. The imagery of liquefaction is symptomatic for a similar dynamization: not only does Tarde identify currents and rivers, '*Ströme . . . Flüsse*,' in physics, but he includes also the field of social deed 'where imitations form the streams' ('*wobei die Nachahmungen die Flüsse bilden*'). Alongside liquefactions, the equally forceful metaphors of radiance (*Ausstrahlung*), dilation (*Ausdehnung*) and contagion (*Ansteckung*) find their rightful place in the fluidity of the social and cultural model of the circulation of knowledge. Thus Tarde refers to the streams (*Nachahmungsflüssen*), rays (*Nachahmungsstrahlen*) and chains (*Nachahmungsketten*) of imitation alternatively, as well as to their extensions and intersections (*Ausdehnung* and *Kreuzungen*).

In Tarde's view, education and knowledge have always been products of social circulation. Not only does imitation mean that ideas and notions, just as acts, are imitated and assimilated, but it also suggests that allegedly new ideas fall into line with existing ones. Also, discoveries and inventions – that sit at the opposite pole to imitation – are structured: 'these combinations in turn are imitated and combined in new elements and more complex combinations, and it may be concluded that there is an evolutionary tree of such a successful initiative'.[31] The history of knowledge knows no grounded origins (*arché*) but is rather constituted by multiplication and diffusion due to contagion (*contagion imitative*):[32] 'This fund consists of a mass of ancient traditions and of experiences that are unorganized or that have been more or less organized and imitatively transmitted through language, the great vehicle of all imitations.'[33]

Language as the agent of imitation, as pointed out above, refers to a further crucial moment of Tarde's notion of circulation, namely, that the society of knowledge do not regard content and instruction as primary issues; rather, milieus occupy centre stage. Tarde distinguishes between the social, the ethnic and the physical spheres (*milieu social*, *milieu ethnique*, *milieu physique*) – all of which he understands according to Positivism. Yet milieus are also (to a certain extent) the cultural- and socio-technical mediation of knowledge. A milieu such as language is to him 'a sphere' ('*eine Sphäre*'), where an 'idea may be appropriately promulgated' ('*in der sich eine Idee verbreiten kann*') also through great distances and periods of time. This way, Tarde also transfers biological genetics on to the history of knowledge, since he understands such diffusion as reproduction (*Fortpflanzung*), as development, indeed as progress (*Fortschritt*). Reproduction and perfecting may happen at various speeds and intensities, namely, either nearly imperceptibly and 'slowly and gradually' ('*langsam und allmählich*') over a prolonged period of time ('*langer Dauer*'), or suddenly, shockingly, as a catastrophe with the power of 'a cyclone, epidemic or insurrection' ('*von einem Orkan, einer Epidemie und einem Aufstand*'):

> A cyclone whirls from neighbourhood to neighbourhood; none of its blast ever tears from it to leap over intervening space and carry its virus to a distance. An epidemic on the other hand rages in a zig-zag line; it may spare one house or village among many, and it strikes down almost simultaneously those which are far apart. An insurrection will spread still more freely from workshop to workshop, or from capital to capital. It may start from a telegraphic announcement.[34]

It is quite significant that in the idea of propagation of news telegraphy, a technical channel enters the stage. The circulation of knowledge is made comprehensible once more as a process of intermediation made possible by media such as language and telegraphy; it applies synchronically as well as to space, and likewise is valid diachronically and temporally. Not only are the history of knowledge, the history of ideas or the history of education the result of processes and techniques of the circulation of news, but so also essentially is the history of knowledge. Language and the technical medium of telegraphy also include physical media such as waves and currents or, again, biological media such as viruses (relating to the semantics of contagion or *Ansteckung*). This also implies that Tarde's notions of imitation and tradition are not understood as a manifestation of conservativism; on the contrary, they are parameters of a liberalistic idea of enclosing and trespassing media processes.

The circulation of knowledge stands out due to a universal tendency. As a matter of fact, the circulation of so-called currents of imitation is potentially unlimited along various forms of assimilation with regard to chronological and spatial views, as well as social and the cultural perspectives. Circulation aims for 'universal exchange' ('*universellen Austausch*' or 'échange universal'), for 'general circulation' ('*allgemeine Zirkulation*' or '*circulation general*'). The waves (*Wellen*) and the rays (*Strahlen*) of knowledge trespass boundaries across cultures. Moreover, boundaries are modified in their significance from obstacle (*Hindernis*) to the actual site of circulation, that is thereby understood as a diasporic non-place of passage, i.e. of transit:

> Men of different civilizations come into mutual contact on their respec-

> tive frontiers, where, independently of war or trade, they are naturally inclined to imitate one another. And so, without its being necessary for them to displace one another in the sense of checking the spread of one another's examples, they continually and over unlimited distances react upon one another. . . . Here we have the first principle of history. Let us note closely the continuity, the power and the irresistibility of its action. Given the necessary time, it will inevitably reach out to the ends of the earth.[35]

Tarde's model for the circulation of knowledge is associated with an idea of transculturality *avant la lettre*. As argued in his concepts, when circulation is universal it embraces all cultures. Furthermore, the way it dissolves old European ideas of origin and identity, the very same way it questions the 'inhabitants' of nations and their cultures.

A similar universalized theory of imitation is thereby open to the future in a non-teleological sense, and it opens into the 'mental image of unlimited progress' ('*Vorstellung vom unbegrenzten Fortschritt*'). In this vein, according to Tarde, the issue is less an intellectual image – such as the idea of a progressive rationality or freedom (as in Hegel's philosophy of history) – and more the focal point of a way of open social and cultural utopia: the circulation of knowledge connects humanity in an ever-increasing manner. Tarde conceives progress as imminent (despite his metaphor of the soul or *Seele*); that is to say, progress aims not to reach a telos but rather transcends any notion of a final stage (of evolution). The focal point then is far from a closing product; the issue is rather the open process of history: 'the utmost law of imitation tends to be limitless progression. This kind of immanent and unconditioned striving is the soul of the Universe.'[36] Whenever applied to the cultural and to the social, universal imitation fosters a growing harmonization. To Tarde, society is not so much the site of 'a struggle' or '*Kampf*' (against Darwinists such as Spencer and Marx), as it is the site of 'fusion' ('*Verschmelzung*') of class and peoples:

> There is yet a further analogy: the continuing play of imitation . . . result in that which is called democratic equality, that is in the fusion of all classes in one single class where imitation is so mutual that both parts conceive it as superior. . . . It [imitation] creates a sort of confederation among peoples.[37]

The effect of the progress of the circulation of knowledge by imitation is a necessary constituent of a post-nationalistic conception of democracy. In this respect, Tarde is not only optimistic about progress but is also a liberal politico-social utopian: 'thus the aspiration after cosmopolitan and democratic blending is the inevitable tendency of history'. In a future time – as imagined by Tarde – different cultures shall not struggle against each other as 'trapped and entrenched peoples' do ('*eingeschlossene und verschanzte Völker*'). The universalized circulation of the pursuit of emulation rather leads to

> the prospect of a future, alas, not soon unification of the different parts of humanity into one family with no belligerent conflicts. Such a vague and persistent idea of unlimited progress gains a clear and exact direction from this perspective only. The laws of imitation engender the necessity to go a step further, namely towards a far, yet apparent, goal that – despite momentary setbacks – seems easier to achieve, namely the birth of one society, its evolution and its universal expansion.[38]

Safe and protected identities (psychological, social, cultural and national) are dissolved by ideas and knowledge in Tarde's universalized process, without origin or unlimited equalization, without assimilation or hybridization. Where mankind's different cultures gradually assimilate and are merged, where knowledge is scattered – there 'gradually the boundaries among castes, classes and nationalities are laid' ('*allmählich die Grenzen der Kasten, Klassen, Nationalitäten*').

Finally, it is quite striking that universal circulation stretched out to the utopian is also explained relating to notions of media. In more precise terms, the condition that it necessarily needs is a channel without resistance, or, in more positive terms, 'an utterly elastic milieu' ('*ein vollkommen elastisches Milieu*'), that is, 'an ethereal or airy milieu' ('*ätherisches oder luftiges Milieu*' or '*milieu éthéré ou aérien*') whereby Tarde consciously and 'analogously' ('*analog*') discusses the 'elasticity of ethers' ('*Elastizität des Äthers*' or '*l'élasticité de l'éther*'). The metaphor of the 'ethereal milieu' ('*ätherische[n] . . . Milieu[s]*') intended for an 'elastic' ('*elastisches*') medium, which as such may fulfil the functions of transmission that has no form or resistance, carries manifold meanings. For Tarde, the metaphor has the same value and significance as Novalis' alchemic and magnetic media based on nature. In other words, it is not entirely by pure chance that both emphasize flexibility. The metaphor makes the circulation of knowledge within a society understandable with a scientific analogy.

Our final step is to illustrate the multiform analogy of ether in more detail. On the one hand, the focus is on the elasticity of ether, especially since Augustin Jean Fresnel's widespread idea in scientific discourse of a mechanic luminiferous ether that is constituted by elastic solid matter, which is to be further developed in the most disparate manifestations. On the other hand, Tarde's universal circulation may be connected not only to the modern scientific question of the constitution of ether, but also lies upon earlier philosophical concepts that conceive ether simply as *the* continuum securing substance. Thereby ether fulfils the function of confuting the idea of an empty space, a vacuum, where any form of circulation is impracticable. In 1878, in his entry on 'Aether' in *Encyclopaedia Britannica*, James Clark Maxwell summarized as follows:

> To those who maintained the existence of a plenum as a philosophical principle, nature's abhorrence of a vacuum was a sufficient reason for imagining an all-surrounding aether, even though every other argument should be against it. To Descartes, who made extension the sole essential property of matter, and matter a necessary condition of extension, the bare existence of bodies apparently at a distance was a proof of the existence of a continuous medium between them.

However, not only in relation to the philosophical function as substance for the propagation among bodies, but also with reference to the non-resistance of media, Tarde's metaphorical definition of circulation is ethereal (*ätherisch*). Inasmuch as the fact that ether (as waves of a transmitting medium for science) is a persistent concern and at the same time a free space for speculation due to its lack of resistance and the fact of it being inconceivable. That is one of the reasons why, during the nineteenth century, ether was mainly described in the nature of its being a medium that secretly conceals, i.e. that performs as a '*fantôme mathématique*', despite the difficulty of rendering ether empirically feasible in its physical consistency. As far as the twentieth century goes, ether was an important hypothesis of physics to explain distant effects and the propagation of light.

As a means that joins everything and enables exchange processes also at a distance, ether proves itself as a suitable and therefore obvious scientific metaphor for Tarde's universalistic conception of circulation. With this scientific paradigm, i.e. of an elastic and uncatchable means of circulation, Tarde succeeds in a notion of circulation that corresponds to the alchemistic *menstruum universale* of Novalis and his mesmeric conceived 'absolute elastic fluid' ('*absolut elastischen Fluidum*') is consequent in the form and function of a scientific analogy. Both Novalis and Tarde base their model of circulation in a coeval scientific hypothesis of a solid mediality that apparently explains the movements and effects of energies such as magnetism, light and gravity. Analogously, their model makes it possible to delineate how knowledge ideally spreads and circulates on social and epistemological levels.

At the end of the nineteenth century with Tarde – just as with Novalis previously – the circulation of knowledge was accompanied by the idea of a universal transgressive mediality (mediation, transfer). Whilst the universal transgressive mediality according to Novalis gave reasons principally to a post-Enlightenment, as well as post-idealistic, universal science of interactions, Tarde employed it as the basis for a globalizing democratic society of knowledge that builds cosmopolitanism and universalism on reciprocal imitation and recognition.

Notes

1 Novalis (1960–88): 361. Vgl. die Einleitung zur kritischen Edition des *Allgemeinen Brouillon* von Hans-Joachim Mähl, eine der wenigen Arbeiten zu Novalis' Enzyklopädie-Projekt: Novalis (1960–88): 207–41.

2 Ibid.: 366.

3 Ibid.: 434.

4 Paul (1927–63): 135.

5 Novalis (1960–88): 101.

6 Ibid: 268.

7 Zedler (1961–64).

8 Auch Novalis verwendet den Begriff des 'Vitalismus', wobei er auf die *Versuche und Beobachtungen über die Fortpflanzung der Wärme in Flüssigkeiten* (in *Annalen der Physik,* 1799) des Grafen von Rumford verweist. Novalis (1960–88): 198.

9 Hufeland (1800): 407f.

10 Novalis' Frage: 'W[as] i[ist] Synkretismus?' ist, wie Hans-Joachim Mähl überzeugend dargelegt hat, vor dem Hintergrund von Kurt Sprengels Rede vom 'verderblichen Synkretismus' in seinem *Versuch einer pragmatischen Geschichte der Arzneikunde* (1792–1794) zu sehen, woraus Novalis für sein Enzyklopädie-Projekt exzerpierte. Vgl. Hans-Joachim Mähl (1963): 139–250.

11 Novalis (1960–88), Vol. 3: 278.

12 Ibid., Vol. 2: 646.

13 Ibid., Vol. 3: 597.

14 Ibid.: 434.

15 Ibid.: 280.

16 Ibid.: 272.

17 Ibid., Vol. 2: 534.

18 Ibid., Vol. 3: 425.

19 Ibid.: 259.

20 Ibid.: 410. Zum epistemologischen Begriff des Witzes um 1800 vgl. Kilcher (2004): 261–80.

21 Novalis (1960–88), Vol. 2: 434.

22 Hüber (1746).

23 Mesmer (1781): 47. Als 'Fluidum' verstand Mesmer einen Stoff, der sowohl den menschlichen Organismus mit seinem Nervensystem wie auch das gesamte All durchflutet: 'Diese Weltkörper wirken auch geradezu auf alle wesentliche Bestandtheile lebendiger Körper, vorzüglich aber das Nerven=System, vermittelst einer alles durchdringenden Flüssigkeit. Ich bestimmte die Art dieses Einflusses, und sagte: Dass er die Eigenschafften der Materie und der organischen Körper, z.B. die Schwere, Zusammenhang, Schnellkraft, Reitzbarkeit und Elecktricität, bald verstärke bald schwäche.' Vgl. Ibid.: 8f.

24 Vgl. Gabriel Tarde (1908): 107. Vgl. Herbert Spencer, der 1857 schreibt: 'the law of organic progress is the law of all progress'. Aus Spencer (1891): 10.

[25] Tarde (2009): 92.
[26] Ibid.: 86. Vgl. die französische Ausgabe. Gabriel Tarde (1993): 58.
[27] Tarde (2009): 29.
[28] Ibid.
[29] Ibid.
[30] Ibid.: 30.
[31] Ibid.: 69.
[32] Ibid.: 40. (im französischen Text p. 13). Vgl. zu diesem Komplex auch das verwandte Kulturkonzept der 'Pfropfung'. Dazu Uwe Wirth, ed. (2011).
[33] Tarde (2009): 38.
[34] Ibid.: 57f.
[35] Ibid.: 73.
[36] Ibid.: 389.
[37] Ibid.: 392.
[38] Ibid.: 19.

References

Hüber, Johann (1746), *Curieuses und reales Natur- Kunst- Berg- Gewerck- und Handlungs-Lexicon.*

Hufeland, Christoph Wilhelm (1800), *System der practischen Heilkunde,* Vol. I, Jena.

Kilcher, Andreas (2004), 'Lessings Cheangant#sic?#. Der Witz als enzyklopädische Textur', *Zeitschrift für Ästhetik und Allgemeine Kunstwissenschaft*, 2: 261–80.

Mähl, Hans-Joachim (1963) 'Novalis und Plotin', in *Jahrbuch des Freien Deutschen Hochstifts*: 139–250.

Mesmer, Franz Anton (1781), *Abhandlung über die Entdeckung des thierischen Magnetismus,* Karlsruhe.

Novalis (1960–88), *Schriften: Die Werke Friedlich von Hardenbergs*, edited by Paul Kluckhohn and Richard Samuel, 5 vols, Stuttgart, Vol. 3.

Paul, Jean (1927–63), *Sämtliche Werke: Historisch-kritische Ausgabe*, edied by Eduard Berend, I. Abt., 19 vols, Weimar and Berlin, Vol. I.

Spencer, Herbert (1891), *Progress: Its Law and Cause: Essays,* Vol. 1, London.

Tarde, Gabriel (1908), *Die sozialen Gesetze: Skizze einer Soziologie,* aus dem Französischen von Hans Hammer, Leipzig.

——— (2009), *Die Gesetze der Nachahmung*, Frankfurt a. M.: Suhrkamp; French edition: *Les lois de l'imitation,* réimpression du texte de la deuxième édition de 1895, Paris, 1993.

Wirth, Uwe, ed. (2011), *Impfen, Pfropfen, Transplantieren,* Berlin.

Zedler, Johann Heinrich (1961–64), *Grosses vollständiges Universal-Lexicon aller Wissenschaften und Künste,* 64 Bde. und 4 SupL#Suppl. ?#-Bde., Halle, Leipzig 1732–1754, Nachdruck Graz, Vol. 2, Sp. 1909.

Difference in Similarity

On a mode of aesthetic comparison in Hofmannsthal, Trakl, Novalis and Thomas Mann[1]

Rüdiger Görner

In *Das Allgemeine Brouillon*, Novalis noted that 'Instinct and space are quite similar', because every object represents a fulfilled desire.[2] In his play, *The Famous Ones*, Thomas Bernhard places this quote in the mouth of the 'Publisher', who uses it to justify the publication of a new series of books that he wants to name after Otto Weininger's legendary *libre fatal*, *Gender and Character*, in order to ensure the success of the series.[3] In this scene the Publisher – like all of the actors in Bernhard's play – has a puppet of a 'famous' role model sitting next to him which he brings to life, thus *performatively* integrating similarity into the scene.

Bernhard's theatrical constructs of similarity – which can also be found in works such as *Minetti* or *Ritter, Dene, Voss* – can thus be understood as processes of representation that presuppose the manufacturability of similarity. He thus fulfils Novalis' precept that the 'wit' *creates* 'comparisons' in two ways.[4] I will discuss Novalis' work within this context later in this essay, but as far as Bernhard's play is concerned, one can argue that his characters end up collapsing under the weight of their desire to be similar to the greats – from Toscanini to Max Reinhardt, from Richard Tauber to Lotte Lehmann. The philosophical question, 'What is the relationship between similarity and identity?', is dealt with here in the form of 'witty' performance guidelines. This question can also be found in the later postmodernity of contemporary literature as illustrated by Thomas Meinecke's controversial (non-)novel *Lookalikes*, in which characters from the Düsseldorf jet-set scene literally play out their physical similarities to celebrities such as Josephine Baker, Marlon Brando and Serge Gainsbourg on the Königsallee.[5]

These few examples already allow us to draw an initial general conclusion: the problem of the similar in art illustrates a structural phenomenon as an aesthetic quality. Literary modernism responded to questions of similarity, especially in the works of Hugo von Hofmannsthal. Towards the end of his tragedy, *Electra*, Orestes asks his sister if she thinks that she looks similar to her mother Clytemnestra. Electra answers him with 'wild' gestures: 'Like me? No, no. But you are not / To look her in her face. When she is dead / We'll look into her face together.'[6] What Electra wants to deny, however, is confirmed by Richard Strauss' musical score in the play, in which both parts, daughter and mother, are accompanied by 'similar' chromatic sound figures.

The problem of similarity was also central in other works by Hofmannsthal. In the notes on his great narrative fragment, *Andreas* – in many respects his life-work – we find the following reference: Andreas mistakes 'similar people' for one another because of his 'uncertainty in recognizing' them again. This in turn is driven by the 'uncertainty of his inner sense'. Furthermore, 'he remembered that he was also unsure if the street he was on was the same'.[7] Hofmannsthal clearly planned to incorporate a grand 'conversation about similarities' into his story. The most important aspect of such a discussion is that Hofmannsthal's Andreas expected mistakes and self-delusions to be the result of inadequately evaluated similarities. In a sense, the narrative of *Andreas* celebrates ambiguity. Consequently, similarities depend on forms of memory and constellations such as those that Baudelaire called 'correspondences', or that T.S. Eliot called 'objective correlations'. Metaphors create similarities. They vouch for the eidetic in speaking and writing, which is to say: similarities reflect certain views of the world. They thus belong to the category of the visual or of making something visual with language. The aesthetics of similarity thus amount to a theory of 'how', and can be understood as a contribution to the problem area of comparison and as an expression of intentions that lead to comparisons.[8]

Aesthetic action – such as playing, as Schiller might say – works *with* similarities. In discourse about aesthetics, however, similarity sometimes approaches the limits of hermeneutics and thus moves into an area of uncertain relationships – the open, the undecidable, and approximations. Similarity cannot, therefore, be an analytical term; at most it can be – in a Kantian sense – a synthetic concept that belongs more to the category of 'as well as' than the category of 'either–or'. Still, it is important to continually root out the 'subtle difference' between similarity on the one hand, and sameness – in the sense of identical with oneself – on the other. Seen from the perspective of the history of ideas, this subtle difference is based on the concept of Heraclitus' 'the One differentiated in itself', the *hen diapheron eautō*. As long as this 'distinction in and of itself' is understood as something contingent, as 'remaining true to itself', it serves to determine identity. But if this distinction is exposed, then it can contribute to this 'subtle difference' in comparative situations and can thus be used to determine similarities.

The Similar as an Artistic Factor

In the field of art, similarity plays a role in the aesthetics of production and reception. But what does similarity mean with respect to the aesthetics of reception and production? An example might be drawn from the following constellation: within Wolfgang Rihm's *Gesänge op. 1 for piano and vocals*, we find his handwritten notes on Georg Trakl's poem, 'Landscape'. In reference to Trakl's lines, 'and the yellow flowers of autumn / bend wordlessly over the pond's blue countenance', Rihm notes: 'see Hölderlin = Half of Life = similarity of a situation'.[9] It is clear that this 'similarity' in poetic-motivic constellations kept the composer from setting this poem to music; instead he chose Trakl's poems 'Decline' and 'Spiritual Twilight'. In 'Landscape', Trakl obviously worked with the material provided by 'Half of Life': Hölderlin's 'yellow pears' become his 'yellow flowers of autumn'; the shore hanging into the lake transforms into bending over the pond. The emphatic 'speechless' remains unchanged but now refers to the flowers and not to walls as it does in Hölderlin. The blue that can only be indirectly inferred from Hölderlin's poem is explained by Trakl in relation to the yellow flowers and their poetic complementary colour.[10] This constellation provides us with an example for manufactured similarity, which we must distinguish from unintentional similarity such as that found between the overtures in Mozart's early comic opera, *Bastien and Bastienne*, and the beginning of Beethoven's *Eroica*; in this case, we have no evidence that Beethoven was aware of the earlier composition.

Trakl's poem 'Decline', set to music by Rihm, points to another philological aspect of problems related to similarity. There are actually five different versions of this poem, all of which exhibit structural similarity with regard to poetic material, motifs and linguistic pictures, and after the second version in the three-stanza structure of the poem.[11] An example illustrates this point: the line 'The winds sound quietly on the lonely hill' becomes 'The past winds tone on the lonely hill', which then changes to 'The winds fall quietly on the lonely hill', before finally shifting in the last version to 'The white walls of the city ever ring.'[12] The poetic nuances here are a result of variations and shifts in the immediate lexical environment of the linguistic motif. The similarities prove to be so dominant that they suddenly change in the final version to an image that was not present before ('The white walls of the city'). In contrast, the acoustic motif remains unchanged and is only partially replaced in the third version ('fall quietly'); in this case, the emphasis shifts entirely from the verb to the adverb, and thus remains discrete from the other versions.

If we understand similarity as 'almost the same', then our focus must shift to the artistic process of variation. From the perspective of production aesthetics, similarity becomes particularly evident in the (compositional) principle of variation, as well as in repetition where that which is repeated is clearly not identical with the original because it is part of a chronological progression and is thus implicitly subject to changes. In his work, *L' Évolution créatrice* (1930), Henri Bergson called attention to the phenomenon of '*ressemblance*' as a complex interdependency that stems from interactional relationships arising during the process of production.[13] Building on Bergson's work, Gilles Deleuze explained his interest in similarity as follows: similarity 'is the identity of that which differs from itself; it proves that the same virtuality actualizes itself in the divergence of series; and it shows the essence subsisting in change, just as divergence shows the change itself at work in the essence'.[14]

Translated into aesthetic contexts, this 'divergence of series' is materialized through the variation of a theme, the 'entity that survives through the change' or the basic character of the theme, whereby such variations are only made possible by an internal differential quality of the theme itself, and its internal plurality only becomes clear through the variations themselves. The variations activate the differential potential of the theme or thematic motif, while the gradual similarity between a set of variations and the original motif arises from genre-typical requirements.

This connection between repetition and similarity is repeatedly presented as ironically broken in Bernhard's *The Famous Ones*. The 'Publisher', who wants to be like Samuel Fischer, for instance, advocates for the most important thesis of aesthetic production, namely, that '[all important artists] produce nothing but a single work / and they always modify intimately incessantly imperceptibly'.[15] And precisely in this – in the subtle creation of similar structures in non-identical repetitions – lies the 'greatness' of art.

Difference and Similarity as 'Simulacrum'

The questions surrounding similarity become more complex if we expand our considerations to (free) improvisations on a topic or theme. In such situations, we must confront the question of what remains of the original theme that the similarities arise from. To put it another way, speaking of similarities only makes sense when something is similar in relation to the original, when the similar is *subtly* different. In this sense, similarity can be understood as the differential in aesthetics.

As Paul de Man wrote in *Allegories of Reading*, questions about the nature of similarity have been connected with problems of dissimilarity since Jean-Jacques Rousseau. De Man identified two levels of discourse about similarity in Rousseau's writing: one based on interpersonal relations and another based on linguistics or, more precisely, on the process of conceptualization:

> The interplay of difference and similarity implied in the encounter between two men is more complex than if the encounter had been between two potentially antithetical entities such as man and woman, as is the case in *Julie* or parts of *Emile*, or man and things, as is the case in the example of the *Second Discourse* [*Discourse on the Origin and Basis of Inequality Among Men*, published in 1754] in which a man is naming a tree instead of naming another man. It seems perverse on Rousseau's part to choose an example based on a more complex situation than that of the paradigm with which he is dealing.[16]

This quotation also addresses the affinities that bridge differences between people, or between things and concepts. When it comes to aesthetics, the question remains open whether sufficient similarity can be manufactured through forming, adaptation or transfers, and if so, to what ends. What underlies our interest in recognizing similarities, and how does such recognition influence the cognitive-psychological side of artistic production? The problem of the 'simulacrum' uses such questions as a starting point. Beginning with Roland Barthes, structuralism conceived of similarity as the result of productive processes driven by awareness:

> The goal of all structuralist activity, whether reflexive or poetic, is to reconstruct an 'object' in such a way as to manifest thereby the rules of functioning (the 'functions') of this object. Structure is therefore actually a *simulacrum* of the object, but a directed, *interested* simulacrum, since the imitated object makes something appear which remained invisible or, if one prefers, unintelligible in the natural object.[17]

In other words, the emergence of the similar as 'simulacrum' does not happen by chance; instead, it must be manufactured from the original object using an aesthetically productive 'activity'. Barthes thus exclusively understood similarity as a pseudo-product – more specifically, as a projection of the original object that allows the specific properties of the original object to become the primary focus of observation.

For its part, one could also view Barthes' approach as a 'simulacrum' in relation to Walter Benjamin's conception of similarity as proposed in January/February 1933. Benjamin's differentiating gaze focused less on the structure and more on the nature of similarity. Today, his conception reads like an encrypted opposing position to the tendency towards enforced conformity of his time, to a non-reflective ideology of sameness that literally celebrated the appearance of uniformity in the torchlight processions of the day.

Benjamin's *Doctrine of the Similar* addresses the aesthetic, philological and anthropological-phylogenic dimensions of similarity. He illustrates these dimensions using the examples of the 'mimetic faculty' in nature and above all in humans, the formation of concepts in different languages and their referents, and the behavioural-psychological necessity for species to assimilate with one another – as he puts it, 'the formerly powerful compulsion to become similar'.[18] Benjamin's decision to explicitly distil an essay, 'On the Mimetic Faculty' (Fall 1933), from his *Doctrine of the Similar* also legitimizes viewing this manifestly aesthetic dimension of similarity as the common denominator between the philological and anthropological qualities of similarity. This also follows from the small experimental layout that he proposes to determine philological similarity: 'If, from the different languages, one were to arrange words meaning the same thing around what they mean as their centre, then it would be necessary to examine how these words, which often have not the slightest similarity to each other, are similar to that meaning in their centre.'[19]

'*Baum*', '*l'arbre*' and 'tree', all refer in different ways to a woody plant – whether as a botanical reality, as a symbolic tree of life or as a phylogenetic family tree. The interlingual similarities emerge from comparable cultural contexts and semantic fields that for the most part refer to the stability and branched nature of that which is being described. In addition to the cultural contingency of similarity, Benjamin also described the specific 'time-moment' in the 'perception of similarities', and emphasizes the spontaneous, the momentary, the 'instantaneous flash' in the perception and recognition of similar phenomena.[20] With regard to linguistic mimesis, on the other hand, this temporal quality corresponds to an auditory quality in the form of the onomatopoeic character of certain words or phrases which seek to approximate the designated natural sounds with a certain articulation and intonation. Benjamin, however, did not reflect further on the performative or playful character of this mimetic conception of similarity.

Similarity as a Classificatory Quality

Benjamin's approach was complemented on two fronts: by Ludwig Wittgenstein's *Philosophical Investigations* – specifically, sections 66 and 67 under the heading 'family resemblance'[21] – on the one hand, and by Henri Poincaré on the other, who wrote as early as 1905 about the problem of similarity and perception.[22] Poincaré's writing in particular would later be picked up by Ludwik Fleck, who posed the question of whether the 'intersubjective similarity of sensory impressions is an indispensable prerequisite for the natural sciences'.[23] Fleck observed:

> Poincaré emphasized that the hypothesis of intersubjective similarity of impressions is fundamentally undecidable. We don't have any way of convincing ourselves how another person perceives or even whether he perceives. Foreign impressions are always closed to us. Everything that is objective and intersubjective must be expressible and communicable through language. Our own impressions, and more specifically their quality, can never be expressed to another person.[24]

Wittgenstein himself approached the same topic by offering an analysis of similarities from the perspective of 'looking'. In contrast to Poincaré, Wittgenstein claims that similarities can indeed be recognized through analytical seeing but not through intellectual effort. As an example he cites the wide variety of games we are familiar with – from board games to ball games, from tennis to children's games – that depend on intersubjective understanding and action. Using processes of classification and categorization, he establishes groups of games in which we can see 'similarities crop up and disappear'.[25] This leads him to the following conclusion: '[W]e see a complicated network of similarities overlapping and criss-crossing: sometimes overall similarities, sometimes similarities of detail.'[26] Wittgenstein calls this 'network' of overlapping 'similar' properties a 'family' that is composed of all games. For their part, games (including his subsequent 'language games') stand out due to the fact that they are limited by rules, but these rules do not determine every element of the game; to illustrate the latter point, he uses the example of tennis, which has many rules but none that specifies how high one can throw the ball during the serve.[27] Wittgenstein turns our attention to the phenomenological nature of similarities, the conditions necessary to perceive similarities and the visual nature of their effects. But he also refers to the categorizing function of similarities, that is, their role in the recognition of structural inter-relationships – in the sense of a group or a 'family'. The two main examples of reflections on similarity that follow also point in this direction.

Perceptual-Psychological Variations of Similarity in Novalis

In the fourth section of the introduction to his reflections on poetic politics, *Faith and Love or The King and Queen*, Novalis writes about the 'lovingly begotten similarity' which leads to 'poetic philosophizing'.[28] The passage itself reads thus: 'One finds what one lives everywhere, and sees similarities everywhere. The greater the love the more extensive and manifold is this similar world. My beloved is the abbreviation of the universe, the universe is the extension of my beloved.'[29] According to Novalis, what is required is a sympathetic gaze that *wants* to see similarities, or at least one that does not look away or even deny their existence. The results are not just analogies or metaphors but actual states of being: under these circumstances the beloved *can* actually *be* an extract of the universal.

For Novalis, the semantics of the concept of similarity fluctuate between the common and the unusual. Between these categories lies his observation that a novel is similar to an 'English garden', because it is entirely 'poetic' and no part of it is just 'flat nature'.[30] What is unusual about Novalis' use of concept can be illustrated by three examples. First is his thesis that 'contrasts' are 'inverse similarities' – a phenomenon that he classifies as belonging to the nature of logic.[31] Second, he associates 'encyclopaedistics' with the relativist or perspectivist determination of relationships (of which similarity is one kind), whereas he is concerned with 'the effects of the sciences on one another'. And third, he argues for the 'similarity between thinking and seeing' as long as one mathematically trains both the eye and thought; this latter point is especially relevant with respect to Wittgenstein's theories of similarity.[32] Accordingly, Novalis assumes a 'similarity between light and thought' since 'both are associated with vibration'.[33] What he postulates here is the 'similarity of perception with thought',[34] or, as he put it, 'the power of [revenge] and memory', which – in a very literal sense – form the relational foundation of poetics. For Novalis, art represents 'a creative act of perception controlled by intentionality', as Friedmar Apel has put it.[35] A more modern equivalent of this line of argumentation – particularly regarding similarity – can be seen in a quote from Paul Klee's 'Creative Credo' (1920): 'Art does not reproduce the visible but makes visible.'[36]

But what connects Novalis' diverse reflections on similarity? All of them suggest a combination of approaches from a comparative psychology of perception with a universal phenomenology, and see difference or 'contrast' as negative kinships – such as those between a loving and an analytical view. The insights provided by these two views might differ but they both have the same principal value – especially within the context of this poetic philosopher's encyclopaedic project.

In order to more strongly argue for the 'similarity between light and thought', Novalis referred to the example of music, and to the strings of an instrument in particular, whose vibrations are necessary to make sound. He used this method of drawing analogies as if it were self-evident, and from his perspective, there was no need to reflect on it any further. Indeed, from his perspective, as the source of similarities – including those created using metaphors – such analogizing had become second nature for philosophical poetry and the poetic philosophizing of a scientifically conscious poet.

The Similar as Elective Affinity in Thomas Mann

Another variation on a poetics of similarity can be found in the work of Thomas Mann. Here, the different is reflected upon as an ironic quality of the similar by explaining the question of identity as an object of irony. A prime example of the considerable importance of similarity as a motif in Mann's work can be found in the conversation between August von Goethe and Charlotte Kestner in his novel, *Lotte in Weimar*.[37] In this scene, August names his 'chosen one' for the first time: Ottilie von Pogwisch. At first Charlotte only hears 'Ottilie' and notes (with reference to Goethe's *Elective Affinities* and the way that work dealt with similarities): 'It is like in the novel.'[38] August corrects her, saying that would 'make Ottilie your daughter', which Charlotte brusquely rejects. August von Goethe then takes a moment to explain in more detail what he means:

> I am not jesting – or scarcely. I was not speaking of an actual likeness, that would be strange indeed. I meant a kinship – and that happens thousands of times in the world. . . . What do we mean by a resemblance? I do not mean a similarity of single features, but the likeness as a whole, the identity of type. It is the same: delicate, charming, slender – in both; and this it is could make you sisters, or make Ottilie your daughter.[39]

Later in the novel Goethe picks up on his son's ideas and carries them over to his own works, whereby he distinguishes them according to their degree of brotherly and sisterly relations to one another, and, somewhat surprisingly, claims that *Divan* and *Werther* are such spiritual siblings, 'or better said: the same thing at different levels, ascent to a climax, repetition and refinement of life'.[40] The different in the similar, the related, is connected to the question of the aesthetic and psychological effect of repetition: is repetition a form of generating similarity? In *Lotte in Weimar*, Mann plays through this problem using the example of a fictional classical constellation whose starting point is the question of how similar the aged Charlotte Kestner and her younger fictional *Urbild*, Werther's Lotte, can really be with one another. The same goes for the figure of Goethe portrayed in the novel. At the same time, the plot of the story centres on the question of how significant this problem of similarity really is, and whether or not every form of similarity is the result of a construction – especially when it is associated with memory.

This thesis is also confirmed by Goethe's claim that 'culture [is] parody',[41] and yet parody works as a special form of variation in the generation of similarities. The reader of *Lotte in Weimar* is confronted by the most impressive form of similarity when, in a conversation with his similarity-aware son, Goethe compares the pyramids with 'sun-monument, giant crystals', and calls them 'mammoth imitations by man of cosmic immaterial concepts'.[42] According to the Goethe of the novel, the 'crystallographic system' exemplifies the 'form and structure . . . continuously reproduced' of these geometric structures, which were also quasi-natural symbols due to their 'affinity . . . for light and the transmission of light'. After August von Goethe refers to 'family resemblances' in the Wittgensteinian sense in his conversation with Charlotte Kestner, his father transcends this form of similarity into the mythical and cosmic without abandoning an earthly framework in the forms of crystals and pyramids.

For Thomas Mann, there was yet one more type of similarity to be found in a downright suggestive comparison, between Goethe and himself. This aspect of similarity has not yet been discussed here, namely, the aspect of representational similarity. In his lecture on 'Goethe as a Representative of the Bourgeois Era' (1932), Mann construed a similarity between himself and Goethe through their common efforts to transform the bourgeois to the 'Überbourgeois': into the cosmopolitan. He saw both Goethe and himself as representatives of the bourgeoisie but also as its last representatives, which in turn hinted at yet another similarity. Goethe had nourished the promising 'dual souls' of art and science by looking back to the Renaissance in order to reconceptualize it as a vision of the future. This was why he 'mistook' the 'Renaissance court of Ferrara' in *Tasso* with the Weimar court, and why he translated Benvenuto Cellini's autobiography.[43] Thomas Mann attempted to do something similar with his drama *Fiorenza* and the story 'Gladius Dei', although he focused more on the state of decay in the Renaissance understanding of art and presented it as a projection of the late-bourgeois problem of art. In *The Magic Mountain*, Mann shaped the actual 'dual soul' of art and science into a novel.

The decisive point for our discussion here is clearly that similarity in the form of representation, an alleged – one could even say a consciously 'styled' – relationship, always operates at the edge of the ironic, even the ridiculous. One could also consider the emptiness of the purely representative existence that results from a superficial similarity with real power in Mann's novel, *Royal Highness*. Hans Blumenberg also expressed this aspect of 'irony and similarity' as it relates to the problem of representation in his parable, *In Frankfurt*. This story describes Schopenhauer's only encounter with Rossini, in which he was appalled by Rossini's outward appearance because it did not seem at all similar to the composer's music.

Schopenhauer was obviously unable to bring his musically based expectation of Rossini in line with the actual appearance of the composer himself. It is, of course, telling that Schopenhauer must have assumed there would be such a similarity at all. The fact that Rossini did not look like his music – at least according to Schopenhauer, as told by Blumenberg[44] – conforms with the more general observation that musicians do not represent that which their music (in the sense of an ontology of appearances) actually *is*.

The counterpart to Thomas Mann's discourse on similarity based on Goethe can be found in his 'Indian legend', *The Transposed Heads*, a mythic narrative about the differences and similarities between two friends, Schridaman and Nanda. The narrative is based on the following premises:

> The friendship between the two youths was based on the diversity in their I- and my-feelings, those of the one yearning towards those of the other. Incorporation, that is, makes for isolation, isolation for difference, difference makes for comparisons, comparisons give rise to uneasiness, uneasiness to wonderment, wonderment tends to admiration; and finally admiration turns into a yearning for mutual exchange and unity.[45]

In this story, similarities and differences are literally balanced on the edge of a sword. The question here is, which spirit belongs to which body? The head of the spiritual merchant's son Schridaman on the body of the muscular and goat-nosed Nanda begins to take on the body's characteristics, but also weakens it for the sake of spirituality. The same happens in reverse for Nanda's head on Schridaman's body. Sita, for whom the self-decapitations take place in world-mother Durga's shrine, becomes entangled in a series of apparent similarities and differences until, in the end, she sacrifices herself in an exalted parody of love after a second mutual decapitation by her lovers. By swapping her lovers' heads in the Temple of Durga, Sita – half consciously, half subconsciously – seeks to compare the two to generate similarity in difference, and this in the form of a sacral-profane act (of love) that requires divine help in order to generate a perverse (or, more objectively, hybrid) corporeality. What also become similar here are elements such as erotic fantasy, existentiality and appearance. Schridaman summarizes this as follows: '[A]ll beings have two sorts of existence: one for themselves and one for the eyes of others. They are, and also they are to be seen as, soul and image; and ever is it sinful to let oneself be influenced by the image only and not to heed the soul.'[46]

And yet all aesthetics of similarity live from the figurative. He who is able to visualize thoughts can compare them with one another and identify similarities and dissimilarities. Jean Paul also made reference to this situation in his *Introduction to Aesthetics*, which in part clearly privileges the problem of similarity. At one point he explains that 'the judgment about their resemblance' requires 'an acquaintance with the original'.[47] Likewise he critically investigates the use of language, and finds that the expression 'distant resemblance' essentially means that something is dissimilar.[48] From this he deduces that the spirited joke is produced by shrewd comparison, which recognizes things as similar but not the same. He uses examples such as *to spice the spice*, or word-play that generates similarity and, in the right context, humour through mirroring: an *exchange of letters (Briefwechsel)* and the *letter of exchange* (*Wechselbrief*), in the sense of an issuance of bonds.[49]

Jean Paul understood word-play as the fundamental substance of all poetry, which he described as a 'game with images, then with the sounds of rhyme and metre'. He spoke of the poetic 'sound of the sign' as an 'echo of the thing', and claimed that the 'identical echoes' between things suggested their fundamental similarity.[50] But he also quoted from Johann Joachim Eschenburg's *Model of a Theory and Literature of Belles-Lettres* (1783),[51] which noted that we connect things with 'our souls' through similarities, but also through the 'counterplay and contrasts of concepts' with the objects they refer to. This means that we internalize what we perceive through the relations, similarities and dissimilarities that we observe. What both Eschenburg and Jean Paul left open is the question of whether the similar – in the sense of a sympathetic vibration – or the dissimilar, the contrastive and dissonant, leave a stronger mark on the human soul. Answering such a question would be part of a perceptual-psychological analysis of the phenomenon of similarity, one that, incidentally, Karl Philipp Moritz implied in his *Experimental Spiritual Teachings* (*Experimentalseelenlehre*), published around the same time as Eschenburg's work. According to Moritz, people must overcome their tendency towards the successive and exercise their faculties in comparing things; this is the only way that harmonies can be created.[52] For the most part Moritz conceived of similarity acoustically, and in such a way that Thomas Mann might have described as the 'eavesdropping insight into the fracture of a . . . clever music'.[53]

Even Thomas Mann's smaller and lesser known works portray an aesthetics of similarity as a way of describing concrete artistic gaming. To conclude my remarks, I would like to point to one such example from Mann's 1921 *Preface to a Portfolio* with 'graphical fantasies' about Wolfgang Born's *Death in Venice*. This is thus an example of similarity in the realm of so-called intermediality; Mann refers to it in a terminologically gratifying way as the 'transfer of views'.[54]

This small text deals with a 'strange and almost secret seeming' similarity between Born's visual depiction and Mann's own intentions. Born could not have known that the narrator of the story, Aschenbach, was 'modelled' on Gustav Mahler, and yet he created a final image in which the protagonist, sitting on a beach, sees Tadzio as an exposed mystagogue, and looks similar to Gustav Mahler in both his posture and his semi-profile. Referring to this image, Thomas Mann notes (once more invoking Goethe) that the illustrating artist should pay more attention to the 'intention of he who speaks as opposed to his words', if he wants to produce similarity. In other words, similarities are created from that which is hidden, or, as Mann writes, 'in the loose and hidden connections of things'.[55] In this sense, that which conceals the dogmatic insistence of difference becomes the breeding ground for similarity. For – all things considered – the value of difference exists in its potential for the similarities that might emerge from it. Indeed, it is possible that difference only becomes viable and capable of consensus when the similar, the congenial, emerges from it.

Notes

1 The original version of this essay appeared in Görner (2014). The version included in this volume has been reworked and significantly expanded.
2 Novalis (2007): 141.
3 Bernhard (1983): 461–546, 569.
4 Ibid.: 135 (§ 732).
5 Meinecke (2011).
6 Hofmannsthal (1908): 73.
7 Hofmannsthal (1992): 105.
8 My considerations here seek to expand on an approach that I recently introduced as a core problem of comparison: Görner (2009).
9 Schmidt-Bergmann, ed. (2012): 133.
10 Trakl (2005): 42.
11 The final version, published posthumously in a collection titled *Sebastian im Traum*, emphasizes this trinity by placing each verse in three lines. See Trakl (2005): 72. There is no translation of the variations; see the German original: Trakl (1987): 386–89.
12 Ibid.
13 Cf. Bergson (1930): 246.
14 Deleuze (2003): 40.
15 Bernhard (1983): 521.
16 de Man (1979): 152.
17 Barthes (1972): 214–15.
18 Benjamin ([1933] 1979).
19 Ibid.: 67.
20 Ibid.: 66.
21 Wittgenstein (1986): 32.
22 Poincaré (1920).
23 Fleck (2011): 310–19.
24 Ibid.: 314f.

[25] Wittgenstein (1986): 32.
[26] Ibid.: 32.
[27] Ibid.: 33.
[28] Novalis (1997): 85f.
[29] Ibid.
[30] Novalis (1999): 835.
[31] Novalis (2007): 5.
[32] Ibid.: 92.
[33] Ibid.: 57.
[34] Apel (2010): 67.
[35] Ibid.
[36] Klee (1961): 76.
[37] Surprisingly, no systematic works have yet been written about the motif of similarity in this novel. One exception that could be built upon is Ingeborg Roble's 'Ähnlichkeit und Differenz in Thomas Mann's frühen Erzählungen' (Roble 2006). In Thomas Mann's work, 'similarity' can even take on a social tone, such as in his novel *Royal Highness*, when Imma Spoelann, the German–American daughter of a billionaire, compares Prince Klaus Heinrich with her chauffeur and sees similarities between the two despite all the class boundaries between them: 'Imma had noticed the likeness between Klaus Heinrich and him [the driver] the first time she saw the Prince. It was of course a similarity not of features, but of expression.' (Mann 1979: 233).
[38] Mann (1990): 273.
[39] Ibid.: 274–75.
[40] Ibid.: 319.
[41] Ibid.: 287.
[42] Ibid.: 362.
[43] Mann (1974b): 301.
[44] Cf. Blumenberg (2010): 123.
[45] Mann (1969): 4.
[46] Ibid.: 25.
[47] Richter (1973): 149.
[48] Cf. ibid.: 120.
[49] Cf. ibid.: 121.
[50] Ibid.: 137.
[51] Eschenburg (1783).
[52] Cf. Moritz (1993): 93f.
[53] Mann (1974a): 766.
[54] Ibid.: 584.
[55] Ibid.

References

Apel, Friedmar (2010), *Das Auge liest mit: Zur Visualität der Literatur*, München: Hanser.

Barthes, Roland (1972), 'The Structuralist Activity', in *Critical Essays*, translated by Ricahrd Howard, Evanston: Northwestern University Press.

Benjamin, Walter ([1933] 1979), 'Doctrine of the Similar', *New German Critique*, Vol. 17: 65–69; available at doi:10.2307/488010, JSTOR, accessed 5 March 2017.

Bergson, Henri (1930), *L'Évolution créatrice*, Paris.

Bernhard, Thomas (1983),'Die Berühmten', in *Die Stücke 1969–1981*, Frankfurt am Main: Suhrkamp; an unofficial translation by Douglas Robertson in *The Philosophical Worldview Artist* is available at shirtysleeves.blogspot.de.

Blumenberg, Hans (2010), *Care Crosses the River*, Palo Alto, CA: Stanford University Press.

Deleuze, Gilles (2003), *Desert Islands and Other Texts 1953–1974*, edited by David Lapoujade, translated by Michael Taorminar, Los Angeles and New York: Semiotext(e).

de Man, Paul (1979), *Allegories of Reading: Figural Language in Rousseau, Nietzsche, Rilke and Proust*, New Haven and London: Yale University Press.

Eschenburg, Johann Joachim (1783), *Entwurf einer Theorie und Literatur der schönen Wissenschaften: Zur Grundlage bey Vorlesungen*, Berlin u.a.: Nicolai.

Fleck, Ludwik (2011), *Denkstile und Tatsachen: Gesammelte Schriften und Zeugnisse*, edited by Sylwia Werner and Claus Zittel, Frankfurt am Main: Suhrkamp.

Görner, Rüdiger (2009), 'Der Vergleich als geistige Form: Versuch einer Methodenreflexion', *Comparatio*, nos. 1 and 2, Heidelberg: Carl Winter: 277–90.

——— (2014), *'Bruchflächen funkeln lassen': Aufsätze zu einer literarischen Morphomatik*, Freiburg im Breisgau: Rombach.

Hofmannsthal, Hugo von (1908), *Electra*, translated by Arthur Symons, New York: Brentano's.

——— (1992), *Andreas*, edited by Mathias Mayer, Stuttgart: Reclam.

Klee, Paul (1961), 'Creative Credo', in *Notebook – Volume 1, The Thinking Eye*, edited by Jürg Spiller, London: Lund Humphries.

Mann, Thomas (1969), *The Transposed Heads*, New York: Vintage.

——— (1974a), 'Vorwort zu einer Bildermappe', in *Gesammelte Werke in dreizehn Bänden*, Vol. XI: *Reden und Aufsätze 3*, Frankfurt am Main: Fischer: 582–84.

——— (1974b), 'Goethe als Repräsentant des bürgerlichen Zeitalters', in Ders., *Gesammelte Werke*, Vol. IX: *Reden und Aufsätze 1*, Frankfurt am Main: Fischer.

——— (1979), *Royal Highness*, translated by A. Cecil Curtis, New York: Penguin.

——— (1990), *Lotte in Weimar*, Berkeley, CA: University of California Press.

Meinecke Thomas, (2011), *Lookalikes*, Berlin: Suhrkamp.

Moritz, Karl Philipp (1993), 'Aussichten zu einer Experimentalseelenlehre', in *Werke*, Vol. III: *Erfahrung, Sprache, Denken*, edited by Horst Günther, Frankfurt am Main: Suhrkamp: 85–99.

Novalis (1997), 'Faith and Love or The King and Queen', in *Philosophical Writings*, Albany: State University of New York Press.

——— (1999), *Das Allgemeine Brouillon*, in Ders., *Werke, Tagebücher und Briefe Friedrich von Hardenbergs*, Vol. II: *Das philosophisch-theoretische Werk*, edited by Hans-Joachim Mähl and Richard Samuel, Darmstadt: Wissenschaftliche Buchgesellschaft: 471–720.

——— (2007), *Notes for a Romantic Encyclopaedia – Das Allgemeine Brouillon*, edited and translated by David W. Wood, Albany: State University of New York Press.

Poincaré, Henri (1920), *La valeur de la science*, Paris.

Richter, Jean Paul (1973), *Horn of Oberon: Jean Paul Richter's School for Aesthetics*, with an introduction and translated by Margaret Hale, Detroit, MI: Wayne State University Press.

Roble, Ingeborg (2006), 'Ähnlichkeit und Differenz in Thomas Mann's frühen Erzählungen', in *Thomas Mann Jahrbuch*, 19: 51–70.

Schmidt-Bergmann, Hansgeorg, ed. (2012), *Etwas Neues entsteht im Ineinander: Wolfgang Rihm als Liedkomponist: Die Gedichtvertonungen*, Karlsruhe: Rombach.

Trakl, Georg (1987), *Dichtungen und Briefe: Historisch-Kritische Ausgabe in zwei Bänden*, Vol. 1, edited by Walther Killy and Hans Szklenar, Salzburg: Müller.

——— (2005), *Poems and Prose: A Bilingual Edition*, Evanston: Northwestern University Press.

Wittgenstein, Ludwig (1986), *Philosophical Investigations*, translated by G.E.M. Mascombe, Oxford: Blackwell.

Kakanian Mélange

Habsburg Central Europe and the shift from the study of identity to the study of similarity

Johannes Feichtinger

Central Europe was, and is, one of the most diversified spaces on the continent: polyglot, pluricultural and multi-denominational. The Habsburg monarchy, which gave Central Europe its political structure, was already being characterized by contemporaries as a 'state of contrasts', that combined 'the most glaring contradictions in terms of the physical landscape, population and intellectual culture', and in which 'the . . . people [did] not consistently inhabit sharply demarcated, separate territories, but in many regions' blended into one another. 'The blend of different nationalities', as Friedrich Umlauft put it, was to be 'observed nowhere in Europe in such evident form . . . as in our very fatherland'.[1] This fatherland was inhabited by 'eleven peoples' (*Völker*) whose 'greatest vitality', according to György Konrád, lay buried in 'the state of being mixed', and who managed 'somehow to get along'[2] because the 'contradictions' – as Robert Musil noted – had begun to 'merge into one another'.[3] For Hugo von Hofmannsthal, another determining factor was a 'certain ability to identify with others, from which springs that which cannot be learned: tact'.[4]

Habsburg Central Europe therefore represented a historical territory, realm of experience and sphere of action in which identities were constructed in a very particular way. 'Fluid borders'[5] allowed contradictions to be over-ridden, and similarities to be recognized and utilized, in guiding action and determining processes of identity formation.

This essay will show different but specific modes of identity formation against the background of the 'pluriculturality' (Anil Bhatti) of Habsburg Central Europe. The term 'pluriculturality' describes a social practice characterized by similarities, overlappings, syncretism and ambiguities, while multiculturalism is understood as the parallel coexistence of diverse linguistic, cultural and religious groups that are often defined in terms of 'ethnicity'.[6] In pluricultural life-worlds, specific modes of practice develop that also shape 'the relation of Self to Other' – as Homi Bhabha defines identity.[7] What the example of Habsburg Central Europe makes visible is that this relationship is not 'simply dualistic',[8] but 'refuse[s] to separate into fixed binary oppositions'.[9]

According to Sigmund Freud, processes involving identity are 'social phenomena'.[10] Differences are not naturally given but are socially constructed, arbitrary. In Habsburg Central Europe, the significance ascribed to cultural difference grew in the late nineteenth century. Processes of nationalization used linguistic difference as an argument for the construction of national or ethnic and cultural difference, which in turn was used to legitimize the political demands of certain groups.[11] In social practice, however, action continued to be guided by similarity. It is not surprising, therefore, that nationalist activists 'worked hard' to delineate the cultural boundaries which, they claimed, separated national communities in pluricultural areas.[12] In daily practice, situational bi- or multilingualism, verbal and non-verbal transcultural and interdenominational communication, go-betweens (agents, translators, brokers, intermediary institutions), national indifference, etc.,[13] enabled interactions and secured the good terms for getting along that appeared constantly under threat from the strategies of nationalist activists to acquire and maintain power.

Knowledge production was crucial here. Against a backdrop of ambivalence towards difference and similarity, two different approaches emerged in the humanities. One gave itself the task of defining what, within Habsburg Central Europe, was modern or backward, civilized or primitive, still classed as the Occident or already part of the Orient.[14] Prevailing social practices based on regional, social and cultural similarities were not taken into consideration – conceptions of a cultural homogeneity attained through assimilation and/or dissimilation provided the frame of reference instead. In their work, therefore, identity researchers of this kind substantiated the nationalists' political activism. Other academics respected the experience of difference but did not discount similarity, using it to develop new models of social coexistence that are relevant to a contemporary theory of similarity. Their approach was critical and reflexive. The most important keywords for these models, which I explore below, are trauma, tradition and memory, rules and entanglement, ambiguity, diversity and indeterminacy. The originators of these models include Alois Riegl, Ernst Mach, Sigmund Freud, Hans Kelsen, Otto Neurath and Ludwig Wittgenstein.

Using these thinkers' theories and concepts makes it possible to approach the complex way in which identities, differences and similarities are structured, and to rehabilitate similarity in two ways – as a social practice and as a heuristic concept. Both functions of similarity were crucial to the reflexive study of identity in Vienna in the period around 1900. They can therefore be described as *the study of similarity avant la lettre*.

Thesis

My thesis is that during the process leading to the nationalization of Habsburg Central Europe, which started in the late nineteenth century, attempts were made to eradicate similarity as a lived practice. Nationalist activists constructed ethnic or national and cultural differences out of linguistic differences, and brought oppositions into being. The pluricultural world was downplayed and it became imbued with the idea of backwardness. Even today, social practice shaped by similarities, overlappings, syncretisms and ambivalence still appears as such. Against this background, cultural homogeneity created through assimilation and/or dissimilation emerged as society's natural physical state. While the academic establishment investigated ways and processes for the creation of cultural homogeneity, those working with a more critical and reflexive approach recognized similarity's heuristic potential, exploiting it in their concepts and theories,[15] which, given the increasingly heterogeneous make-up of contemporary societies, are once again finding application. Until now, however, this significant aspect of intellectual life in *fin-de-siècle* Vienna has remained underexplored.

Habsburg 'Similarities and Differences'[16]

Bukovina was the most heterogeneous crownland in the Habsburg monarchy. A relatively poor eastern province with a population of around 800,000, it was inhabited by six linguistic groups (Ruthenians, Romanians, Germans, Jews, Poles, Magyars) belonging to four different religions (Eastern Orthodox, Catholic and Protestant Churches, and Judaism). In terms of size, the linguistic and religious groups were more or less balanced. During the Austro–Hungarian era, Bukovina and Czernowitz served as a model of peaceful coexistence, notwithstanding the great diversity the inhabitants experienced in everyday life. The situation was different in the economically prosperous heartlands of the monarchy (Austria, Bohemia/Moravia and Hungary). Here German speakers and Magyars made up the majority in terms of numbers, and they also held a more dominant political position. Most of the population were members of the Catholic Church; a comparatively low number were Greek Orthodox; Jews and Protestants were to be found in the Austro–Hungarian half of the dual monarchy.

Despite similarities with regard to religion and widespread use of German as the *lingua franca*, the idea of difference increasingly came to determine social relationships. Thus, for example, linguistic differences between German and Czech speakers were used as an argument in the construction of differences along ethnic and national lines. In Hungary, ethnic/national differences between, for example, Slovaks (often Lutherans) and Magyars (often Calvinists) were established and overplayed to the detriment of denominational similarities. These constructed ethnic/national differences came to the fore in what was known as the nationality struggle, which was not pacified by fundamental changes to the law. Thus the Czechs and Slovaks made no attempt to form a joint state before 1918, despite the 'pressure to Magyarize' felt by the latter. The southern Slavs (Croats, Serbs and Slovenians) likewise failed to find common ground. They were united by a similar language, but divided by writing system, religion and membership of different halves of the empire. The Slovenians (belonging to the Austrian half) used the Latin script and were predominantly Catholic, as were the Croats, whose multilingual kingdom of Croatia–Slavonia remained in the Hungarian half. The majority of Serbs (independent since 1878, proclamation of the Kingdom of Serbia in 1882) used the Cyrillic script and belonged to the Serbian Orthodox Church.

The comparison between the periphery (Bukovina) and the centre (Austria, Bohemia, Hungary) of the monarchy shows that similarities and differences were not necessarily translated into law, and that cultural differences did not automatically lead to conflict. At the same time, relative prosperity did not promise harmony or poverty discord. Tellingly, the nationality struggle was fought most fiercely in the most highly developed regions. Whether groups got along with one another or not depended on the significance ascribed to ethnic or national differences within the social structure, differences that had first been invented, then propagated in the media, and which were used to legitimize the claims of particular groups to a position of dominance.

Similarity and Social Practice

Taking Sigmund Freud's concept of the 'narcissism of minor differences',[17] we can say that the greater the similarity between two cultures, the harder it is to delineate them but the greater becomes the necessity to find – or construct – differences. As such, the Hungarian politician and political philosopher Josef von Eötvös (1813–1871) recognized early on that 'the idea of nationality' 'was championed with the greatest zeal' in that part of Europe in which the majority of 'mixed races' lived.[18] In contrast, the greater the differences between cultures, the more possibility there seems to be for appreciating similarities and acting upon them. It is unlikely that the Slovenian chestnut roaster, the Silesian linen trader and the Italian salami seller, all living in Vienna, asked themselves what made them different from one another. In any case, in a climate stirred up by nationalist rhetoric, what divided them was clear: their nationality. But this big difference meant little in everyday life, because the context of interaction remained intact in spite of ethnic or national differences. In social practice, getting along with one another was more important than understanding one another. One means to this end might have been situational multilingualism, or forms of non-verbal, transcultural and inter-denominational communication, which are characteristic of everyday practice in pluricultural societies.[19]

The Eradication of Similarity

The following section shows how the multilingual, pluricultural and supranational Habsburg empire was transformed into a multi-ethnic or multi-national state. The central concern for linguistic nationalists was the vision of 'complete equality' between nationalities. The creation of this equality demanded the construction of ethnic/national differences between linguistic groups. For nationalist activists, these differences were 'natural differences' of which the various nationalities had become aware: 'The closer the kindred is drawn together,' wrote Bohemian politician František (Franz) Palacký (1798–1876), 'the more the foreign is repelled.'[20]

At the same time, the fact that this vision of 'natural difference' did not correspond to social practice was emphasized by Josef von Eötvös:

> When we observe the different nationalities in our part of the world, so we find between them hardly any difference greater than that of dress. The fabric and the main components are the same; only in colour, in the proportion of individual parts, in the cut does difference lie and in the better educated classes, this too ceases so that – at least in Europe – the similarity, which we discover between the moral life and ideas of the different peoples, depends far more on their level of education than on their racial affinity.[21]

While the liberal publicist Eötvös may have supported the demand for individual equality and freedom, he cautioned against collective rights for national groups. For, in the Austrian empire, he argued, the nationalities appeared 'so blended together' that

> in each region that nationality which forms the majority, [would] oppress the others, to be repaid richly by the oppressed where the majority fell to their nationality, until finally, following the natural development of things, mutual oppression in our fatherland would reach its peak and national differences would degenerate into open hostilities.[22]

For Eötvös, the consequences of a process of nationalization were obvious: the 'disarray of all relationships', the 'systematization of language wars' and, ultimately, the disintegration of the 'Austrian state'.[23]

Many of the liberal founding fathers of the Austro–Hungarian dual monarchy, of which Eötvös – as Hungarian Minister for Religion and Education from 1848 to 1851, and again from 1867 onwards – was one, were aware of the destructive force inherent in the principle of nationality. For this reason, the making of legislation for the Fundamental Law of 1867 and Nationalities Law of 1868 was carried out carefully: these laws guaranteed the right of each inhabitant to individual freedom and equality, and to preserve and cultivate his or her nationality and language, but no form of recognition was given to the nationalities as legal entities.

In the Austrian half of the monarchy, no official language was introduced. The use of the language classified as customary for a particular region was permitted in government offices and schools.[24] The Hungarian Nationalities Law attempted to curb the demands of the separate nationalities through three central principles: (i) 'the inseparable, unified Hungarian nation', which was formed of 'all inhabitants of Hungary' regardless of 'the nationality to which they belong'; subordinate to this principle, (ii) 'the equality' between 'the different languages customary in the country', in so far as this does not endanger 'the unity of the land';[25] but (iii) only on the basis of individual rights. Use of minority languages was permitted at a local level and in schools, but the Magyar language was introduced as the official state language.

The Fundamental Law of 1867 and Nationalities Law of 1868 in no way met the demands of the nationalist activists since individual fundamental rights did not protect nationalities from discrimination. This deficit meant that liberal gains were soon put to the test.

In the Austrian half of the empire, the state administration made concessions to some nationalities while denying others. Over time, the individual right to preserve and cultivate nationality and language was transformed into a sort of 'ethnic group right' (*Volksgruppenrecht*) through legal teachings and court judgments. This allowed the nationalities to give the impression of being the bearers of collective rights.

In the Hungarian half of the empire, the Magyars, as the largest nationality proportionally, used the lack of protection afforded to national groups as a chance to gain dominance. Soon they gave the impression of being the only legitimate official nationality. From the late 1870s onwards, a huge wave of Magyarization swept across Hungary, starting with the School Law of 1879. Teaching in Magyar became compulsory. In the period from 1880 to 1910, the proportion of the Magyar population rose from 44.9 per cent to 54.6 per cent.

The sobering conclusion is that the central authorities failed to find ways and means to halt the nationalities' trajectory of self-empowerment. Because cultures were mixed within territories, this necessarily brought with it the loss of individual freedom. Robert Musil's ironic comment on this process was that while the government hoped to maintain its supremacy, to do so it allowed the nationalities' 'unsatisfied urge . . . to play at games of statehood' free rein, which played out as 'dollhouse imperialism'.[26] Strong evidence of these concessions to the nationalist activists can be seen in the censuses, the ban on 'forced' language learning and the national compromises.

The censuses carried out in Austria from 1880 onwards did not gather data on mother tongue but on language of habitual use.[27] Respondents could choose between German, Bohemian–Moravian–Slovakian, Polish, Ruthenian, Slovenian, Serbo–Croat, Italian–Ladin, Romanian and Magyar. Pieter M. Judson has pointed out that the nationalists knew how to exploit census results for their own ends.[28] By cleverly conflating the stated language of habitual use with national belonging, the censuses advanced the idea that nations were located in particular territories. The result of a relative majority in the census for *one* language of habitual use in a province gave rise to claims of national dominance for the group using it. Linguistic borders were drawn up on maps, and language islands discovered and exploited by nationalist activists. The census did not record the multilingualism that was so crucial to everyday life.

The Eradication of Multilingualism

In Habsburg Central Europe, bi- or multilinguality was 'politically' important. The Czech poet, philosopher and physiologist Jan Evangelista Purkyn (1787–1869) saw this importance in the way it resulted in different peoples 'drawing closer', peoples who were 'united in Austria under one government'.[29] For this reason, for a long time the state cultivated bi- or multilinguality in everyday dealings (trade, military, administration). In the supranational Austrian empire (1804–67), polyglotism was by no means limited to the elite urban classes, but was widespread in rural backwaters as well. 'We have cases', wrote Purkyn in his essay 'Austria polyglotta,' 'where the long-serving Bohemian soldier not only understands his mother tongue and the habitual German used in drill, but also Italian, Hungarian, Polish and even Romanian and speaks them tolerably as well.' He noticed a similar versatility among low-ranking bureaucrats who 'move all around Austria from time to time', and that polyglotism had done much to facilitate trade.[30] The last surviving evidence of polyglotism are diaries written in three languages and multilingual cookery books. They demonstrate that everyday practices such as individual recollection or culinary skill, for example, were recorded in the language in which a situation was experienced or with which a particular recipe was associated.[31]

The eradication of multilingualism was officially ushered in by the Fundamental Law of 1867. Article 19, paragraph 3 contained the so-called *Sprachenzwangsverbot* or 'ban on forced language use', in which the Constitution's authors conceded to the demands of nationalist activists and removed the obligation to learn the 'second language of the land'.[32] The number of bilingual primary and general secondary schools as well as grammar schools declined rapidly as a result: primary and general secondary schools from 9 per cent (1870–71) to 1.1 per cent (1912–13), and grammar schools during the same period from 7.3 to 5.6 per cent.[33] The Viennese historian Hanna Burger writes of the 'expulsion of multilingualism'.[34]

Compromises and Separations

In the decade before the First World War, the nationalities were granted national autonomy through so-called *Ausgleiche* or compromises. The Moravian Compromise (1905) was the first, followed later by compromises agreed to with Bukovina (1910) and Galicia (1914).[35] The aim of the compromises was to protect the rights of the inhabitants who found themselves demoted to the status of national minority by eradicating competition between the nationalities. The impact was felt in local and school administration. The electorate, which was still composed of various *Kurien* or estates (great landowners, cities, chambers of commerce, municipalities), were registered in so-called 'national cadastres', i.e. lists of voters by nationality. The authorities attempted to ascribe a nationality to each voter objectively using indicators such as language use, parentage, membership of associations and choice of school. The supervision of schools and local administration was also split along ethnic/national lines. For example, in Bohemia, the local, district and provincial school boards were divided into national sections, as were the boards for agricultural matters in Tyrol, Moravia and Austrian Silesia.

The compromises and separations raised ethnic/national segregation to a guiding principle. The result was that the supranational Habsburg empire became a multinational state, which wore itself out in the nationality struggle. Bilingual teaching in schools was abolished, the nationality of individual inhabitants was determined by the authorities on the basis of language of habitual use, and suffrage at a regional level was subject to nationality. Here we see the paradox that – as Eötvös had foreseen long ago – the seemingly supranational constitutional state actually aided the formation of a 'new type of caste system',[36] within which a social practice shaped by linguistic and cultural diversity, situational multilingualism and similarity was attacked or even destroyed by the pressure to assimilate. The national reforms, presented as a 'milestone on the road to an ideal social order', ultimately turned out to be, as Robert A. Kann aptly put it, 'the exact antithesis of transnational state thinking along pluralistic lines'.[37]

The Legacy that Blinds Us

Appropriation of an understanding of identity that rests primarily on cultural difference and ethnic or national sameness is perhaps the greatest legacy of nationalism, and one that continues to blind us to 'the paradigm of similarity in the theory of culture'.[38] Jeremy King writes of the 'ethnicist approach',[39] Rogers Brubaker of 'groupism',[40] and Tara Zahra justifiably highlights this deficit which renders us oblivious to the way that 'national indifference'[41] shaped everyday life. The nation continues to function as the foundational premise of scholarship, and the prefix 'trans' shifts the problem without solving it. It is important to mention two variant arguments of 'methodological nationalism'[42] here. In the first, the past is measured using the yardstick of the respective present. This line of argument can be seen already in the nineteenth century. Josef von Eötvös pointed out that in his day, non-Magyar nationalists were propagating the idea that 'the Hungarian nation (*Volksstamm*)' had been 'a wedge' 'which had been driven into the body of the Slavic nation and prevented the unification of the northern limbs with the southern'. 'It seems to me', wrote Eötvös, that 'this view is based on the frequent fallacy by which we apply the ideas of a more recent era to past centuries and, when assessing individual events, take into consideration not the circumstances of the day, but rather our own contemporary situation.'[43]

We see the other formation of methodological nationalism when past ideas, terms and concepts continue to be adopted, brought up to date and used either in academic or commonplace contexts. Cultural differences are overemphasized and similarities overlooked. For the late Habsburg monarchy, Pieter M. Judson shows that in everyday life, cultural differences played nowhere near the role ascribed to them by nationalist actors.[44] In view of the indifference shown towards nationality by large parts of the population, talk of cultural difference is at times not only misleading but also dangerous, since the continued academic use of politically weighted historical terms as analytical terms consciously or unconsciously legitimizes inclusion and exclusion. Two examples show this. In the 1930s, German national politicians, jurists and historians drew on the Austrian Nationalities Law of the nineteenth century in order to establish an 'Ethnic Groups Law' (*Volksgruppenrecht*) which allowed them to define 'ethnicities' (*Volkstümer*) as being essentially different from one another. Karl Gottfried Hugelmann (1879–1959), an anti-Semitic, National Socialist legal historian and politician, viewed this use of the imperial Nationalities Law as its 'greatest lasting glory'.[45] Ultimately, as would be seen, this 'Ethnic Groups Law',[46] as he named it, was used to justify the 'exclusion of the Jewish population from the community of German people' (*deutsche Volksgemeinschaft*).[47]

This aim was also pursued by other academics during the *Ständestaat* (1933/34–1938), a period of authoritarian, corporatist state rule that was Christian and German national in character, using the argument of spiritual and intellectual difference. Representatives of a clerical, Catholic tradition of scholarship were able to classify Jews as foreign, not on the basis of their 'racial difference' but on the basis of their 'cultural and spiritual difference'. Two Viennese cultural researchers, pre-historian Oswald Menghin (1888–1973) and ethnologist Wilhelm Schmidt (1868–1954), endeavoured to define the concept of Jews' otherness in terms of culture rather than biology. The 'intellect', wrote Menghin, would 'overcome blood'.[48] As representatives of the so-called *Kulturkreislehre*, both researchers insisted on a sharp division between a Jewish and a Christian (-German) essence. In their eyes, this difference manifested itself in an unbridgeable 'difference in culture and spirit', which must not be relinquished since it protected the 'national character of the German people' from impurities. Heredity made 'race' uncertain and transient, whereas the spirit and the intellect, which they believed shaped ethnicity and culture, were stable and permanent.[49] These Catholic national anti-Semites of the inter-war years were therefore in favour of dissimilation since assimilation, 'the adoption of Judaism as part of Germanness . . . , given the current status of the essence of each, would doubtless threaten to alter the national character of the German people'.[50]

The Study of Similarity avant la lettre (Mach, Freud, Kelsen & Co.)

Hugelmann, Menghin and Schmidt were typical proponents of an attitude in the sciences, prevalent in Austrian universities during the inter-war years, which sought to lend credence to political developments. Scholars of this kind focused on developing concepts of cultural, i.e. Christian-German identity. They defined identity through difference, and utilized concepts such as culture, spirit and race to determine who belonged or did not belong to the people's community (*Volksgemeinschaft*). However, a different strand of research – conducted outside the university by scientists I describe as critical and reflexive – rejected the fiction of homogeneity and developed concepts that showed how identity could be produced beyond constructions of difference. A model of similarity is discernible in these concepts which allowed the critical and reflexive strand of research to overcome the unworldliness of scholarship in 'Kakania', an unworldliness that was politically desirable but which Robert Musil criticized in chapter 72 of *The Man without Qualities*. Under the ironic and alienating, chapter heading 'Science smiling into its beard, or a first full-dress encounter with Evil', he wrote

> that the needs of life are different from the requirements of thought. What happens in life is more or less the opposite of whatever the trained mind is accustomed to. Life places a very high value on natural distinctions and congenialities; . . . In short, what we think and what we do coexist in an intricate compromise.[51]

Those representing a critical and reflexive study of identity discarded essentialist concepts of identity.[52] Rather, they focused on social practice, and used this to develop alternative models of togetherness which still have relevance in the twenty-first century.

Ernst Mach (1838–1916), a Viennese physicist, philosopher and physiologist of the senses, led the way here. He declared the concept of ego as substance to be irredeemably lost, and defined it in more abstract terms as complexes of sensations which are put together and presented as a unity for the purposes of provisional orientation. The dissolution of the essentialized ego would, Mach believed, lead to 'a more enlightened view of life, which will preclude the disregard of other egos and the overestimation of our own'.[53] Taking up Mach's criticism of the concept of substance, Hans Kelsen (1881–1973), a professor of law, rejected the dominant organicist concept of the state in German legal thinking, to develop what he himself termed a 'science of the state without a state'.[54] Likewise, in his 'psychology without a soul', as Kelsen put it, Sigmund Freud bid farewell to a scholastic understanding of the soul.[55] It is within this de- and reconstruction that figures of thought and arguments appear which point to the concept of similarity.

In his final large-scale work, *Moses and Monotheism*, published in 1939, Sigmund Freud transformed the biblical Moses, the founding figure of the Jewish people, into an Egyptian. From this starting point, he set about returning the (partially) forgotten history of entanglement between Judaism and Christianity to memory. Through this he demonstrated to a broad public that Jews and Christians were not 'fundamentally different' but kindred spirits, i.e. similar to one another. What Jews and Christians shared was 'Moses and Monotheism'. Freud was on the trail of that 'which we might call historical truth'.[56] According to this truth, a sense of shared identity was not based on having the same heritage, ethnicity or race, but on 'something ideal', a tradition: on 'the possession they had in common of certain intellectual and emotional values'.[57] For Freud, this tradition was founded in the historicity of past events and the processes (forgetting, traumatization and the 'return of the repressed' after long intervals) linked to these incidents.[58] The past events singled out by Freud had not been worked through, and had therefore buried the similarity between Jewish and Christian monotheism. Psychoanalysis opened up a pathway for Freud to approach the 'historical truth', i.e. the similarity between Judaism and Christianity, and to expose the idea of essentialized difference as an illusion.

This was the illusion feeding the rampant anti-Semitism that Freud was attempting to combat by highlighting other, non-essentialist models of identity. In his eyes, that which held Jews and Christians together, and at the same time divided them, was not cultural or racial difference or commonality. Ancestry was not a category of identity: 'Admixture of blood made little difference.'[59] Rather, Freud located the difference between Christians and Jews in the processes of transmission, conscious and necessarily unconscious, of trauma over the centuries. This had concealed the similarity between the two monotheistic religions, or – to borrow from Jan Assmann – cultural repression had acted as a 'form of retention and stabilization'.[60] From Freud's point of view, assimilation and dissimilation – by then the dominant forms for dealing with difference in Central Europe – were nothing other than operations of a reductive concept of identity based on the illusion of 'one state, one people, one culture'. If the history of the division between Jews and Christians was to be told anew, the unmastered trauma underpinning it worked through, and therefore the similarities between the two religions lent new significance, then two things would become unnecessary: the pressure to assimilate, and the unarticulated but soon to be undertaken attempt to exterminate what could not be assimilated.

Like Freud, Hans Kelsen, the Viennese professor of law and theorist of democracy, also refused to close his eyes to the concrete challenges of life. The pluricultural lived reality of Habsburg Central Europe showed him that the state could not be defined as an internally homogeneous 'natural organism'[61] that exercised power, but instead had to be conceived in abstract terms, i.e. in legal and formal terms as a 'legal concept' (*Rechtsbegriff*). Kelsen defined the state as the sum of positive and therefore mutable rules of conduct: the state was law, not substance.[62] In the state so defined, it was also possible to generate identity so that, in a social world fissured by 'opposing interests',[63] no group injured the value structure of another. Kelsen therefore took a stand against the dogma of homogeneity which was keenly championed by his main opponent, the German political philosopher Carl Schmitt.

What differentiated Schmitt and Kelsen was how they dealt with differences in social reality. In particular, this can be seen in their diametrically opposed concepts of democracy. Kelsen conceptualized democracy as a technique for resolving conflict through compromise, while Schmitt, in his constitutional theory, premised democracy on the 'homogeneity of the people' and on the 'identity of ruler and ruled, governing and governed, commander and follower'.[64] For Schmitt, '[d]emocracy's precise state form can be grounded only on a precise and substantial concept of equality', which refers to the 'possibility of inequality'.[65] 'Political democracy', he continued, rested on 'ideas of common race, belief, common destiny and tradition'.[66] If the nation was understood as 'the essential substantive element of democratic equality', then the nationally homogeneous state would appear as 'something normal' whereas the state lacking homogeneity had an 'abnormal quality'.[67] If homogeneity was not achieved through 'separation or gradual, peaceful *assimilation* to the ruling nation',[68] there remained 'if the need arises – the elimination or eradication of heterogeneity'.[69] In the National Socialist era, Schmitt wrote of 'ethnic identity' as a necessary condition of the National Socialist state.[70]

It was towards this supposedly abnormal state that Hans Kelsen directed his full attention. For Kelsen, the 'homogeneity' Schmitt spoke of was neither evident in social reality nor necessary for the democratization of the state. It was enough that individuals agreed on rules for getting along with one another; sharing the same ancestry, language or culture was not a requirement. The only requirement was that the set of rules agreed upon – the state as the highest normative instance – were accepted as the basis for action. In contrast to Schmitt, Kelsen defined the state and democracy in legal, normative and performative terms. Citizens had equal rights because they submitted to the agreed coercive order and, by doing so, participated in the decision-making process. Kelsen dismissed any demand for national homogeneity as a condition of democracy. Heterogeneity was acceptable in any democracy,[71] since the task of democracy was not to create sameness but to guarantee the individual freedoms of the largest possible number of people through compromise, 'peacefully and gradually'.[72] This model, which implicitly underpins the concept of similarity, rests on the idea that the agreement of a set of rules renders the fiction of homogeneity unnecessary. As concerns a cultural theory of similarity, therefore, it makes it clear that rejecting the dichotomy of identity and alterity demands a high measure of reflexivity with regard to how those rules are devised and applied.

The theories and approaches of other Viennese cultural historians, sociologists and philosophers working in the period around 1900 also pointed towards the concept of similarity. Alois Riegl, for example, reassessed the artistic production of previous eras and discovered similarities in ornamentation that indicated a long history of entanglement between Orient and Occident.[73] Ludwig Wittgenstein and Otto Neurath reappraised language with regard to similarities. What had been the most important symbol in the pursuit of the creation of national identity through division since the nineteenth century was rehabilitated by both as a central means of communication. In language, the philosopher Wittgenstein discovered an analogy with play,[74] while Neurath, a philosopher of science, examined its function as a means of communication between the different disciplines within science.[75] Both dissociated themselves from the exact descriptive processes used in the natural sciences since these – from their point of view – were in a position to give only an unsatisfactory description of the world. Wittgenstein distanced himself from the idea that language was a copy of reality, Neurath from the concept of the system as a model for the so-called unified science of logical empiricism.

Wittgenstein studied the communicative function of language and, in this context, compared the way language was used to games. While there was no characteristic that was shared by all games, they resembled one another on the basis of being governed by rules. And like games, no language had a unique essence that allowed clear distinctions between individual languages to be made. Languages are related and, like games, are connected by a 'complicated network of similarities overlapping and criss-crossing'.[76] Language-games bear 'family resemblances'[77] to one another and yet are as varied as are the different forms of life. The meaning of words is determined only by how those words are used.

Similar arguments were put forward by Otto Neurath. His aim was to use a 'Universal Jargon' to bring together propositions made in the different scientific disciplines.[78] In 'shared' knowledge, based on the 'actual store of expressions which people have in common all over the world',[79] he saw an important step towards a democratic public sphere. The expressions used must, according to Neurath, be 'based on conventions which could never be definite or authoritative', for '[p]luralism is the aura of this scientific world community of the common man'.[80] However, the attempts at logical systematization undertaken by his colleague Rudolf Carnap appeared to him suspect, and he rejected them as metaphysics. 'We do *not* arrive at "*one*" system of science that could take the place of the "real world" so to speak; everything remains ambiguous and in many ways uncertain.' Science does not rest on global but on 'local systematizations', on 'multiplicity' and 'uncertainty'. The system, on the other hand, is a leveller; it is the 'great scientific lie'.[81] Neurath preferred the 'encyclopaedia as a model' to the 'system as a model'. In contrast to the system, the encyclopaedic approach would orchestrate the multiplicity of the sciences without destroying it.[82]

Conclusion

In this overview of similarity and cultural difference in everyday life, politics and scholarship, I have focused attention on how similarity was dealt with in social practice and as a heuristic concept in Habsburg Central Europe. I have tried to show that in Vienna, in the period around 1900, a critical and reflexive branch of the study of identity addressed the way cultural difference was being used to lend political credence to national identity; and in doing so, it rehabilitated similarity as a heuristic concept. While the complex process of nationalization in the Habsburg monarchy and Austria as a successor state made assimilation and dissimilation the preferred form for dealing with cultural difference, figures of thought emerged in the sciences which are of value for a cultural theory of similarity: the figure of trauma in connection with tradition, memory and reflection (Freud); the figure of the rule (Kelsen and Wittgenstein); the figure of entanglement (Riegl); and a scientific attitude that valued the ambivalence and indeterminacy of lived reality (Wittgenstein and Neurath).

The proposed scientific models that arose in connection with these figures of thought, from Freud to Kelsen and the other scientists mentioned above, fulfilled *avant la lettre* that function which today the concept of similarity in combination with the concept of difference promises to fulfil. These models turn out to be an antidote to a 'methodological nationalism' in science, which is still taking the concepts (culture, ethnicity, race) and processes (assimilation and dissimilation) once used in nationalization and rendering them useful and applicable to the formation of collective identities today. The models shown here delegitimize a concept of identity that sanctifies the idea of difference, be it cultural or ethnic/national. The scientists discussed here replace it with a vision of community according to which assimilation and dissimilation are not an adequate form for dealing with difference in pluricultural societies. What binds and differentiates people is not origin, language or heritage (*Volkstum*), but the joint endeavour to find a 'historical truth' which values similarities as well as the willingness to agree to binding rules as the basis for action and the willingness to reflect on culture. Social practice shows that culture does not recognize boundaries and that social spaces elude 'stark cultural barriers',[83] as Alois Riegl named them. Ultimately, language has also been deprived of its value as a political symbol and returned to its function as a means of communication that enables the uncertainties (anything that is similar, rather than not the same or completely different) of everyday life to be dealt with. The perspective presented here on Habsburg Central Europe and beyond draws on postcolonial theory. The attempt has been to show how a critical analysis of the fiction of homogeneity allows the emergence of new approaches to thought and action shaped by the concept of similarity.

Notes

[1] Umlauft (1876): 1f.
[2] Konrád (1986): 88.
[3] Musil (1995): 405.
[4] Hofmannsthal ([1922] 1979b): 195f.
[5] Hofmannsthal ([1921] 1979a): 474.
[6] See Bhatti (2016b) and Bhatti (2016a).
[7] Bhabha (1994): 52.
[8] Ibid.
[9] Hall (2000): 216.
[10] Freud (1999a): 73.
[11] On the nationalization process, see Cohen (2008); Judson (2006); Wingfield, ed. (2003).
[12] See Judson (2005): 4 and Judson (2016b).
[13] On multilingualism and non-verbal communicative practices, see Csáky (2010; 2014).
[14] See Feichtinger (2016b) and Feichtinger (2013).
[15] See Feichtinger (2010) and Feichtinger (2012).
[16] For a detailed discussion, see Kann (1962).
[17] See, for example, Freud ([1939] 1999b): 197.
[18] Eötvös (1851): 1f.
[19] See Csáky (2016).
[20] Palacký (1866): 13.
[21] Eötvös (1865): 85f.
[22] Ibid.: 111.
[23] Eötvös (1859): 83.
[24] See *Staatsgrundgesetz vom 21, December 1867.*
[25] *Ueber die Gleichberechtigung der Nationalitäten* (1872).
[26] Musil (1990): 93.
[27] See Brix (1982).
[28] See Judson (2016b): 309–12 and Judson (2016a).
[29] Purkyn (2002): 353.
[30] Ibid.: 356.
[31] See Luthar (2016).
[32] See *Staatsgrundgesetz vom 21, December 1867.*
[33] See Burger (1997): 42.
[34] See ibid.
[35] See Kuzmany (2016).
[36] Eötvös (1865): 176.
[37] Kann (1975): 51, 53.

[38] See Bhatti *et al.* (2011), and Bhatti (2014).
[39] See King (2001).
[40] Brubaker (2007).
[41] Zahra (2010); Judson and Zahra (2012).
[42] See Smith (1979).
[43] Eötvös (1865): 40.
[44] See Judson (2016a).
[45] Hugelmann, ed. (1934): 281.
[46] Ibid.: 282.
[47] Fahlbusch (2008): 693.
[48] Menghin (1934a): 596.
[49] Schmidt (1964): 278, 274.
[50] Menghin (1934b): 171f., 163. See also Schmidt (1936).
[51] Musil (1995): 329.
[52] See Feichtinger (2016a).
[53] Mach ([1886] 1991): 20, 23.
[54] Kelsen (1922): 208.
[55] Kelsen ([1923] 1989): 54.
[56] Freud (1996): 108.
[57] Ibid.: 158.
[58] Ibid.:109.
[59] Ibid.: 158.
[60] Assmann (1997): 161.
[61] Jellinek (1929).
[62] Kelsen (1922): 114–204 (Section III: 'Kritischer Beweis der Identität von Staat und Recht') and 205–18 (Chapter: 'Der Staatsbegriff als Substanzbegriff').
[63] Kelsen (1929): 22.
[64] Schmitt (2008): 264.
[65] Ibid.: 257f.
[66] Ibid.: 258.
[67] Ibid.: 262.
[68] Ibid.
[69] Schmitt ([1923] 1926): 14. He continues: 'The political power of a democracy is manifested in its ability to remove or keep away the foreign and the different, that which threatens homogeneity.' ('Die politische Kraft einer Demokratie zeigt sich darin, daß sie das Fremde und Ungleiche, die Homogenität Bedrohende zu beseitigen oder fernzuhalten weiß.')
[70] Schmitt (2001): 48.
[71] See Lübbe-Wolff (2007): 124f.
[72] Kelsen (1925): 361.
[73] See Riegl (1985).
[74] See Wittgenstein ([1953] 1984).
[75] See Neurath (1981).
[76] Wittgenstein (2009): 36e (Number 66).
[77] Ibid.: (Number 67).
[78] Neurath ([1946] 1983b): 236.
[79] Ibid.: 242.
[80] Ibid.
[81] Neurath ([1935] 1983a): 116.
[82] Neurath ([1946] 1983b).
[83] Riegl (1995): 108.

References

Assmann, Jan (1997), *Moses the Egyptian: The Memory of Egypt in Western Monotheism*, Cambridge, MA: Harvard University Press.

Bhabha, Homi K. (1994), *The Location of Culture*, London, New York: Routledge.

Bhatti, Anil (2014), 'Ähnlichkeit', in Özkan Ezli and Gisela Staupe, eds, *Das neue Deutschland: Von Migration und Vielfalt*, Konstanz: Konstanz University Press: 161–63.

——— (2016a), 'Heterogeneities and Homogeneities: On Similarities and Diversities', in Johannes Feichtinger and Gary B. Cohen, eds., *Understanding Multiculturalism: The Habsburg Central European Experience*, Austrian and Habsburg Studies 17, Oxford and New York: Berghahn: 17–46.

——— (2016b), 'Plurikulturalität', in Johannes Feichtingerand Heidemarie Uhl, eds, *Habsburg neu denken: Vielfalt und Ambivalenz in Zentraleuropa, 30 kulturwissenschaftliche Stichworte*, Wien, Köln and Weimar: Böhlau: 171–80.

Bhatti, Anil *et al.* (2011), 'Ähnlichkeit: Ein kulturtheoretisches Paradigma', *Internationales Archiv für Sozialgeschichte der deutschen Literatur*, 36 (1): 261–75.

Brix, Emil (1982), *Die Umgangssprachen in Altösterreich zwischen Agitation und Assimilation: Die Sprachenstatistik in den zisleithanischen Volkszählungen 1880 bis 1910* (Veröffentlichungen der Kommission für Neuere Geschichte Österreichs 72), Wien, Köln and Weimar: Böhlau.

Brubaker, Rogers (2007), *Ethnizität ohne Gruppen*, Hamburg: HIS.

Burger, Hanna (1997), 'Die Vertreibung der Mehrsprachigkeit am Beispiel Österreichs 1867–1918', in Gerd Hentschel, ed., Über Muttersprachen und Vaterländer: *Zur Entwicklung von Standardsprachen und Nationen in Europa*, Frankfurt am Main u.a: Peter Lang: 35–49.

Cohen, Gary B. (2008), 'Nationalist Politics and the Dynamics of State and Civil Society in the Habsburg Monarchy, 1867–1914', *Central European History*, 40: 241–78.

Csáky, Moritz (2010), *Das Gedächtnis der Städte. Kulturelle Verflechtungen – Wien und die urbanen Milieus in Zentraleuropa*, Wien, Köln and Weimar: Böhlau.

——— (2014), *Kulinarik und Kultur: Speisen als kulturelle Codes in Zentraleuropa*, edited by Georg Christian Lack, Wien, Köln and Weimar: Böhlau.

——— (2016), 'Culture as a Sphere of Communication', in Johannes Feichtinger and Gary B. Cohen, eds, *Understanding Multiculturalism: The Habsburg Central European Experience*, Austrian and Habsburg Studies 17, Oxford and New York: Berghahn.

Eötvös, Joseph von (1851), *Ueber die Gleichberechtigung der Nationalitäten in Oesterreich*, Wien: Jasper, Hügel and Manz.

——— (1865), *Nationalitäten-Frage*, Pest: Ráth.

——— (1859), *Die Garantien der Macht und Einheit Oesterreichs*, Leipzig: Brockhaus.

Fahlbusch, Michael (2008), 'Südostdeutsche Forschungsgemeinschaft', in Ingo Haar and Michael Fahlbusch, eds, *Handbuch der völkischen Wissenschaften: Personen–Institutionen–Forschungsprogramme–Stiftungen*, München: Saur: 688–97.

Feichtinger, Johannes (2010), *Wissenschaft als reflexives Projekt: Von Bolzano über Freud zu Kelsen: Österreichische Wissenschaftsgeschichte 1848–1938*, Bielefeld: Transcript Verlag.

——— (2012), '"Staatsnation", "Kulturnation", "Nationalstaat": The Role of National Politics in the Advancement of Science and Scholarship in Austria from 1848 to 1938', in Mitchell G. Ash and Jan Surman, eds, *The Nationalization of Scientific Knowledge in the Habsburg Empire (1848–1918)*, Houndmills, Basingstoke: Palgrave Macmillan: 57–82.

——— (2016a), 'Intellectual Affinities: Ernst Mach, Sigmund Freud, Hans Kelsen and the Austrian Anti-Essentialist Approach to Science and Scholarship', in Ian Bryan, Peter Langford and John McGarry, eds, *The Foundation of the Juridico-Political*

Concept Formation in Hans Kelsen and Max Weber, New York: Routledge: 117–39.

——— (2016b), 'Modernisierung, Zivilisierung, Kolonisierung als Argument: Konkurrierende Selbstermächtigungsdiskurse in der späten Habsburgermonarchie', in Christof Dejung and Martin Lengwiler (eds), *Ränder der Moderne. Neue Perspektiven auf die europäische Geschichte (1800–1930)*, Peripherien: Neue Beiträge zur Europäischen Geschichte 1, Köln, Weimar and Wien: Böhlau: 147–81.

Feichtinger, Johannes and Johann Heiss (2013) 'Distant Neighbors: Uses of Orientalism in the Late Nineteenth-Century Austro-Hungarian Empire', in James Hodkinson, John Walker and Shaswati Mazumdar, eds, *Deploying Orientalism in Culture and History: From Germany to Central and Eastern Europe*, Studies in German Literature, Linguistics and Culture, Rochester and New York: Camden House.

Feichtinger, Johannes and Gary B. Cohen, eds (2016), *Understanding Multiculturalism: The Habsburg Central European Experience*, Austrian and Habsburg Studies 17, Oxford and New York: Berghahn.

Freud, Sigmund ([1921] 1999a), 'Massenpsychologie und Ich-Analyse', in *Gesammelte Werke. Band XIII. Jenseits des Lustprinzips/Massenpsychologie und Ich-Analyse/ Das Ich und das Es*, edited by Anna Freud *et al.*, Frankfurt am Main: Fischer: 71–161; English edition: London: Imago Publishing Co., 1940.

——— ([1939] 1999b), 'Der Mann Moses und die monotheistische Religion', in *Gesammelete Werke. Banks XVI. Werke aus den Jahren 1932–1939*, edited by Anna Freud *et al.*, Frankfurt am Main: Fischer: 101–246; English edition: London: Imago Publishing Co., 1950.

——— (1996), *Moses and Monotheism*, translated by Katherine Jones, New York: Random House.

Hall, Stuart (2000), 'Conclusion: The Multi-Cultural Question', in Barnor Hesse, ed., *Un/ settled Multiculturalisms: Diasporas, Entanglements*, London: Zed Press: 209–41.

Hofmannsthal, Hugo von ([1921] 1979a), 'Bemerkungen', in *Reden und Aufsätze II 1914–1924* (Gesammelte Werke in zehn Einzelbänden), Frankfurt am Main: Fischer: 473–77.

——— ([1922] 1979b), 'Wiener Brief [II] ', in *Reden und Aufsätze II 1914–1924* (Gesammelte Werke in zehn Einzelbänden), Frankfurt am Main: Fischer: 185–96.

Hugelmann, Karl Gottfried, ed. (1934), *Das Nationalitätenrecht des alten Österreich*, Wien and Leipzig: Braumüller.

Jellinek, Georg ([1900] 1929), *Allgemeine Staatslehre*, fifth expanded reprint of the 1914 edition, reviewed and expanded by Walter Jellinek, Berlin: Springer.

Judson, Pieter M. (2005), 'Constructing Nationalities in East Central Europe', in Pieter Judson and Marsha L. Rozenblit, eds, *Constructing Nationalities in East Central Europe*, Austrian and Habsburg Studies 6, Oxford and New York: Berghahn.

——— (2006), *Guardians of the Nation: Activists on the Language Frontiers of Imperial Austria*, Cambridge, MA: Harvard University Press.

——— (2016a), 'Do Multiple Languages Mean a Multicultural Society? Nationalist "Frontiers" in Rural Austria, 1880–1918', in Gary B. Cohen and Johannes Feichtinger (eds), *Understanding Multiculturalism: Central Europe and the Habsburg Experience*, Austrian and Habsburg Studies 17, Oxford and New York: Berghahn: 61–82.

——— (2016b), *The Habsburg Empire: A New History*, Cambridge, MA and London: Harvard University Press.

Judson Peter and Tara Zahra (2012), 'Introduction', *Austrian History Yearbook*, 43, (Schwerpunktthema: 'National Indifference').

Kann, Robert A. (1962), *Werden und Zerfall des Habsburgerreiches*, Graz u.a.: Styria.

——— (1975), 'Die Habsburgermonarchie und das Problem des übernationalen Staates', in

Adam Wandruszka and Peter Urbanitsch, eds, *Die Habsburgermonarchie 1848–1918: Verwaltung und Rechtswesen*, Vol. 2, Wien: Verlag der Österreichischen Akademie der Wissenschaften: 1–56.

Kelsen, Hans (1922), *Der soziologische und der juristische Staatsbegriff: Kritische Untersuchung des Verhältnisses von Staat und Recht*, Tübingen: Mohr.

——— (1925), *Allgemeine Staatslehre*, Berlin: Springer Verlag.

——— (1929), *Vom Wesen und Wert der Demokratie*, Tübingen: Mohr.

——— ([1923] 1989), 'Gott und Staat', in *Staat und Naturrecht: Aufsätze zur Ideologiekritik*, edited by Ernst Topitsch, Munich: Fink.

King, Jeremy (2001), 'The Nationalization of East-Central Europe: Ethnicism, Ethnicity, and Beyond', in Maria Bucur and Nancy M. Wingfield, eds, *Staging the Past: The Politics of Commemoration in Habsburg Central Europe, 1848 to the Present*, West Lafayette: Purdue University Press: 112–52.

Konrád, György (1986), 'Der Traum von Mitteleuropa', in Erhard Busek and Gerhard Wilfinger, eds, *Aufbruch nach Mitteleuropa: Rekonstruktion eines versunkenen Kontinents*, Wien: Herold: 87–97.

Kuzmany, Börries (2016), 'Habsburg Austria: Experiments in Non-Territorial Autonomy', *Ethnopolitics*, 15 (1): 43–65.

Lübbe-Wolff, Gertrude (2007), 'Homogenes Volk – Über Homogenitätspostulate und Integration', *Zar: Zeitschrift für Ausländerrecht und Ausländerpolitik*, 4: 121–27.

Luthar, Oto (2016), 'The Slice of Desire: Intercultural practices versus national loyalties in the peripheral multiethnic society of Central Europe at the beginning of twentieth century', in Johannes Feichtinger and Gary B. Cohen, eds, *Understanding Multiculturalism: Central Europe and the Habsburg Experience*, Austrian and Habsburg Studies 17, Oxford, New York: Berghahn.

Mach, Ernst ([1886] 1991), *Die Analyse der Empfindungen und das Verhältnis des Psychischen zum Physischen*, Mit einem Vorwort von Gereon Wolters, Darmstadt: WBG.

Menghin, Oswald (1934a), 'Geist und Blut. Zur Rassenfrage', *Schönere Zukunft*, 9 (24), 11 March: 595–97.

——— (1934b), *Geist und Blut: Grundsätzliches um Rasse, Sprache, Kultur und Volkstum*, Wien: Anton Schroll & Co.

Musil, Robert ([1919] 1990), 'Anschluss with Germany', in *Precision and Soul: Essays and Addresses*, translated and edited by Burton Pike and David S. Luft, Chicago: University of Chicago Press: 90–98.

——— (1995), *Man Without Qualities*, translated by Sophie Wilkins, edited by Burton Pike, London: Picador.

Neurath, Otto ([1945] 1981), 'Die Orchestrierung der Wissenschaften durch den Enzyklopädismus des Logischen Empirismus', in *Gesammelte philosophische und methodologische Schriften*, edited by Rudolf Haller und Heiner Rutte, Vol. 2, Vienna: Hölder, Pichler, Tempsky.

——— ([1935] 1983a), 'The Unity of Science as a Task', in Robert S. Cohen and Marie Neurath, eds, *Philosophical Papers: 1913–1946*, Dordrecht: D. Reidel Publishing Company: 115–20.

——— ([1946] 1983b), 'The Orchestration of the Sciences by the Encyclopaedism of Logical Empiricism', in Robert S. Cohen and Marie Neurath (eds), *Philosophical Papers: 1913–1946*, Dordrecht: D. Reidel Publishing Company: 230–42.

Palacký, Franz ([1865] 1866), *Oesterreichs Staatsidee*, Prague: Kober.

Purkyn , Jan Evangelista ([1867] 2002), 'Austria polyglotta', in *Tschechische Philosophen von Hus bis Masaryk*, selected, with introductions and an afterword by Ludger Hagedorn, Stuttgart, München: DVA: 303–68.

Riegl, Alois ([1893] 1985), *Stilfragen. Grundlegungen zu einer Geschichte der Ornamentik*, with an Afterword by Otto Pächt, München: Mäander Verlag.

——— ([1905] 1995), 'Entwurf einer gesetzlichen Organisation der Denkmalpflege in Österreich', in Ernst Bacher, ed., *Kunstwerk oder Denkmal: Alois Riegls Schriften zur Denkmalpflege*, Studien zu Denkmalschutz und Denkmalpflege 15, Wien, Köln and Weimar: Böhlau: 49–144.

Schmidt, Wilhelm (1936), 'Rassen und Rassenpflege im Bereich des deutschen Volkes', *Schönere Zukunft*, 11 (17), 26 January: 425–27.

——— ([1935] 1964), 'Rasse und Weltanschauung', in *Wege der Kulturen: Gesammelte Aufsätze*, Bonn: Anthropos-Institut St. Augustin: 269–84.

Schmitt, Carl ([1923] 1926), *Die geistesgeschichtliche Lage des heutigen Parlamentarismus*, München, Leipzig: Duncker & Humblot.

——— (2001), *State, Movement, People: The Triadic Structure of Political Unity*, translated and edited by Simona Draghici, Corvallis: Plutarch Press.

——— (2008), *Constitutional Theory*, translated and edited by Jeffrey Seitzer, Durham and London: Duke University Press.

Smith, Anthony D. (1979), *Nationalism in Twentieth Century*, New York: New York University Press.

Staatsgrundgesetz vom 21. December 1867, über die allgemeinen Rechte der Staatsbürger für die im Reichsrathe vertretenen Königreiche und Länder, StF: RGBl. Nr. 142/1867 http://www.ris.bka.gv.at.

Ueber die Gleichberechtigung der Nationalitäten, 44, Gesetzartikel vom 6. Dezember 1868, in: Landesgesetz-Sammlung für die Jahre 1865, 67 und 1868, Pest: Ráth 1872: 270–78.

Umlauft, Friedrich (1876), 'Einleitung', in *Die Oesterreichisch-Ungarische Monarchie. Geographisch-statistisches Handbuch mit besonderer Rücksicht auf die politische und Kultur-Geschichte für Leser aller Stände*, Wien and Pest: Hartleben Verlag.

Wingfield, Nancy M., ed. (2003), *Creating the Other: Ethnic Conflict and Nationalism in Habsburg Central Europe*, Austrian and Habsburg Studies 5, Oxford and New York: Berghahn.

Wittgenstein, Ludwig ([1953] 1984), 'Philosophische Untersuchungen', in Id., *Werkausgabe*. Vol 1 (stw 501), Frankfurt am Main: Suhrkamp.

——— (2009), *Philosophical Investigations* (Number 66), translated by G.E.M. Anscombe, P.M.S. Hacker and Joachim Schulte, Oxford: Blackwell.

Zahra, Tara (2010), 'Imagined Noncommunities, National Indifference as a Category of Analysis', *Slavic Review*, 69 (1): 93–119.

The Similarity and Difference of Religion(s) 1750–1850

Rudolf Schlögl

I

Within cultural studies, the idea and concept of similarity has developed in three different dimensions. Although Foucault identified a significant discontinuity in the history of the concept, similarity has left a broad wake in European discourse from the Renaissance to today.[1] This influence is not only due to the continued effect of ancient traditions of thought in which similarity represented an irreducible point of reference for the formation of order.[2] Given this, similarity also represents a prerequisite for the generation of human knowledge and thus takes on an epistemological dimension alongside its historical-discourse dimension. The third dimension emerges when similarity is juxtaposed with alternative concepts that determine its application to social practices. Not only does the concept of similarity provide access to the world, it also orders the social world. It orders the world differently and has different consequences for social practices than the concept of equality, which pushes for assimilation where diversity exists. Similarity also orders the world differently than the concept of difference, which calls for the exclusion of the other.

Similarity mediates. It anticipates the inherent overlapping qualities of things so that both differing and related elements can be identified and placed next to one another. It emphasizes the compatible, the related in the diverse, and minimizes the importance of the different. This is why similarity, and not identity and difference, should be the frame of reference in complex social situations. Of course, history rarely provides such clear-cut examples of such insights. A look at the field of religion, for instance, reveals a tradition of thought that originated in the epistemic dimension of similarity, and has had an effect on other schools of thought and practice as well. Recognition of the similar is always based on the perspective of the observer, and thus clearly allows for an orientation towards normative benchmarks; indeed, it almost demands such benchmarks. This is why the comparative observation of global religions, which culminated in the concept of a collective singular at the end of the eighteenth century, was almost without exception accompanied by a marked heirarchization of world religions according to their 'similarity' to European Christianity.

II

After the mid-nineteenth century, discourse about world religions combined with the missionary expansion of Europe led to the institutional formation of a new scientific discipline: religious studies.[3] This process was accompanied by intense reflection about the methods to be used in the new science, and the concept of similarity played a critical role.[4] The phenomenon of religion was only able to be isolated as a globally unique and independent social truth because world religions could be identified as having similar core elements. This view was shared by both the founding fathers of religious studies: Max Müller and Edward Burnett Tylor.[5] Both of them also agreed that the best way to identify such similarities was comparative observation, which is why they declared chronologically and geographically comparative approaches to be the gold standard of methodology in the new science. They then posed the question of how similarity could be explained within such a methodology, and believed that the search for an explanation alone would establish the scientific character of the study of the human phenomenon that is religion.

In answering this question, Müller and Tylor referred to entirely different scientific traditions. Müller explicitly argued from a linguistic perspective. In his view, fundamental similarities present in the historical variety of religions could be explained by the fact that they all combined a very limited number of initial elements in new ways. Both the variety and the similarity of religions were thus based on a common underlying general structure. Thus, the core task of religious studies should be to identify these rules of combination through comparative observations, and to develop a generative grammar (including a syntax and perhaps even a semiotics) of the social phenomenon of religion.[6] Tylor, on the other hand, looked to natural history as a model. He believed that a comparison of religions would allow for their categorization according to their type and subtype. By identifying the respective development logics of each religion, it would be possible to describe all religions as an evolutionary development from one or more original prototypes.[7] In this view, similarity in the diversity of religions can thus be explained genetically. Despite these argumentative differences, both theologians were unified in another important point: that European Christianity had nothing to fear from such comparative operations, because it represented the highest and most superior form of religion.

With their methodological considerations, both Max Müller

and E.B. Tylor took for granted something that had not yet been widely accepted by the middle of the eighteenth century: a general concept of religion – a collective singular of the phenomenon. In Volume 31 of his 1742 universal lexicon, Zedler defined religion/*religio* as the service and worship of the 'true God' based on either rationality or the revelation of the Holy Scripture. Because it was hard to find any examples of a people that lived without any knowledge of revealed divine will, Zedler divided religions into the one true religion and the many false religions, which 'themselves are very different from one another'.[8] The entry continues by describing the various religions of different continents: Africa, America, Asia and Europe. In this way, the article defined religion based on the vast diversity and difference of religions and confessions around the globe. Authors who wrote about religion at the end of that century or at the beginning of the next – historians such as Christoph Meiners and Johann Christoph Adelung, philosophers such as Immanuel Kant and Georg Friedrich Wilhelm Hegel, or theologians such as Friedrich Schleiermacher – on the other hand, used a more universal concept of religion that was no longer based on orthopraxy, but rather on a social, spiritual or civilizing cultural phenomenon.[9] This made the many different religions of the world similar. So similar, in fact, that the special status of Christianity in the emergence of the collective singular faded, or was at least relativized to such an extent that authors from Friedrich Schleiermacher to Georg Wilhelm Friedrich Hegel and Friedrich Wilhelm Joseph Schelling attempted to re-establish this special role of Christianity based on philosophical arguments and arguments concerning the history of civilization. Original theological arguments were largely missing because the Christian revelation had become a victim of bible criticism to such an extent that, at best, commentators could postulate a sort of 'original' revelation that would allow religion to be explained as a constitutive part of human history and the human experience. This new arrangement conformed with the observation that the various religious parties of Europe had coalesced around the confessions of European Christianity, and that the national societies that were forming at the time increasingly committed themselves to plurality instead of tolerance.[10]

A recognition of the geographical and historical breadth of the phenomenon of religion emerged from the comparative observation of religions found in the historical and global world of the eighteenth century. The similarity between all of these religions was established by connecting them together in a common history of religion that was either based on the more general history of civilization or stood on its own as a separate phenomenon. Either way, this approach put religious scholars in a position to identify the common core of all religions while at the same time recognizing the differences between them.

III

It is possible to differentiate between the various historiographic strategies used by religious scholars over time, and here I would like to selectively focus on a series of texts written between 1750 and 1850. The first strategy that sought to identify similarities and differences between religions was the aforementioned theory of 'original' revelation. In 1738, William Warburton sought to explain the laws of Moses in order to counter free thinker and libertine claims that ordered civil society was possible without religion, and that such a society could even be founded based on the sinful nature of man alone. Such arguments led Warburton to cite the ancient Egyptians as the first to recognize the close connection between a 'civil society' and a belief in gods and an afterlife. This allowed Warburton to conclude that Moses – as the founder of the Old Testament religion – also must have had a direct influence on the social and religious order of the present, because he had not foreseen an afterlife in his teachings. Warburton embedded this argument in a narrative about the development of religion which began with an original revelation that took place at creation. But this revelation was lost, and led to astral religions and the worship of ancestral law-givers as gods, finally ending in the worship of animals as in ancient Egypt. This is where the development of religions split: priests and wise men overcame the crude worship of things and ultimately developed a theology in which the recognition of the one God was connected with teachings about the afterlife. Warburg then went on to demonstrate the existence of this connection between an esoteric and an exoteric side of religion through the entirety of ancient philosophy.[11]

Warburton's complicated argument sought to do two things. First, he sought to unify the possibility of a natural human religion – which emerged from the nature of man and the necessities of his socialization – with the original revelation and the presence of God in the Old Testament. At the same time, he wanted to emphasize the fundamental difference between Judaism and Christianity, in order to argue that Judaism was unsuited to be the basis for a civil society.

From 1724 to 1730, John Hutchinson undertook a similar attempt at placing natural religions and revelatory religions on good terms with one another. He asked himself the question of why ancient heathens had access to wisdom and knowledge that the Christians did not, despite the fact that the latter had been given the words of God's revelation. His answer was that God had first revealed himself to man by teaching him through the emblematic contemplation of nature. In this way, religious texts represented a sort of secondary source because they formulated insights that the heathens had already gained through their symbolic understanding of nature. Over time, Christians who oriented themselves to the written word of God then lost their ability to emblematically decrypt nature.[12]

At this point I would like to jump forward in time to the year 1808, and to Freidrich Schlegel's work *Language and Wisdom of the Indians*, which sought to illustrate the kinship between the languages of Europe and the Orient, and to describe the reasons for such a connection. Schlegel focused his considerations on religious texts, which he compared with one another. He too built his reconstruction of reciprocal relationships and influences on the idea of an original revelation, and he claimed that this revelation was then lost to mankind as it turned away from God. He then reinterpreted the poetry and philosophy that came afterwards as an expression of horror at the fall from God. This enabled him to evaluate the religions of India, China and the ancient world against a philosophically interpreted Christian monotheism. He claimed that the religious texts of Indians in particular provided evidence that they had observed the darkness that came after the fall from grace with particular clarity. Following Johann Gottfried von Herder, Schlegel then described the further history of similarities and relations between Europe and the Orient as the result of contacts, migration and processes of colonization.[13]

Attempts to establish a constructive relationship between the revelation and natural religion wore out the more they were repeated. David Hume, who (in light of his profession) was in no way bound to theology, was able to escalate the doubt caused by deism. He connected the development of religion with the character of man; not with the highly regarded better faculty of rationality but rather with the traits that emerged from his ignorance. He began his investigations on the *Natural History of Religion* by posing the question of the source of religion. He claimed that it was certainly based on rationality, because all of nature is clearly the manifestation of an *intelligent author*. But this is the rationality of the creator, and not of man. When it comes to man, we must assume a secondary principle, because we cannot prove the existence of an original religious instinct. This led Hume to identify ignorance and fear of natural forces as the basis of religion, which, appropriately, first emerged as polytheism. According to Hume, at this stage of development man was not yet even capable of the kind of rationality-based, causal observation of nature that could have provided him with knowledge of the creator. In other words, philosophy and knowledge of nature helped man come to believe in the one true God. For Hume, the remainder of history consisted of a fluctuation between these two forms of religion, and he utilized this fundamental distinction to diagnose the mixture of polytheism and monotheism in the Christianity of his time. In doing so, he was able to forego a heirarchization of theism and polytheism, because he assumed that even the most pure human concepts of God would transform into superstitious piety.[14] In this sense all religions were similar to one another, but human irrationality made the mistake of seeing them as the same.

The result was not much different in those instances where religion was seen as a positive factor in the formation and developmental history of the human spirit. Here we can distinguish between two different variations: the philosophical phenomenology of the absolute spirit as paradigmatically formulated by Hegel, and linguistic and poetic theories of religious myths which saw religious texts as evidence for a human history of semiotics and poetological forms. These variations have often been mixed together as well.

In the phenomenology of the absolute spirit, religion was considered an epiphenomenon in a different way than found in the negative histories from Voltaire to Constant. God became the world because he had to differentiate himself from himself. The history of religion could thus be framed as a history of the self-revelation of the human spirit that occurred because man reflected upon himself. In his *Lectures on the Philosophy of Religion*, Hegel attempted to explain the diversity and randomness of historical events as necessary, given this phenomenological foundation. He differentiated natural religions into those of sublimeness and beauty, and those of utility. This led to a depiction of religion that was more geographical than historical or genetic. The typology of Hegel's description followed the abstractive forms of the human spirit, and thus the structure of the relationship between subject and object. This is also why Hegel was convinced that Christianity, as a revelatory religion, was the highest form of religion: in Christianity, the concept of religion became concrete and objective in and of itself. In other words, the spirit was able to observe itself in the form of religion.[15]

In 1810, Friedrich Creuzer published the second edition of his *Symbolism and Mythology of the Ancients*, in which he added an extended section on the Persian and Indian systems of religion. Creuzer also considered Christianity to be the highest form of religion, even though he equated it with the Greek mysteries of the spiritual form; as a public cult, he saw the Greek myths as a necessary precursor to Christianity. Creuzer drew this conclusion by dividing the textual products of the ancient religions into symbolic texts and mythical texts, and he also identified the 'scientific consideration' of the Greeks as a form of epistemic reference to the world.

Creuzer connected this stepwise development of abstractive form with a semiotic of signs from the symbol to the allegory. He also combined it with a theory of media designed to explain the connections between the discursive speech of the Greeks and their alphabetic writing as an analogy of merged semiotic elements.[16] In 1828, Friedrich Wilhelm Joseph Schelling began holding his lectures on the *Philosophy of Mythology*, which were directed against Hegel's view and referred back to Creuzer's depiction in order to portray the history of religion until the Greeks (which Christian history necessarily followed) as a theogonic process. He described the emergence of a monotheistic concept of God as the incremental upward development of the consciousness and reflection about the human spirit. This process ultimately resulted in a revealed religion that developed a concept of something beyond rationality, because it could not only explain the quality of being but could also justify the existence of being at all.[17]

IV

At this point, I must cut short my presentation of the different attempts to describe the similarity between religions with a universal concept of religion. It should be clear by now that within this discourse, the concept of 'similarity' was not conceived of without difference or hierarchization.

This leads us to a more general suggestion that once more emphasizes the epistemological origins of this connection. In his 1938 work, *Experience and Judgement*, Edmund Husserl established the recognition of sameness and similarity as the fundamental operation of all worldviews. He believed that the comparative observation of conscious objects was so fundamental that he also applied it to describe 'the constitution of the consciousness of generality and, at the highest level of all, for that of the consciousness of essence'. For him, the formation of concepts was the result of eidetic identification and the formation of arbitrary comparative relationships. This form of similarity spans the gap between equality and partial similarity. Husserl described the importance of comparison for the 'constitution of empirical generalities'. Consciousness is able to recognize the 'pure generalities' using the method of 'an intuition of essences'. By this Husserl meant the generalization of an experienced or imagined representation to an arbitrary example, and to expand from that example to an infinite number of other variations. The differences between these variations allowed the 'invariable *what*' among them to be seen, which is the Platonic ideal of the object. The idea of difference is thus tightly intertwined with the 'identically common'. Difference remains the element that cannot be brought into agreement with the others. '[O]n the other hand, it is clear that *things cannot enter into conflict which have nothing in common*' (emphasis in the original). For this reason, the process of ideation includes the 'active identification which brings out the congruent over against the differences'.[18]

We must accept that the same goes for the concept of religion, with all of the political consequences it entails. My impression is this: similarity and difference were not evenly distributed across the globe. The Christian confessions of Europe were similar, while difference was to be found outside of Europe. A necessary condition for the Christian mission – an operation of assimilation – was that similarity could be found outside of Europe as well. Thus, similarity seems to offer only limited protection against the accentuation of difference from case to case and where it is deemed to be necessary.

Notes

1 Cf. Foucault (2002): 219–32; cf. Otto (1992).

2 For both Aristotle and, even later, Thomas Aquinas, similarity was the only thing that could create order, because both difference and sameness are combined within it. Cf. Aristotle (1926): 1156b and 1159b; Aquinas (1955–57), Book III.1: 263–277 (Ch. 79–82), Book III.2: 114–124 (Ch. 111–114), available at http://dhspriory.org/thomas/

3 Cf. Gründer (1992): Ch. 10–17.

4 Cf. Kippenberg (2002).

5 Cf. Müller (1872); ([1871] 1920).

6 Cf. Müller (1872): XI–XV, and XXIf on the usefulness of theology for missionary work.

7 Cf. Tylor, Vol. II ([1871] 1920): 14–27.

8 Zedler (1731–1754), Vol. 31: col. 443–495.

9 Cf. Schlögl (2013): 369–94.

10 Cf. ibid.: 139–56.

11 Cf. Warburton (1738): esp. 87–95, 349ff.

12 Cf. Hutchinson ([1930] 1748), Vol. III: v–xx, xcviif.

13 Schlegel (1860): 473ff., 489–95, 500ff., 513ff.

14 Cf. Hume ([1757] 1957): 21–29, 47 ff., 53, 63–70.

15 Cf. Hegel (1984): 221–30.

16 Cf. Creuzer ([1816] 1890): 21f, 38, Ch. 3.

17 Cf. Schelling (1857) Vol 2.2: 11, 20–29, 350–63, 671.

18 Husserl (1973): 152ff, 214–30, 403 ff, 409–20.

References

Aristotle (1926), *Nikomachean Ethics*, in 23 volumes, Vol. 19, translated by H. Rackham, Cambridge, MA: Harvard University Press, London: William; available at perseus.tufts.edu.

Aquinas, Thomas von (1955–57), *On the Truth of the Catholic Faith*, translated by Anton C. Pegis, James F. Anderson, Vernon J. Bourke and Charles J. O'Neil, Vols 1–5, New York: Doubleday.

Creuzer, Friedrich ([1816] 1890), *Symbolik und Mythologie der alten Völker besonders der Griechen*, Leipzig, Darmstadt: Heyer und Leske.

Foucault, Michel (2002), The Archaeology of Knowledge, Abingdon, New York: Routledge.

Gründer, Horst (1992), *Welteroberung und Christentum: Ein Handbuch zur Geschichte der Neuzeit*, Teil II, Gütersloh: Gütersloher Verlaghaus Mohn.

Hegel, Georg Friedrich Wilhelm (1984), *Lectures on the Philosophy of Religion*, edited by Peter C. Hodgson, Vol. 1, Berkeley: University of California Press.

Hume, David ([1757] 1957), *The Natural History of Religion*, Stanford: Stanford University Press.

Husserl, Edmund (1973), *Experience and Judgment: Investigations in a Genealogy of Logic* edited by Ludwig Landgrebe, and translated by James S. Churchill and Karl Ameriks, London: Routledge.

Hutchinson, John ([1730] 1748), *Moses's Sine Principio: Represented by Names, by Types, by Words, by Emblems. With an Introduction shewing the Nature of Body and Soul, the first State of Man ... that by Reasoning of Man's Nature and of his Fall, Persons, Things, and Actions where represented by Substitutes ...*, Vol. III, London: John Hutchinson.

Kippenberg, Hans G. (2002), *Discovering Religious History in the Modern Age*, Princeton, NJ: Princeton University Press.

Müller, Max (1872), *Chips from a German Workshop*, Vol. 1: *Essays on the Science of Religion*, New York: Scribner; available at archive.org.

Otto, Stephan (1992), *Das Wissen des Ähnlichen: Michel Foucault und die Renaissance*, Frankfurt am Main u.a.: Lang.

Schelling, Friedrich Wilhelm Joseph von (1857), *Philosophie der Mythologie*, in Ders., *Sämtliche Werke*, Vol. 2.2, Stuttgart u.a.: Cotta.

Schlegel, Friedrich (1860), 'On the Language and Wisdom on the Indians', in *The Aesthetic and Miscellaneous Works of Frederick von Schlegel*, translated by E.J. Millington, London: Bohn; available at archive.org.

Schlögl, Rudolf (2013), *Alter Glaube und moderne Welt: Europäisches Christentum im Umbruch 1750–1850*, Frankfurt am Main: Fischer.

Tylor, Edward Burnett ([1871] 1920), *Primitive Culture: Researches into the Development of Mythology, Philosophy, Religion, Language, Art, and Custom*, Vols. I–II, London: Murray; available at archive.org.

Warburton, William (1738), *The Devine Legation of Moses demonstrated on the Principles of a Religious Deist, from the Omission of the Doctrine of a Future State of Reward and Punishment in the Jewish Dispensation*, Vols. 1–6, London; available at Google Books.

Zedler, Johann H. (1731–1754), *Großes vollständiges Universallexikon aller Wissenschaften und Künste*, Leipzig (nach der Digitalisierung der Bayerischen Staatsbibliothek und der Herzog August Bibliothek), available at zedler-lexikon.de.

Comparison and Classification in Religious Studies

Indigenous discourses as case study

Johan Strijdom

'The "end" of comparison', claims Jonathan Smith, 'cannot be the act of comparison itself.' Instead, he argues, the purpose of comparison should be to provoke thought that would enable us to 'see things in a new, and frequently unexpected, light'. Not only should comparison lead to 'the redescription of the exempla (each in light of the other)', but also, importantly, to 'a rectification of the academic categories in relation to which they have been imagined'.[1]

In this essay I engage with the issue of comparison, with its constituent terms 'similarity' and 'difference', from the perspective of the academic study of religion. I do so by assessing the work of two prominent scholars in the discipline, Jonathan Z. Smith and David Chidester, before I turn to a cross-cultural comparison of indigenous discourses and practices as my chosen example to illustrate and problematize ideological assumptions and power relations at work in comparative intellectual experiments in the human, cultural and social sciences.

For Jonathan Smith, it was an early fascination with the classification of plants that led to and influenced his lifelong interest in comparisons, classifications and definitions. His subsequent engagement with philosophy, linguistics, history and cultural anthropology assisted him in developing crucial theoretical and methodological insights in the comparative study of religions. Just as he was completing his Yale doctoral dissertation on Frazer's *Golden Bough*, which he found particularly weak in comparative theory and method, he was recruited by the University of Chicago, where he devoted the early 1970s to the formulation of an appreciation, a critique and the development of alternatives to aspects of the work of his senior colleague, Mircea Eliade. The debate has since for Smith come to centre on the relationship between diachronic and synchronic comparisons, monothetic and polythetic classifications, emic and etic categories, and, most importantly, between essentialist and historical views of culture and religion – entangled issues that he illustrates by means of pertinent examples.

Although Smith emphasizes that 'comparison' and 'classification' are inseparable, he nevertheless indicates that he has focused in some publications more on the one and in other publications more on the other.[2] His reflection on *synchronic and diachronic modes of comparison* was a result of relating his interest in botanical taxonomies to Eliade's morphological analysis of religious phenomena in the latter's *Patterns in Comparative Religion* (first published in French in 1949). It was specifically Cassirer's article, 'Structuralism in Modern Linguistics' (1945), that not only alerted Smith to 'a crucial analogy between morphology in biology and structuralism in linguistics',[3] but also drew his attention to Goethe's *Metamorphosis of Plants* – readings that helped Smith to assess Eliade's morphological analysis of religious phenomena.[4]

While Goethe was visiting the botanical garden in Padua, he was struck by the extraordinary variety of plants. He observed differences not only between species, but even on the same parts of a single plant. Against Linnaeus' rigid classification of plants on the basis of one arbitrarily chosen feature alone (their reproductive parts) frozen in time, Goethe instead proposed a dynamic classification that would take the form of the whole organism seriously and arrange the variety in a sequence of development that commenced with an *Urpflanze* (*ur*plant) from which the variety of plants and their parts metamorphosed (i.e. 'changed form') over time, either progressively from simple to more complex differentiation, or retrogressively so that the differentiation would come to a halt or disappear. Hidden beneath these observable differences, Goethe insisted, lay an *innere Identität* (an inner identity or similarity), a simple *Urform* (archetype, imagined by him as a relatively undifferentiated leaf), from which the diverse forms subsequently evolved.

Smith shows that this notion of an inner identity that transformed into diverse species[5] had a profound impact on Eliade's conception of religious forms.[6] In his morphological classification of religious phenomena in *Patterns in Comparative Religion*, Eliade attempted to identify the primal image or religious archetype (in his view, to be found in the transcendental order of primordial cosmogonies) that became manifested in different concrete religious phenomena. The first duty of a student of religion, he insisted, 'is to grasp the original *meaning* of a sacred phenomenon and then to interpret its history'.[7] Smith argues that Eliade planned a second volume to *Patterns* that would have addressed the historical perspective, but only published a few chapters of it, which actually gave an indication of how he would have done it.

Where does that leave Smith on the issue of morphological (or synchronic) and historical (or diachronic) comparisons of religious phenomena?[8] Smith agrees with Carlo Ginzburg that integration of the two perspectives is a noble aspiration but one that is difficult to achieve.[9] In his own work, Smith has experimented with both diachronic and synchronic analyses, but come to share Wittgenstein's view that synchronic synopsis of data is crucial to see connections (i.e. similarities) and their transformations.[10] The tension between synchronic and diachronic analyses in both the natural and the human sciences, as two ways of looking at the same data, has not yet been resolved, according to him.

Closely linked to Smith's argument on synchronic and diachronic comparisons is his reflection on *monothetic and polythetic classifications* of data. Whereas a monothetic approach groups members of a class together on the basis of a single characteristic that they share, a polythetic approach – as advanced by Wittgenstein – groups members of a class together on the basis of 'family resemblances', which means that each member of the class possesses a number of characteristics, with each characteristic being shared by a large number in the group but not every characteristic being possessed by every member.[11] As an example to illustrate the point, Smith chose early Judaism.[12] By using circumcision and diverse indicators of Jewish identity from funerary inscriptions, he contested the traditional monothetic classification of early Judaism and instead argued for a 'variety of Judaisms, each of which appears as a shifting cluster of characteristics which vary over time'.[13]

What interested Smith particularly was the classification, description and explanation of relative proximity and distance between species. Building on the anthropologist Robert Redfield's postulate that the 'primitive mind' characteristically constructs a binary opposition between us and them, Smith specified four ways in which humans have constructed this relative relationship of similarity and difference: '(1) They are LIKE-US, (2) They are NOT-LIKE-US, (3) THEY ARE TOO MUCH-LIKE-US, or (4) WE ARE-NOT-LIKE-THEM.'[14] The third type, the constructed perception of 'the proximate other', has persistently fascinated Smith, as is clear from his study of early Judaisms. He holds[15] that these intracultural or 'intraspecific' negotiations are often characterized by hierarchies, by intense power struggles over rankings and prestige, and are thus fundamentally political.

Equally important, however, are 'occasions when a difference that is unrelated to the proximate other appears as a severe cognitive shock', an intercultural issue that Smith has increasingly focused on since the 1990s, and exemplified by means of historical studies of the European 'discovery' of the Americas and the invention of the category of 'race'.[16] Pertinent to our theme is the move from monogenetic to polygenetic accounts of the encountered 'others'. Viewing native Americans through the lens of the monogenetic myth of Genesis, Columbus until his death would regard them (in his mind 'Indians') as descendants of Adam and Eve. This explanation of human unity and similarity as a result of diffusion from common primal ancestors came to be seriously challenged after Columbus, once the differences between American and European fauna and flora were admitted. Individuals in the seventeenth century thus posited a polygenetic explanation that celebrated biological and anthropological difference. 'While these radical conclusions would be debated throughout the seventeenth and eighteenth centuries,' Smith holds, 'they contributed to the formation of the first new western theory for explaining human similarities and differences, the theory of race, the possibility that the genus *homo* might be divided by essential rather than accidental characteristics into separate species of differing lineages' – an attempt that was 'limited by the unfortunate eighteenth-century decision to correlate biological and cultural characteristics'.[17] Monogenetic accounts that stress historical diffusion from a common origin and polygenetic theories that emphasize independent development have continued to generate central debates in cross-cultural anthropology since the eighteenth century.

Smith finally accepts the Foucauldian argument that power instrumentalizes classification, but insists that this presents 'the study of religion with an occasion for rectification, not resignation or renunciation'.[18] The fact that nineteenth-century colonial scholars of religion, such as Max Müller, instrumentalized classifications to divide and conquer should not lead us to reject classification, comparison and explanation, since these are simply fundamental to intellectual engagement with the world.[19]

The necessity to construct *etic* or *second-order scholarly categories* for the sake of critical thinking is defended as foundational to the study of religion and culture.[20] 'Nativists',[21] who insist on the reproduction of *emic or insider categories* on the basis of the uniqueness or incommensurability of their cultures, reject not only the legitimacy of translation from one culture to another, but also the possibility of comparative research as such within the human, cultural and social sciences. Their conservative model remains at the level of paraphrase, and condemns us 'to live in the world of Borges's Pierre Menard; in which a tale must always be identically "twice-told", where a word can only be translated by itself'.[22] Smith further illustrates its uselessness for critical thinking from Borges' parable, 'Exactitude in science', which I quote in full for its aptness:

> In that Empire, the Act of Cartography attained such Perfection that the map of a single Province occupied the entirety of the City, and the map of the Empire, the entirety of a Province. In time, these Unconscionable

> Maps no longer satisfied, and the Cartographer's Guild struck a Map of the Empire whose size was that of the Empire, and which coincided point by point with it. The following generations, who were not so fond of the Study of Cartography, as their Forebears had been, saw that that vast Map was useless, and not without some Pitilessness was it, that they delivered it up to the Inclemencies of Sun and Winters. In the Deserts of the West, still today, there are Tattered Ruins of that Map, inhabited by Animals and Beggars; in all of the Land there is no other Relic of the Discipline of Geography.[23]

Among 'nativists' like these Smith includes not only biblicists who apply structuralist methods to merely paraphrase their textual data, but also philologists and phenomenologists in Religious Studies who adopt 'a sort of common-sense descriptive discourse' and summarize texts 'as if their citation is, by itself, sufficient to guarantee significance'.[24] At one point he admits, however, that Africanists who insist on the importance of native categories have – in the case of the study of magic (both a first-order and second-order category) – 'generated a number of important interpretative strategies', but emphasizes that these in the end carry 'little explanatory power' for which second-order categories are of vital importance.[25]

The argument is that it is precisely the incongruence between map and territory, the gap between model and data, the difference between conceptual category and phenomena that creates puzzlement, defamiliarization, surprise and thought. The way surprise is then reduced but never fully overcome, Smith proposes, is by means of translation – whether intercultural or intracultural, whether in the natural or human sciences, 'by bringing the unknown into relations to the known, relations of similarity and difference, relations of analogy and homology, relations of metonymy and metaphor' – a procedure well illustrated by Durkheim's 'translation' of the language of religion (the unknown) into the language of society (the known), or better, in Lévi-Strauss' formulation, of substituting a less intelligible complexity with a more intelligible one.[26] The result might not meet with the approval of the insiders, but that, according to Smith, is 'perfectly justifiable and is, in fact, normal procedure'.[27] Translation as generalization is 'necessarily incomplete' and 'highly selective', and must therefore be continuously subjected to comparison, critique and rectification.[28]

What divides scholars of religion most deeply 'when the chips are down', to use Smith's colloquial expression,[29] is the fault-line between *essentialists* and *historians*. *Ontologists* focus on transcendence as the unique essence of the sacred/holy, whereas *historical anthropologists* view the sacred as a social construct that may unite or divide a group. Smith has elaborated his choice for the latter mostly in debate with Mircea Eliade, who favoured the former theory.

Although Smith appreciates Eliade's almost limitless expansion of data for the comparative study of religions, and although he argues that Eliade insisted on the importance of a historical study of religious phenomena (i.e. their metamorphosis), he expresses his concern with the fact that Eliade barely treats the historical in *Patterns*.[30] Or rather, more accurately, it is not so much the synchronic method of analysis – which he values, as noted above – that concerns Smith, but Eliade's ontological or 'incarnational' (even 'sacramental') view of the sacred as revelation of 'the Other' that he cannot accept. According to Eliade, the transcendent is universal, and remains singular/undivided and suprahistorical/non-temporal as it falls downward or regresses into ever-more concrete and diverse human particularities, or as the latter aspire upwards or progress towards their original form (*Urform*/archetype) to restore the original equilibrium/order.

In his analysis of gnosticism, however, Smith shows an alternative structural possibility – one that radically challenged or reversed this order, clearly served the interests of an imperialist elite, and which scholars like Eliade continued to maintain through their monovalent synchronic analyses. Instead, Smith argues, the dominant order and its reversal along with other structural possibilities need to be examined within their specific social-anthropological and historical contexts. Whereas the romantic view holds to the *immediacy* of a primordial religious experience, Smith insists that an understanding of religious phenomena is always socially and historically *mediated* – a position that is of utmost importance for the comparative enterprise.

In summarizing his work in Comparative Religious Studies, Smith thus underlines as first procedure, historical and anthropological description.[31] The first requirement, he insists, is that 'we locate a given example within the rich texture of its social, historical and cultural environments that invest it with its local significance'. He continues:

> The second task is that of reception history, a careful account of how our second-order scholarly tradition has intersected with the exemplum. That is to say, we need to describe how the datum has become accepted as significant for the purpose of argument. Only when such a double contextualization is completed does one move on to the description of [at least] a second example undertaken in the same double fashion.

It is only then that we are ready to compare the two (or more) exempla 'with respect to some category, question, theory, or model of interest to us'. And, as already highlighted above, 'the aim of such a comparison is [both] the redescription of the exempla (each in light of the other) and a rectification of the academic categories in relation to which they have been imagined' for the sake of seeing 'things in a new, and frequently unexpected, light'.

I turn now to David Chidester's problematization of the comparative method in the study of religions. Chidester studied in the United States of America, and describes himself as part of the Santa Barbara and Chicago tradition of Comparative Religious Studies.[32] He has been working at the University of Cape Town for the last three decades, and has from this location published significant postcolonial critiques of both colonial uses of religions and of the imperial academic study of religions. Chidester's emphasis is not in the first place on the comparative method as such, but rather on the ideological/political uses to which comparisons of religions were put during the colonial period – with particular reference to South African contexts. In elaborating his critique, he engages with 'a variety of academic disciplines [that] have worked to relocate the production of knowledge within the power relations of colonial situations', notably anthropology, comparative literature, history and gender studies.[33]

Although colonialism is often simply taken to refer to an asymmetrical power relationship in which colonizers of a territory benefited economically from the exploitation of the colonized, Chidester emphasizes that these encounters changed both parties and that the agency of the colonized needs our attention too.[34] If it is true that European colonists dehumanized 'barbarians' in colonized territories and considered it their task to civilize them, it is equally true that indigenous peoples developed a variety of ways to deal with these encounters. Some submitted to the dominating culture, but others resisted it by reworking indigenous traditions. Nineteenth-century Xhosa, for example, reconfigured their myths of the sea by identifying Europeans with the sea, whence Europeans arrived and where they should have stayed. The land belonged not to the European invaders but to the indigenous people (i.e. to 'the autochthons', to use a term that will be further explored later in this essay). The Zulu similarly reinterpreted their cosmogonic myth to make sense within the colonial situation of the opposition between black and white, land and sea.

The comparative study of religions as an academic discipline emerged under nineteenth-century colonial conditions. European colonists initially considered indigenous people encountered on colonial frontiers as lacking 'religion', taking Christianity as their norm for comparison, or as having only 'superstitions' – a binary hierarchy, Chidester holds, that portrayed 'indigenous people as living in a different world', and served to justify imperial conquest and denial of 'indigenous rights to land, livestock' and 'control over their own labour'.[35]

When, in the second half of the nineteenth century, European administrators came to acknowledge the existence of indigenous religions, it was not, in Chidester's view, 'necessarily a breakthrough in human recognition', but rather served the colonial administrative system to *classify* and thereby *contain* indigenous people.[36] The colonial administrators' 'discovery' of the Xhosa, Zulu and Tswana-Sotho religious systems, which came to be seen as members of the same 'Bantu' religion, served to keep indigenous people in their place. At the same time, colonists constructed genealogies that questioned the indigenous status of the Zulu, Xhosa and Sotho-Tswana by imagining each group as having originated *from elsewhere*, from different ethnic groups in the Near East. Both colonial strategies – of *containment* and *displacement* of indigenous people through ideological classifications – served the colonial administration of political power.[37]

The late nineteenth-century founders of the comparative study of religions, by devising an evolutionary hierarchy of religions, supported the colonial project and were complicit in dehumanizing indigenous groups. By using reports from European adventurers, missionaries and administrators in the colonies, who had obtained their information in turn from indigenous informants and collaborators, theorists of religion in European metropoles typically constructed an evolutionary scheme with 'primitive' religion at the bottom and Christianity at the top, which justified the imperial *mission civilisatrice*. Chidester points out that the late nineteenth-century founders of Religious Studies and Anthropology not only foregrounded difference and distance in their comparisons and evolutionary models, but their classification of religions was also used as a means of control and domination of indigenous groups.[38] Max Müller, often considered the founder of Comparative Religious Studies, could thus take the old imperial saying, '*Divide et impera*' and freely translate it as 'Classify and conquer'.

Given this horrible legacy of the comparative study of religions, how are students of comparative religion to proceed? Chidester maps two opposite positions in postcolonial studies that may inform the future of Comparative Religious Studies.[39] At one extreme are the *indigenists*, whose aim it is to recover and promote authentic, pure roots, which they claim have remained essentially the same 'since time immemorial', even though they were temporarily suppressed during colonialism. At the other extreme are those who question such romantic nostalgia for precolonial purity by arguing that cultures are always subject to *historical change* and *hybridity* due to continuous migrations and cultural interaction.

Although Chidester would follow the second approach in his study of religions, he is nevertheless sympathetic to those indigenists who have instrumentalized an essentialist notion of indigenous traditions as a strategy to liberate and restore dignity to those who had been marginalized and dehumanized under colonialism. Among such indigenists he includes:

- Fanon, as a post-romantic indigenist who linked the recovery of a suppressed past with his violent struggle against inhumane colonialism and for a new humanity;
- *Hindutva*, as a Hindu nationalist movement that searches for and aims to recover a pure, precolonial 'Hinduness' as a marker of Hindu identity; and
- proponents of a postcolonial African renaissance, who reject 'colonial constructions of African mentality', and instead search for and promote the notion of a pure 'Africanness' characterized by 'visions of African humanity and personality, communalism and socialism'.

In a previous contribution I had problematized Chidester's juxtaposition of *Hindutva* and African indigenism by drawing on Anil Bhatti's analysis of postcolonial India. I argued that the violent trail of exclusionary, essentialist religious nationalisms – whether Buddhist, Hindu, Christian or Muslim – should alert us to the dangers of postcolonial Afrocentric discourses as well.[40] Bhatti, in his article 'Diversität und Homogenisierung: Postkoloniale Anmerkungen aus Indien',[41] not only identifies the same two contradictory tendencies as Chidester in postcolonial theory, but also, importantly, shows in no uncertain terms the destructive consequences of a closed nativist paradigm that searches for original, pure roots. In contrast to this attitude, which is actively propagated by *Hindutva* and its political arm, the nationalist Bharatiya Janata Party (abbreviated as BJP), and the supportive international Vishwa Hindu Parishad (abbreviated as VHP), he presents us with an alternative vision of postcolonial India as an open, multilayered palimpsest that has been formed by diverse religions, languages and ethnicities, which must be respected in order to avoid intolerance and violent conflict – a vision embodied in India's anti-colonial struggle, by Gandhi's respect for Islam and Christianity, and by Nehru's vision of a secular state that would deal equally with all religions.

The dangers of exclusionary indigenist discourses and practices in postcolonial Africa have indeed been the subject of recent anthropological analyses by Peter Geschiere and Francis Nyamnjoh.[42] To illustrate the importance of contextualized interpretations for valid comparisons of similar problems, I will first examine their analyses of pertinent cases in postcolonial Africa, and then introduce classical Athens as a further case study from another time and another place. These historically and geographically nuanced comparative analyses of a similar problem will problematize the generalized, unqualified, decontextualized and ahistorical claims of human rights discourses on behalf of indigenous groups.[43]

In an essay titled '"Ever-diminishing circles": The paradoxes of belonging in Botswana', Nyamnjoh argues that although essentialist constructs of ethnic identity are contradicted by the reality of change, migrations and mixtures, one needs to emphasize that such reified notions have been instrumentalized by colonial and postcolonial state apparatuses, resulting in ethnic hierarchies and exclusions.[44]

Ethnic identities were constructed and classified under colonialism and apartheid, often with disregard of local histories, and imposed not only for purposes of indirect rule but also to justify a civilizing mission to 'primitive natives'. Tensions have been ongoing among ethnic groups in postcolonial African states about purity, belonging and entitlements, as Nyamnjoh demonstrates in the case of the resurgence of indigeneity in Botswana since the mid-1980s.

Although the nation-state of Botswana guarantees citizenship to all indigenous groups within its territory, and has tried to unite all its citizens by means of a national anthem, a sports stadium and other public structures, it has not been able to resolve resurgent ethnic divisions, hierarchies and tensions. Owing to their privileged position under British colonialism (as administrators and converts), the Tswana have become the most prominent group, as is reflected in the name of the modern state itself. This position has been contested by the minority BaKalanga's educated elite, themselves products of colonial privileging, who demand greater recognition and representation in government structures due to their having been in the area before the Tswana. The response from certain Tswana circles, however, is a stereotyping of the BaKalanga as darker-skinned *makwerekwere* ('total outsiders') who originate from Zimbabwe and further north, and are therefore not authentic citizens of Botswana.

Ironically, the Khoesan (Bushman) minority, which can legitimately claim to have been there prior to all other ethnic groups, has been relegated to the lowest end of the hierarchy and is the least represented in government structures. The Khoesan are looked down upon by all these groups as hunter-gatherers who have failed to establish agricultural villages as a condition for entitlement to land. Nyamnjoh aptly summarizes the point:

> Although legal provisions might promise civic citizenship to all in principle, in practice inequalities prevail among individuals and groups,

> especially along rigid lines of politically constructed indigeneity. Being indigenous thus becomes a matter of degree and power relations, thereby making some less Batswana than others, even as they are armed with the same . . . Identity Card and inspired or protected in principle by the same constitution.[45]

Nyamnjoh however continues to show that even the Constitution, mentioning only the eight major Tswana 'tribes', was accused by the minorities of a 'rigid hierarchy of indigeneity' that discriminates between, rather than protects, the equality of all citizens. A commission was appointed to investigate, but its recommendations met with resistance from the Tswana majority who wanted to retain their dominant position in the national House of Chiefs. A redraft introduced additional members from districts with minority ethnic groups, but still privileged the Tswana. It was adopted by parliament, but most minority ethnic groups rejected it as an entrenchment of Tswana domination.

Against such rigid, hierarchical and exclusionary concepts of indigeneity, such 'ever-diminishing circles', Nyamnjoh insists on a more fluid view of indigeneity, by which he means a cosmopolitan vision that would acknowledge the reality of historical change, value diverse and mixed group identities, and be inclusive of and hospitable to 'outsiders'.[46] 'The emphasis', he concludes, 'should be on the freedom of individuals and communities to negotiate inclusion, opt out and opt in with flexibility of belonging in consonance with their realities as straddlers of a kaleidoscope of identity margins.'[47]

In his book, *The Perils of Belonging: Autochthony, citizenship, and exclusion in Africa and Europe*, Peter Geschiere similarly argues that the political construct and instrumentalization of rigid ethnic identities tend to lead to increasing fragmentation, exclusion and violent conflict.[48] Although he focuses on Cameroon, where he has done fieldwork for more than thirty years, he compares autochthonous discourses and practices there with examples from elsewhere in Africa and Europe. He thus analyses the destructive effect of indigenism not only in the Ivory Coast with Gbagbo's disastrous *Opération Nationale d'Identification* in the eastern Democratic Republic of Congo and in South Africa's recent xenophobic outbursts, but also in the Netherlands, Flanders, France and even in ancient Athens, as the cradle of the discourse.

In the case of postcolonial Cameroon, he distinguishes between the role of ethnic belonging during the dictatorship of the 1960s–80s, on the one hand, and its role after the introduction of multi-party elections in the 1990s, on the other.

After the Second World War, Francophone Cameroon under the leadership of Ahmadou Ahidjo (from the Muslim north) called for unification with Anglophone Cameroon in the struggle for independence. Although a northern group within British Cameroon voted to become part of the Nigerian federation, the southern sector decided to join Ahidjo and formed a unified federation in 1961. Independent Cameroon quickly settled into a dictatorship under Ahidjo. Citizens were exhorted to unite behind the President and to enact their loyalty in stiff national ceremonies enforced from above. Expression of local ethnic loyalties was banned and traitors were to be denounced. When Ahidjo unexpectedly stepped down in 1982, he appointed Paul Biya, a Beti from the Christian south, as his successor. Biya continued the suppression of dissidents until 1990, when, due to international political economic pressure (particularly from development organizations like the World Bank and the International Monetary Fund), multi-party elections were introduced. Under this new dispensation, Biya however found new strategies to stay in power, one of them being the use of autochthonous discourse and policies to divide the opposition. Three main parties emerged, each with its own regional and associated ethnic strongholds:

- Biya's party in the Centre, South and East Provinces (with the Beti ethnic group as majority);
- the opposition led by John Fru Ndi in the Anglophone Northwest and Southwest provinces, as well as in the Francophone West Province (with the Bamileke as the main ethnic group); and
- the main party in the Muslim north (associated primarily with the Fulbe).

These regions do not form homogenous blocks but are internally deeply divided, which Biya exploited in his favour by supporting specific ethnic groups. In the north, Biya supported the Kirdi who never converted to Islam and sought liberation from the Fulbe. In the western part, there was a divide not only between Anglo- and Francophones, but also amongst Anglophones themselves, caused by northern highlanders migrating to the richer southwestern coastal and forest areas for job opportunities. Biya's government exploited these tensions by siding with the coastal minority of Bakweri and Douala, who claimed autochthony and complained about being swamped by Bamenda migrants from the Anglophone northwest and Bamileke from the Francophone west. Participating in funerary rituals in one's village of origin became the ultimate test of belonging, of deciding who were autochthons and who allochthons, contributing to suspicion, fragmentation and conflict.

Like Nyamnjoh, Geschiere would consider as a crucial alternative the cultivation of a historical sensitivity open to change and a cosmopolitan attitude that values diversity and mixtures. Geschiere concludes:

> This drastic exclusionary tendency and this quest for purity make autochthony discourse problematic in Africa as well as in other parts of the globe. Already in the classical Athenian example this implied a view in which staying in place is the norm and migration the exception. All the more important to emphasize that migration is as old as human society and that autochthony's 'Otherless universe' is therefore an impossibility. There may be considerable wisdom in Kwame Appiah's plea for a combination of cosmopolitanism and identity, or, to put it more concretely, in his idea that we need common stories in order to live together, but that these stories must address diversity and allow for conversation across differences.[49]

The comparison of political uses of autochthonous discourses and practices in modern Africa and Europe with those in ancient Athens illustrates not only the possibility of synchronic comparisons across historical eras, but also of diachronic analyses of influences or reception history. Particularly helpful here is Marcel Detienne's critical reflection on the comparative method and his analysis of autochthony as a key political problem.

Detienne argues against classical philologists and nationalist historians who have propagated the idea of an unbroken continuity between an idealized, unique Greece and modern western nations, and have used this idea of incomparability/incommensurability/uniqueness to claim superiority of the west over the rest of the world.[50] Instead of embracing these limiting, homogenizing and exclusionary discourses that extol autochthony and nationalism, often concerned with primordial roots and legitimized by myths of pure origin within a specific territory, Detienne maintains that we need to deconstruct and destabilize ideas of fixed identities, and break down arrogant attitudes of self-congratulation which characterize the mind-set of fundamentalist western nationalist historians and classicists – an objective to be achieved by means of historical and comparative research. It is indeed, he insists, the anthropological comparison of cultures across spaces and times that will assist us in reflecting anew on key political notions, and stimulate insight beyond the fixation on narrow nationalist and disciplinary barbed-wired boundaries.

The Athenian obsession with pure descent and its myth of autochthonous origins arose, according to Detienne, between 450 and 340 BCE. The mentality is clear from archaeological evidence like the building of the

Erechtheum on the Athenian acropolis, and from texts like Euripides' *Ion* and Plato's *Menexenos*, and its contestation by Thucydides – texts that I have analysed in more detail elsewhere.[51] Suffice it to say that Euripides' play centres on the Athenian foundation myth of autochthony (of being 'born from the earth' of Athens), which, though problematized in the course of the drama, is reconfirmed in the end. In *Menexenos*, Plato has Socrates perform a funeral speech in honour of the fallen autochthonous heroes of Athens. Socrates claims to have learned the speech from Pericles' concubine, Aspasia. It is precisely by means of the regular state ritual of funeral orations, Detienne argues, that the autochthonous myth was ingrained in the imagination of the Athenians. 'All you had to do', Detienne says, 'was to listen to the established deliverers of funeral orations, an earlier and more modest version of the professors of nineteenth- and twentieth-century nations, officials trained to swell every breast with passionate national sentiment':[52] exclusionary attitudes that we need to move away from in order to live within our current multicultural and mixed societies.

In the case of ancient Greece, this may be achieved by taking a broader view of history and by means of cross-cultural comparisons. It is, for example, important to emphasize the foundation of Greek colonies in the seventh and sixth centuries in Sicily, Graeca Magnia and on the shores of the Black Sea by landless Greek migrants, and of the law-giver Solon's encouragement of 'residents and immigrants of Attica to become citizens of Athens'[53] a century before Pericles' much more restrictive law around 450 BCE, according to which only those qualified for citizenship whose father and mother were both Athenians. Thucydides, furthermore, at the very time of the invention of the autochthonous myth, seems to avoid the term *autochthon*, and 'explains Athens' pre-eminence instead in reference to its success in attracting immigrants (the *metoikoi*)'. Nicole Loraux in my view rightly concludes that 'an insistence of having remained on the same spot is a basic denial of history, which always implies movement'.[54]

What have we then achieved in this essay? Which insights about the comparative method and its constituent elements of 'similarity' and 'difference' have we gained here? And in which ways have we illustrated these theoretical points with reference to the issue of indigenous claims and practices across space and time? I agree with Jonathan Smith that once we have chosen a particular issue for comparison (for instance, indigeneity in this essay), we need to first offer a synchronic description of a case within its socio-political context and a diachronic review of what preceded and followed it (in this case, indigeneity in modern Cameroon); we then need to repeat this process for a second case study (for example, indigeneity in ancient Athens) and possible further case studies (possibly indigeneity in contemporary Europe, or Tibet, or Australia or the United States). Only then, when we follow such an approach that focuses on change rather than essence, will we, according to Smith's argument, be able to offer a historically nuanced anthropological comparison of the issue under consideration. Only then will we, in his view, be able to specify how similar (proximate) or different (distant) the case studies are with respect to the chosen problem that we are investigating. What we are aiming for, as Smith emphasizes, is not exact description of our territory but rather a mental map that uses etic categories not only as a means to throw new, unexpected light on the problem that is studied across time and space, but also as a challenge to adapt our etic/academic categories for even better analysis of the chosen problem.

David Chidester's contribution, I have shown, takes this concern with the comparative method further by focusing on the uses to which it has been put under colonial conditions. He convincingly argues that the categories of 'similarity' and 'difference' were instrumentalized by colonial explorers, missionaries, administrators and academics (notably anthropologists and scholars of religion) to first deny religion amongst indigenous people, and later – after acknowledging the existence of indigenous religion – locate indigenous religion at the bottom of an evolutionary scale. In both cases, the produced knowledge served to dehumanize colonized people – a shameful legacy that needs to be rectified in the postcolonial comparative study of religions. It is this consciousness that makes Chidester sympathetic to approaches that strategically use essentializing discourses to recover previously suppressed indigenous traditions. In my argument I have sounded a warning against this sympathy with reference to the disastrous consequences of *Hindutva* as well as the case studies from postcolonial Botswana and Cameroon.

The critical questions here concern political power relations that are at work in the autochthonous claims and practices. We need to persistently ask the moral question: Who is making the claims and who is institutionalizing them? Whose interests are served by the claims and practices, and at whose expense is this done? My case studies above do not explore these fundamental questions sufficiently, but merely point the way. More case studies are needed, and more historical and anthropological nuance is called for. Is it, for example, acceptable when Geschiere considers post-1990 Dutch or French claims to autochthony as similar to those in post-1990 African states? Or, to extend the comparison, how are these claims and practices similar to and different from indigenous claims of native Americans under formally democratic political systems, or – more critically – to Tibetan and Muslim minorities under an authoritarian Chinese state?[55] Or to those of San and Afrikaners respectively in contemporary South Africa? Finally, how do these questions relate to and problematize third generation human rights for indigenous peoples?

Most importantly, if indigenist and nationalist claims are morally problematic when they become rigid and exclusionary, what alternatives can we imagine? It is at this point, I would argue, that a cross-cultural and historical-critical comparison of types of cosmopolitan attitudes,[56] including that of a rooted cosmopolitanism, becomes a moral duty of liberal educators who intend to contribute to the social and political well-being of people – not least of those living on the African continent.

Notes

1 Smith (2004): 29–30, 197.
2 Ibid.: 20–21.
3 Ibid.: 4.
4 Ibid.: 63–73.
5 Ibid.: 70–72.
6 Ibid.: 64–67 and 71, where Smith notes the influence of Goethe's *Metamorphosis of Plants* not only on biological thought, but also on the cultural, linguistic and literary theories of Hegel, Darwin, Spengler, Propp, Wittgenstein, Chomsky and Derrida.
7 Eliade, in Smith (2004): 67.
8 Smith (2004): 72 prefers the terms 'morphological' and 'historical', but considers these to be 'analogous to synchrony and diachrony in Saussure's formulation'. Elsewhere he distinguishes between 'analogical' and 'homological' modes of comparison to make a parallel point: cf. ibid.: 14, 24–25, 92–93.
9 Ibid.: 64, 27.
10 Ibid.: 63–64, 67.
11 Cf. Smith (2000a): 37.
12 Smith (2004): 22.
13 The classification of 'religions' as species of the genus 'religion' has been of particular interest to Smith as a historian of religion (see Smith 2000a: 38–43; Smith 2004: 179–96). He emphasizes that these categories and classifications have been constructed in numerous ways by intellectuals, particularly since the discovery of the Americas, and that like the invented categories of 'language' and 'speech', they crucially serve the task of critical analysis.
14 Smith (2004): 27.
15 Ibid.: 27, 245–46.
16 Ibid.: 25, 28.
17 Ibid.: 314–15.
18 Ibid.: 43.
19 Cf ibid.: 173–74. Cf also, ibid.: 174: 'So classify we must – though we can learn from the past to eschew dual classifications . . . which finally reduce to "ours" and "theirs"'; and ibid.: 175: 'Classification, by bringing disparate phenomena together in the space of a scholar's intellect, often produces surprise, the condition which calls forth efforts of explanation.'
20 Ibid.: 201.
21 Smith seldom uses the terms 'emic' and 'etic', but did write the following entry in the *HarperCollins Dictionary of Religion*: 'a distinction between an act of

cultural understanding by the actors themselves (emic) and an understanding of that culture by trained outsiders (etic)' (Smith 1995; cf Smith 2004: 398). He prefers 'first-order' and 'second-order' respectively, and in the case of emic categories, often refers to them as 'native' (ibid.: 134, 204, 208, 221), or as exemplifying 'nativism' (ibid.: 175). Elsewhere (Smith 2000a: 35), he considers Hobbes' prioritization of 'the giving of names to names' as a scientific 'second-order activity' over 'the naming of things' as a utilitarian 'first-order activity', which he finds similar to the 'fabled report of the Bakiri of Brazil, often cited by advocates of "primitive prelogical thinking"; while the Bakiri have names for each sort of parrot or palm, they have no word for the genus parrot or palm.'

22 Smith (2004): 372.

23 Ibid.: 209.

24 Ibid.: 7, 206, 368.

25 Smith (2000a or 2000b?): 219, 221–22.

26 Smith (2004): 30, 208.

27 Ibid.: 207.

28 Ibid.: 31.

29 Ibid.: 1.

30 Ibid.: 81–82, 90–91.

31 Ibid.: 29, 197.

32 Cf. Chidester (2012): xii.

33 Chidester (2000): 423–24.

34 Ibid.: 424.

35 Ibid.: 428.

36 Ibid.: 429.

37 Chidester (1996) offers a detailed analysis of this historical process. Cf. also Chidester (2014) for subsequent elaboration of his analysis.

38 Chidester (2000): 430.

39 Ibid.: 432–36.

40 Cf. Strijdom (2009).

41 Bhatti (2005); also Bhatti (2014) for a development of this argument.

42 Cf. Strijdom (2012).

43 Cf. Niezen (2003) for the historical emergence of the third generation of human rights for indigenous groups. Pelican (2009) pertinently argues that autochthonous discourses in postcolonial Cameroon had political consequences that the United Nations has not anticipated in its propagation of indigenous rights.

44 Nyamnjoh (2007).

45 Ibid.: 311.

46 Ibid.: 323.

47 Ibid.: 325.

48 Geschiere (2009).

49 Ibid.: 224.

50 Detienne ([2000] 2008).

51 Cf. Strijdom 2012.

52 Detienne (2007): 79.

53 Ibid.: 80.

54 In Geschiere (2009): 12.

55 For an excellent analysis, see Gladney's monograph, *Dislocating China*, which resulted in his being refused a visa to enter China (Gladney 2004).

56 Pertinent here would be engagement with the work of Sen (2009), Nussbaum (2011), Appiah (2006), Benhabib (2011) and Calhoun (2007).

References

Appiah, Kwame Anthony (2006), *Cosmopolitanism: Ethics in a world of strangers*, New York: W.W. Norton & Company.

Benhabib, Seyla (2011), *Dignity in adversity: Human rights in troubled times*, Cambridge (UK): Polity.

Bhatti, Anil (2005), 'Diversität und Homogenisierung: Postkoloniale Anmerkungen aus Indien', available at http://www.goethezeitportal.de/index.php?id=1431, accessed on 18 December 2016.

——— (2014), 'Heterogeneities and Homogeneities: On Similarities and Diversities', in Johannes Feichtinger and Gary Cohen, eds, *Understanding Multiculturalism and the Habsburg Central European Experience*, New York: Berghahn.

Calhoun, Craig (2007), *Nations Matter: Culture, History and the Cosmopolitan Dream*, London, New York: Routledge.

Chidester, David (1996), *Savage Systems: Colonialism and Comparative Religion in South Africa*, Charlottesville, VA: University Press of Virginia.

——— (2000), 'Colonialism', in Willi Braun and Russell McCutcheon, eds, *Guide to the Study of Religion*, London, New York: Cassell.

——— (2012), *Wild Religion: Tracking the Sacred in South Africa*, Berkeley, Los Angeles, London: University of California Press.

——— (2014), *Empire of Religion: Imperialism and Comparative Religion*, Chicago: University of Chicago Press.

Detienne, Marcel (2007), *The Greeks and Us: A Comparative Anthropology of Ancient Greece*, Malden, MA: Polity.

——— ([2000] 2008), *Comparing the Incomparable*, Stanford: Stanford University Press.

Geschiere, Peter (2009), *The Perils of Belonging: Autochthony, Citizenship, and Exclusion in Africa and Europe*, Chicago, London: University of Chicago Press.

Gladney, Dru (2004), *Dislocating China: Muslims, Minorities, and Other Subaltern Subjects*, Chicago: University of Chicago Press.

Niezen, R. (2003), *The Origins of Indigenism*, Berkeley: University of California Press.

Nussbaum, Martha (2011), 'The capabilities approach and ethical cosmopolitanism: The challenge of political liberalism', in Maria Rovisco and Magdalena Nowicka, eds, *The Ashgate Research Companion to Cosmopolitanism*, Burlington, VT: Ashgate.

Nyamnjoh, Francis (2007), '"Ever-diminishing circles": The paradoxes of belonging in Botswana', in Marisol De la Cadena and Orin Starn, eds, *Indigenous Experience Today*, Oxford, New York: Berg.

Pelican, M. (2009), 'Complexities of indigeneity and autochthony: An African example', *American Ethnologist*, 36 (1): 52–65.

Sen, Amartya (2009), *The Idea of Justice*, Cambridge, MA: Harvard University Press.

Smith, Jonathan Z. (1995), 'Emic/etic', in Jonathan Smith, ed., *The HarperCollins Dictionary of Religion*, New York: Harper San Francisco.

——— (2000a), 'Classification', in Willi Braun and Russell McCutcheon, eds, *Guide to the Study of Religion*, London, New York: Cassell.

——— (2000b), 'Epilogue: The "end" of comparison: Rectification and redescription', in K.C. Patton and B.C. Ray, eds, *A Magic Still Dwells: Comparative Religion in the Postmodern Age*.

——— (2004), *Relating Religion: Essays in the Study of Religion*, Chicago and London: University of Chicago Press.

Strijdom, Johan (2009), 'Nationalizing religion: The violent path of religious nationalism', *Alternation*, 3: 254–69.

——— (2012), 'Problems with indigeneity: Fragmentation, discrimination and exclusion in post-colonial African states', *Image & Text*, 19: 24–32.

Navigating Identities, Similarities and Differences

An anthropological comparison

Thomas G. Kirsch

Work on this article started while I was analysing the data from my ethnographic fieldwork in present-day South Africa, which brought me to the conclusion that crime prevention measures are not always concerned with maintaining identitary distance to anticipated offenders, but, surprisingly, attempt at times to attain a certain degree of similarity to them. My thoughts about this can be found in the second part of the present article. In the process of this analysis, however, I became increasingly aware that the attention ethnographers pay to such practices of similarity necessitates a more general reflection on the ways and modalities in which anthropology itself is dependent on certain forms of thinking in similarities. This issue will be discussed in the first part of the article.

Introduction

The discipline of anthropology has a long and fraught history of the observation of others and of self-observation. Questions of identity, difference and similarity are not only part of the discipline's founding myth and basic legitimation, but have also repeatedly given rise to new thematic focus and epistemological self-positioning. This history is also fraught in part because it involves contradictory movements of thought. On the one hand, anthropology is perhaps the only discipline in the canon of western sciences that has been so clearly defined since its origins by socio-cultural processes of drawing boundaries, as a existence of radical alterity long served as the touchstone for the identitary self-assurance of anthropological modernity. On the other hand, most cultural and social anthropological theories continue even today to be based on the pre-empirical, often implicit assumption that there are certain transcultural commonalities within humanity which can accentuate the anthropological ethos of interpreting sympathetically the actions and thoughts of other people, even beyond notions of difference. Assumptions of similarity, in the sense of Adolf Bastian and Franz Boas' 'principle of the *psychic unity of mankind*',[1] have thereby become the condition of possibility for a hermeneutics of the other.

One deficiency of the recent history of academic anthropology seems to be, however, that the intellectual enthusiasm for difference, alterity and understanding the other has eclipsed many of the questions dealing with relations of similarity. Precisely these questions of similarity characterized proto-anthropological reflection on intercultural encounters in European expansionist movements of the sixteenth and seventeenth centuries, since 'if diversities in culture were puzzling to thoughtful men during the Renaissance, so also were similarities'.[2] With the institutionalization of anthropology as a discipline and its subsequent prominence as a science concerned with 'culture(s)' in the first decades of the twentieth century, there was, however, an increased emphasis on thinking in differences, which can be traced back in part to the remarkable success of approaches based on cultural relativism. As an epistemic stance that seeks to enable understanding the other beyond normative horizons of meaning, cultural relativism has paved the way for a methodological programme and research ethic for open-ended cognitive encounters in the 'global ecumene'.[3] But, 'because cultural relativism is primarily directed to differences, it tends to undervalue universals, which are treated as constants and therefore of limited utility in the interpretation of behaviour in specific settings'.[4] Drawing on a comment by Jean Baudrillard, we can therefore speak of an anthropological 'orgy of discovery, exploration and "invention" of the other',[5] which is characterized by the fact that 'the other is . . . no longer there to be exterminated, hated, rejected or seduced, but instead to be understood, liberated, coddled, recognized'.[6] The otherness of the other nevertheless remains ambivalent:

> Our present obsession with difference is motivated by the politics of diversity. This politics has a stake in favouring difference over similarity. But even before identity politics gathered steam, anthropology had a built-in bias for difference. It was differences, after all, that attracted the attention of the traveller and the anthropologist. Differences generated romance and danger; they captivated and enticed, or repelled and disgusted, but they did not leave us neutral.[7]

In contrast to this fixation on difference, in this article I will explore how thinking in similarities can be made fruitful for current anthropological research. This is *not* meant to be a plea to return to the search for anthropological constants or 'human nature'.[8] Nor is it my intention to shift the conceptual apparatus of my own research from a perspective of difference to a perspective of similarity, as Martin Sökefeld, for example, proposed in his seminal article about anthropological research on identity: 'After many decades in which difference was the paradigm for conceiving of the others' selves, it might be useful to try a paradigm of more similarity.'[9] Instead, I would like to pursue a heuristic strategy that has proven to be productive in recent decades of anthropological research, namely, making concepts of scientific self-reflection the object of empirical studies in other life-worlds. If the term *othering* – as introduced in anthropology by Johannes Fabian[10] – was initially used in the context of postcolonial debates on (academic) Orientalism, over the course of time, anthropological research with this term was able to transcend this context and provide revealing insights into how powerful processes of *othering* could emerge not only between colonizing (examining) and colonized (examined) societies, but also *within* postcolonial societies.

In the following, I use this heuristic procedure in order to plumb the potential of the concept of 'similarity' for the understanding of a specific ethnographic issue, namely, the lay-criminological etiology of crime in South Africa.[11] In contrast to the aforementioned fixation on questions of cultural difference, my focus here is on emic interpretations of *intersociality*, that is, the relationship between different segments of South African society and forms of sociality. In terms of my anthropological material, I am thus concerned with sense-making processes when dealing with certain 'internal others' in a society – namely, people who are presumed to be involved in asocial or even anti-social actions, and who are categorized as 'criminals'.

In order to illustrate the advantages that such an approach offers, it is worthwhile to recall some of the traces left in the cultural memory of the global North by the events of 11 September 2001. The hermeneutics of suspicion that rapidly gained currency in the aftermath of those events are strikingly expressed in the figure of the 'sleeper', that is, of a terrorist who lives inconspicuously in a society of the global North, waiting to suddenly be activated to carry out an attack. The social anxieties connected with the ominous figure of the 'sleeper' – which could already be identified historically in secret service agencies during the Cold War, and which have been associated since 11 September 2001 with members of the so-called Hamburg terror cell – could be described in two different ways. On the one hand, the distinction between 'frontstage' and 'backstage',[12] as defined by Erving Goffman, can be found in mass media and popular culture presentations, whereby sleepers are depicted as leading an apparently normal life that is actually focused on an ambush. On the other hand, it has been repeatedly noted that the members of the terror cell lived very inconspicuously in Germany for many years. The news magazine *Der*

Spiegel put this succinctly in its headline about one of the assassins on 6 October 2001: 'The only thing that was conspicuous was his inconspicuousness.'[13] This second mode of description does not classify terrorists from the outset as 'different', situating them at a limited distance to the identities of mainstream society, but rather places them in an intermediate identitary space of similarity, which conceals a problematic potential to become different that can be activated at any time. 'Sleepers' are thus an interesting example for the heuristic value of the concept of 'similarity', which – as Anil Bhatti, Dorotheė Kimmich, Albrecht Koschorke, Rudolf Schlögl and Jürgen Wertheimer emphasize in a jointly written article on the issue – lies in 'replacing or supplementing well-known oppositions such as homogeneity and heterogeneity, or identity and alterity'.[14]

This example establishes the perspective applied in the ethnographic part of this article. Just as in the so-called war on terrorism, in the discourses and practices of crime prevention in South Africa that will be discussed below, assumptions of similarity play a significant role in efforts to identify, socially (re)integrate or isolate potential offenders. In other words, as an 'internal other' in South African society, (potential) offenders are not classified as absolutely identical with the members of mainstream society; at the same time, they are not always, or not in every aspect of identity, considered to be absolutely different from them. For the majority actors involved, the practical configuration of the crime prevention measures they employed is instead dependent on the question if and how they presume the existence of similarities between themselves and (potential) offenders.

As mentioned above, the ethnographic analysis of assumptions of similarity in specific empirical contexts makes it necessary to address the ways in which anthropology itself has adopted certain forms of thinking in similarities. The first part of this article is thus a selective, self-reflective excursus on the history of anthropology. This excursus provides insights into two different modalities of thinking in similarities, which then inform the subsequent analysis of my own empirical research.

First of all, we can identify a mode of thinking in similarities that refers to similarities between objects of scientific observation. Such a mode of thinking forms the basis, for example, of Jean and John Comaroff's analysis of occult economies in the age of neoliberalism. The Comaroffs argue that the imaginary figure of the zombie is remarkably similar throughout various regions of the world and different historical periods: 'This kaleidoscopic figure, the ultimate embodiment of flexible, "nonstandard", asocial labour, comes to us in a range of ethnographic, historical, and literary accounts that point both to subtle differences and to *nonco-*

incidental similarities.'[15] For this reason, their study can be regarded as a 'comparative archaeology of similar signs and practices to ascertain where else, and in what circumstances, parallel discourses might be found'.[16]

Second, there is a mode of thinking in similarities that relates to the self-reflective question about the similarity of a scientific observer to the (human) object of scientific observation. As I will explain below, two varieties can be distinguished in this context, since it is either assumed that scientific understanding requires a certain underlying similarity between the (human) subject and the (human) object of cognition, or, on the contrary, the existence of such an underlying similarity is seen as an impediment or obstruction to the potential for scientific knowledge. Both variants of this mode are concerned with assumptions of similarity, not *between* different objects of scientific observation but rather *in the observer's relation to* the object of observation.

In methodological terms, my comparison here of anthropological and lay-criminological assumptions of similarity will adopt the former mode, since, for heuristic reasons, I examine the discipline of anthropology from a comparative and symmetrizing perspective. In terms of content and with an eye to my own ethnographic material, however, I am interested in certain specific empirical manifestations of the second mode mentioned above, that is, the question how assumptions of similarity are incorporated into the drafting of crime prevention measures in South Africa.

Anthropological Thinking in Similarities

The category of 'similarity' has played a significant role in the self-understanding of modernity wherever it has sought to distinguish itself from the non-modern other. This is apparent in social theories that introduce such a distinction through fundamental oppositions such as 'homogeneous/heterogeneous' and 'nondifferentiated/differentiated'. For example, Émile Durkheim's work on 'organic' and 'mechanical solidarity'[17] has a prominent place in the history of anthropological theory. Durkheim ascribes mechanical solidarity to 'simple' societies ('*societies primitives*') with relatively small populations. According to him, such societies comprise 'a system of homogeneous segments similar to one another',[18] whose members in turn are similar in the sense that they all heed the common interest. Because they also share the same living space and engage in similar activities, homogeneity and a 'mechanical' form of solidarity prevail here, upheld by shared religious beliefs, emotions and states of consciousness. 'The solidarity that derives from similarities is [thus] at its *maximum* when the collective consciousness completely envelops . . . total consciousness, coinciding with it at every point. At that moment . . . individuality is zero.'[19] As is well known, Durkheim contrasts this 'solidarity through similarities'[20] with the 'organic' solidarity of modern societies differentiated functionally and through a division of labour, which he describes as internally heterogeneous, individualizing and organized through the interdependence of the specialized tasks of their members.

The assumptions of similarity articulated here with respect to non-modern societies have proven to be astonishingly persistent, not only in the theoretical history of anthropology and other scientific disciplines concerned with non-modern socialities, but also in popular culture discourses of the past and the present. They point to the difficulties and aversions in modern thought to developing a sense for the *internal* differentiation of a categorical other. There was a long tradition of ethnographers who, on the basis of such assumptions of similarity, let selected key informants speak for an entire society, presuming without hesitation that statements made by men would also be valid for women who had not been interviewed by the researchers. They sometimes even drew conclusions in a metonymic gesture about the entire 'cultural community' on the basis of research in a clearly limited, small-scale locality – that is, *one* village. At the latest, since the 'writing culture' debate of the 1980s,[21] it has generally been accepted that homogenizing ethnographic depictions, in which members of non-modern societies are reduced to a collective singular based on similarity (as in references to 'the Azande' or 'the Nuer'), are extremely problematic.[22] It is nevertheless surprising how little attention was long paid to certain early insights about the relativity and manipulability of cultural components within a society, such as those by Bronislaw Malinowski in his pointed criticism at that time of 'the dogma of the automatic submission to custom [that] dominates the whole inquiry into primitive law'.[23]

In addition to assumptions of similarity regarding the general social and cultural constitution of non-modern societies, the category of 'similarity' has also repeatedly been used as a marker of difference in anthropological and philosophical attempts to distinguish modern and non-modern modes of thought. Thus, for James Frazer, the actions of a 'primitive magician'[24] represent a spurious science whereby two principles of magic can be differentiated as extreme types: the 'Law of Contact or Contagion' and the 'Law of Similarity'. Regarding the Law of Similarity, according to Frazer, 'the magician infers that he can produce any effect he desires merely by imitating it',[25] thereby erroneously 'assuming that things which resemble each other are the same'.[26] In this view, the magician's positing the existence of real connections based on similarity, when, according to Frazer's understanding of science, these do not in fact exist, becomes the criterion by which science establishes a socio-cultural distinction between itself and the (magically thinking) other. The capacity to differentiate 'realistic' categories is thereby reserved only for scientific rationality.

Reflecting on anthropological modes of thinking in similarities can help anthropologists avoid repeating such pejorative distinctions. There is, for instance, a certain irony in the fact that Frazer's selection of empirical examples for the Law of Similarity follows a similarity principle itself. Frazer exemplifies his argument with a compilation of magical practices from a vast spectrum of regions throughout the world and across historical epochs which share specific characteristics. They are related to one another in Frazer's remarks in a radically decontextualized way. Arnold van Gennep's famous comparative treatise on rites of passage is also based on such a practice. Gennep asserts therein that 'we encounter a wide degree of general similarity among ceremonies of birth, childhood, social puberty, betrothal, marriage, pregnancy, fatherhood, initiation into religious societies, and funerals'.[27]

This form of cultural comparison based on similarity, which was very popular at that time, was replaced within the parameters of (structural) functionalist theories by an alternative convention of anthropological systematization that no longer emphasized the comparison of similar or different elements, but instead focused on the structural interplay of *copresent* socio-cultural elements.[28] In this convention, cross-cultural references to empirical similarities assume a different status, namely, that of an analogy for the purpose of intercultural heuristics.[29] Melford Spiro has described this transformation of anthropological depictions that accompanied a rise in cultural relativism:

> Because the diversity of cultures was now viewed as comprising not a scale of cultural evolution, but rather the range of cultural variability, its aim was taken to be the discovery of principles and theories that might explain the diversity in cultural and social systems. With that change in aim, the rationale for focusing on primitive peoples correspondingly changed. No longer viewed as similar to one another – each being an instance of an archaic type of society – they were now chosen for study precisely because . . . they were viewed as different, each different from every other, and all, in turn, from Western peoples.[30]

In addition to concentrating on socio-cultural differences, there were also attempts in the early history of anthropology to identify underlying similarities between modern and non-modern societies. This is also apparent in the role that the category of 'similarity' assumed in distinguishing different modes of thought. According to Lucien Lévy-Bruhl, in the pre-logical thinking of the 'primitive mind', all objects and entities of the world appear tied into a system of mystical participation which gives the world coherence and order, and which is beyond the rules of formal logic. Characteristic for this mode of thinking, for example, is the statement that 'to them the things which are unseen cannot be distinguished from the things which are seen'.[31] For Lévy-Bruhl, this mode of thought has to be understood as a culturally specific system that is internally coherent and rational, and that does not challenge the basic capacities of the 'primitive mind'. He asks, 'Why is it that primitive mentality shows such indifference to . . . the discursive operations of thought, of reasoning, and reflection . . . ?'[32] In answering this question, he places special emphasis on the existence of common ground between self and other:

> It is due neither to incapacity nor inaptitude, since those who have drawn our attention to this feature of primitive mentality expressly state that among them are 'minds quite as capable of scientific thought as those of Europeans' and we have seen that Australian and Melanesian children learn what the missionary teaches them quite as readily as French or English children would do.[33]

As my comments above indicate, regarding developments in anthropology and related disciplines describing others as being prone to 'thinking in similarities' often has a pejorative character, and, in implementing a powerful othering, has historically been used repeatedly to demarcate the self from the other. Attributing the presence or (supposed) absence of differentiated thinking thus becomes the point of departure for practices of socio-cultural distinction.[34] However, it also becomes clear that there are gradual differences in how absolutely this distinction is implemented. Whereas some authors in these debates were convinced that differences in the modes of thinking in modern and non-modern societies could be traced back to biological (that is, racial) causes, others – such as Lévy-Bruhl cited above – referred to the existence of a shared horizon of human possibilities shaped only by divergent cultural conditions. Taking up this second line of thought, Adolf Bastian and Franz Boas advocated the concept of 'the psychic unity of mankind' as the axiomatic point of departure for anthropological research. This position was not only based on an anti-racist programme grounded in the Enlightenment, but also addressed the very conditions of possibility of anthropological understanding.[35]

A question that has often been posed in the history of anthropology – if and/or how intercultural understanding is possible – can be translated into another question: to what extent can the hiatus between identity and alterity be bridged by the existence of similarities? In the context of the present article, I am less concerned with studies on incommensurability, inconceivability and untranslatability.[36] Instead, in several theoretical traditions, there have been attempts to define the ontological foundation of interpersonal understanding on the basis of similarity. In anthropological approaches influenced by philosophical and sociological phenomenology, the issue, for example, is the actual 'direct understanding'[37] of the life-worlds investigated and, accordingly, the attempt 'to describe human consciousness in its lived immediacy'.[38] In the introduction to his anthology, *The Anthropology of Experience,* Edward Bruner clearly identifies what is significant in this conception as the foundation of the process of understanding: 'We understand *other* people and their expressions on the basis of *our own* experience and self-understanding.'[39]

Anthropologists inspired by the cognitive sciences have also emphasized personal experience and physical practices in their research. Maurice Bloch, for example, has argued that greater attention should be paid to the non-verbal forms of practical learning, both when conducting anthropological research and when writing about it:

> Perhaps we should make much more use of description of the way things look, sound, feel, smell, taste and so on – drawing on the realm of bodily experience – simply for heuristic purposes, to remind readers that most of our material is taken from the world of non-explicit expert practice and does not only come from linear, linguistic thought.[40]

According to Bloch, physical being-in-the-world allows the scientist, in the process of participatory observation, to gain similarity-based knowledge about other life-worlds that would be inaccessible to a study conveyed exclusively on the level of language.[41]

From the perspective of these and comparable approaches, research experience that results in intercultural understanding does not have to be of a physical nature. In his renowned essay, 'Grief and a Headhunter's Rage: On the Cultural Force of Emotions',[42] Renato Rosaldo describes how it was only due to the painful experience of his wife dying suddenly during their fieldwork together among the Ilongot in the Philippines that he was able to comprehend the connections between 'grief' and 'rage' characteristic of the Ilongot headhunters. It nevertheless continues to be debated in anthropology today whether empathy – in the sense of a similarity-based connection rooted in experience or emotion – can be considered a (legitimate) foundation for scientific understanding.[43]

The question about the conditions of possibility and modalities of intercultural understanding was transferred early on also from the domain of scientific methodology to that of ethnographies. In implementing a 'reverse anthropology',[44] books such as Julius Lips's *The Savage Hits Back:*

Or The White Man through Native Eyes[45] and a series of important later publications[46] addressed non-western efforts to deal with colonial experiences and other power-related configurations whereby particular attention was paid to mimetic-imitational forms. With respect to the phenomenon of spirit possession, mimesis was understood as a process of a physical, symbolic 'conforming with something else or an other',[47] serving the presentation, interpretation and appropriation of the powerful other.[48] At the same time, it was interpreted as a non-intellectual epistemic practice in which the separation between the subject and object of knowing dissolves into a formula of similarity.

Regarding the history of anthropology, we must ask whether the epistemic interest of anthropological research was always (only) focused on the foreignness of the other, or on its similarity as well. In her fascinating treatise on the proto-anthropology of the sixteenth and seventeenth centuries, Margaret T. Hodgen describes how Renaissance intellectuals were puzzled not only by the diversity of cultures, but also by the simultaneous existence of intercultural commonalities.[49] That kind of intellectual anxiety can also be found among modern anthropologists, for example Claude Lévi-Strauss, whose studies on mythology presume the identification of an (apparent) contradiction:

> Mythology confronts the student with a situation which at first sight could be looked upon as contradictory. On the one hand, it would seem that in the course of a myth anything is likely to happen. There is no logic, no continuity. Any characteristic can be attributed to any subject; every conceivable relation can be met. With myth, everything becomes possible. But on the other hand, this apparent arbitrariness is belied by the astounding similarity between myths collected in widely different regions. Therefore the problem: if the content of a myth is contingent, how are we going to explain that throughout the world myths do resemble one another so much?[50]

I cannot discuss in detail here Lévi-Strauss' widely known approach to myth analysis, in which he extracts elementary structures of human thought from socio-cultural diversity. It should be emphasized, however, that the problem identified by Lévi-Strauss is fundamental for the discipline of anthropology as a comparative science.

In his essay, 'The Limitations of the Comparative Method of Anthropology',[51] Franz Boas distinguished between two modalities of scientific comparison: one that seeks to specify commonalities and another that seeks to identify differences. Beyond this distinction, which initially appears rather straightforward, however, the practical implementation of an anthropological comparison of society and culture presents a number of epistemological and methodological challenges. On the one hand, the units of the comparison have to be determined, for which James A. Boon has offered a – certainly appropriate – general warning: 'the comparison of cultures requires not that we reduce them to platitudinous similarity'[52] in the sense of an overly reductive 'lowest common denominator' approach.[53] Nevertheless, Boon's insistence that the cultures being compared are to be understood as 'integrated systems of differences'[54] would face well-founded criticism from representatives of poststructuralist and postmodern positions, especially in light of recent works on cultural hybridizations and processes of socio-cultural translation.

On the other hand, from a methodological perspective it should be noted that 'relations of similarity and difference are not given in the empirical phenomena themselves but are generated by people who act on them and decide, using criteria of their own choosing, to which class, category or concept they conform'.[55] For anthropologists, therefore, the act of comparing involves the more or less conscious establishment of comparability, in which the 'objects of comparison'[56] do not exist *a priori* but are produced performatively according to particular (comparative) points of view. The existence of intercultural and timeless similarities is thus inextricably dependent on the standpoint of the respective observer and of the respective approach: 'If one looks hard enough one can find ideas anticipated long before their time, or one can trace their similarity through time. Yet, when one looks again, and considers other ideas, the sense of similarity vanishes.'[57]

Starting in the mid-twentieth century, the postcolonial independence of countries in the global South and the transnational transfer of knowledge finally led to a situation in which it became commonplace for anthropologists to turn the focus of their research to their own countries ('*anthropology at home*').[58] Another effect of these developments was that scholars of the global South who had been trained in the global North increasingly returned to their respective home countries, where they conducted ethnographic research. As Akhil Gupta and James Ferguson have shown,[59] these processes undermined the partitioning of the world into distinct socio-spatial research fields according to historically established scientific conventions, in which representatives of academic anthropology were assigned the 'savage slot' of the non-modern global South.[60] Within the discipline of anthropology, this socio-spatial division is reflected in the distinction between 'field' and 'home', and in the persisting expectation that '*real* anthropologists' have to travel to distant places to conduct their research:

> After all, if 'the field' is most appropriately a place that is 'not home', then some places will necessarily be more 'not home' than others, and hence more appropriate, more 'fieldlike'. All ethnographic research is thus done 'in the field', but some 'fields' are more equal than others – specifically, those that are understood to be distant, exotic, and strange.[61]

In an absurd reversal, one of the consequences of this logic was that African-American graduate students were long discouraged by their academic supervisors at American universities from doing ethnographic fieldwork on the African continent, since they were assumed to lack the objectivity necessary for such research.[62] Such advice expressed 'seemingly nonsensical assumptions about what race is, how identity is constituted, and who one's "own" people are'.[63] At the same time, this example shows that (ostensible) identitary proximity between the human subjects and the objects of anthropological research is often seen as detrimental in gaining objective, valid and legitimate knowledge.

The example of African-American anthropology students suggests that such attributions of legitimacy according to identitary categories should be interpreted against the background of the specific political discourses in which they are embedded. For some anthropologists, existing similarities between researchers and the objects of their research tend to delegitimize the findings of that research. In contrast, other anthropologists criticize a *lack* of such similarity when, for example, an ethnographer conducts research on 'others' who have a different identity. Furthermore, it is neither politically nor ethically neutral when anthropologists presume that the people they are researching are either different from themselves (*othering*) or actually 'like themselves' (*nostrification*). For this reason, there have been repeated calls, especially in recent anthropological work, for an awareness of ethical problems regarding the relationship between the researcher and the object of research. One example of this is David Graeber's plea for 'dialogic relativism', which he describes as consisting of 'a mutual recognition of, and respect for, difference founded on the recognition of an even more fundamental similarity (hence, equality) that makes such recognition possible'.[64] In this passage, the 'fundamental similarity' of people is presented as a prerequisite for both 'equality' and the recognition of 'difference'. This demonstrates in exemplary fashion how the concept of 'similarity' is frequently conflated with other – morally and politically loaded – concepts, thereby rendering an ambiguous picture-puzzle that integrates contradictory elements which can be invoked at will depending on the particular discursive context.

In the following analysis of my own ethnographic research on thinking in similarities in the lay-criminological etiology of crime in South Africa, two aspects in particular that can prove heuristically fruitful can be gleaned from the above remarks. First, there is a mode of thinking in similarities in this empirical context which – from the perspective of members of mainstream society – refers to similarities between certain forms of 'asocial alterity', and which makes it possible in a complexity-reducing gesture to classify *all* '(criminal) internal others' of South African society to a common category. Second, we encounter here the following question, which should be familiar given my previous remarks: do similarities between people who implement crime prevention measures and those others from whom the former wish to protect themselves have a beneficial or detrimental effect on these efforts?

Thinking in Similarities from a Lay-Criminological Perspective

Since the official end of apartheid in 1990, South Africa has been caught up in a long and difficult transformation process. While the first democratic general elections in April 1994 did ensure the equality of all population groups as guaranteed in the Constitution, the transition from apartheid to a democracy grounded in basic civil rights also led to a series of profound political, economic and socio-cultural problems. The 'new South Africa' thus faces the challenge of bringing about a comprehensive socio-political transformation that integrates previously discriminated segments of the population as well as previously privileged ones while confronting the institutional, infrastructural and cultural legacy of the apartheid regime. Dealing with past injustices through the Truth and Reconciliation Commission,[65] for example, requires prolonged and contentious negotiation processes in the struggle for a new social order in a pluralist, democratic South Africa.

Many of these conflicts have been triggered by concrete socio-political problems. In addition to unemployment and the HIV/AIDS pandemic, another issue that carries considerable weight is the rise in crime that is often associated with South Africa and which substantially impacts all areas of society in the country today. Until the early 1990s, the African National Congress (ANC) under Nelson Mandela still assumed that violence and crime were reactive side-effects of the systematic oppression of the non-white population. With the end of apartheid widespread peace in civil society was anticipated in the country. Thus, for a long time, the ANC had no political programme targeting issues of crime prevention and control. Not until the ANC took control of the government in 1994

> did the party begin [to see] crime and violence as issues of order. There were several reasons for this change in approach. First, violence and crime undermined the party's legitimate claim to rule. Second, large segments of the South African population became preoccupied with crime and violence as the most serious problem facing society.[66]

Against the background of the politicization of violence and crime that has burdened South Africa's past, present debates on these issues have led to discourses on 'normalcy' and 'deviance' as well as on practices of social inclusion and exclusion that express competing ideas of social order. This configuring of the social order in reference to its categorical opposite – that is, 'crime' – is taking place not only as a reaction to and within the framework of state jurisdiction. There have also been diverse crime prevention efforts by governmental and non-governmental actors in present-day South Africa. These socio-cultural, infrastructural and technological measures represent attempts to anticipate criminal activities at everyday and institutional levels in order to develop counter-strategies proactively. Crime prevention thus presumes the potentiality of future conflicts. At the same time, this potentiality is inscribed into the socio-cultural and material space of South Africa by the crime prevention measures. This anticipation based on experience with crime, stereotypes and fantasies, as well as political ambitions, becomes an independent reality that influences not only the present but also the future shape of social life in South Africa.

Two aspects of this ethnographic constellation are particularly significant in the context of my argument here. First, we should emphasize that the selected crime prevention strategies are always fragile, and have to be continually adapted or readjusted since they are confronted with imaginary, potential or real offenders who threaten to undermine the measures. Second, we need to pay attention to the emic experiences and expectations of the actors of mainstream society. When these actors develop fantasies, assumptions and conclusions about the groups of people they need to be protected from, statements are also made, more or less implicitly, about precisely how and in what area of life the crime prevention measures are to be applied, and – especially important for my argument – what the causes of these criminal acts are.

As suggested above, my research is based on a heuristic approach that views the people I interviewed and observed in present-day South Africa as 'lay criminologists'. Thus, drawing on a concrete empirical example, I analyse their assessments as lay criminologists in order to comprehend the social construction and significance of assumptions about identity, difference and similarity in the field of crime prevention.

According to the 'labelling theory' in sociological crime research as developed by Howard S. Becker, 'deviance' represents a culturally dependent category of social attribution through which norm-setting social differentiation is implemented.[67] In the field of crime prevention, such differentiation reflects specific socio-cultural and socio-political configurations based on the guiding distinction of 'social/asocial'. As part of a recursive social (self-) observation of sociality, a parallel, contrasting duality is also embedded here from the perspective of members of the mainstream society, in which 'sociality' is associated with 'identity' and 'asociality' with 'alterity'. In contrast to discourses of alterity in intercultural contexts, which generally presume foreignness, in the context of actions labelled as 'asocial' and 'criminal' among people within the same social unit, it is not even clear whether one can actually speak of 'alterity'. At first glance, (potential) offenders appear in such contexts as a group of 'internal others', that is, as a group that – in the sense of Louis Dumont's discussion of 'hierarchical opposition' – stands as representatives of 'asociality' in structural opposition to representatives of 'sociality', but who at the same time are structurally included in the latter group (that is, the representatives of 'sociality').[68] After a closer anthropologically informed examination, however, it becomes obvious that this descriptive model is too facile because it is a simplification. Turning from a lay-criminological perspective to the etiology of crime in South Africa, it is clear that several (potential) causal factors have been introduced here that vary with regard to the respective emphasis and inter-relation of social identity, difference and similarity.

In lay-criminological discourses in present-day South Africa, the following factors are regarded as causes of crime (depending on the speaker and the context, but also in various mixed forms and emphases): the 'racial identity' of the offender, biological sex, economic poverty, pessimism about the future, having been socialized in a 'culture of violence', as well as opportunism and political efforts to redress socio-economic inequalities after the end of apartheid.

Some of the aforementioned factors follow a logic of binary opposition, through which the distinction between 'identity' and 'difference' is emphasized and the possibility of intermediate similarities is factored out. For example, a recurring narrative strategy of women I talked to in South Africa was to describe their own sociality as that of a *female victim* of a criminal act and to radically differentiate that from the asociality of the *male offenders*, thus dissociating themselves in an identitary, absolutizing manner. Other lay-criminological interpretations have racist connotations: for example, when the racial affiliation of a person is named as an indication of the future probability of that person's criminal behaviour. The arbitrariness of classifying people according to such racial features evidently does not make people uncomfortable enough to curtail the widespread practice among lay criminologists (particularly among the South African middle and upper classes) of profiling potential perpetrators according to a bipolar, black-and-white model.

Both of these lay-criminological etiologies of crime assume the existence of a naturally determined and thus immutable causation principle for criminal acts (e.g., biological sex or race), thereby distinguishing 'social identity' from 'asocial alterity', leaving neither space for intersocial similarities nor any option for transforming 'asocial alterity' into its positively connoted opposite through socialization or cultural adaptation.

Another lay-criminological etiology of crime that I repeatedly encountered during my field research in South Africa interprets crimes as an expression of a politically motivated desire for socio-economic compensation by segments of the population that have historically been subjected to discrimination. Like the two aforementioned perspectives, this approach is based on a binary opposition, namely, the categorical distinction between privileged and discriminated people. In contrast to the other perspectives, however, a notion of gradual mutability is implied here, in which collective efforts to address the history of apartheid – combined with socio-economic restructuring programmes (such as land reform) – are supposed to lead to gradual dissolution of the binary opposition. Through this process 'difference' should turn into 'identity'. The question of 'similarities', which after all are 'vague circumstances, diffuse dynamics and imprecise relations',[69] does not play a significant role in this socio-political emancipatory programme.

In present-day South Africa there are, however, also lay-criminological perspectives of the etiology of crime that allow a great deal of leeway for assumptions of similarity. One example is the argument that crime is related to the economically precarious situation of large segments of the population. This also takes into account the transformation processes of the past twenty years and the resulting economic decline of once-privileged social strata. These processes have increasingly made 'poverty' into a relative concept – and not only with respect to categories ('poverty' as the opposite of 'affluence'), but also in terms of identitary configurations, since different population groups now increasingly find themselves in *similar* economic situations.

Assumptions of similarity also play a role in lay-criminological explanatory models that emphasize the great impact of a South African 'culture of violence'. Among the people I spoke to, some said that such a 'culture of violence' existed only within specific segments of the population, with my black interlocutors in the townships referring to the violent police apparatus of the apartheid regime and the white people mentioning violence in the townships. Further, I was sometimes told that *all of* South African society was suffused with a 'culture of violence' that had developed historically and interdependently. This notion of an interface of (white) militarism and (black) violent criminality presumes a systemic similarity among different groups in the population.

Finally, I should mention a lay-criminological approach that, in contrast to the other positions, identifies an essential commonality between the actors of mainstream society and (potential) offenders, namely, 'opportunism'. According to this perspective, all people are identical to the extent that they pursue their own interests, and, after rationally assessing gains and risks and considering their practical options, (can) in fact decide to commit criminal acts.

It would be easy to expand the discussion of different lay-criminological interpretations of the causes of crime in South Africa. But let us stop here and, in summary, point out that such approaches express different ideas about how actors in mainstream society relate to (potential) offenders, giving different weight to commonalities, differences and similarities. It should be also emphasized that these lay-criminological etiologies of crime are not purely discursive or classificatory, but are also reflected in the concrete manifestation and practical implementation of crime-preventive measures. In the remainder of this article I thus address the question of how – with an eye toward empirical manifestations of the distinction between 'difference' and 'similarity' – the transition between these categories is shaped in practice or becomes the focus of social negotiations.

It is widely known that racist social discrimination of the apartheid era was tied to a categorical black-and-white schema. What is less well-known, however, is that the socio-spatial segregation of white and black segments of the population in large parts of the country was placed in the hands of a group of people referred to as 'coloureds', which can be understood as an intermediate identitary category. Recruitment of this group of people – 'hybrids', in the problematic biologistic sense of the word – for the military, police and security apparatus of the apartheid regime was disproportionately high; thus they served as a buffer between two social groups whose relations were considered fundamentally antagonistic. They were also given this role because the 'coloured' population was attributed qualities that had a certain similarity to both 'whites' and 'blacks'. An intersocial zone of 'similarity' was therefore created between 'identity' and 'difference' that served both segregating and communicating functions.

As I discovered during my fieldwork, identity, difference and similarity also play an important role in crime prevention discourses and practices in present-day South Africa. I repeatedly witnessed controversies between local actors about which forms of social relations could be regarded as 'promoting crime' and which as 'preventing crime'.[70]

A private security company that I studied took care, when hiring new employees, to ensure that they were not related to anyone on the existing staff. This did not mean that family structures were viewed as irrelevant. On the contrary, company employees were regularly visited at home by their superiors in order for company management to get an impression of the family environment. From the perspective of management, the ideal situation was for staff to live in nuclear families. Extended families, on the contrary, had a reputation for potentially promoting crime. Furthermore, the security company made sure that security guards placed in department stores and businesses remained resistant to attempts at criminal infiltration – that is, that social distance to the staff and customers was maintained. Finally, the employees working for the security company were encouraged to establish informal, friendly contact with security guards in neighbouring businesses (i.e. with the employees of other security companies) so that they could assist each other if necessary.

An employee of this security company who was working as a security guard described his employer's crime prevention precepts as follows: in private life he was supposed to live in a clearly defined nuclear family; at the security company he was supposed to fit into the military-like, hierarchical order; during his work shift he was expected to maintain his personal autonomy, but also to cultivate friendly contact with the staff of other security companies. Various forms of sociality are combined in this ensemble to form a complex constellation that aims to prevent crime among potential offenders both within and outside the security company. In order to achieve this, there were systematic attempts to promote certain forms of relationship in certain contexts and to prevent others.

The contextuality of such configurations also becomes apparent if the security guards are accompanied to their homes after work, as I did during my fieldwork. It then becomes evident that many things considered crime-promoting in the context of the security company serve to reduce crime in the context of the private lives of security guards: for example, having an extended family living in close proximity or even contacts with local gangs. In the poor and conflict-laden townships where most of the employees of the South African security companies live, it would be downright dangerous for them to follow the crime prevention precepts of security companies in their private lives and to insist on rigorous distinctions to potential offenders. In some urban spaces in present-day South

Africa, one can survive only by adopting the conventionalized habits of a small-time criminal and not shying away from occasionally engaging in violence in a way that attracts public attention.

Despite their differences, the crime prevention practices discussed here have in common that they all incorporate lay-criminological interpretations about the kinds of sociality through which crime can be limited or even prevented. Also, these interpretations all address the question whether crime prevention should be based on a *principle of similarity* or a *principle of difference*: the aforementioned security company essentially follows the principle of difference, since it sets 'formal hierarchical structures' against 'informal network structures'. In contrast to this, the employees of this company often follow the principle of similarity in their private lives, attempting through a kind of identitary adaptation to establish a protective compatibility with those forms of social relations experienced on the ground as 'criminal'. Characteristic of partial adaptation as a crime prevention practice is the actor's engagement with the gradual, delicate and ambivalent boundary between internal and external, similarity and difference. Remaining in this border zone and mimetically aligning themselves with the '(criminal) internal others' who populate it is at once a prerequisite and a hazard to their own actions and even to their existence. Such similarity-based alignment always also raises suspicions about whether the line between legality and illegality has been crossed, and whether moral identity has become amoral alterity.

Conclusion

The French sociologist Luc Boltanski recently published a book tracing the emergence of the literary genre of detective stories and spy novels back to transformation processes of modern societies and the modern state since the nineteenth century. Boltanski argues that the 'new ways of problematizing reality'[71] that are negotiated in this literature reflect certain parallel developments in the empirical social sciences. In his book, he seeks

> to pin down the social and political conjuncture in which, in the late nineteenth and early twentieth centuries, the thematics of mystery and conspiracy became tropes destined to play a prominent role *both* in fiction *and* in the interpretation of historical events and the workings of society. The thesis proposed here *links* questions about the representation of reality with changes that affected the way reality itself was instituted during the period in question.[72]

In contrast to this, my discussion here of various manifestations of anthropological and lay-criminological thinking in similarities has *not* sought to identify historical links between these manifestations, or to equate anthropological references to 'external others' with lay-criminological references to '(criminal) internal others'. Instead, my aim has been, first of all, to explore the heuristic value of a comparison by means of 'similarities', thereby complementing the version of comparison by means of 'differences' preferred by Clifford Geertz (see above). Using this comparative approach, it has become clear that – considering in each case the different categorical and moral assessments of the respective other – a certain structural similarity exists, in that an attempt is made in both fields of social practice to maintain a balance perceived as problematic and challenging between closeness and distance to the other. Just as anthropologists engaged in participatory observation seek to maintain knowledge-generating proximity while simultaneously trying to avoid an identitary entanglement with the object of their observation, many of the practices of crime prevention discussed above require a balance when dealing with similarities that could become ensnaring.

Second, a review of the history of anthropology shows that thinking in similarities was repeatedly invoked in the discipline as a way of making pejorative distinctions regarding the non-modern other, while reserving for modern rationality the capacity to produce accurate categorical distinctions. In order to counteract this form of othering with regard to my own ethnographic research, I have made the discipline of anthropology itself the object of my reflections and have identified some of those modalities of thinking in similarities that were – and to some extent still are – characteristic of anthropology (as well as other related disciplines).

Some of the insights presented in the first part of this article regarding the history of anthropology as a discipline and proto-anthropological precursors can be distilled into one significant distinction. There are two types of mind among scholars. There are those who, in their efforts to understand the world, submit to the methodological principle of specification or particularization. When drawn into making comparisons, they resist assertions of likeness, similarity, analogy, unity. The phenomenon of differentness in culture prevails against even the most persuasive arguments from likeness. The other type adheres to the principle of homogeneity; to the fruitfulness in explanation of arguing from the similar, the corresponding, the parallel or the identical.[73]

As I have shown in the second, ethnographic part of this article, this distinction can also be made with respect to the lay-criminological etiology of crime. In the discourses and practices of crime prevention in present-day South Africa, there are diverging interpretations of the relationship between actors in mainstream society and (potential) offenders.

These interpretations differ from each other in the way they emphasize and inter-relate social 'identity', 'difference' and 'similarity'. In crime prevention strategies, assumptions of similarity establish an intermediate identitary space and an intersocial contact zone in which members of mainstream society align with '(criminal) internal others' while simultaneously endangering their own sociality. 'Similarity' is inevitably ambivalent in this context, as much a promise as a gamble.

Notes

1 On Adolf Bastian see Köpping (1983); see also Boas (1910).
2 Hodgen (1964): 295.
3 See Hannerz (1989).
4 Brown (2008): 370.
5 Baudrillard (1993): 124.
6 Ibid.: 124–25.
7 Miller (1997): 17.
8 See Bloch (2005).
9 Sökefeld (1999): 431.
10 See Fabian (2002).
11 In this chapter, 'lay criminology' refers to any reflections by non-professional social actors about the causes (etiology) of – and options for possible prevention measures for – any asocial or antisocial actions that are classified in their respective social contexts as 'criminal'.
12 See Goffman (1959).
13 Gebauer (2001).
14 Bhatti *et al.* (2011): 247.
15 Comaroff and Comaroff (2003): 150 (emphasis added).
16 Ibid.: 170.
17 Durkheim ([1984] 2014): 101–02.
18 Ibid.: 142.
19 Ibid.: 101.
20 Ibid.: 117.
21 Clifford and Marcus, eds (1986); see also Berg and Fuchs, eds (1993).
22 Homogenizing representations of this kind were possible in part through cultural theories that understood 'culture' as a horizon of meaning tied to an ethnic identity largely shared within a society and also clearly distinguishable in social terms from other 'cultures'; for a critique of these theories, see Abu-Lughod (1991).
23 Malinowski (1926): 14. Malinowski counters this dogma with a situational approach oriented around an individual's interests and options for action, in which 'his observance of the rules of law under the normal conditions, when it is followed and not defied, is at best partial, conditional, and subject to evasions; that it is not enforced by any wholesale motive like fear of punishment, or a general submission to all tradition, but by very complex psychological and social inducements – all this is a state of affairs which modern anthropology has so far completely overlooked' (ibid.: 15).
24 Frazer (2002): 11.
25 Ibid.
26 Ibid: 12.
27 Gennep (1960): 3.

[28] Exceptions to this are of course studies that identify *regional* socio-cultural patterns; see for example Schoffeleers, ed. (1978).

[29] A classic example of such analogies is the term 'argonauts' in the title of Bronislaw Malinowski's *Argonauts of the Western Pacific* (1922). In contrast to this are cultural comparisons based on the identification of differences. Clifford Geertz has described the heuristic advantages of this with reference to his research in Morocco and Indonesia: 'The dissimilitudes of Morocco and Indonesia do not separate them into absolute types, the sociological equivalent of natural kinds; they reflect back and forth upon one another, mutually framing, reciprocally clarifying. Or so they seem to do for me. I learned more about Indonesia when, shaken by the disturbances of the mid-sixties, I decided it the better part of valour to work in Morocco, than I would have had I gone back then directly to Indonesia. And I learned more about Morocco when, after things had settled down again in the seventies, I returned, not without trepidation, to Indonesia, than I would have by confining myself, as beginning to find my feet in another civilization, I was tempted to do, thenceforth to North Africa' (Geertz 1996: 28).

[30] Spiro (1986): 277.

[31] Lévy-Bruhl (([1923] 1966): 61.

[32] Ibid.: 29.

[33] Ibid.: 29–30. The problem of different modes of thinking in modern and non-modern societies was discussed not only in the early period of anthropology, but has had continued relevance. This became apparent in the heated debate in the 1990s between Marshall Sahlins and Gananath Obeyesekere about whether or not the British seafarer and explorer James Cook was viewed as a 'god' (*lomo*) by the Hawaiians in the eighteenth century. See Sahlins (1995); Obeyesekere (1997).

[34] See also Latour (1993).

[35] The 'psychic unity of mankind' is characterized by Boas as follows: 'It would seem . . . that the weight of evidence is, on the whole, in favour of *an essential similarity of mental endowment in different races*, with the probability of variations in the type of mental characteristics.' (Boas 1910: 372, emphasis added).

[36] See, for example, Povinelli (2001); Port (2005). Some anthropologists doubt that 'intercultural untranslatability' is even conceivable. Ernest Gellner has pointed out that 'no anthropologist, to my knowledge, has come back from a field trip with the following report: their concepts are so alien that it is impossible to describe their land tenure, their kinship system, their ritual.' (Gellner 1985: 86)

[37] Jackson, ed. (1996): 2.

[38] Ibid. See also Hastrup and Hervik, eds (1994).

[39] Bruner (1989): 6 (emphasis added).

[40] Bloch (1991): 193.

[41] For a general discussion of the role of taxonomic similarities ('features') and 'similarity judgments' in cognitive anthropology, see D'Andrade (1995).

[42] Rosaldo (1984).

[43] See also Kirmayer (2008).

[44] Kirsch (2006).

[45] Lips (1937).

[46] For example, Ferguson (2002); Kramer (1993); Taussig (1993).

[47] Kramer (1993): 250.

[48] See also Bhabha (1994).

[49] See Hodgen (1964).

[50] Lévi-Strauss (1963): 208.

[51] Boas (1896).
[52] Boon (1982): ix.
[53] Geertz (1973): 43.
[54] Boon (1982): ix.
[55] Holý (1987): 16. See also Gingrich and Fox (2002).
[56] Niewöhner and Scheffer (2010): 9.
[57] Strathern (1987): 253.
[58] See Jackson, ed. (1987); Peirano (1998). Another postcolonial context in which conditions of similarity have become the focus of anthropological studies is the question of organizational formalization in the process of globalization, which, for example, is covered by the neo-institutionalistic concept of 'isomorphism' (see, for example, Kirsch 2003; and Rottenburg 2009). Due to space limitations, these studies cannot be discussed in the present article.
[59] See Ferguson and Gupta (1997).
[60] See Trouillot (1991).
[61] Ferguson and Gupta (1997): 13.
[62] Amory (1997): 109f.
[63] Ibid.: 110.
[64] Graeber (2007): 289–90.
[65] See Wilson (2001).
[66] Jensen (2001): 109.
[67] See Becker (1973).
[68] Dumont (1980) speaks of 'encompassing'.
[69] Bhatti *et al.* (2011): 236–37.
[70] For example, it is striking that a single institution for crime prevention can be interpreted in radically different ways. For example, whereas the Community Policing Forums (CPFs) are seen by some South African citizens as a welcome and morally positive form of civil society engagement in crime prevention, the CPFs' programmatic inclusiveness also embraces potential offenders, which has led to great mistrust of the CPFs by other South African citizens; see Kirsch (2010).
[71] Boltanski (2014): xiv.
[72] Ibid.: xv, emphasis added.
[73] Hodgen (1964): 295.

References

Abu-Lughod, Lila (1991), 'Writing against Culture', in Richard Fox, ed., *Recapturing Anthropology*, Santa Fe: School of American Research Press: 137–62.

Amory, Deborah (1997), 'African Studies as American Institution', in James Ferguson and Akhil Gupta, eds, *Anthropological Locations: Boundaries and Grounds of a Field Science*, Berkeley: University of California Press: 102–16.

Baudrillard, Jean (1993), 'The Melodrama of Difference (Or, The Revenge of the Colonized)', in *The Transparency of Evil: Essays on Extreme Phenomena*, translated by James Benedict, New York: Verso: 124–38.

Becker, Howard S. (1973), *Outsiders: Studies in the Sociology of Deviance*, New York: The Free Press.

Berg, Eberhard and Martin Fuchs, eds (1993), *Kultur, Soziale Praxis, Text: Die Krise der ethnographischen Repräsentation*, Frankfurt am Main: Suhrkamp Verlag.

Bhabha, Homi (1994), 'Of Mimicry and Man: The Ambivalence of Colonial Discourse', in *The Location of Culture*, London: Routledge: 85–92.

Bhatti, Anil *et al.* (2011), 'Ähnlichkeit: ein kulturtheoretisches Paradigma', *Internationales Archiv für Sozialgeschichte der deutschen Literatur*, 36 (1): 233–47.

Bloch, Maurice (1991), 'Language, Anthropology and Cognitive Science', *Man* (26): 183–98.

——— (2005), 'Where Did Anthropology Go? Or the Need for "Human Nature"', in *Essays on Cultural Transmission*, Oxford: Berg: 1–20.

Boas, Franz (1896), 'The Limitations of the Comparative Method in Anthropology', *Science*, new series 4 (103): 901–08.

——— (1910), 'Psychological Problems in Anthropology', *The American Journal of Psychology*, 21 (3): 371–84.

Boltanski, Luc (2014), in Catherine Porter, trans., *Mysteries and Conspiracies: Detective Stories, Spy Novels and the Making of Modern Societies*, Cambridge, MA: Polity.

Boon, James A. (1982), *Other Tribes, Other Scribes: Symbolic Anthropology in the Comparative Study of Cultures*, Cambridge: Cambridge University Press.

Brown, Michael F. (2008), 'Cultural Relativism 2.0', *Current Anthropology*, 49 (3): 363–83.

Bruner, Edward M. (1989), 'Experience and its Expressions', in Victor W. Turner and Edward M. Bruner, eds, *The Anthropology of Experience*, Chicago: University of Illinois Press: 3–30.

Clifford, James and George Marcus, eds (1986), *Writing Culture: The Poetics and Politics of Ethnography*, Berkeley: University of California Press.

Comaroff, Jean and John Comaroff (2003), 'Ethnography on an Awkward Scale: Postcolonial Anthropology and the Violence of Abstraction', *Ethnography*, 4: 147–79.

D'Andrade, Roy G. (1995), *The Development of Cognitive Anthropology*, Cambridge: Cambridge University Press.

Dumont, Louis (1980), *Homo Hierarchicus: The Caste System and Its Implications*, translated by Mark Sainsbury, Louis Dumont and Basia Gulati, Chicago: University of Chicago Press.

Durkheim, Émile ([1984] 2014), *The Division of Labour in Society*, translated by W.D. Halls, New York: Free Press.

Fabian, Johannes (2002), *Time and the Other: How Anthropology Makes its Object*, New York: Columbia University Press.

Ferguson, James (2002), 'Of mimicry and membership: Africans and the "New World Society"', *Cultural Anthropology*, 17 (4): 551–69.

Ferguson, James and Akhil Gupta (1997), 'Discipline and Practice: "The Field" as Site, Method, and Location in Anthropology', in Ferguson and Gupta, eds, *Anthropological Locations: Boundaries and Grounds of a Field Science*, Berkeley: University of California Press: 1–45.

Frazer, James G. (2002), *The Golden Bough*, abridged edition, Mineola, NY: Dover. Unabridged republication of the abridged version, edited by the author, London: Macmillan, 1922.

Gebauer, Matthias (2001), 'Vita des Attentäters Marwan al-Shehhi: Auffällig war nur seine Unauffälligkeit', in *Der Spiegel*, 6 October; available at www.spiegel.de/politik/ausland/vita-des-attentaeters-marwan-al-shehhi-auffällig-war-nur-seine-unauffäelligkeit-a-161098.html.

Geertz, Clifford (1973), *The Interpretation of Cultures*, New York: Basic Books.

——— (1996), *After the Fact: Two Countries, Four Decades, One Anthropologist*, Cambridge, MA: Harvard University Press.

Gellner, Ernest (1985), *Relativism and the Social Sciences*, Cambridge: Cambridge University Press.

Gennep, Arold van (1960), *The Rites of Passage*, translated by Monika B. Bizedom and Gabrielle L. Caffee, Chicago: University of Chicago Press.

Gingrich, André and Richard G. Fox (2002), *Anthropology, by Comparison*, London, New York: Routledge.

Goffman, Erving (1959), *The Presentation of Self in Everyday Life*, New York: Doubleday.

Graeber, David (2007), *Possibilities: Essays on Hierarchy, Rebellion and Desire*, Edinburgh: AK Press.

Hannerz, Ulf (1989), 'Notes on the Global Ecumene', *Public Culture*, 1 (3): 66–75.

Hastrup, Kirsten and Peter Hervik, eds (1994), *Social Experience and Anthropological Knowledge*, London: Routledge.

Hodgen, Margret (1964), *Early Anthropology in the Sixteenth and Seventeenth Centuries*, Philadelphia: University of Pennsylvania Press.

Holý, Ladislav (1987), 'Introduction: Description, Generalization and Comparison', in Holý, ed., *Comparative Anthropology*, Oxford: Blackwell: 1–12.

Jackson, Anthony, ed. (1987), *Anthropology at Home*, London: Tavistock.

Jackson, Michael, ed. (1996), *Things as They Are: New Directions in Phenomenological Anthropology*, Bloomington: Indiana University Press.

Jensen, Steffen (2001), 'The Battlefield and the Price: ANC's Bid to Reform the South African State', in Thomas Hansen and Finn Stepputat, eds, *States of Imagination*, Durham: Duke University Press: 97–120.

Kirmayer, Laurence J. (2008), 'Empathy and Alterity in Cultural Psychiatry', *Ethos*, 36 (4): 457–74.

Kirsch, Stuart (2006), *Reverse Anthropology: Indigenous Analysis of Social and Environmental Relations in New Guinea*, Stanford: Stanford University Press.

Kirsch, Thomas G. (2003), 'Church, Bureaucracy, and the State: Bureaucratic Formalization in a Pentecostal Church of Zambia', *Zeitschrift für Ethnologie*, 128 (2): 213–31.

——— (2010), in Thomas G. Kirsch and Thilo Grätz, eds, 'Violence in the Name of Democracy: Community Policing, Vigilante Action and Nation-Building in South Africa', *Domesticating Vigilantism in Africa*, Oxford: James Currey: 139–62.

Köpping, Klaus-Peter (1983), *Adolf Bastian and the Psychic Unity of Mankind: The Foundations of Anthropology in Nineteenth Century Germany*, St. Lucia: University of Queensland Press.

Kramer, Fritz (1993), *The Red Fez: Art and Spirit Possession in Africa*, translated by Malcolm R. Green, London, New York: Verso .

Latour, Bruno (1993), *We Have Never Been Modern*, translated by Catherine Porter, Cambridge, MA: Harvard University Press.

Lévi-Strauss, Claude (1963), 'The Structural Study of Myth', in Claude Lévi-Strauss, ed., *Structural Anthropology*, translated by Claire Jacobson, New York: Basic Books: 206–31.

Lévy-Bruhl, Lucien ([1923] 1966), *Primitive Mentality*, translated by Lilian A. Clare, Boston: Beacon Press.

Lips, Julius (1937), *The Savage Hits Back: Or, The White Man Through Native Eyes*, translated by Vincent Benson, London: Lovat Dickson.

Malinowski, Bronislaw (1922), *Argonauts of the Western Pacific*, London: E.P. Dutton and Co., New York: George Routledge and Sons.

——— (1926), *Crime and Custom in Savage Society*, London: Routledge & Kegan Paul.

Miller, William I. (1997), *The Anatomy of Disgust*, Cambridge, MA: Harvard University Press.

Niewöhner, Jörg and Thomas Scheffer (2010), 'Introduction. Thickening Comparison: On the Multiple Facets of Comparability', in Niewöhner and Scheffer, eds, *Thick Comparison: Reviving the Ethnographic Aspiration*, Amsterdam: Brill.

Obeyesekere, Gananath (1997), *The Apotheosis of Captain Cook: European Mythmaking in the Pacific*, Princeton, NJ: Princeton University Press.

Peirano, Mariza G.S. (1998), 'When Anthropology is at Home: The Different Contexts of a Single Discipline', *Annual Review of Anthropology*, 27: 105–28.

Port, Mattijs van der (2005), 'Circling Around the Really Real: Spirit Possession Ceremonies and the Search for Authenticity in Bahian Condomblé', *Ethos*, 33 (2): 149–79.

Povinelli, Elizabeth A. (2001), 'Radical Worlds: The Anthropology of Incommensurability and Inconceivability', *Annual Review of Anthropology*, 30: 319–34.

Rosaldo, Renato (1984), 'Grief and a Headhunter's Rage: On the Cultural Force of Emotions', in Edward M. Bruner, ed., *Text, Play and Society: The Construction and Reconstruction of Self and Society*, Washington D.C.: American Ethnological Society: 178–95.

Rottenburg, Richard (2009), *Far-Fetched Facts: A Parable of Development Aid*, translated by Allison Brown and Tom Lampert, Cambridge, MA: MIT Press.

Sahlins, Marshall (1995), *How 'Natives' Think: About Captain Cook, For Example*, Chicago: University of Chicago Press.

Schoffeleers, Matthew, ed. (1978), *Guardians of the Land: Essays on Central African Territorial Cults*, Gwelo: Mambo Press.

Sökefeld, Martin (1999), 'Debating Self, Identity, and Culture in Anthropology', *Current Anthropology*, 40 (4): 417–47.

Spiro, Melford E. (1986), 'Cultural Relativism and the Future of Anthropology', *Cultural Anthropology*, 1 (3): 259–86.

Strathern, Marilyn (1987), 'Out of Context: The Persuasive Fictions of Anthropology', *Current Anthropology*, 28 (3): 251–80.

Taussig, Michael (1993), *Mimesis and Alterity: A Particular History of the Senses*, New York: Routledge.

Trouillot, Michel-Rolph (1991), 'Anthropology and the Savage Slot: The Poetics and Politics of Otherness', in Richard G. Fox, ed., *Recapturing Anthropology: Working in the Present*, Santa Fe: SAR Press: 17–44.

Wilson, Richard (2001), *The Politics of Truth and Reconciliation in South Africa: Legitimizing the Post-Apartheid State*, Cambridge: Cambridge University Press.

Chains of Similarity and Struggles for Hegemony

The Turkish Republic at a turning point[1]

Levent Tezcan

Introduction

In this essay, I deal with the topic of 'similarity' by focusing on a distinction from the powerful grand narrative of 'modernization': namely, the opposition of 'orient/occident' or – to put it in another way for purposes of this analysis that is both more up to date and specific – 'Islam/west'. Thus 'Islam' and the 'west' are not considered as individual categories of interest here but rather in their connected appearance, their referentiality to each other. Unlike the 'orient' of Orientalism, which existed only in the imaginary – based on an alliance of power politics and knowledge practices – Islam actually exists as a religion. There is a community of believers who live, act, speak and negotiate as Muslims.

The distinction appears disguised in various other conceptual juxtapositions – Islam and science, Islam and democracy, Islam and women, Islam and gender equality, Islam and homosexuality, Islam and human rights, Islam and violence, Islam and politics (the state), Islam and secularism, etc. – to which the juxtaposition Islam and integration is added in the context of migration. In all of these relations, we find simultaneous definitions of self and other. Whether it is Muslims describing themselves or westerners, the 'other' of Islam in these relations is always the 'west'. It is a powerful idea that calls for formative interventions that shape the social life of individuals and political structures of societies.

The 'culturalizing' effects of this conceptual distinction have often been referred to, and getting rid of this distinction is no simple task. Its analytical use may be in doubt, but as a category the relevance of this distinction cannot be ignored. From the very beginning, the most challenging task for the Republic of Turkey has been to determine a proper relation between the two parts that make up this distinction, namely, 'Islam' and the 'west'. Both categories have been put into use to establish a chain of similarities at the ideological level, in institutional arrangements and in cultural practices.

Theoretical stimulation for my analysis comes from the sociology of Gabriel Tarde, for whom the fundamental social operation is imitation.[2] Somewhere an innovation appears and dreams, 'like Alexander, of conquering the world'.[3] Similarities (naïve or reflected) are brought forth by fashion, customs, sympathy and obedience, or education. In terms of a discussion on similarity that asks how this term is related to the more prominent concept of 'difference', it is important to note that for Tarde – whose theoretical credo is, 'To exist is to differ' – there is no juxtaposition between them.[4] Tarde's sociology helps also to consider other prominent concepts involved in this debate from a different point of view. It is the repetition of different parts (a multitude of imitations) that creates a chain of similarity. But this is only operational and similarity is never total – it is always partial and fragile. To put it in other words: entities are already heterogeneous at their core. Therefore, similarities are always the result of operations of *making* similar.

Turkey as a 'Model'?

Turkey can be taken as an interesting exemplar for a discussion on similarity. Paradigms might have changed since the foundation of the Republic in 1923, but Turkey was again and again considered as a 'model', both in her self-understanding and in the perceptions of those outside.

Two historical paradigms can be discerned as crucial here. The first, when Turkey was mentioned as a 'model' within the framework of the theory of modernization. Turkey's official laicism supported at that time, without any serious objections, the general idea of the progress of history. The decline of religion counted as a necessary part of this universal development that started in Europe and spread to the whole world. Secularism is one of the essential components of the modernization theory. Modern Turkish elites were socialized within the culture of this universalism. They articulated the radical transformation that reached its peak with the Republic, with the help of the orient/occident distinction.

For them, this historical moment was no less than a civilizational shift. Their ambitious motto was 'to attain the level of contemporary civilization'. A series of reforms were undertaken: abolition of the Sultanate and Caliphate completed the legal transition, while other reforms directly affected the everyday life of people. One of the most important reforms concerning gender equality and the public visibility of women deserves to be highlighted as a radical intervention into the moral organization of Turkish society, hitherto mainly shaped by religion – especially since religion would return to the political agenda at the end of the twentieth century as a core issue of the 'politics of counter-imitation'.

The second historical paradigm could be discerned in the last quarter of the twentieth century. This period witnessed the replacement, or at least a substantial modification, of the classical modernization paradigm. Increasing attention to culture was fuelled by religious resurgence and Islamic movements (starting with the Iranian revolution), and this played a crucial part in the paradigmatic shift. Within the political and cultural parameters of this new situation, Turkey's laicism could no more serve as proof of societal progress. The secularization theory itself was about to undergo an overall revision.[5] Its universalism could not any more determine debates unquestioned; rather, its Christian genealogy was increasingly gaining mention.

The revision of the secularization theory corresponded to a new note with regard to descriptions of modernity. Shmuel N. Eisenstadt reconceptualized the modernity narration with his approach on 'multiple modernities'.[6] Instead of a directed and universal form of modernity (characterized by the decline of religion), this concept spoke of different modernities whereby religious traditions played a formative role for different institutional modes of modernity. The former distinction between modern and pre-modern had obviously become obsolete in a world thoroughly pervaded by modern institutions. The question now to be asked concerned the specific regional and cultural formations of this globally spread modern society. It is not surprising that Turkey's secular orientation and ideological universalism lost their paradigmatic relevance and also had practical effects, as we will see in the last sections of this essay.

Thus, after a short interim, Turkey has once again returned to the Islam/west agenda, but is now considered as a case which proves that Islam is *not* an obstacle to modernity but rather its motor; that Islam and democracy can go well together. At the end of this essay we will come back to this issue by embedding it in the concrete historical context, namely, the new strategic role of Turkey as a regional power. Here, only one aspect should be mentioned: the former chain of similarities is now about to be replaced by another. This new orientation seeks strategic touches more than it does cultural commonalities.[7]

Beneath the 'Official Narrative'

'Islam and the west' is an official narrative with a long history, a narrative that has nurtured the visions of Turkish Republicans as well as their critics. It is not my intention here to reject it as a 'wrong' conception and replace it with a 'true one'. But this narrative has never stated the whole story of modern Turkey. Beneath this narrative, which was actually challenged in the 1990s, other distinctions have been dominant in public space.

Turkey's political space in the second half of the twentieth century was captured by movements circulating globally. Student movements in the 1960s did not stop at the allegedly 'cultural borderlines' – a phrase used anachronistically in our time. The 1970s especially were characterized by the dominant global conflict paradigm of left/right. The civilization issue, formerly decisive for the construction of political space, was deactivated within this new conflict paradigm. Islam was articulated as the common denominator of the anti-communist, right-wing alliance (conservatives, fundamentalists and fascists). Left-wing groups, on the other hand, were trying to neutralize the political use of religion. Whilst opposing US hegemony with an international anti-imperialist rhetoric, the lifestyle of the left-wing groups was actually compatible with the prevailing global cultural trends. It is remarkable that this part of recent Turkish history cannot be narrated any more due to the dominant parameters of current culturalist discourse.

Related to this is another issue which helps to relativize the grand narrative of Islam/west in its local version. The history of military coups in Turkey has been told in the last decade in such a way that these coups (of 1960, 1971, 1980 and the so-called postmodern coup of 1997) are now narrated as a near-'eternal' struggle between 'secular Kemalist political and military elites' on the one hand, and the 'Muslim people' on the other. A closer look, however, reveals the particular nature of each one of these military interventions. The first, in 1960, was indeed partially motivated by fear for the very existence of the Republic due to the oppressive measures implemented by the premier Menderes in his third term in office, when he was about to lose power. But this was only a part of the intervention against an increasingly oppressive politics. The army put an end to a democratically elected government, and it is a paradox that the most democratic Constitution in Turkish history (1961) was passed under the army's reign.

In the second and third cases of military intervention, any relation to the grand narrative of 'Islam/west' was missing. The coup of 1980 was by far the most brutal, and far from attacking religion, the new regime deployed religion as a power medium. For instance, compulsory religious education was introduced in state schools and adopted in the Constitution. Turkish–Islamic synthesis – an anti-communist nationalist project of right-wing intellectuals – was appropriated as a sort of official ideology. Later generations of Islamists grew up in this climate of affirmation of religion with a political mission. It is not surprising that conservative religious leaders, such as the powerful Imam Fethullah Gülen, did not hesitate to eagerly support these military interventions.

Of all these anti-democratic interventions, only the attempted coup in 1997 could be considered as decisively directed against religious groups. And it was mainly after this intervention and the power struggles that followed (which Erdoğan successfully turned to his advantage) that a new idiom was born which spoke of 'white Turks' vs. 'common Muslims' or 'black Turks'.[8]

What I wish to make clear by recalling these particular stories is that the recent history of Turkey as it is now being told is quite to the contrary. The current hegemonic position of Erdoğan and his party, the AKP (Party for Justice and Development), has succeeded in establishing an alternative narrative based around the subject-type of the 'persecuted conservative democrat'. By devaluing the modernist subject of the Kemalist approach as 'forced' on society, this new subject claims to originate authentically from Turkish–Islamic culture. And it was and is, by far, accepted in the global arena as being able to reconcile Islam with modernity and democracy.

This conservative democrat constitutes another chain of similarities. On the level of everyday life, the cultural reforms of modernization are being questioned and partially modified, especially since 2011. Similarities here lean towards those with Islamic countries. We will later see that this intellectual and political project of the 'conservative democrat' – or 'moderate Islam', the term that is geopolitically used – corresponds to the current strategies of US hegemony. It is due to this proximity that secular opposition today subscribes gladly to conspiracy theories to explain the dramatic change in power relations. By totally underestimating the social and cultural dynamics, they see only a game of foreign powers. Thus it is literally traumatic for them if some western powers currently prefer the Islamist movement, which in turn definitely dislikes the everyday cultural trappings of those who are secular with their westernized lifestyle. But this fits exactly into the hegemonic perception, within the parameters of the culturalist paradigm described as coexistence of 'multiple modernities'.

Counter-similarities: Body as Battlefield

The above explanations have sketched a picture of Turkish political history that helped to modify the grand narrative, presenting different types of conflicts in different historical settings. The ideological construct of 'oppressed Muslims' or 'black Turks' has also to be questioned critically, because nearly throughout the period since 1950, cultural conservative parties with explicit reference to Islam (including Islamists) have reigned in Turkey. Affirmative concern for Islam is more than a rhetorical hint. For instance, the Office for Religious Affairs has been successively extended with regard to its resources and tasks, and the capacity of 'Preacher schools' has been expanded. However, this struggle – related to the ideological construct of 'oppressed Muslims' or 'black Turks' – has remained mainly within the ideological framework of the secular Republic. In all these historical cases, religion was certainly a part of an ideological struggle, without, however, being the main source of power and form of representation. An Islamic identity politics came up only in the 1980s; here too not just as a unique event but as part of a global transformation.

From the 1990s onwards, when new social classes (mainly new migrants in the cities of western Turkey and Anatolian entrepreneurs in more rural cities) joined the religious discourse, the situation changed radically. This process reached its peak when the AKP subsequently came to power. The same process of a religious movement in its own terms could simultaneously be observed in other Muslim countries as well as among migrants in Europe originating from Muslim countries. The point I want to make strongly regarding this religious discourse is that a new chain of similarities is about to be formed. It is a political endeavour to reverse the hegemonic narrative. It could be called 'counter-similarity', inspired by the term 'counter-imitation' in the sense of Tarde. For Nilüfer Göle, the practical presence of cultural similarity with the west established in everyday life feeds contrary ambitions to make the difference stronger. Islam in this new discourse embodies – as Göle puts it – the 'fear of similarity'.[9] This reaction reveals itself in different forms of visibility that underline being different. One important area for experiencing and demonstrating difference is gender relations. The female body, largely debated with reference to the veil, is of crucial importance for the new cultural regime. Here I do not intend to review the vast literature on the veil. I only wish to show, using the example of covering the body, how strongly the macro-politics of modernization and the Islamization of modernity in reverse are connected to the micro-politics of body.

Republicanism challenged orthodox religious morality in its very own domain, namely, the organization of relations between the sexes. By abolishing the gender separation that was the structural principle of social organization, public space was desexualized. The introduction of co-education, political rights for women and the aesthetic visibility of a woman's body radically revolutionized – culturally, politically and aesthetically – the social fabric of Turkish society. Feminists today point critically to the desexualized nature of the Republican female subject.[10] Different from the Islamist approach, however, this critical revision still shares the paradigmatic framework designed by Republicanism.

Any particular power seeks to establish a specific model of the 'body'.[11] The aesthetic representation of the body in public space represents a cultural break with the former organization of social life – the ambitious goal of the secular Republic and far more than a simple change in the political system. The Republican subjects have been modelled as a young man and woman standing hand in hand behind Atatürk, who disposes off the Republic to them as warrantors of the future. What is scandalous here from the perspective of Islamic morality is the public visibility of the female body. But the representation of the body is already offensive for this kind of sentiment.

This struggle between two imaginaries of the body is more than an abstract dissent. Visions of social order immediately affect the human body (in particular, the female body). The question is about the particular relation between the body and the moral–social order. The Republican subject is not imagined in the light of a sexual morality that covers the body, but as exactly the contrary, with characteristics such as being young and athletic, eyes directed to the horizon and head held up high. Here too a morality is being constructed, but it does not have sexual connotations. Göle pointed out the crucial role of women for the 'civilizational conversion' performed by Kemalist modernism:

> Photographs of women unveiled, women in athletic competitions, women pilots, women professionals and photographs of men and women in European fashion depicted the modernist representations of the 'prestigious life'. Civilized Republican individuals went to tea salons, mixed-gender dinners and balls. Yet, against Ottoman cosmopolitanism, Kemalist women were serious, modest and devoted – accommodating the presumed pre-Islamic Anatolian culture and thereby embodying the Turkish nationalist project.[12]

Radical change embodied within this Republican body-regime reveals itself fully only if we compare it with the religious mode of body regulation. For a set of religious ethics, as conceived in its dominant variant, the organization of social order is performed by certain mechanisms to shut off paths leading to 'sinful behaviour'. This is to banish all possibilities of 'seduction' from the social space beforehand. This is the socio-logic of separation of the sexes that is a specific technique of self. This technique regulates sentiments and hormones. It was again Göle who formulated it directly, without however having come back to this crucial point of relation between ethics and politics:

> Today, Islamist politics seeks to curb the free public space by limiting women's visibility through veiling, which is essentially an effort to con-

> trol women's sexuality by regulating the social encounter between the sexes. . . . Hence, in a Muslim context, the existence of a democratic public space depends on the social encounter between the sexes and on the eroticization of the public sphere. In short, while in Western societies it is the issue of abortion and freedom of reproduction that provokes collective passions, in the non-Western Islamic context the issue is the freedom of seduction.[13]

The new Islamist movement has introduced a new form of subjectivity. Whilst the Republican model was based upon mixing and revealing, the specificity of Islamic subjectivity consists in separating and covering. Here, a different chain of similarities (political, cultural and historical) is being formed.

Of course, both regulation mechanisms do not practically exist in pure forms. Effects also do not always point clearly to a certain direction. After all, the veil currently is not simply a medium of exclusion from the public sphere, but rather has been a vehicle for young educated women to gain access into the public sphere. How this process will evolve further depends on whether a historical arrangement will be made between opposing power groups.

The Bio-politics of the 'Conservative Democrat'

The new Islamic movement, and specifically the new female subjectivity, has been researched and discussed widely. Among the other merits of this academic research is its having brought to the fore the different dynamics inherent in the veil.[14] On the other hand, such research has not yet proved adequately sensitive for the institutional dimensions of the subject at hand. The reasons for this lack are indeed comprehensible. First of all, Islamist body-politics presented itself in public debate mainly as the claim of a protest movement against a partially authoritarian modernism. Students were the primary objects of research, and were observed as individual participants in a mass movement. The most powerful manufactures of the Islamic self, namely, brotherhoods and new types of communities, were not collected in the samples of scholars, although these groups were habitats for the Islamic way of life at the grassroots level. Attention to these faith-based communities would immediately have given an idea of the will to power which motivationally carries the current religious discourse.

It has been only a few years since an Islamic bio-politics performed by the state has taken visible forms within the state apparatus. In Turkey, this is especially true of the AKP government's recent years. Municipal authorities have already successfully paved the way for the success of such politics at the central level. It was only in the third term of his premiership (since 2011), when he gained control over all the power centres, that Erdoğan declared, offensively, the goal of training a religious generation. This programme counters, in a way, the Republican project of forming a 'contemporary Turkish youth'. Erdoğan cited a poem by a prominent Turkish poet and leading right-wing nationalist of a youth yet to come, who 'commits to his language, religion, honour, home, and hatred'.[15] Erdoğan's call can also be read as an attempt to build his own sustainable base – in competition especially with the 'Golden Generation' of the powerful 'Gülen movement'.[16] In any case, the programmatic goals of the Republic have undergone a dramatic change, something not seen since Atatürk.

The most powerful instruments for the formation of 'religious youth' are schools and the Office for Religious affairs. Both help to construct an alternative chain of similarities. The amount of religious education imparted in schools has been increased by the addition of three new optional subjects. The Office for Religious Affairs, on the other hand, has proclaimed its strategic plan to diffuse religion to the niches of society. Originally, the Office was supposed to keep religion under control, but this task has been turned subsequently into a proactive Islam policy. Currently, new restrictions on alcohol and dress codes format the behaviour of individuals in public spaces.

After the Arab Spring, religious bio-politics conducted by the state has become more explicit.

Arab Rebellion, Huntington's Vision, Turkey's New Role

When people marched on the streets throughout the Arab world, for a brief moment it appeared as though the sun of rebellion had chased away the long shadow of Huntington. It seemed that dividing the world along cultural differences had lost its glamour. For a long time the Arabs had been called a lethargic people who did not stand up for change. Islamic resurgence did not give way to new interpretations because Muslim activism had only brought more authoritarian, if not totalitarian, movements. The new situation of rebelling Arabs could not be ranked within the well-known pattern of secular modernization vs. Islamic resurgence.

At least in the beginning, the Arab movement attended to another chain of similarities. Its motto, 'honour, justice and freedom', expressed experiences that were also common to other revolutions, such as those of 1789, 1848 and 1989. We are not discussing here how far an Islamic background was an effective factor in this, beyond the Islamic groups. But soon Islamic parties became the victors of the rebellion, although they were not an active part of it at the beginning.

This is not the place to give a detailed sketch of the Arab rebellion and its implications, nor to discuss the dramatic turn of the Spring into a deadly Winter. The significance of the Arab rebellion for the subject under discussion in this essay is that in the new situation, Turkey's relevance as a regional power increased. Turkey as a country which, according to this perception, managed to reconcile democracy and Islam, could probably be an exemplar for new Arab regimes where parties came to power having originated from a similar Islamist political tradition as Erdoğan's AKP.

In 2005, within the then prevailing civilization paradigm, Erdoğan had already obtained recognition due to his efforts towards a Dialogue of Civilizations. Together with Zapatero, then premier of Spain, he initiated an 'Alliance of Civilizations' within the framework of the United Nations.[17] That fitted perfectly into a situation where western countries, alienated by terror, were looking for instances of power that could care for order. Since then a lot of significant changes have taken place in the world, especially in the Near East. The Alliance of Civilizations is facing a hard test. Forced by the dramatic changes in power structures in the region, not least caused by his own failed interventionist politics in Syria, Erdoğan is manoeuvring Turkey between Russia and the USA at huge risk. He is about to cut the long-reaching ties between Turkey and the western world. Meanwhile, the subject-type of 'conservative democrat', hailed for a short while as a new model for Muslim countries, has been widely demystified. The 'conservative democrat' is going to turn into a dictator with a strong tendency towards fascism that is religiously implemented.[18]

Conclusion

The notion of similarity is useful to deconstruct collectives which are surrounded by the myth of being a necessary expression of their authentic nature – whether this nature is determined by the idea of 'historical progress' or is the comeback of a culturalist essence. In both cases, here attached to two different paradigms, similarity helps to present the contingent dynamics behind these homogenized entities. In this sense the Republican subject, declared as an agent of progress and emancipation, was a hegemonic concept that was forced, not without resistance. The same goes for the 'conservative democrat'. It is not simply the revision of an 'injustice' by which the allegedly authentic representatives of a suppressed culture are now being given back their rights; rather, it has to do with power struggles revolving around different concepts of society and individuals. The concept of similarity makes us aware of the fragility of collectives. These emerge as a result of similarities of ideas and institutional arrangements.

From a normative point of view, similarity as a concept favours a certain type of humanism. This minimalist humanism is based upon the idea that human beings are not separated from each other by insurmountable cultural borders. Simultaneously, it does not ignore the existence and significance of such borders in social life. We are expected to pay attention to their fragility, heterogeneity and complexity.

Notes

1 This essay was originally written just before significant events such as the protests in Gezi Park in Istanbul (June 2013). The politics of the AKP (Adalet ve Kalkınma Partisi) government under Recep Tayyip Erdoğan had not yet evolved into an overall totalitarian offensive. The turn of the Turkish Republic into a sort of religious fascist regime was to be accomplished at the beginning of 2017.
2 Tarde, ed. (2009).
3 Tarde (2012): 60.
4 Ibid.: 40.
5 Casanova (1994).
6 Eisenstadt, ed. (2002).
7 Due to the recent rapid changes in the Near East, this 'new' orientation within the Euro-American alliance is now outdated. Erdoğan is seeking a new ally in Russia.
8 The failed coup attempt on 15 July 2016 was apparently undertaken by Gülen followers in the Turkish army. There are, however, many questions still open about the real background of this very curious intervention.
9 Göle (2002; 2008).
10 Kandiyoti (1997).
11 Turner (1996): 67.
12 Göle (2002): 78.
13 Ibid.
14 Two prominent studies for this thesis: for Turkey, Göle (1996) and for Germany, Nökel (2002).
15 For the original poem, see Kısakürek (2012).
16 The failed coup of June 2016 gave Erdoğan the chance to create a militant mass movement, hitherto absent. Fully aware of the situation, he perceived this event as a 'present of God'. He has taken the best advantage of this 'present' to hit out at not only the Gülen movement, but the entire opposition.
17 United Nations Alliance of Civilizations (UNAOC) (2005).
18 A systematic comparison between fascist movements from the 1920s and the current Islamic fundamentalists (the nomadic war machines of the Islamic State as well as the former legalist AKP under Erdoğan) is still lacking. Therefore there are a lot of indications that are waiting to be taken as relevant.

References

Casanova, José (1994), *Public religions in the modern world*, Chicago: Chicago University Press; available at http://www.loc.gov/catdir/description/uchi052/93037485.html.

Eisenstadt, Shmuel Noah, ed. (2002), *Multiple Modernities*, New Brunswick, NJ: Transaction Publishers.

Göle, Nilüfer (1996), *The Forbidden Modern: Civilization and Veiling*, Critical perspectives on women and gender, Ann Arbor: University of Michigan Press; available at http://www.loc.gov/catdir/description/umich051/96018179.html.

——— (2002), 'The Freedom of Seduction', *New Perspectives Quarterly*, 19, DOI: 10.1111/0893-7850.00466.

——— (2008), 'Anverwandlungen: Der Islam in Europa zwischen Kopftuchverbot und Extremismu', Politik bei Wagenbach 598, Berlin: Wagenbach; available at http://deposit.d-nb.de/cgi-bin/dokserv?id=3103401&prov=M&dok_var=1&dok_ext=htm.

Kandiyoti, Deniz (1997), 'Gendering the Modern: On Missing Dimensions in the Study of Turkish Modernity', in Sibel Bozdoğan, ed., *Rethinking Modernity and National Identity in Turkey*, Publications on the Near East 7, Seattle: University of Washington Press.

Kısakürek, Necip Fazıl (2012), *Necip Fazıl Kısakürek'in gençli e hitabesi*; available at http://t24.com.tr/haber/necip-fazil-kisakurekin-genclige-hitabesi,198090, zuletzt geprüft am 06.01.2017.

Nökel, Sigrid (2002), *Die Töchter der Gastarbeiter und der Islam: Zur Soziologie alltagsweltlicher Anerkennungspolitiken*, Eine Fallstudie 1, Aufl., Globaler lokaler Islam, Bielefeld: Transcript Verlag; available at verfügbar unter http://dx.doi.org/10.14361/9783839400449.

Tarde, Gabriel (2009), *The Laws of Imitation*, reprint, BiblioLife.

Tarde, Gabriel (2012), *Monadology and Sociology*, Melbourne: re.press.

Turner, Bryan S. (1996), *The Body and Society: Explorations in Social Theory* (Theory, culture and society), second edition, London: Sage; available at http://www.loc.gov/catdir/enhancements/fy0656/96068999-d.html.

United Nations Alliance of Civilizations (UNAOC) (2005), http://www.unaoc.org/, zuletzt geprüft am 02.01.2017.

The Similar Yields Divergence

Global notions of 'social welfare' and the making of 'informality' in twentieth-century India[1]

Ravi Ahuja

I

India's rudimentary and extremely uneven welfare regime rarely guarantees liveable social minimum standards and often targets specific demographic segments instead. Indian welfarism thus seems to epitomise the subcontinent's irreducible otherness: the universalist claims of capitalist 'modernity'. Will they not fail by necessity in a country where 'community' appears to consistently defy the imperatives of capitalist socialization? 'Western' welfare regimes may display similarity and family resemblances, but isn't India's welfare regime best understood as an instance of primordial 'difference' precluding any meaningful comparison? This essay contests such a view, but before we develop our argument we need to take account, if only in passing, of the hegemonic current of academic thought that we are up against.

Problems of similarity and difference, or of convergence and divergence, are at the heart of many contemporary academic debates on South Asia's cultural, social and political history. At the theoretical level, many influential academic interventions operate in a framework marked out by a mechanistic dualism that appears to have turned upon the head rather than demolished the dichotomies of old-style orientalism. Time-worn binaries of 'tradition' and 'progress', of 'occident' and 'orient', thus have been reproduced in inverted form rather than transcended. Such revalued binaries include, among others, those of indigenous versus post-enlightenment discourses, of eastern 'custom' versus western 'law', or of primordial identities versus the universalist claims of capitalist 'modernity'. While 'east' and 'west' are thus reinterpreted beyond recognition, Kipling's claim stands confirmed that the twain shall never meet. The 'dilemma' of irreducible cultural incommensurability has thus enjoyed remarkable longevity as a trope in both academic and non-academic writings during the long twentieth century.

If the procedure of revaluing established dichotomies of value has commanded intellectual influence even in recent decades, it is precisely because it bears an innovative, irreverent, radical appearance without challenging the prevailing, seductively clear-cut but intrinsically mechanistic intellectual habit of carving up the world into cognitively incommensurable and practically irreconcilable binaries. Such strategies of inverting dichotomies of value rather than breaking them up have been particularly attractive in the historical context of our own times, when intellectual sensibilities continue to be shaped by a crisis of progressivist notions of a unity of world history, and by the concomitant hegemony of inherently anti-historical identity politics – upending prevailing normative structures seemed to provide, for instance, the ultimate tactical device in many subaltern and not-so-subaltern struggles for recognition. Of late we are witness, once again, to the effortless appropriation of such strategies by dominant social groups for seemingly 'populist' and substantively authoritarian political projects.

This essay does not attempt another general critique of this familiar and institutionally well-embedded intellectual current. Rather, it explores one possible pathway that may permit to circumvent what I perceive to be a cognitive roadblock to serious engagement with the emergence of qualitatively new relations and practices from existing social structures. The essay thus explores the utility of the concept of 'similarity': it appears to be more open to phenomena of movement and change, not merely in the sense of mechanical motion, 'fluidity' or 'dance of the fragments', but also in that implying *differentiation* or the emergence of new qualities from fields-of-forces constituted by contending historical actors. In other words, our objective is to trace the *politics of similarity* that emerge from specific historical constellations.

The concept of 'similarity', however, can be appropriated to a wide range of competing or even irreconcilable theoretical perspectives. If we look for alternatives to mechanic-dualistic conceptualizations of difference, the turn to the concept of similarity *can* but does not necessarily provide such an alternative. Is the fragmented and identified to be seen as diametrically opposed to the connected and similar? If some propound, even celebrate, the 'dilemma' that foundational concepts of 'modernity' are both unavoidable and incommunicable across cultural identities, can we refute this assertion by simply staking the normative counter-claim that similarity enables a universal if selective communicability? In short, will identifications reflecting, producing and fortifying difference recede to the background compliantly as we choose to highlight similarity and its potentials?

My own approach would be to reconstruct concrete historical

movements between the conceptual 'poles' of difference and similarity. For both concepts are, in my understanding, crude though legitimate simplifications, attempts at making sense of the dazzling complexity and dynamism of the world. The modality of this simplification is that of turning a *moment* of a dynamic process into a distinct, seemingly stable phenomenon in order to render it more easily comprehensible. This is admittedly an unavoidable initial stage of cognition, which can be overcome, however, by then discovering dynamism, by tracing unfinished movement within and between such static, quasi-photographic depictions – in other words: by way of historicization. Blockages in social communication or the resilience of social institutions, in this perspective, may result not so much from unresolvable 'dilemmata' than from tensions not yet resolved and tendencies not yet realized. In other words, what appears to contemporary observers as a timeless 'dilemma' may in fact be a stalemate that could last for longer periods but is temporally limited and just as perishable as the historical actors locked into it.[2] Moreover, from a historical perspective, the connected often seems to suffer fragmentation only to endow the fragments with new compatibilities that permit to reconnect them in new ways.[3] Conversely, the identical can be observed to differentiate into the similar, which may in turn dissolve and diverge into new mutually exclusive identities – a process we will briefly discuss at the end of this essay.

Tensions are resolved, stalemates released and structures differentiated through the conflictual encounters of social actors, which is to say, by way of essentially *political* processes. This is why the above abstract hypotheses provide material for forging analytical tools that are applicable to very concrete historical phenomena. Here I attempt, accordingly, to sketch out how the politics of similarity and difference played out in one particular case, namely, the Indian offshoot of the global turn towards extended 'social welfare' policies in the middle decades of the twentieth century. More specifically, I try to show how in this case *the similar yielded divergence*, by reconstructing the trajectory of labour-centred notions of 'social policy' or 'welfarism' in India during a period that spanned the final stage of colonial rule, the Second World War and the formative phase of the postcolonial state. Since my research is still in its early stages, the provisional arguments will be roughly outlined in three steps, while a detailed discussion of historical material will be deferred to another occasion.

II

I approach this phenomenon of labour-centred Indian welfarism from its point of dissolution. In order to illustrate this dissolution of a historically specific regime of labour regulation and social policy, I will quickly look at two comparatively minor but telling contemporary incidents. The year 2012 turned out at least two remarkable cases of industrial violence in India: the first went almost unnoticed; the second, although strikingly similar in many ways, resulted in a wider public debate. On 27 January 2012, the first incident affected Regency Ceramics, a major Indian manufacturer and exporter of tiles that employed 1,200 workers in its factory at Yanam, a territory administered from Puducherry but located in the Andhra coastal region in southeastern India. Industrial conflict had been looming large in this factory for months, but when a respected local trade union leader succumbed to severe chest injuries in police custody after a violent police baton charge on picketing workers, sections of the workforce and local population set fire to parts of the factory premises while others attacked the General Manager in his house, who subsequently died in hospital from serious head injuries.[4]

The second incident occurred on 18 July 2012 in one of the factories of India's largest car manufacturer, Maruti, of which the Japanese Suzuki concern owns a majority of shares. The factory is located in Manesar on the periphery of the National Capital Region (NCR) Delhi, in the state of Haryana. At the time of the incident it employed 3,300 workers, of whom 1,500 were regularly employed while the rest consisted of so-called 'contract labour' with much lower wages and reduced entitlements. This factory had a history of industrial conflict, the last major strike having occurred in 2011. The events of 18 July seem to have been sparked off by a minor incident: a supervisor showered caste abuse on a worker who belonged to the Dalit community, which led to a scuffle. When trade unionists demanded disciplinary action against the supervisor, the Dalit worker was fired and local strongmen were allegedly mobilized by the company to restore order. Sections of the workforce were reported to have reacted to this violently by setting fire to parts of the factory and assaulting management personnel. After hours of violence, the factory's Human Resources Manager was found burned to death in one of the factory sheds.[5]

A comparison between the two incidents reveals both crucial differences and important commonalities. While the first generation Manesar workforce confronted a powerful multinational corporation, the Japanese motor vehicle giant Suzuki which enjoyed full support from a particularly 'business-friendly' Haryana state government, the incident at Regency Ceramics in Yanam was coloured by the regional and caste politics of the Puducherry and Andhra Pradesh polities in peculiar and complex ways. Despite these and other differences, both eruptions of violence resembled each other, in that each was preceded by a long period of largely peaceful and largely unsuccessful labour conflicts and actions. The experience at both Yanam and Manesar, shared by many workers across India, was that existing protective labour and industrial disputes legislation remained non-enforceable due to state administrations and courts actively blocking their implementation. In both cases, this experience crystallized around two key issues. First, the freedom of association, i.e. of creating and joining a trade union of one's own choice (as guaranteed by the Indian Trade Union Act of 1926), which the respective managements forestalled both in Yanam and Maruti by victimizing activists and through other time-honoured means of union-busting. Secondly, the conflicts focused on workers' demands to abolish the differences in legal status, wages and benefits within one factory between the 'regular' or directly employed workforce and the so-called 'contract workers', i.e. those employed through a contractor (the latter often receive less than half of their 'regular' colleagues' salaries even though they are often employed over years for the same tasks). The workers' demands were raised on the basis of the Contract Labour Act of 1970, which stipulates that contract workers employed in perennial non-seasonal work should receive a regular contract. In Yanam, an apparently moderate, politically unambitious local trade union leader who had risen from the ranks of the Regency Ceramics workers had used the full repertoire of a state-led labour welfare regime, including negotiations with local MLAs, to little effect, only to die under suspicious circumstances in police custody.[6] In Manesar, full utilization of the legal right to strike had failed to secure a recognition of the workers' preferred trade union: legal and peaceful means of self-organization were exposed to be totally ineffectual when the union proved to be unable even to protect an individual worker from caste abuse.

Public reactions to these incidents were fairly predictable at first. Outsiders and 'undesirable' or radical 'fringe elements' were held responsible for souring industrial relationships;[7] militant unions and irresponsible workers were accused of shaming the 'brand name India'.[8] The chairman of WIPRO, Azim Premji, demanded that 'government should act ruthlessly' against the social unrest that was building up within the country;[9] and Adi Godrej, President of the Confederation of Indian Industries (CII), likened industrial violence to terrorism that needed to be stamped out, not explained.[10] A *Times of India* lead story identified the workers' union as the culprit to be taken to task for allowing industrial conflict to deteriorate into 'barbaric violence', and the *Indian Express* demanded 'legal safeguards against unreasonable and militant trade union activity'.[11] Numerous tweets and letters to newspaper editors reflected a middle-class consensus condemning the 'irrational' and undisciplined behaviour of the workers using tropes of distinguished orientalist pedigree. In the meantime, the powers of the state came down heavily on the workforce, i.e. not only on those who had actually committed the crimes but potentially on all who had participated in previous labour protests. In Manesar, the Haryana police indiscriminately jailed hundreds of workers. The Maruti company likewise fired a third of its 1,500-strong regular workforce without it having been established by the courts that these workers had actually been involved in the riot of 18 July.[12] In Yanam, the politically engineered detentions of workers and local residents – whose participation in the assault on the manager or the factory premises was never proven – led to the suspension from service of two policemen several months later, while the circumstances of the trade unionist's death remained unexamined.[13] The complete workforce of Regency Ceramics continued to be locked out even a year after the incident.[14] This pattern of inflicting collective punishment upon workers in cases of industrial violence rather than relying on formal criminal proceedings against individual perpetrators would have been observable, too, under British rule in the 1920s and 1930s.

After the Manesar incident, however, less predictable reactions could also be heard in public. Congress politician Mani Shankar Aiyar saw the incident as an 'expression of an immense frustration' with growing inequalities among the lower middle classes and the proletariat in urban India,[15] and Labour Minister Mallikarjun Kharge even declared that 'Enforcement of labour laws has to be followed strictly. Failure in this area has led to the recent flaring up of incidents like Maruti Suzuki in Haryana, Regency Ceramics, Yanam, Puducherry and Neyveli Liginite Limited in Tamil Nadu.'[16]

More significantly, a new debate set in among business circles. A few months earlier B.P. Pant, the head of the labour bureau of the Federation of Indian Chambers of Commerce and Industry (FICCI), had still insisted that 'India's labour laws were mostly designed in the British times when conditions were quite different and workers needed protection'. This need having supposedly disappeared, he asked for major changes in laws 'relating to registration of trade unions, participation of non-employees in unions, restrictions on closing factories, contract labour and strikes'.[17] Demanding, in public, the repeal of presumably 'archaic' or 'obsolete' protective legislation while disregarding, in practice, the existing labour laws as courts and 'business-friendly' state governments looked the other way – an approach to industrial relations that had served employers well for decades.

The Manesar incident, according to high-ranking spokeswomen of the employer, 'sent shock waves in the corporate board rooms of companies both at home and abroad',[18] and gave 'the industry and other stakeholders an opportunity to look for long-term solutions that will help in preventing such outbreaks in future'.[19] In business circles, the argument gained some currency that disregarding the freedom of association, evading existing labour laws and establishing two-tiered workforces where contract labour received only a fraction of the compensation granted to those regularly employed had proved to be risky options – options that provoked desperate industrial violence and put India's investment climate at peril.[20] The president and senior vice-president of FICCI and the president of the Employers' Federation of India, in a joint press statement in September 2012, responded by cautiously and incrementally modifying their approach to labour issues with direct reference to the incident of industrial violence in Manesar: they insisted on the need for a 'simplification' of the labour law (a euphemism for the repeal of protective legislation) while conceding somewhat vaguely that contract labour was entitled to social security benefits and skill development measures. New emphasis was given, however, to involving 'all stakeholders' in this process, to generate a 'code of understanding and behaviour for all stakeholders' and 'recognize the importance of labour laws'.[21]

Placed in a longer historical perspective, such statements seem to suggest that a labour regime that has prevailed in India for roughly three decades is reaching its limits as older problems of labour control begin to resurface. While the labour legislation of the 1940s to the 1970s was not formally repealed in the period of 'liberalization' (the beginning of which is conventionally dated to 1991, though the process may have commenced earlier), it came to be regarded generally as an economically harmful labour market rigidity. Backed by this hegemonic consensus, labour laws came to be honoured in the breach not merely in individual cases but as a rule. Without anyone lighting the funeral pyre, the previous regime of labour regulation and labour-centred welfare was reduced to ashes.

A sense of frustration has been growing among workers. Forms of industrial violence that marked out the Indian worker as culturally 'different' in colonial accounts seem to have reappeared on the scene. Despite the (officially counted) number of industrial disputes in India having plunged to pre-Second World War standards in the 2000s in spite of a much larger industrial workforce, there is still a sense today in business circles of a growing and threatening 'labour unrest'.[22] Unpredictable, uncontrolled and dangerously violent forms of industrial conflict had been more common before the 1950s.[23] Sir Ardeshir Dalal, an influential director of the Tata concern, had uttered a complaint in 1948 that is echoed almost verbatim by today's business spokes persons: 'A tendency to use personal violence against the superior staff has grown of late.'[24] Such concerns, among other factors, had induced employers at that time to grudgingly assent to a labour-centric social policy and a finely tuned industrial relations policy. The FICCI statement may thus reflect a recognition that things have come full circle in a way that might affect the business climate and slow down foreign direct investment (FDI). However, a simple return to the 1940s brand of regulatory policies is clearly not on the cards, as demonstrated by the 'deregulatory' rhetoric and authoritarian practice of an Indian government elected to power in 2014 with unprecedented corporate support.

III

In order to understand both a regulatory regime that appears to have reached its point of exhaustion and the tendencies set free by this decline, we need to take a wider view and step back in both temporal and spatial terms. If the middle decades of the twentieth century saw the emergence of a specific labour-centred social policy in India that gave the postcolonial state a particularly prominent role in regulating the country's world of labour, this process was clearly rooted in a global context in the precise sense: events of truly global impact had resulted in connected or even similar social experiences, and cleared the way for policy changes that resembled each other to some extent in various parts of the world. The two world wars and the 'Great Depression' of 1929 were events that marked out what Eric Hobsbawm appropriately called the 'age of catastrophe'.[25] They precipitated a labour-centred social policy in various ways.

First, as Beverly Silver has clearly demonstrated, the post-war crises after 1918 and 1945, each led to a global upsurge of labour strikes induced by a drop in employment and living standards for the industrial working classes. Interestingly, this surge was even more pronounced *outside* the North Atlantic world region after the Second World War.[26] These findings are corroborated by Indian evidence that indicates a rise of strike movements and the emergence of numerous trade unions in a process that was triggered off by the deep social and political crisis in the aftermath of the 'Great War', and sustained by recurring cycles of industrial unrest throughout the inter-war period.[27] The extreme bitterness and intensity of these struggles, measurable in extraordinarily high 'losses of man-days' despite the smallness and local restrictedness of the industrial working class, has been emphasized by historians and other labour scholars ever since:[28] almost 32 million 'man-days' were 'lost' in industrial conflicts in 1928 that affected about half a million of workers, implying an average involvement in strikes (or lockouts) of 64 days per worker.

Historians have been less alert with regard to a major strike movement that began at the close of the Second World War and extended into the early years of independence (1946–1950). Officials registered a 'phenomenal increase' of industrial disputes[29] and V.V. Giri considered the post-war years, in hindsight, as a period of 'industrial strife unprecedented in the history of India'.[30] At its peak in 1946 and 1947, this strike movement was far less intensive than that of the late 1920s (with 16.5 million 'man-days lost' in 1947 or about half of the 1928 figure), but involved almost four times as many workers (about 2 million in 1946). Though 57 per cent of these disputes were still concentrated in the provinces of Bengal and Bombay, i.e. in established labour movement strongholds, the strike movement nevertheless was spread more widely than ever before across industrial sectors and geographical space, which was indicated by the unprecedented number of strikes and lockouts. Strike movements had been transformed from incidents of highly visible, intense but localized unrest into supralocal events that were increasingly considered to be of national import by the ruling forces.[31]

Apart from the specific social content of these movements, a wider implication was that 'labour' emerged in the course of the three decades preceding India's independence as a major as well as legitimate *political category* that was appropriated by a wide range of political forces far beyond the socialist and communist left, though the latter also experienced their most dynamic growth exactly in this period. Hence, most major nationalist politicians engaged to some degree with the labour question, even though Gandhi remained wary of the political uncontrollability of the urban worker. The burgeoning movement of former 'untouchables' or Dalits, including its towering leader B.R. Ambedkar, experimented in the 1920s and 1930s with constituting itself as a *labour* movement (for instance, in the form of an Independent Labour Party).[32] In the early decades of the postcolonial state, labour ministers like Jagjivan Ram, V.V. Giri and Gulzarilal Nanda were political heavyweights who could officiate as prime ministers or even rise to the office of the President of India.[33] Labour became a subject of extensive official and unofficial reports.[34] It became a field measured and, to some extent, administered by a growing labour bureaucracy. It became the focus of liberal reform activities by associations akin to today's NGOs; and the topic of doctoral dissertations and academic studies,[35] of socially engaged novels in various Indian languages,[36] and of popular non-fiction monographs by authors like the eminent and politically influential journalist B. Shiva Rao.[37] Labour, crucially, was increasingly understood as the section of India's population most urgently in need of 'welfare' measures, of a social policy that was distinct from older forms of philanthropic 'charity'.

The second crucial turning point was the Great Depression that set in, in 1929. In India, as elsewhere, it was soon perceived as a fundamental crisis of the policy precepts of classical political economy and of 'liberal capitalism' as such, that required a reassessment of the role of the state in general and of the need for planning in particular. The 1930s, and even more so the early 1940s, saw the publication of various plans for the 'development' of India's economy and society, as nationalists, big business and others prepared themselves for a political independence that became increasingly tangible.[38] 'Planning' was regularly extended to matters of social policy focusing on industrial labour in two ways. First, 'social security' or 'welfare' measures were propagated as means to increase the productivity of labour by way of reducing absenteeism, stabilizing the workforce, and improving its physical stamina and skill level through social insurance, medical, educational as well as housing schemes.[39] Second, 'social policy' was advocated as the most effective instrument for containing and regulating industrial conflict, and various international comparisons were drawn in this regard – the International Labour Organization (ILO), of which 'British India' was a founding member in 1919, commanded much attention, and so did the notion of 'tripartism' that was propagated by it.[40] Soviet planning also caught some interest, though the abolition of private property in means of production did not seem to be a desirable option to most currents of the political spectrum. Moreover, in the 1930s, despite the sincere anti-fascism of Nehru and other protagonists of the nationalist left, Mussolini's authoritarian policy of 'corporativism' as a 'third way' between liberal capitalism and communism met with sympathy and interest among India's intellectuals and political class as much as it did in other countries like the United States of America (USA), Brazil or Great Britain.[41]

The third set of events that figured as relevant turning points were the world wars themselves. As has been pointed out by Schivelbusch and others, 'bellicism' or the warfare state served in many ways as the launching pad for the welfare state.[42] This in turn led to state-planned and state-directed production and distribution during the wars, and the concomitant expansion of state apparatuses (demonstrated compellingly for India during the Second World War by Indivar Kamtekar[43]) generated means and incentives for a more extensive 'social policy'. This tendency was observable globally as early as during the 'Great War' but was far more pronounced during the next global military confrontation. Hence 'social policy' assumed new meanings and dimensions both in Britain and India during the Second World War. Proponents as well as adversaries of this development noticed the transformative potential of the wars even at the time. William Beveridge, whose 1942 report influenced the spate of British welfare reforms between 1944 and 1948, considered the war as 'a revolutionary moment in history', while the British Employers' Federation complained to government that '[w]e did not start this war with Germany in order to improve our social services'.[44] Similarly, B.R. Ambedkar, Labour Member of the Government of India between 1942 and 1945, pointed out in 1943 that it was doubtful whether labour welfare, and particularly the establishment of tripartism as a principle of industrial relations, 'would have taken concrete shape so quickly if the war had not made the maintenance of labour morale an urgent and immediate necessity'. And he added that tripartism was 'to last beyond the war. It is going to be an institution which will have a permanent place in the economic structure of the country.'[45] This prediction would remain correct for decades, providing further evidence for the observation that many of the regulatory devices forged during the Second World War, including key mechanisms of economic planning and social engineering, were seamlessly absorbed into the postcolonial state's administrative set-up.[46]

In sum, the *same* crucial and truly global events of the 'age of catastrophe' generated *similar* experiences and evoked *similar* political responses in regions of the world that were otherwise following very distinct historical trajectories of their own. The rise of 'labour' as a major and legitimate political category, the increasing acceptance of state planning as an economic necessity, and growing administrative efforts to provide 'social welfare' with a focus on industrial labour were the most crucial of these responses, and this global context of similarity clearly extended to India too. At the international level, the ILO's Declaration of Philadelphia of 1944 reflected these global trends by envisaging the 'progressive application' of universal labour standards to all parts of the world including the 'dependent' states or colonies, even though the need for differential temporal schedules of implementation was conceded. Historian Daniel Maul has considered this a 'quantum leap' in the ILO's policy as it abolished an earlier two-tier conception of the world of labour, where the colonial world largely remained outside the ambit of social policies.[47]

IV

If a set of globally momentous events generated similar experiences and responses, divergences were simultaneously prompted at three different levels at least: (i) the structural preconditions for the experience of these events; (ii) the differential impact of the events themselves; and (iii) the diverging choices made by political actors when confronted with the range of options delimited by these events. As for the structural preconditions, suffice it for our purposes to state that India's colonial regime and largely agrarian economy differed substantially, of course, from the more democratic polities as well as industrialized and competing economies of the North Atlantic region, which implied divergent political pressures, social needs and economic resources.

That key global events impacted differentially is particularly evident for the two world wars, in which India was heavily involved both as a recruiting ground for soldiers and non-combatant military labour (1.5 million in the First World War and 3 million in the Second World War), and as a dependent hinterland providing resources for the British war economy.[48] In India, as in several other non-European parts of the world, the world wars and the connected constriction of world trade provided a kind of protectionist umbrella that facilitated and prompted a quick growth and diversification of its industrial base. Employment in perennial factories rose by 62 per cent, from 1.46 million in 1939 to 2.37 million in 1945,[49] and the Second World War proved to be a highly profitable period for Indian capital, while real wages declined due to inflation.[50] Industrial tensions and the incidence of work stoppages were therefore high, even as the right to strike was severely restricted by the Defence of India Rules.[51] The surge of industrial conflict after the end of the war was thus not unexpected, and labour market policies were therefore placed close to the centre of government attention.

As Indivar Kamtekar has pointed out, the effects of the world wars on the different social groups and classes diverged far more radically in India than in European countries. Despite the large numbers, only certain social classes and regional sections of the population became the principal recruitment grounds for the army – battlefield experience was far less general than in European societies where conscription was introduced. Moreover, the socio-economic implications of the war were more unevenly distributed among the different social classes. The wars were enjoyed as a period of unmitigated prosperity both by urban business groups and propertied peasants, while inflation and disease badly hit the urban wage-earning classes, including the industrial workforce, and even more severely the agricultural labourers, sharecroppers and other poor country dwellers, as was brought out most dramatically by the severe Bengal famine of 1943. Hence, the Second World War bore not even the appearance of a 'people's war' in India – an appearance that was, in Europe, sufficiently rooted in reality to make more similar or comparable the social experiences of members of different social classes who came into social communication with each other in new ways as military conscripts, and were affected, though surely not to the same extent, by bombing raids and food scarcity.[52] In Britain, for instance, the 'people's war' prepared the ideological ground for, and rendered politically unpreventable, a more generalized and radical welfare reform that aimed at *national minimum standards*.

This was not the case in India, where the war was not accepted by large parts of the population as their war and where the experiences of war diverged more sharply. This was only partly made up for by the 'heroic illusion' of Indian independence, an event that seemed to hold the promise of social betterment for all Indians, including the poor, and did have limited but nevertheless substantial effects as borne out by growing life expectancy or broader access to education. However, while proclamations of welfarism became more ambitious and wide-ranging in India too, in the course and aftermath of the Second World War, they remained, as a rule and with significant exceptions, more targeted at specific social groups, particularly at the industrial workforce. They deferred to more prosperous times the establishment of social minimum standards available to the population as a whole, thus excluding the subcontinent's vast 'informal' economy and its workforce.

Before the First World War, labour legislation in India had been mainly confined to regulating and guaranteeing the labour contract and to factory laws, while issues of social reproduction remained strictly outside the ambit of legislation, with the partial exception of plantation labour. In the 1920s, the need to address problems of social reproduction – specifically, compensation in the event of work accidents (Act of 1923) and the urban housing question – came to be pressed on government more frequently, and became a matter of policy and of social planning. This tendency, initially rather precarious and fragile, was consolidated to some extent after 1937, when the Indian National Congress headed most provincial governments, until the beginning of the war. Labour policy was thus increasingly turned into a more expansive *social policy*, a process that was further accelerated during the Second World War, and resulted in extensive political debates and a spate of legislation in the late 1940s and 1950s. Roughly one decade after independence, the main pillars of India's labour and social policy were in place – pillars that would be undercut only from the 1980s.

An analysis of the related political debates in this period suggests, at first sight, that the agenda was rather *similar* to that in other parts of the globe – for instance, in Britain. Public housing and rent control, the establishment of health insurance and pension funds, the provision of free elementary education and of industrial training, even the issue of unemployment – in other words, Beveridge's famous five 'Evil Giants' (Want, Disease, Ignorance, Squalor and Idleness) – all figured and were identified as the targets of social policy. An eminent trade unionist, parliamentarian and social reformer, N.M. Joshi, demanded a Beveridge plan for India in 1944,[53] while the famous 'Bombay Plan', drafted by leading Indian industrialists in the same year, quoted Beveridge's assertion that if 'the giant Idleness can be destroyed, all other aims of reconstruction come within reach'.[54] B.P. Adarkar, the author of a 'Report on Health Insurance for Industrial Workers' (1944), was, perhaps somewhat disparagingly, dubbed a '*chhota* Beveridge' (little Beveridge) by the strongman of Indian conservatism, Vallabhbhai Patel;[55] Beveridge himself was indeed officially approached with the request to evaluate a 'Social Security Plan for India' a year later.[56] Social policy in the debates of the final years of colonial rule, as well as in early postcolonial India, seemed to aim at society as a whole and not merely at a small section of the wage-earning population.

Nor was the distinction between what was later called the organized or formal and the unorganized or informal sector very apparent at the level of the burgeoning social movements of the post-war years. Indian trade unions today appear as a historical phenomenon largely confined to large factories of the 'organized sector', but an analysis of labour movements in the 1930s and 1940s discloses a picture that was very different from the one that emerged in subsequent decades. In July 1946, the journal *Eastern Economist* noted, for instance, that 'Recent strikes have shown clearly that the strike is no longer a weapon of the factory operatives only', pointing out that even sweepers, clerks and agricultural labourers now turned to this device.[57] New research on labour movements of the 1930s and 1940s corroborates this impression by recovering trade union activities in artisanal workshops, domestic worksites and occupations that are today typically associated with the 'informal sector', but were at that time clearly not considered to be in a separate societal or labour market category.[58]

At this point it is important to emphasize that the 'informal sector' should not be understood as a pre-existing traditional or quasi-natural constituent of economies outside the North Atlantic region, but as a very recent phenomenon. The term itself came into use not before the early 1970s, when it was first applied to African economies. More importantly, as Prabhu Mohapatra has repeatedly pointed out, the 'informal sector' has been consistently defined as a residual category for all workers who are employed outside the 'organized sector' and consequently not covered by labour law; or, according to a more recent definition, for all workers not receiving any social benefits.[59] In this sense, the 'informal sector' was produced along with the 'formal sector' by way of legislation; 'formal' labour was to be regulated mainly by law, 'informal' labour was to be regulated mainly by extra-legal means such as informal debt or kinship bonds. This division came into being as soon as a more extensive social policy began to assume legal form in the 1920s. Reading the debates on social legislation, one notices that frequently, more energy was expended on defining the ambit of a law than on its actual content. Employers, but also state officials, were intent to keep the area of application of labour laws and other social legislation as narrow as possible. Social legislation thus became a structure of exclusion right from its inception. Debates in the 1930s and 1940s, and particularly nationalist contributions to it, stressed, however, that improving the living conditions of the comparatively small industrial working class (no more than 5 per cent of the total workforce) was only intended as a first step. More and more workers, so it was envisaged and propounded, would be absorbed by a growing 'organized' sector, and an economically prospering independent India would be able to extend social benefits to wider sections of the workforce including the vast number of agricultural labourers.[60]

Yet, despite all declarations of intent and projections of an inclusive nation, the actual historical dynamics, shaped by a field of forces dominated by the growing rural and urban middle classes and increasingly self-confident business interests, pointed in the opposite direction. Social policy measures reaching beyond the workforce of the 'organized sector', starved of funds and reluctantly implemented, often ran out of steam. Thus the Government of India's housing programme, recommended by the 'Industrial Truce Resolution' of 1947 and announced in 1948, to provide one million houses for industrial workers within one decade was replaced by a less ambitious one only two years later, which in turn bore even more modest results.[61] The Bombay Rent Control Act of 1947 had attempted to cap the costs of working-class housing but, in the absence of major public investment in housing for the poor, it exacerbated the scarcity of cheap accommodation and triggered instead the establishment of cooperative housing societies that mainly benefited the urban 'middle classes'.[62] The Employees' State Insurance Act of 1948, intended by its architect Adarkar and propagated by Labour Minister Jagjivan Ram as a first step towards a general social insurance scheme, has remained confined to the 'formal sector' until today.[63] The Minimum Wages Act of the same year has remained largely unenforceable in the informal economy, though it does serve even today as a reference in conflicts over the wages of contract workers especially in the public sector.[64] Diverging from the Keynes-inspired model of social policy, despite the many references to it in public debate, full employment and the guarantee of a national minimum standard never became the basis of Indian welfare policy.

Further, in the context of the mentioned upsurge of strike movements in 1946, the suppression of 'labour unrest' and the establishment of a 'machinery' of industrial disputes arbitration became a major political issue in the midst of the turmoil of the newly acquired independence and the catastrophic partition. The notion that strikes amounted to disloyalty to the nation for lowly, 'selfish' reasons became a regular feature of official and press criticism of labour movements in the late 1940s.[65] Legal instruments for curbing labour militancy had been forged already in early 1947 under the interim government. Taking its cue from the 1929 Indian Trades Disputes Act, from the 1938 Bombay Industrial Disputes Act and from the wartime Defence of India Rules, the industrial disputes legislation of 1947, initiated even before formal independence and basically in place until today, gave the state strong powers of compulsory arbitration, of limiting the right to strike and of recognizing 'representative trade unions'.[66]

There were a few voices critical of this policy even among the protagonists of the nationalist mainstream, namely V.V. Giri, who stated that the 'present tendency after India obtained independence is to secure settlement in industrial disputes more through methods of compulsory adjucation or through the intervention of government rather than through the machinery of collective bargaining and voluntary negotiations'.[67] Independent India's industrial relations regime was presented publicly as an offspring of the ILO's model of tripartism but resembled authoritarian forms of corporativism more closely in some ways, with its almost unilateralist emphasis on state regulation and by effectively linking a trade union's bargaining power to its equations with the governing party.

However, the attempt at 'pacifying' labour movements had limited success only – the period between 1966 and 1984 was in fact one of sustained industrial unrest,[68] and militant, extra-legal forms of worker protest were prominent especially in the old labour movement strongholds in Maharashtra and West Bengal.[69] This does not imply a comprehensive ineffectiveness of the postcolonial state-focused regime of industrial relations: one pervasive consequence appears to have been that trade union activities came to be confined more rigidly to the 'organized sector' than had been the case in the 1930 and 1940s.

As Jan Breman has rightly insisted for decades,[70] the boundaries between informal and formal employment were never as absolute as to constitute a dual economy. This is also visible in the fact that the so-called 'formal sector' – persistently encompassing about 5 to 6 per cent of the workforce – was internally hollowed out in terms of employment relations right from the beginning of its existence. While so-called *badli* or contract labour had been employed in capitalist enterprises through *sardars* (labour intermediaries) alongside 'regular' workers throughout the colonial period, the very process of formalizing labour relationships that is observable for the 1940s and 1950s preserved differences in the status of employees within the same industrial establishment and endowed it with legal sanction.[71] The Industrial Employment (Standing Orders) Act of 1946 thus allowed for a differentiation between various categories of workers ('permanent, temporary, apprentices, probationers or *badlis*') with differential wages and social security entitlements.[72] This has remained a key issue of political and legal conflict for decades, and so far a losing battle for Indian labour movements: according to 2009/10 figures, 58 per cent of the workforce of the 'organized sector' are estimated to be contract labourers[73] – a crass indication of the pace of what has been called an informalization process.

The social policy that emerged between the 1930s and 1950s, with its focus on formally employed industrial labour, had relevance for larger sections of the population in that it provided avenues for inter-generational upward mobility for otherwise underprivileged social groups such as Dalits, and in that it created new horizons of aspiration.[74] Yet it remained confined to a fraction of the workforce, and has increasingly been conceived of in public discourse since the 1980s as an unwarranted minority 'privilege' and a labour market rigidity-preventing investment. While various political parties in power have presided over the erosion of labour-centred social policy ever since in India, the present dispensation has vowed to break down formally even its remaining all-but-empty shell.[75] Aspirations produced in the past can no longer be fulfilled. The consequent frustrations may result in the foreseeable future, as the Yanam and Manesar accounts suggest, in a vicious cycle of desperate and dispersed industrial violence and its repression by an increasingly authoritarian state.

'Informality' today appears as the main marker of a fundamental *difference* not only of the Indian labour market but of its society as a whole. Social policy has not been relinquished altogether – arguably it saw a remarkable comeback during the first Manmohan Singh government (most prominently in the shape of the National Rural Employment Guarantee Scheme (NREGS), which even a chest-thumping BJP government finds difficult to do away with). But this more recent social policy has assumed a form that is based on an acceptance of informality, as it ceases to regulate existing employment relationships (as Prabhu Mohapatra has pointed out).[76]

Indian social policy is presently not recognized as a familiar structure by scholars of North Atlantic welfare regimes, while Indian informal labour is usually perceived as belonging to a realm of difference with clear colonial antecedents. At the same time, however, a contrary tendency is discernible that may indicate another strategic shift within the politics of difference and similarity. Informality is increasingly re-evaluated, no longer interpreted as a remnant of the past but as a mainstay of entrepreneurial initiative, economic growth and employment generation. In the aftermath of another great depression, informalization is even recommended as a precept for revitalizing stagnant economies in the North Atlantic rim – as a remedy whose universal application presumes similarity of the patients.[77] In this rendering, a realm of difference (the 'informal sector' of 'developing' economies) is conceived of as a resource for the production of similarity (the globalization of practices of informalization), the purpose of which, however, is not the elimination but rather the reconstitution of difference. The informalization of labour relations as a global process does not aim, after all, at evening out wage differentials the world over, but at gaining comparative cost advantages over competing economies.

The introductory section of this essay argued that similarity and difference should be understood as *moments* of the *same* process. Historical reconstruction, our case study confirms, reveals that the contradictory tendencies of familiarization/assimilation and differentiation/dissimilation imply and mirror each other. Together, they mark out a dynamic field in which contending social forces confront each other. In itself, then, the concept of 'similarity' does not allow for more humane forms of social life than that of 'difference'. For the story of informalization suggests that we have travelled a long way from similarity to divergence only to be confronted with a new, as yet partly utopian but not necessarily benign proposition of similarity once again.

Notes

[1] This article was written in 2012, revised for publication in 2014 and the discussion of contemporary developments in India in section II takes account of information available at that time. It is now published with some delay. An update discussing more recent developments under the Modi-led NDA government may be desirable, but would not change my argument substantially both in theoretical and empirical terms. In fact, despite its announcement of a radical labour reform and 'simplification' of labour laws, the Modi government appears to have largely continued the labour policy of its predecessors.

[2] For a similar exposition of this elementary problem of historical and political analysis, see Gramsci (2000): 190f.

[3] For a related theoretical idea, see Febvre (2003): 316.

[4] See detailed reports in *The Hindu* (especially 28 and 29 January 2012).

[5] The incident was covered widely in the Indian press. A particularly useful analysis was provided by the journalist G. Sampath: 'Can India Inc. Face the Truth about the Manesar Violence?', http://www.dnaindia.com/analysis/column_can-india-inc-face-the-truth-about-the-manesar-violence_1721167, accessed on 29 March 2013.

[6] For the prehistory of the Yanam incident, see 'Casual Workers Demand Regularization of Services', *The Hindu*, 24 January 2012. See also *Yanam Fights*

Back! A Trade Union Solidarity Committee Report 2012, available at http://sanhati.com/articles/5121/, accessed on 29 March 2013.

[7] See, for instance, for the Yanam case, the statements of south Indian employers' associations as reported in 'Industry for Yanam Probe', *The Times of India*, 3 February 2012.

[8] Suhel Seth in a roundtable discussion on NDTV, 'Manesar mayhem: Should there be a crackdown on militant trade unionism?', 20 July 2012, available at http://www.ndtv.com/video/player/left-right-centre/manesar-mayhem-should-there-be-a-crackdown-on-militant-trade-unionism/240028?v_also_see, accessed on 29 March 2013.

[9] *The Hindu Business Line*, 24 July 2012.

[10] 24 August 2012, available at http://www.youtube.com/watch?v=rHmqlYmSAos, accessed on 29 March 2013.

[11] *The Times of India*, 23 July 2012; *The Indian Express*, 23 July 2012.

[12] *The Hindu Business Line*, 16 August 2012 and 26 September 2012.

[13] See, for example, 'Yanam Fast Turning into Ghost Town', *The Hindu*, 8 March 2012; 'Policemen Suspended', *The Hindu*, 20 October 2012.

[14] *The Hindu*, 26 and 28 January 2013.

[15] Roundtable discussion on NDTV, 'Manesar mayhem: Should there be a crack-down on militant trade unionism?', 20 July 2012.

[16] *The Economic Times*, 28 September 2012.

[17] *The Times of India*, 6 November 2011.

[18] FICCI President R.V. Kanoria, according to FICCI Press Release, 21 July 2012, available at http://www.ficci.com/press-releases.asp#, accessed on 29 March 2013.

[19] FICCI Press Release, 11 September 2012, available at http://www.ficci.com/press-releases.asp#, accessed on 29 March 2013.

[20] See for instance: 'Beyond Maruti: India's Progress Calls for a New Set of Labour Laws and Labour Relations', editorial, *The Economic Times*, 23 July 2012; 'The Lessons of Manesar', *Business Standard*, 23 July 2012; 'Maruti Manesar Violence: Its Time India Inc Complies with the Contract Labour Act', *The Economic Times*, 26 August 2012; 'India Inc Grapples with Growing Labour Unrest', *Business Today*, 26 October 2012. For a relevant publication by the All India Organization of Employers, see 'Industrial Relations and Contract Labour in India', available at http://www.ficci.com/publication-page.asp?spid=20189, accessed on 2 April 2013.

[21] FICCI Press Release, 11 September 2012.

[22] See, for instance, All India Organization of Employers, 'Industrial Relations and Contract Labour in India': 1f; 'India Inc Grapples with Growing Labour Unrest', *Business Today*, 26 October 2012.

[23] Cf. Chandavarkar (1998): Ch. 5.

[24] '"No Conditions for Industrial Truce": Sir A. Dalal Denies Reported Socialist Charges', *The Times of India*, 3 March 1948.

[25] Hobsbawm (1994).

[26] Silver (2003).

[27] Statistics of industrial disputes in India are available from 1921 and can be culled, for the earlier decades, from *Indian Labour Gazette* and, for later decades, from *Indian Labour Journal* and the yearbook *Indian Labour Statistics*. My extensive essay (in preparation), 'Produce or Perish: The crisis of the late 1940s and the place of labour in postcolonial India', will provide a more systematic analysis of long-term trends in industrial disputes.

[28] See, for instance, Bhattacharya (1988); Chandavarkar (1998); Das Gupta (1994).

For a fresh and meticulous analysis of the 1929 jute mill strike in Calcutta, see Sailer (2013).

[29] *Indian Labour Gazette*, 5/11 (1948): 763.

[30] Giri (1965): 85.

[31] My extensive essay, 'Produce or Perish' (in preparation, see note 27 above), will provide a detailed analysis of this strike movement and a more systematic analysis of long-term trends in industrial disputes.

[32] Cf. Bhattacharya (1988).

[33] For an interesting though uncritical account of a career trajectory of this kind, see Kalhan (1997).

[34] With regard to official reports, the following publication, supplemented by numerous detailed evidence volumes, was a milestone that set standards for subsequent surveys: see Government of India (1931). A number of specific reports followed in the 1940s. As for unofficial reports, intellectuals involved with the Servants of India Society were notable in particular for making effective use of this form of creating a 'counter-public'. For an example, see Social Service League (1928).

[35] See for instance, Burnett-Hurst (1925) and Das (1941).

[36] See, for example, Yashpal's *Dada Kamred*, first published in 1941.

[37] Shiva Rao (1939).

[38] Cf. Zachariah (2005), especially chapter 5; Zachariah (2010): 547–78.

[39] This argument was brought forward by the Indian Industrial Commission as early as in 1918, but was taken up time and again afterwards, for instance, by the Royal Commission of Labour in India (which published its report in 1931), by the National Planning Committee (1938) under Nehru's chairmanship, and by the 'Bombay Plan' (1944) of India's leading industrialists.

[40] A thorough historical analysis of this labour-centred social policy discourse is not yet available and is one objective of my ongoing research. A systematic summary of the key notions of this discourse as they had emerged by the 1950s can be found, however, in Giri (1965).

[41] For developmental discourses in late colonial India, see Zachariah (2005) and Framke (2013). For the reception of fascist economic policy in the Anglo-Saxon political discourses of the 1930s, see Schivelbusch (2005), especially chapter 2.

[42] Schivelbusch (2005): 50 and 42–51.

[43] Indivar Kamtekar's pathbreaking research, embodied in his 1988 Cambridge thesis and a brilliant conference paper, 'Freedoms Lost and Gained: A Perspective on the Impact of the Second World War on India' (2007), are unfortunately not yet available in published form.

[44] Quoted from Glennerster (1995): 22f.

[45] Ambedkar ([1942] 1943): 4f.

[46] Cf. Rothermund (1983): 81–94; Kamtekar (2002).

[47] Maul (2007): 391f and 108–21.

[48] A useful overview of the social consequences of the world wars is provided in Bhattacharya (2001): 182–96.

[49] *Indian Labour Gazette*, 1/8 (1944): 191; 2/3 (1944): 90–94; 4/4 (1946): 123.

[50] Kamtekar (2002): 187–221.

[51] See note 24 above.

[52] I owe this argument to Kamtekar (2002).

[53] Cut Motion in the Central Assembly on 16 March 1944, quoted in *Monthly Report of the Delhi Branch Office of the International Labour Organization for March 1944*: 2.

[54] Thakurdas *et al.* (1945): 71.

[55] Joshi ([1978] 2011): 221.

[56] *Monthly Report of the Delhi Branch Office of the International Labour Organization for September 1945*: 16; *Monthly Report of the Delhi Branch Office of the International Labour Organization for October 1945*: 30f.

[57] *Eastern Economist*, 26 July 1946, excerpted in *Monthly Report of the Delhi Branch Office of the International Labour Organization for July 1946*: 65.

[58] This is pointed out, for instance, in the contributions by Ahmad Azhar, Shahana Bhattacharya and Tanika Sarkar in Ahuja, ed. (2013).

[59] Cf. Mohapatra (2005; 2012).

[60] This is a running theme, for instance, in V.V. Giri's influential work (1965). A systematic analysis of these debates will be presented elsewhere.

[61] 'Million Houses for Workers', *The Times of India*, 2 April 1948; 'Housing Plan for Workers', *The Times of India*, 4 November 1949; 'Plans for Industrial Housing to Receive High Priority', *The Times of India*, 1 August 1950; 'Industrial Housing in India', *The Times of India*, 30 August 1950. For a brief summary of this largely abortive scheme, see Giri (1965): 310–14.

[62] Cf. Collective Research Initiatives Trust (2007): 5, 51, 76.

[63] '"New Chapter in the History of Labour Legislation": State Insurance Bill Passed in Dominion Parliament', *The Times of India*, 3 April 1948; see also *Monthly Report of the Delhi Branch Office of the International Labour Organization for April 1948*: 90–93.

[64] For a brief account on the content of this Act and the parliamentary debate about it, see Monthly Report of the Delhi Branch Office of the International Labour Organization for February 1948: 22–26.

[65] See, for instance, Jawaharlal Nehru's All India Radio talk on 18 January 1948, reproduced in *Indian Labour Gazette,* 5/8 (1948): 553. My extensive essay (in preparation), 'Produce or Perish', will provide a more systematic analysis of long-term trends in industrial disputes.

[66] For a useful summary of trade union and industrial disputes legislation up to the 1950s, see International Labour Office (1957): 71–86.

[67] Giri (1965): 504.

[68] The number of industrial disputes ranged consistently between 2,000 and over 3,000 per year during that period, experiencing a limited dip only during the Emergency years of 1975 and 1976 – a level never reached again, before or after.

[69] The fabric of this often violent tradition of labour militancy is brought out for the case of Bombay clearly in Adarkar and Menon (2004).

[70] See especially Breman's (1976) classic series of articles.

[71] For an excellent discussion of the changing fortunes of the labour intermediary in the textile industry, see Chandavarkar (1998).

[72] *Monthly Report of the Delhi Branch Office of the International Labour Organization for April 1946*: 5.

[73] Cf. Mohapatra (2012).

[74] Fascinating oral history accounts illuminating this potential for appropriating industrial labour by Dalit workers are, for instance, contained in Janaki Nair's documentary film, *After the Gold* (1997).

[75] See, for instance, See, for example, 'Govt bid to make labour laws investor-friendly', *The Times of India*, 12 June 2014.

[76] Cf. Mohapatra (2012).

[77] For a critical discussion, see Breman and Linden (2014).

References

Adarkar, Neera and Meena Menon (2004), *One Hundred Years, One Hundred Voices: The Millworkers of Girangaon*, Kolkata: Seagull.

Ahuja, Ravi, ed. (2013), *Working Lives and Worker Militancy: The Politics of Labour in Colonial India*, New Delhi: Tulika Books.

Ambedkar, B.R. ([1942] 1943), Presidential Address to the 2nd Plenary Session of the Tripartite Labour Conference, New Delhi (6 and 7 September 1942), quoted in *Monthly Report of the Delhi Branch Office of the International Labour Organization for August 1943*, http://www.uni-goettingen.de/en/324221.html.

Bhattacharya, Sabyasachi (1988), 'Swaraj and the Kamgar: The Indian National Congress and the Bombay Working Class, 1919–1931', in R. Sisson and S. Wolpert, eds, *Congress and Indian Nationalism: The Pre-Independence Phase*, Berkeley/Los Angeles: University of California Press.

Bhattacharya, Sanjoy (2001), 'Colonial India: Conflict, Shortage and Discontent', in P. Liddle *et al.*, eds, *The Great World War, 1914–45*, Vol. 2: *The People's Experiences*, London: HarperCollins.

Breman, Jan (1976), 'A Dualistic Labour System? A Critique of the "Informal Sector" Concept', *Economic and Political Weekly*, 11 (48–50).

Breman, Jan and Marcel van der Linden (2014), 'Informalizing the Economy: the Return of the Social Question at a Global Level', *Development and Change*, 45(5): 920–40.

Burnett-Hurst, A.R. (1925), *Labour and Housing in Bombay: A Study in the Economic Conditions of the Wage-earning Classes in Bombay*, London: P.S. King & Son.

Collective Research Initiatives Trust (2007), *Housing Typologies in Mumbai*, Mumbai: CRIT.

Chandavarkar, Rajnarayan (1998), *Imperial Power and Popular Politics: Class, Resistance and the State in India, c. 1850–1950*, Cambridge: Cambridge University Press.

Das, Rajani Kanta (1941), *History of Indian Labour Legislation*, Calcutta: University of Calcutta,.

Das Gupta, Ranajit (1994), *Labour and Working Class in Eastern India: Studies in Colonial History*, Kolkata: K.P. Bagchi.

Febvre, Lucien (2003), *A Geographical Introduction to History: An Introduction to Human Geography*, London: Kegan Paul.

Framke, Maria (2013), *Delhi - Rom - Berlin: Die indische Wahrnehmung von Faschismus und Nationalsozialismus 1922–1939*, Darmstadt: Wissenschaftliche Buchgesellschaft,.

Giri, V.V. (1965), *Labour Problems in Indian Industry,* Mumbai: Asia Publishing House; reprint of second enlarged 1959 edition.

Glennerster, Howard (1995), *British Social Policy since 1945*, Oxford: Blackwell.

Government of India (1931), *Report of the Royal Commission on Labour in India*, Calcutta: Central Publication Branch, Government of India.

Gramsci, Antonio (2000), in D. Forgacs, ed., *The Antonio Gramsci Reader: Selected Writings 1916-1935*, New York: New York University Press.

Hobsbawm, Eric (1994), *The Age of Extremes: The Short Twentieth Century 1914–1991*, London: Michael Joseph.

International Labour Office (1957), *Labour Legislation in India*, New Delhi: ILO.

Joshi, S.P. ([1978] 2011), 'Social Security Legislation in India', in K.D. Gangrade, *Social Legislation in India*, Vol. 2, Delhi: Concept Publishers.

Kalhan, Promilla, (1997), *Gulzarilal Nanda: A Life in the Service of the People,* Mumbai: Allied Publishers.

Kamtekar, Indivar (2002), 'A Different War Dance: State and Class in India 1939–1945', *Past and Present Society*, 176 (1): 187–221.

——— (2007), 'Freedoms Lost and Gained: A Perspective on the Impact of the Second World War on India', unpublished conference paper.

Maul, Daniel (2007), *Menschenrechte, Sozialpolitik und Dekolonisation: Die Internationale Arbeitsorganisation (IAO) 1940–1970*, Essen: Klartext.

Mohapatra, Prabhu (2005), 'Regulated Informality: Legal Construction of Labour Relations in Colonial India 1814–1926', in S. Bhattacharya and J. Lucassen, eds, *Workers in Informal Sector: Studies in Labour History 1800–2000*, East London: Macmillan.

——— (2012), 'Shifting Boundaries of Freedom: Genealogies of Informalization and Informal Labour in India', unpublished paper presented at the workshop 'Boundaries of "Free Labour": XIX and XX Century Perspectives', IGK Work and Human Lifecycle in Global History, Berlin, 21–22 June.

Rothermund, Dietmar (1983), 'Die Anfänge der indischen Wirtschaftsplanung im Zweiten Weltkrieg', in P. Hablützel *et al.*, eds, *Dritte Welt: historische Prägung und politische Herausforderung: Festschrift zum 60. Geburtstag von Rudolf von Albertini,* Wiesbaden: Steiner.

Sailer, Anna (2013), '"Various Paths are Today Opened": The Bengal Jute Mill Strike of 1929 as a Historical Event', in R. Ahuja, ed., *Working Lives and Worker Militancy: The Politics of Labour in Colonial India*, Delhi: Tulika Books.

Shiva Rao, B. (1939), *The Industrial Worker in India*, London: George Allen and Unwin.

Schivelbusch, Wolfgang (2005), *Entfernte Verwandschaften: Faschismus, Nationalsozialismus, New Deal 1933-1939,* Munich/Vienna: Hanser.

Silver, Beverly (2003), *Forces of Labor: Workers' Movements and Globalization since 1870,* Cambridge: Cambridge University Press.

Social Service League (1928), *Seamen in India: Report of an Enquiry into the Conditions of Their Life and Work*, Bombay: N.M. Joshi, Servants of India Society.

Thakurdas, Purshotamdas, J.R.D. Tata, G.D. Birla *et al.* (1945), *Memorandum Outlining a Plan of Economic Development for India,* Parts I and II, Harmondsworth: Penguin.

Yashpal ([1941] 2010), *Dada Kamred*, Delhi: Lokbharti Prakashan-Rajkamal Prakashan.

Zachariah, Benjamin (2005), *Developing India: An Intellectual and Social History*, Delhi: Oxford University Press.

——— (2010), 'The Creativity of Destruction: Wartime Imaginings of Development and Social Policy, *c.* 1942–1946', in H. Liebau, K. Bromber *et al.*, eds, *The World in World Wars: Experiences, Perceptions and Perspectives from Africa and Asia,* Leiden/Boston: Brill: 547–78.

Select Bibliography

Ahuja, Ravi (2013), 'Das Ähnliche speist den Unterschied: Die globale Wohlfahrtsdebatte und die Erzeugung "informeller Arbeit" im Indien des 20. Jahrhunderts', in H-J. Burchardt, S. Peters and N. Weinmann, eds, *Arbeitspolitiken in globaler Perspektive: Informalität und Prekarisierung als Herausforderung*, Frankfurt am Main, New York: 123–44.

Allolio-Näcke, Lars, Britta Kalscheuer and Arne Manzeschke, eds (2005), *Differenzen anders denken: Bausteine zu einer Kulturtheorie der Transdifferenz*, Frankfurt am Main, New York.

Ambedkar, B.R. (2014), *Dr Babasaheb Ambedkar: The Annihilation of Caste*, with commentary and edited by S. Anand, introduced by Arundhati Roy's essay, 'The Doctor and the Saint', New Delhi: Navayana.

Amin, Samir (1998), *Spectres of Capitalism: A Critique of Current Intellectual Fashions*, New York: Monthly Review Press.

Aquinas, Thomas von ([2009] 2013), *Summa contra gentiles libri quatuor*, Darmstadt: Lambert Schneider.

Arber, Agnes Robertson (1946), 'Analogy in the History of Science', in M.F. Ashley Montagu, ed., *Studies and Essays in the History of Science and Learning offered in Homage to George Sarton on the Occasion of his Sixtieth Birthday, 31 August 1944*, New York: 219–33.

Arduini, Stefano and Robert Jr Hodgson, eds (2001), *Similarity and Difference in Translation: Proceedings of the International Conference on Similarity and Translation*, New York City: Bible House.

Arendt, Hannah (1955), *Elemente und Ursprünge totaler Herrschaft*, Frankfurt am Main: Europäische Verlagsanstalt.

Aristotle (1984), *Poetik*, German translation and edited by Manfred Fuhrmann, Stuttgart.

——— (1995), *Nikomachische Ethik: Philosophische Schriften*, Vol. 3, Darmstadt.

——— (2002), *Rhetorik*, translated by Christof Rapp, in *Werke*, Vol. 4, German translation by Hellmut Flashar, Berlin.

——— (2003), *Metaphysik*, translated by Thomas A. Szlezák, Berlin.

——— (2007), 'Über die Teile der Lebewesen' (translated by Wolfgang Kullmann), in *Werke in deutscher Übersetzung*, edited by Hellmut Flashar, Vol. 17: Zoologische Schriften II, 1, Berlin.

Arroyo, Gustavo (2006), *Wittgensteins analogisches Denken*, Berlin.

Assmann, Aleida (2006), 'Kulturen der Identität, Kulturen der Verwandlung', in

Aleida Assmann and Jan Assmann, eds, *Verwandlungen* (Archäologie der literarischen Kommunikation, Vol. IX), München: 25–45.

——— (2011), 'Zeitkonzepte im Wandel – von der Modernisierungstheorie zur Gedächt-nistheorie', in Mario Grizelj and Oliver Jahraus, eds, *Theorie Theorie: Wider die Theorie-müdigkeit in den Geisteswissenschaften*, München: 273–88.

——— (2012), 'Authentizität – Signatur des abendländischen Sonderwegs?', in Michael Rössner and Heidemarie Uhl, eds, *Renaissance der Authentizität: Über die neue Sehnsucht nach dem Ursprünglichen*, Bielefeld: 27–42.

Assmann, Jan (2002), 'Der Fortschritt in der Geistigkeit: Sigmund Freuds Konstruktion des Judentums', *Psyche: Zeitschrift für Psychoanalyse und ihre Anwendungen*, 56: 154–71.

——— (2011), 'Transkulturelle Theorien – am Beispiel von Jaspers' Achsenzeit-Konzept', in Mario Grizelj and Oliver Jahraus, eds, *Theorie Theorie: Wider die Theorie-müdigkeit in den Geisteswissenschaften*, München: 261–71.

Auerbach, Erich (1946), *Mimesis: Dargestellte Wirklichkeit in der abendländischen Literatur*, Bern.

Bachmann, Thomas (1998), *Die Ähnlichkeit von Ereignisbegriffen bei der Analogie-bildung*, München.

Bachmann-Medick, Doris (2007), *Cultural Turns: Neuorientierungen in den Kulturwissenschaften*, Reinbek bei Hamburg: Rowohlt Verlag.

Bader, Lena, Martin Gaier and Falk Wolf, eds (2010), *Vergleichendes Sehen*, München.

Bal, Mieke (2002), *Travelling Concepts in the Humanities: A Rough Guide*, Toronto.

Bambrough, Renford (1966), 'Universals and Family Resemblances', in George Pitcher, ed., *Wittgenstein: The Philosophical Investigations – A Collection of Critical Essays*, Garden City, New York: 186–204.

Barthes, Roland (1966), 'Die strukturalistische Tätigeit', *Kursbuch*, 5: 190–96.

Bellah, Robert N. and Hans Joas, eds (2012), *The Axial Age and Its Consequences*, Cambridge, MA: Belknap Press.

Benjamin, Walter ([1918] 1977, 1991), 'Über das Programm der kommenden Philosophie', in *Aufsätze, Essays, Vorträge: Gesammelte Schriften Vol. II.I*, edited by Rolf Tiedemann and Hermann Schweppenhäuser, Frankfurt am Main: Suhrkamp: 157–71.

——— ([1921] 1991), 'Die Aufgabe des Übersetzers', in *Gesammelte Schriften, Vol. IV (1): Kleine Prosa, Baudelaire-Übertragungen*, edited by Tillman Rexroth, Frankfurt am Main: 9–21.

——— ([1926] 1977, 1991), 'Traumkitsch', in *Aufsätze, Essays, Vorträge: Gesammelte Schriften Vol. II.I*, edited by Rolf Tiedemann and Hermann Schweppenhäuser, Frankfurt am Main: Suhrkamp: 620–22.

——— ([1933] 1977, 1980), 'Über das mimetische Vermögen', in *Aufsätze, Essays, Vorträge: Gesammelte Schriften Vol. II.I*, edited by Rolf Tiedemann and Hermann Schweppenhäuser, Frankfurt am Main: Suhrkamp: 210–13.

——— (1977), 'Die Lehre vom Ähnlichen', in *Gesammelte Schriften, Vol. II, 1*, edited by Rolf Tiedemann und Hermann Schweppenhäuser, Frankfurt am Main: 204–13.

——— (1980), 'Analogie und Verwandtschaft', in *Aufsätze, Essays, Vorträge: Gesammelte Schriften Vol. II.I*, edited by Rolf Tiedemann and Hermann Schweppenhäuser, Frankfurt am Main: Suhrkamp: 43–45.

Berndt, Frauke and Stephan Kammer, eds (2009), *Amphibolie–Ambiguität–Ambivalenz*, Würzburg: Königshausen and Neumann.

Bhatti, Anil (2003), 'Kulturelle Vielfalt und Homogenisierung', in Johannes Feichtinger, Ursula Prutsch and Moritz Csáky, eds, *Habsburg Postcolonial: Machtstrukturen und kollektives Gedächtnis (Gedächtnis – Erinnerung – Identität 2)*, Innsbruck: 55–68.

——— (2007), '"... zwischen zwei Welten schwebend...": Zu Goethes Fremdheitsexperiment im Westöstlichen Divan', in Hans-Jörg Knobloch and Helmut Koopmann, eds, *Goethe: Neue Ansichten*, Würzburg: 103–21.

——— (2009), 'Der Orient als Experimentierfeld: Goethes "Divan" und der Aneignungs-prozess kolonialen Wissens', *Goethe-Jahrbuch*, 126: 115–28.

——— (2010), 'Heterogenität, Homogenität, Ähnlichkeit', in Andrea Allerkamp and Gérard Raulet, eds, *Kulturwissenschaften in Europa: Eine grenzüberschreitende Disziplin?* Münster: 250–66.

——— (2012), 'Die Abwendung von der Authentizität: Postkoloniale Sichtweisen in neueren Romanen', in Heidemarie Uhl and Michael Rössner, eds, *Renaissance der Authentizität: Über die neue Sehnsucht nach dem Ursprünglichen*, Bielefeld: 43–62.

——— (2014), 'Ähnlichkeit', in Özkan Ezli and Gisela Staupe, eds, *Das neue Deutschland: Von Migration und Vielfalt*, Konstanz: 161–63.

Bhatti, Anil and Dorothee Kimmich, eds (2015), *Ähnlichkeit: Ein kulturtheoretisches Paradigma*, Konstanz: Konstanz University Press.

Bhatti, Anil, Dorothee Kimmich, Albrecht Koschorke, Rudolf Schlögl and Jürgen Wertheimer (2011), 'Ähnlichkeit: Ein kulturtheoretisches Paradigma', *Internationales Archiv für Sozialgeschichte der deutschen Literatur*, 36 (1): 261–75.

Bhatti, Ketan (2012), 'Verkörpernde Nachahmung', in Holger Schulze, ed., *Gespür – Empfindung – Kleine Wahrnehmungen: Klanganthropologische Studien*, Bielefeld: 133–43.

Biela, Adam (1991), *Analogy in Science: From a Psychological Perspective*, Frankfurt am Main.

Blumenberg, Hans (1987), *Die Sorge geht über den Fluß*, Frankfurt am Main.

Bolzano, Bernard (2007), 'On the Relations between the Two Peoples of Bohemia: Read on the seventh Sunday after Pentecost, 1816 [July 21]', in *Selected Writings on Ethics and Politics*, translated by Paul Rusnock and Rolf George, Amsterdam: Rodopi: 96–122.

Bourdieu, Pierre and Loïc Wacquant (1996), *Reflexive Anthropologie*, Frankfurt am Main: Suhrkamp.

Braun, Willi and Russell McCutcheon, eds (2000), *Guide to the Study of Religion*, London, New York: Cassell.

——— (2008), *Introducing Religion: Essays in Honour of Jonathan Z. Smith*, London: Equinox.

Breidbach, Olaf (1987), *Der Analogieschluss in den Naturwissenschaften oder die Fiktion des Realen: Bemerkungen zur Mystik des Induktiven*, Frankfurt am Main.

Brockmeier, Peter (2003), 'Der Vergleich in der Literaturwissenschaft', in Hartmut Kaelble and Jürgen Schriewer, eds, *Vergleich und Transfer: Komparatistik in den Sozial-, Geschichts- und Kulturwissenschaften*, Frankfurt am Main: 351–66.

Bronfen, Elisabeth (2009), *Crossmappings: Essays zur visuellen Kultur*, Zürich.

Bronfen, Elisabeth and Benjamin Marius (1997), 'Hybride Kulturen: Einleitung zur anglo-amerikanischen Multikulturalismusdebatte', in Elisabeth Bronfen *et al.*, eds, *Hybride Kulturen: Beiträge zur anglo-amerikanischen Multikulturalismusdebatte*, Tübingen: Stauffenburg Verlag: 1–29.

Burger, Hannelore (1993), 'Der Verlust der Mehrsprachigkeit: Aspekte des Mährischen Ausgleichs', *Bohemia*, 34: 77–89.

Burke, Peter (2009), *Cultural Hybridity*, Cambridge.

Burke, Peter and R. Po-chia Hsia (2007), *Cultural Translation in Early Modern Europe*, Cambridge.

Busch, Werner *et al.*, eds (2010) *Ähnlichkeit und Entstellung: Entgrenzungstendenzen im Porträt*, Berlin.

Cacciari, Cristina (1995), *Similarity in Language, Thought and Perception*, Turnhold.

Canguilhem, Georges (1968), 'Modeles et analogies dans la découverte en biologie', in *Études d'histoire de philosophie des sciences*, Paris: 305–18.

Chatterjee, Margaret (2002), *Hinterlands and Horizons: excursions in search of amity*, Lanham.

Coenen, Hans Georg (2002), *Analogie und Metapher: Grundlegung einer Theorie der bildlichen Rede*, Berlin.

Conrad, Sebastian (2007), 'Vergleich, Transfer, transnationale und globalgeschichtliche Perspektiven: Geschichte der Geschichtsschreibung jenseits des National-staates (am japanischen Beispiel)', in Jan Eckel und Thomas Etzemüller, eds, *Neue Zugänge zur Geschichte der Geschichtswissenschaft*, Göttingen: 230–54.

Croce, Benedetto (1929), 'Bildnis und Ähnlichkeit', in *Kleine Schriften zur Ästhetik*, Vol. 2, Tübingen: 265–70.

Csáky, Moritz (2010), *Das Gedächtnis der Städte: Kulturelle Verflechtungen: Wien und die urbanen Milieus in Zentraleuropa*, Vienna: Böhlau Verlag.

Csáky, Moritz and Johannes Feichtinger, eds (2007), *Europa – geeint durch Werte? Die europäische Wertedebatte auf dem Prüfstand der Geschichte*, Bielefeld.

Damerau, Burghard (2000), 'Das Gesetz vom Ähnlichen: Zu Peter Handkes drei "Versuchen"', in *Gegen den Strich: Aufsätze zur Literatur*, Würzburg: 18–25.

de Man, Paul (2012), *Allegorien des Lesens*, Vol. II: *Die Rousseau-Aufsätze*, edited by Gerhard Poppenberg, translated by Sylvia Rexing-Lieberwirth, Berlin.

Decock, Lieven and Igor Douven (2011), 'Similarity After Goodman', *Review of Philosophy and Psychology*, 2: 61–75.

Deleuze, Gilles (1992), *Differenz und Wiederholung*, München; French edition: *Dif-férence et répétition*, 1968.

——— (2003), *Die einsame Insel: Texte und Gespräche von 1953–1974*, edited by David Lapoujade, translated by Eva Moldenhauer, Frankfurt am Main: Suhrkamp Verlag.

Didi-Huberman, Georges (1999), *Anachronismus und Archälogie: Ähnlichkeit und Berühung Modernität des Abdrucks*, translated by Christoph Hollender, Köln.

——— (2010) *Formlose Ähnlichkeit oder die fröhliche Wissenschaft des Visuellen nach Georges Bataille*, translated by Markus Sedlaczek, München.

Doshi, Tishani (2017), '"I'm here all by myself": The Salman Rushdie interview', 1 September, available at http://www.thehindu.com/books/interview-with-salman-rushdie-on-the-golden-house/article19600953.ece

Eco, Umberto (2000), *Kant und das Schnabeltier*, München.

Eggers, Michael, ed. (2011), *Von Ähnlichkeiten und Unterschieden: Vergleich, Analogie und Klassifikation in Wissenschaft und Literatur, 18/19 Jahrhundert*, Heidelberg.

Eiden, Wolfgang (2002), *Präzise Unschärfe: Informationsmodellierung durch Fuzzy-Mengen*, Stuttgart.

Emcke, Carolin (2016), *Gegen den Hass: Essay*, Frankfurt am Main.

Erdle, Birgit and Siegrid Weigel (1996), *Mimesis, Bild und Schrift: Ähnlichkeit und Entstellung im Verhältnisder Künste*, Köln.

Erel, Umut (2004), 'Paradigmen kultureller Differenz und Hybridität', in Martin Sökefeld, ed., *Jenseits des Paradigmas kultureller Differenz: Neue Perspektiven auf Einwanderer aus der Türkei*, Bielefeld: 35–51.

Eßlinger, Eva *et al.*, eds (2010), *Die Figur des Dritten: Ein kulturwissenschaftliches Paradigma*, Frankfurt am Main, Berlin.

Ezli, Özkan (2007), 'Von der Identität zur Individuation: "Gegen die Wand" – eine Problematisierung kultureller Identitätszuschreibungen', in Levent Tezcan and Monika Wohlrab-Sahr, eds, *Konfliktfeld Islam in Europa*, Baden-Baden: 283–304.

Falkenhayner, Nicole (2010), 'The Other Rupture of 1989: The Rushdie Affair as the Inaugural Event of Representations of Post-secular Conflict', *Global Society*, 24 (1): 111–33.

Feichtinger, Johannes (2003), 'Habsburg (Post)-colonial: Anmerkungen zur Inneren Kolonisierung in Zentraleuropa', in Johannes Feichtinger, Ursula Prutsch and Moritz Csáky, eds, *Habsburg Postcolonial*, Innsbruck: 13–33.

——— (2010), *Wissenschaft als Reflexives Projekt: Von Bolzano über Freud zu Kelsen: Österreichische Wissenschaftsgeschichte 1848–1938*, Bielefeld: transcript.

Feichtinger, Johannes *et al.*, eds (2003), *Habsburg postcolonial: Zentraleuropa – Orte Innerer Kolonisierung?* Innsbruck, Wien, München.

Feichtinger, Johannes and Heidemarie Uhl, eds (2016), *Habsburg Neu Denken: Vielfalt und Ambivalenz in Zentraleuropa: 30 kulturwissenschaftliche Stichworte*, Wien: Böhlau.

Ferguson, James (2002), 'Of mimicry and membership: Africans and the "New World Society"', *Cultural Anthropology*, 17 (4): 551–69.

Fillafer, Franz Leander (2012), 'Imperium oder Kulturstatt: Die Habsburgmonarchie und die Historisierung der Nationalkulturen im 19. Jahrhundert', in Philipp Ther, ed., *Kulturpolitik und Theater: Die kontinentalen Imperien in Europa im Vergleich*, München: Oldenbourg and Wien: Böhlau: 27–54.

Fittler, Doris M. (2005), *'Ein Kosmos der Ähnlichkeit': Frühe und späte Mimesis bei Walter Benjamin*, Bielefeld.

Fliethmann, Axel (2002), 'Gespenstische Ähnlichkeit: Die Renaissance der Bilder', in Matthias Bickenbach and Axel Fliethmann, eds, *Korrespondenzen: Visuelle Kulturen in Früher Neuzeit und Gegenwart*, Köln: 55–74.

Foucault, Michel (1974), *Die Ordnung der Dinge: Eine Archäologie der Humanwissenschaften*, Frankfurt am Main.

——— (1981), *Archäologie des Wissens*, translated by Ulirich Köppen, Frankfurt am Main: Suhrkamp Verlag.

Frazer, James George (1922), *The Golden Bough: A Study in Magic and Religion*, abridged edition, London.

——— (1968), *Der goldene Zweig: Eine Studie über Magie und Religion*, Köln, Berlin.

Freud, Sigmund ([1900] 1972), *Die Traumdeutung*, in *Studienausgabe*, Vol. 2, edited by Alexander Mitscherlich, Angela Richards and James Strachey, Frankfurt am Main.

——— ([1913] 2000), 'Totem und Tabu: Einige Übereinstimmungen im Seelenleben der Wilden und der Neurotiker', in *Studienausgabe*, Vol. 9, edited by Alexander Mitscherlich, Angela Richards and James Strachey, Frankfurt am Main: 287–444.

——— (2010), *Der Mann Moses und die monotheistische Religion*, edited by Jan Assmann, Stuttgart: Reclam Philipp jun. GmbH Verlag: 137–42.

Fromm, Waldemar (1997), 'Inspirierte Ähnlichkeit: Überlegungen zu einem ästhetischen Verfahren des Novalis', *Deutsche Vierteljahrsschrift für Literaturwissenschaft und Geistesgeschichte*, 71 (4): 559–88.

Funk, Gerald, Gert Mattenklott and Michael Pauen, eds (2001), *Ästhetik des Ähnlichen: Zur Poetik und Kunstphilosophie der Moderne*, Frankfurt am Main.

Gabriel, Gottfried (2005), 'Familienähnlichkeit', in *Enzyklopädie Philosophie und Wissenschaftstheorie*, 4 vols, Vol. 2, edited by Jürgen Mittelstraß, Stuttgart, Weimar: 473–74.

Gaier, Martin, Jeanette Kohl and Alberto Saviello, eds (2012), *Similitudo: Konzepte der Ähnlichkeit in Mittelalter und Früher Neuzeit*, München.

Gamm, Gerhard (1994), *Flucht aus der Kategorie: Die Positivierung des Unbestimmten als Ausgang aus der Moderne*, Frankfurt am Main.

Gammerl, Benno (2010), *Untertanen, Staatsbürger und Andere: Der Umgang mit ethnischer Heterogentität im Britischen Weltreich und im Habsburgerreich 1867–1918* (Kritische Studien zur Geschichtswissenschaft 189), Göttingen: Vandenhoeck & Ruprecht.

Gebauer, Gunter and Christoph Wulf (2003), *Mimetische Weltzugänge: Soziales Handeln – Rituale und Spiele – ästhetische produktionen*, Stuttgart.

Gellner, Ernest (1998), *Language and Solitude: Wittgenstein, Malinowski and the Habsburg Dilemma*, Cambridge.

Genette, Gérard (1996), *Mimologiken: Reise nach Kratylien, aus dem Franz*, translated by Michael von Killisch-Horn, München.

Gentner, Dedre and Arthur B. Markman (1997), 'Structure Mapping in Analogy and Similarity', *American Psychologist*, 52 (1): 45–56.

Gentner, Dedre, Arthur B. Markman Kurtz and J. Kenneth (2006), 'Relations, Objects and the Composition of Analogies', *Cognitive Science*, 30: 209–642.

Ginzburg, Carlo (2004), 'Family Resemblances and Family Tree: Two Cognitive Metaphors', *Critical Inquiry*, 30: 537–56.

Giovanelli, Marco (2008), 'Leibniz, Kant, Helmholtz und die philosophische Bedeutung des Kongruenzbegriffs', available at http://www.wpk.uni-tuebingen.de/wp-content/uploads/2008/02/marco-giovanelli-leibniz-kant-helmholtz-und-die-philosophische-bedeutung-des-kongruenz-begriffs.pdf, accessed on 6 November 2013.

Glock, Hans-Johann (1996), 'Family Resemblance', in *A Wittgenstein Dictionary*, Oxford: 120–24.

Gloy, Karin and Manuel Bachmann, eds (2000), *Das Analogiedenken: Vorstöße in ein neues Gebiet der Rationalitätsforschung*, Freiburg, München.

——— (1999), 'Kalkulierte Absurdität: Die Logik des Analogiedenkens', in Gloy, Karin and Manuel Bachmann, eds, *Rationalitätstypen*, Freiburg, München: 213–43.

Godglück, Peter (2008), *Sprache – Zeichen – Analogie: Philologische Aspekte von Ähnlichkeit*, Tübingen.

Goffman, Erving (1974), *Das Individuum im öffentlichen Austausch: Mikrostudien zur öffentlichen Ordnung*, Frankfurt am Main: Suhrkamp.

Goldstone, Robert L. (1994), 'Similarity, Interactive Activation, and Mapping', *Journal of Experimental Psychology: Learning, Memory, and Cognition*, 20: 3–28.

Goldstone, Robert L. and Son Ji Yun (2005), 'Similarity', in Keith J. Holyoak and Robert G. Morrison, eds, *Cambridge Handbook of Thinking and Reasoning*, Cambridge: 13–36.

Goldstone, Robert L., Son Ji Yun, Douglas Medin and Dedre Gentner (1991), 'Relational Similarity and the Non-independence of Features in Similarity Judgments', *Cognitive Psychology*, 23: 222–64.

Gombrich, Ernst H. (1984), 'Maske und Gesicht: Die Wahrnehmung physiognomischer Ähnlichkeit im Leben und in der Kunst', in *Bild und Auge: Neue Studien zur Psychologie der bildlichen Darstellung*, Stuttgart: 105–34.

Goodman, Nelson ([1968] 1976), *Languages of Art: An Approach to a Theory of Symbols*, Indianapolis.

——— (1972), 'Seven Strictures on Similarity', in *Problems and Projects*, New York: 23–32.

Görner, Rüdiger (2010), 'Der Vergleich als geistige Form: Versuch einer Methodenreflexion', in *Form und Verwandlung: Ansätze zu einer literaturästhetischen Morphologie*, Heidelberg: 9–27.

Gruber, Bernhard (2001), *Topographie des Ähnlichen: Aristoteles und die gegenwärtige Kritik an 'Repräsentation'*, München.

Guru, Gopal and Sundar Sarukkai (2012), *The Cracked Mirror: An Indian Debate on Experience and Theory*, New Delhi.

Hagestedt, Lutz (1997), *Ähnlichkeit und Differenz: Aspekte der Realitätskonzeption in Ludwig Tiecks späten Romanen und Novellen*, München.

Hahn, Ulrike and Michael J.A. Ramscar, eds (2001), *Similarity and Categorization*, Oxford.

Hahn, Ulrike and Nick Chater (1998), 'Understanding Similarity: A Joint Project for Psychology, Case Based Reasoning and Law', *Artificial Intelligence Review*, 12: 393–427.

Hahn, Ulrike, Nick Chater and Lucy B. Richardson (2003), 'Similarity as Transformation', *Cognition*, 87: 1–32.

Hampton, James A. (1998), 'Similarity-Based Categorization and Fuzziness of Natural Categories', *Cognition*, 65 (2–3): 137–65.

Hannerz, Ulf (1992), *Cultural Complexities: Studies in the Social Organization of Meaning*, New York: Columbia University Press.

Hattori, Seiji (2006), '"Vergleichen" als ein Ritual des Verstehens aufgrund des Ähnlichkeitsdenkens? Überlegungen zu einer literaturwissenschaftlichen Verfahrensweise am Schnittpunkt von Hermeneutik, Dekonstruktivismus und Kulturwissenschaft', in Nobuo Ikeda, ed., *Rituale des Verstehens – Verstehen der Rituale* (Beiträge des Vierten Internationalen Kolloquiums der Japanischen Gesellschaft für Germanistik an der Doshisha-Universität, Kyoto, 9–10 Oktober 2005), München: 73–93.

Hegel, Georg Friedrich Wilhelm (1993), *Vorlesungen über die Philosophie der Religion, Teil 1*, edited by Walter Jaeschke, Hamburg: Felix Meiner Verlag.

Hentschel, Klaus (2007), 'Zur Bedeutung von Analogien in den Naturwissenschaften', *Scientia Poetica: Yearbook for the History of Literature, Humanities and Sciences*, 11: 241–75.

Herder, Johann Gottfried ([1777] 1893), 'Von der Ähnlichkeit der mittlern englischen und deutschen Dichtkunst', in *Herders sämmtliche Werke*, edited by Bernhard Suphan, Berlin: 522–35, Kommentar 553–54.

Hodkinson, James, John Walker, Shaswati Mazumdar and Johannes Feichtinger, eds (2013), *Deploying Orientalism in Culture and History: From Germany to Central and Eastern Europe* (Studies in German Literature, Linguistic and Culture), Rochester, New York: Camden House.

Hödl, Karl (2017), 'Jewish history beyond binary conceptions: Jewish performing musicians in Vienna around 1900', *Journal of Modern Jewish Studies*, 16, 3: 377–94.

Hofmannsthal, Hugo von (2004), *Gesammelte Werke*, Vol. II: *Dramen und Opernlibretti*, edited by Dieter Lamping, in collaboration with Frank Zipfel, Düsseldorf, Zürich: Artemis & Winkler.

Hofstadter, Douglas and Die Fluid Analogies Research Group (1996), *Die FARGonauten: Über Analogie und Kreativität, aus dem Amerikan*, translated by Ulrich Enderwitz and Monika Noll, Stuttgart.

Hofstadter, Douglas and Emmanuel Sander (2014), *Die Analogie: Das Herz des Denkens, aus dem Amerikan*, translated by Susanne Held, Stuttgart.

Hoenen, Maarten J.F.M. (1992), 'Analogie', in *Historisches Wörterbuch der Rhetorik*, edited by Gert Ueding, 9 vols, Vol. 1, Tübingen: 498–514.

Holz, Harald (1973), 'Analogie', in *Handbuch philosophischer Grundbegriffe*, edited by Hermann Krings, Hans Michael Baumgartner and Christoph Wild, Vol. 1, München: 51–65.

Hume, David (2007), *Eine Untersuchung über den menschlichen Verstand, aus dem Englischen von Raoul Richter, durchgesehen und überarbeitet von Lambert Wiesing*, Frankfurt am Main.

Husserl, Edmund (1972), *Erfahrung und Urteil: Untersuchungen zur Genealogie der Logik*, edited by Ludwig Landgrebe, Hamburg.

Irmscher, Hans Dietrich (1981), 'Beobachtungen zur Funktion der Analogie im

Denken Herders', *Deutsche Vierteljahrsschrift für Literaturwissenschaft und Geistesgeschichte*, 55: 64–97.

——— (1988), 'Die Analogie: Versuch einer Wortgeschichte', *Wissenschaftliche Zeitschrift der Universität Rostock (Geisteswissenschafliche Reihe)*, 37: 4–6.

Itkonen, Esa (2005), *Analogy as Structure and Process: Approaches in Linguistics, Cognitive Psychology and Philosophy of Science*, Amsterdam.

Jean Paul (1990), *Vorschule der Ästhetik: Nach der Ausgabe von Norbert Miller herausgegeben, textkritisch durchgesehen und eingeleitet von Wolfhart Henckmann*, Hamburg.

Judson, Pieter (2016), *The Habsburg Empire: A New History*, Cambridge, MA: The Belknap Press of Harvard University.

Kablitz, Andreas and Gerhard Neumann (1998), *Mimesis und Simulation* (Reihe Litterae, Vol. 52), Freiburg im Breisgau.

Kaelble, Hartmut and Jürgen Schriewer, eds (2003), *Vergleich und Transfer: Komparatistik in den Sozial-, Geschichts- und Kulturwissenschaften*, Frankfurt am Main.

Kaffenberger, Helmut (1998), 'Denkbilder des dritten Raums? Walter Benjamins Theorie des Ähnlichen', in Claudia Breger and Tobias Döring, eds, *Figuren der/des Dritten: Erkundungen kultureller Zwischenräume*, Amsterdam: 36–64.

Kilcher, Andreas (2011), 'Assimilation und Zirkulation: Ein universalistisches Wissensmodell des 19 Jahrhunderts', in Andreas Kilcher and Philip Sarasin, eds, *Zirkulationen* (= *Nach Feierabend* 2011), Zürich: 15–36.

Kimmich, Dorothee (2010), 'Migration und Literatur: Literatur als Kulturkritik', in Andrea Allerkamp and Gérard Raulet, eds, *Kulturwissenschaften in Europa – eine grenzüberschreitende Disziplin?*, Münster: 234–49.

——— (2012), 'Gefährliche Nachbarschaften: Bürgerliche Grenzwüsten bei Stifter und Keller', in Sandra Evans and Schamma Schahadat, eds, *Nachbarschaft – Räume – Emotionen: Interdisziplinäre Beiträge zu einer sozialen Lebensform*, Bielefeld: 141–56.

——— (2012), 'Lob des "Nebeneinander": Zur Kritik kulturalistischer Mythen bei Kafka und Wittgenstein', in Dorothee Kimmich and Schamma Schahadat, eds, *Kulturen in Bewegung: Beiträge zur Theorie und Praxis der Transkulturalität*, Bielefeld: 41–67.

——— (2012), 'Metamorphosen einer Biographie. Bemerkungen zu Feridun Zaimoglus Leyla', in Peter Braun and Bernd Stiegler, eds, *Literatur als Lebensgeschichte: Biographisches Erzählen von der Moderne bis zur Gegenwart*, Bielefeld: 129–43.

——— (2017), *Ins Ungefähre: Ähnlichkeit und Moderne*, Konstanz University Press.

Kippenberg, Hans G. (1997), *Die Entdeckung der Religionsgeschichte: Religionswissenschaft und Moderne*, München.

Kistner, Ulrike (2012), 'Das Ereignis des Unaussprechlichen: Traumdeutung, Sprachmagie, Poesie – und Kritik', in Carlotta von Maltzan, ed., *Magie und Sprache, Jahrbuch für Internationale Germanistik*, Bern: 239–58.

Klee, Paul (1987), *Kunst-Lehre: Aufsätze, Vorträge, Rezensionen und Beiträge zur bildnerischen Form- lehre*, Leipzig.

Kleeberg, Bernhard and Andreas Langenohl, eds (2011), *Kulturalisierung, Dekulturalisierung: Zeitschrift für Kulturphilosophie*, 2: 281–302.

Kluck, Nora (2014), *Der Wert der Vagheit* (*Linguistics & Philosophy 5*), Berlin, Boston.

Kluxen, Wolfgang, Hans Schwarz and Adolf Remane (1971), 'Analogie I–III', in *Historisches Wörterbuch der Philosophie*, edited by Joachim Ritter *et al.*, 13 vols, Vol. 1, Darmstadt: 214–29.

Knapp, Fritz Peter (1975), *Similitudo: Stil- und Erzählfunktion von Vergleich und Exempel in der lateinischen, französischen und deutschen Großepik des Mittelalters*, Wien, Stuttgart.

Knobloch, Eberhard (1989), 'Analogie und mathematisches Denken', *Berichte zur Wissenschaftsgeschichte*, 12 (1): 35–47.

Knörer, Ekkehard (2007), *Entfernte Ähnlichkeiten: Zur Geschichte von Witz und ingenium*, München.

Kohne, Jens (2005), *Drei Variationen über Ähnlichkeit: Eine systematische Einführung in die Eigenschaftsontologie*, Hildesheim, Zürich.

Koschorke, Albrecht (2003), *Körperströme und Schriftverkehr: Mediologie des 18 Jahrhunderts*, München.

——— (2009), 'Wie werden aus Spannungen Differenzen? Feldtheoretische Überlegungen zur Konfliktsemantik', in Heinz Fassmann, ed., *Kulturen der Differenz – Transformationsprozesse in Zentraleuropa nach 1989: Transdisziplinäre Perspektiven*, Wien: 271–86.

Kümmel, Werner Friedrich (1989), 'Einführung in das Thema', in *Analogie in den Wissenschaften* (XXVI: Symposium der Gesellschaft für Wissenschaftsgeschichte, 12–14 Mai 1988, Stuttgart), Berichte zur Wissenschaftsgeschichte, 12 (1).

Kunzmann, Peter (1998), *Dimensionen der Analogie: Wittgensteins Neuentdeckung eines klassischen Prinzips*, Düsseldorf.

Lachmann, Renate (1983), 'Die problematische "Ähnlichkeit": Sarbiewskis Traktat De acuto et arguto im Kontext concettistischer Theorien des 17. Jahrhunderts', in Renate Lachmann, ed., *Gedenkschrift für Dimitrij Tschižewskij (1894–1977)* (= Slavische Barockliteratur, Vol. 2), München: 87–114.

——— (2001), 'Die Mystifikation der Ähnlichkeit: Anmerkungen zu Vladimir Nabokovs Roman Ot ajanie (Verzweiflung)', in Susi Frank *et al.*, ed., *Mystifikation – Autorschaft – Original*, Tübingen: 313–30.

Lakoff, George (1987), *Women, Fire, and Dangerous Things: What Categories Reveal About the Mind*, Chicago.

Langenohl, Andreas (2006), 'Öffentlichkeit und politisch-kulturelle Differenz in Europa: Jenseits von Kulturalismus und Anti-Kulturalismus', in Kathrin Ruhl *et al.*, eds, *Demokratisches Regieren und politische Kultur: Post-staatlich, post-parlamentarisch, post-patriarchal?*, Münster: 177–97.

——— (2010), 'Modernization, Modernity, and Tradition: Sociological Theory's Promissory Notes', in John N. Kim and Richard Calichman, eds, *Rethinking Cultural Difference around the Work of Naoki Sakai*, London: 192–210.

——— (2014), 'Verknüpfung, Kontextkonfiguration, Aspiration: Skizze einer Kulturtheorie des Übersetzens', *Zeitschrift für interkulturelle German-*

istik, 5 (2), special issue: 'Übersetzen: Praktiken kulturellen Transfers am Beispiel Prags', edited by Irina Wutsdorff and Št pán Zbytovský: 17–28.

Latour, Bruno (1986), 'The Powers of Associations', in John Law, ed., *Power, Action and Belief: A New Sociology of Knowledge?*, Sociological Review Monograph 32, London: 264–80.

——— (1998), *Wir sind nie modern gewesen: Versuch einer symmetrischen Anthropologie*, Frankfurt am Main.

——— (2000), *Die Hoffnung der Pandora: Untersuchungen zur Wirklichkeit der Wissen-schaft*, Frankfurt am Main: Suhrkamp.

——— (2005), *Reassembling the Social: An Introduction to Actor-Network-Theory*, Oxford: Oxford University Press.

——— (2009), 'Gabriel Tarde und das Ende des Sozialen', in Christian Borch and Urs Stäheli, eds, *Soziologie der Nachahmung und des Begehrens: Materialien zu Gabriel Tarde*, Frankfurt am Main: Suhrkamp: 39–61.

Leinweber, Jörg (1979), *Mimetisches Vermögen und allegorisches Verfahren: Studien zu Walter Benjamin und seiner Lehre vom Ähnlichen*, Marburg.

Lessing, Gotthold E. (1778), *Ernst und Falk: Gespräche für Freymäurer*, Wolfenbüttel, Göttingen: Dieterich.

——— (1968), *Ernst und Falk: Mit den Fortsetzungen Johann Gottfried Herders und Friedrich Schlegels*, edited by Ion Contiades, Frankfurt am Main: Insel.

——— (1979), 'Ernst und Falk', in *Werke*, Vol. VIII, edited by Herbert G. Göpfert, München: Hanser: 450–88.

Lévy-Bruhl, Lucien (1921), *Das Denken der Naturvölker*, in *Deutscher Übersetzung*, edited by Wilhelm Jerusalem, Wien, Leipzig.

Leyton, Cristian Alvarado and Philipp Erchinger (eds) (2010), *Identität und Unterschied: Zur Theorie von Kultur, Differenz und Transdifferenz*, Bielefeld.

Lobsien, Eckhard (1999), *Kunst der Assoziation: Phänomenologie eines ästhetischen Grundbegriffs vor und nach der Romantik*, München.

Luhmann, Niklas (1980), *Gesellschaftsstruktur und Semantik: Studien zur Wissenssoziologie der modernen Gesellschaft*, Vol. 1, Frankfurt am Main: Suhrkamp.

Mach, Ernst ([1905] 1926, 1991), 'Die Ähnlichkeit und die Analogie als Leitmotiv der Forschung', in *Erkenntnis und Irrtum: Skizzen zur Psychologie der Forschung*, Leipzig, Darmstadt: 220–31.

Mahajan, Gurpreet (2011), *Accommodating Diversity: Ideas and Institutional Practices*, New Delhi.

Mann, Thomas ([1932] 1990), 'Die Einheit des Menschengeistes', in *Gesammelte Werke in 13 Bänden*, Vol. X, Frankfurt am Main: Fischer: 751–55.

——— (1974), *Die vertauschten Köpfe*, in *Gesammelte Werke in dreizehn Bänden*, Vol. VIII: *Erzählungen/Fiorenza/Dichtungen*, Frankfurt am Main: 712–22.

——— (1990), *Königliche Hoheit*, in *Gesammelte Werke in dreizehn Bänden*, Vol. II: *Königliche Hoheit*, Frankfurt am Main.

Mauthner, Fritz (1923), 'Ähnlichkeit', in *Wörterbuch der Philosophie: Neue Beiträge zu einer Kritik der Sprache*, 3 vols, Vol. 1: *Zur Sprache und zur Psychologie*, Leipzig: 21–22.

——— (1923), 'Analogie', in *Wörterbuch der Philosophie: Neue Beiträge zu einer*

Kritik der Sprache, 3 vols, Vol. 1: *Zur Sprache und zur Psychologie*, Leipzig: 45–48.

——— (1982), 'Ähnlichkeit und Sprache', in *Neue Beiträge zu einer Kritik der Sprache*, 3 vols, Vol. 1: *Zur Sprache und zur Psychologie*, Frankfurt am Main: 434–38.

Mengel, Peter (1995), *Analogien als Argumente*, Frankfurt am Main.

Mühr, Stephan (2011), 'Zwischen Xenologie und Assimilation: Anmerkungen zu einer Hermeneutik der Interkulturalität', in Michael Ewert, Renate Riedner and Simone Schiedermair, eds, *Deutsch als Fremdsprache und Literaturwissenschaft: Zugriffe, Themenfelder, Perspektiven*, München: 29–51.

——— (2016), in *Acta Germanica*, 44.

Müller-Funk, Wolfgang and Heidemarie Uhl, eds (2009), *Kulturen der Differenz – Transformationsprozesse in Zentraleuropa nach 1989: Transdisziplinäre Perspektiven*, Göttingen: V&R Unipress: 271–86.

Musil, Robert ([1919] 2000), 'Der Anschluss an Deutschland', in *Gesammelte Werke: Prosa und Stücke. Kleine Prosa. Aphorismen. Autobiographisches. Essays und Reden. Kritik*, Reinbek bei Hamburg: Rowohlt: 1033–42.

——— (1978), *Der Mann ohne Eigenschaften. Roman. I. Erstes und zweites Buch*, edited by Adolf Frisé (Rowohlt Jahrhundert 1), Reinbek bei Hamburg: Rowohlt.

Novalis (1999), 'Das Allgemeine Brouillon', in *Werke, Tagebücher und Briefe Friedrich von Hardenbergs*, Vol. 2: *Das philosophisch-theoretische Werk*, edited by Hans-Joachim Mähl and Richard Samuel, Darmstadt: 471–720.

Opitz, Michael (2000), 'Ähnlichkeit', in Michael Opitz and Erdmut Wizisla, eds, *Benjamins Begriffe*, Frankfurt am Main: 15–49.

Ortony, Andrew (1993), 'The Role of Similarity in Similes and Metaphors', in *Metaphor and Thought*, Cambridge .

Ortony, Andrew and Stella Vosniadou, eds (1989), *Similarity and Analogical Reasoning*, Cambridge.

Osterhammel, Jürgen (2010), *Die Entzauberung Asiens: Europa und die asiatischen Reiche im 18 Jahrhundert*, München: C.H. Beck; English translation forthcoming, Princeton, NJ: Princeton University Press, 2018.

——— (2010), *Die Verwandlung der Welt: Eine Geschichte des 19 Jahrhunderts*, München.

Otto, Detlev (1998), *Wendungen der Metapher: Zur Übertragung in poetologischer, rhetorischer und erkenntnistheoretischer Hinsicht bei Aristoteles und Nietzsche*, München.

Otto, Stephan (1992), *Das Wissen des Ähnlichen: Michel Foucault und die Renaissance*, Frankfurt am Main.

Parsons, Talcott (1972), *Das System moderner Gesellschaften*, München: Juventa.

Patrut, Iulia (2016), in *Zeitschrift für interkulturelle Germanistik (ZiG)*, 7.

Paul, Jean (1990), *Vorschule der Ästhetik: Nach der Ausgabe*, edited by Norbert Miller, critically reviewed and with an introduction by Wolfhart Henckmann, Hamburg: Meiner Felix Verlag.

Peirce, Charles (1965), *Collected Papers*, Vol. 2: *Elements of Logic*, edited by Charles Hartshorne and Paul Weiss, Cambridge (MA).

Petersen, Jürgen H. (2000), *Mimesis – Imitatio – Nachahmung: Eine Geschichte der europäischen Poetik*, München.

Petrarca, Francesco (2005–09), *Familiaria: Bücher der Vertraulichkeiten*, edited by Berthe Widmer, Berlin, New York.

Picht, Robert (1990), 'Schafft die Modernisierung mehr Ähnlichkeit – mehr Nähe? Vom schwierigen Vergleich gesellschaftlicher Entwicklungen', *Dokumente: Zeitschrift für den deutsch-französischen Dialog*, 46 (5): 380–86.

Pieper, Annemarie (1996), 'Kant und die Methode der Analogie', in Gerhard Schönrich and Yasushi Kato, eds, *Kant in der Diskussion der Moderne*, Frankfurt am Main: 92–112.

Putnam, Robert D. (2000), *Bowling Alone: The Collapse and Revival of American Community*, New York: Simon and Schuster.

Quine, Willard van Orman (1969), *Ontological Relativity and Other Essays*, New York: Columbia University Press.

——— (1975), *Ontologische Relativität und andere Schriften*, Stuttgart.

Rapp, Christof (1992), 'Ähnlichkeit, Analogie und Homonymie bei Aristoteles', *Zeitschrift für philosophische Forschung*, 46: 526–44.

Reckwitz, Andreas (2017), *Die Gesellschaft der Singularitäten: Zum Strukturwandel der Moderne*, Berlin.

Rehkämper, Klaus (2002), *Bilder, Ähnlichkeit und Perspektive: Auf dem Weg zu einer neuen Theorie der bildhaften Repräsentation*, Wiesbaden.

——— (2005), 'Ist der Begriff der bildhaften Ähnlichkeit wirklich undefinierbar?', in *Bildwissenschaft zwischen Reflexion und Anwendung*, edited by Klaus Sachs-Hombach, Köln: 242–50.

Reulecke, Anne-Kathrin (2005), 'Täuschend, ähnlich: Das Problem des Plagiats in poetologischen und literarischen Texten: Goethe, Federman, Malerba', in Corinna Laude and Ellen Schindler-Horst, eds, *List – Lüge – Täuschung: Mitteilungen des Deutschen Germanistenverbandes*, 3: 416–27.

Riedel, Wolfgang (2000), 'Archäologie des Geistes: Theorien des wilden Denkens um 1900', in Jürgen Barkhoff, Gilbert Carr and Roger Paulin, eds, *Das schwierige 19. Jahrhundert: Germanistische Tagung zum 65: Geburtstag von Eda Sagarra im August 1998*, Tübingen: 467–85.

Riesman, David (1950), in collaboration with Reuel Denney and Nathan Glazer, *The Lonely Crowd*, New Haven and London: Yale University Press.

Ritzer, Monika (2004), 'Vom Ursprung der Kunst aus der Nachahmung: Anthropologische Prinzipien der Mimesis', in Rüdiger Zymner and Manfred Engel, eds, *Anthropologie in der Literatur: Poetogene Strukturen und ästhetisch-soziale Handlungsfelder*, Paderborn: 81–101.

Rosch, Eleanor and Carolyn B. Mervis (1975), 'Family Resemblance: Studies in the Internal Structure of Categories', *Cognitive Psychology*, 7: 573–605.

——— (1978), 'Principles of Categorization', in Eleanor Rosch and Barbara B. Lloyd, eds, *Cognition and Categorization*, Hillsdale (NJ): 27–48.

——— (1998), 'Family Resemblances: Internal Structure of Categories', in Michael DePaul and William Ramsey, eds, *Rethinking Intuition: The Psychology of Intuition and its Role in Philosophical Inquiry*, Lanham: 17–44.

Rosen, Valeska von (2003), 'Nachahmung (Mimesis)', in *Metzler Lexikon Kunstwissenschaft: Ideen, Methoden, Begriffe*, edited by Ulrich Pfisterer, Stuttgart, Weimar: 240–44.

Rousseau, Jean-Jacques ([1754] 2009), *Discourse on the Origin and Basis of Inequality Among Men*, Auckland (NZ): The Floating Press.

Rudolph, André (2006), *Figuren der Ähnlichkeit: Johann Georg Hamanns Analogiedenken im Kontext des 18. Jahrhunderts* (Hallesche Beiträge zur Europäischen Aufklärung), Tübingen.

Russell, Bertrand ([1923] 1988), 'Vagueness', in John G. Slater and Bernd Frohmann, eds, *The Collected Papers of Bertrand Russell*, Vol. 9, London: 145–54.

Ruthner, Clemens (2018), *Habsburgs 'Dark Continent': Postkoloniale Lektüren zur österreichischen Literatur und Kultur im langen 19. Jahrhundert Francke* (Kultur – Herrschaft – Differenz, Bd. 23), Tübingen: Francke.

Sachs-Hombach, Klaus (2000), 'Ähnlichkeit als kulturabhängiges Phänomen', in *Vom Realismus der Bilder: Interdisziplinäre Forschungen zur Semantik bildhafter Darstellungs-formen*, edited and introduced by Klaus Sachs-Hombach und Klaus Rehkämper, Magdeburg: 89–106.

——— (2003), 'Resemblance Reconceived', in *Looking into Pictures: An Interdisciplinary Approach to Pictorial Space*, edited by Heiko Hecht *et al.*, Cambridge: 167–77.

——— (2005), 'Über Sinn und Reichweite der Ähnlichkeitstheorie', in *Symbole, Systeme, Welten: Studien zur Philosophie Nelson Goodmans*, edited by Jakob Steinbrenner, Oliver R. Scholz and Gerhard Ernst, Heidelberg: 203–26.

——— (2006), 'Bildsemantik', in *Das Bild als kommunikatives Medium: Elemente einer allgemeinen Bildwissenschaft*, Köln: 123–56.

Sakai, Naoki (2006), 'Translation', *Theory, Culture and Society*, 23 (2–3): 71–78.

Sandkühler, Hans Jörg (1990), 'Analogie', in Hans Jörg Sandkühler, ed., *Europäische Enzyklopädie zu Philosophie und Wissenschaften*, 4 vols, Vol. 1, Hamburg: 101–08.

Sangalli, Arturo (1998), *The Importance of Being Fuzzy: And Other Insights from the Border Between Math and Computers*, Princeton.

Schade, Sigrid (1996), 'Posen der Ähnlichkeit', in Birgit Erdle and Sigrid Weigel, eds, *Mimesis, Bild und Schrift: Ähnlichkeit und Entstellung im Verhältnis der Künste*, Köln: 65–81.

Schahadat, Schamma (2012), 'Zwangsgemeinschaften: Erzwungene Nachbarschaft im Lager und im Gefängnis (am Beispiel von Fedor Dostoevskij, Evgenija Ginzburg und Varlam Šalamov)', in Sandra Evans and Schamma Schahadat, eds, *Nachbarschaft – Räume – Emotionen: Interdisziplinäre Beiträge zu einer sozialen Lebensform*, Bielefeld: 157–87.

Schlüter, Dietrich (1971), 'Ähnlichkeit', in *Historisches Wörterbuch der Philosophie*, edited by Joachim Ritter, 13 vols, Vol. 1, Basel: 114–15.

Schmidt-Glintzer, Helwig (2010), 'Chancen für einen globalen Humanismus im Kampf der Kulturen', in Jörn Rüsen, ed., *Perspektiven der Humanität: Menschsein im Diskurs der Disziplinen* (*Der Mensch im Netz der Kulturen – Humanismus in der Epoche der Globalisierung*, Vol. 8), Bielefeld: 407–41.

Schmitt, Carl (1928), *Verfassungslehre*, Humboldt & Duncker: Munchen.

——— (1935), *Staat, Bewegung, Volk: Die Dreigliederung der politischen Einheit* (Der deutsche Staat der Gegenwart 1), Hamburg: Hanseatische Verlagsanstalt.

——— (1936), 'Schlusswort des Reichsgruppenwalters Staatsrat Prof. Dr Carl Schmitt', in *Das Judentum in der Rechtswissenschaft: Ansprachen, Vorträge und Ergebnisse der Tagung der Reichsgruppe Hochschullehrer des NSRB am 3. und 4. Oktober 1936. 1: Die deutsche Rechtswissenschaft im Kampf gegen den jüdischen Geist*, Berlin: Deutscher Rechts-Verlag: 28–34.

Schirra, Jörg (2000), 'Täuschung, Ähnlichkeit und Immersion: Die Vögel des Zeuxis', in Klaus Sachs-Hombach and Klaus Rehkämper, eds, *Vom Realismus der Bilder: Interdisziplinäre Forschungen zur Semantik bildhafter Darstellungsformen*, Magdeburg: 119–35.

Schittko, Martin Paul (2003), *Analogien als Argumentationstyp: Vom Paradeigma zur Similitudo (Hypomnemata: Untersuchungen zur Antike und zu ihrem Nachleben)*, Göttingen.

Schlegel, Friedrich (1808), *Ueber die Sprache und Weisheit der Indier: Ein Beitrag zur Begründung der Altertumskunde*, Heidelberg.

Sennet, Richard (1977), *The Fall of Public Man*, New York: Knopf.

Serres, Michel (1980), *Der Parasit*, Frankfurt am Main: Suhrkamp.

Simmel, George (1908), *Soziologie: Untersuchungen über die Formen der Vergesellschaftung*, Berlin: Duncker and Humblot.

——— (1989), *Aufsätze 1997–1890: Über sociale Differenzierung: Die Probleme der Geschichtsphilosophie (1892)*, edited by Heinz-Jürgen Dahme (= Georg Simmel Gesamtausgabe, Vol. 2), Frankfurt am Main: Suhrkamp.

——— (1992), 'Exkurs über den Fremden', in *Soziologie: Untersuchungen über die Formen der Vergesellschaftung* (Georg Simmel Gesamtausgabe, Vol. 11), edited by Otthein Rammstedt, Frankfurt am Main: 764–71.

Sjoberg, Lennart (1972), 'A Cognitive Theory of Similarity', *Goteborg Psychological Reports*, 2 (10).

Smith, Jonathan Z. (1990), *Drudgery Divine: On the Comparison of Early Christianities and the Religions of Late Antiquity*, Chicago: University of Chicago Press.

——— (2010), 'Reading Religion: A Life in Scholarship', Plenary address, American Academy of Religion; available at http://vimeo.com/20286150, accessed on 18 March 2013.

Sökefeld, Martin (1999), 'Debating Self, Identity, and Culture in Anthropology', *Current Anthropology*, 40 (4): 417–47.

Spaemann, Robert (2011), 'Ähnlichkeit', in *Schritte über uns hinaus: Gesammelte Reden und Aufsätze*, Vol. 2, Stuttgart: 50–57.

Stadler, Ulrich (1999), '"Ich lehre nicht, ich erzähle": Über den Analogiegebrauch im Umkreis der Romantik', *Athenäum Jahrbuch für Romantik*, 3: 83–105.

Stammberger, Ralf M.W. (1995), *On Analogy: An Essay Historical and Systematic*, Frankfurt am Main.

Steinhart, Eric (1994), 'Beyond Proportional Analogy: A Structural Model of Analogical Mapping', *Pragmatics & Cognition*, 2: 95–130.

Strijdom, Johan (2013), 'A political problem in inter-human relations: Autochthony in ancient Greek and modern African thought and practice', *Phronimon*, 14 (1): 79–92.

Strub, Christian (1991), *Kalkulierte Absurditäten: Versuch einer historisch reflektierten sprachanalytischen Metaphorologie*, Freiburg im Breisgau, München.

——— (1995), 'Abbilden und Schaffen von Ähnlichkeiten: Systematische und historische Thesen zum Zusammenhang von Metaphorik und Ontologie', in Lutz Danneberg, Andreas Graeser and Klaus Petrus, eds, *Metapher und Innovation: Beiträge aus philosophischer und literaturwissenschaftlicher Sicht*, Bern: 105–25.

Sulzer, Johann Georg (1771), 'Ähnlichkeit', in *Allgemeine Theorie der schönen Künste*, Vol. 1, Leipzig: 14–16.

Tambiah, Stanley J. (1996), 'Relations of Analogy and Identity: Toward Multiple Orientations to the World', in David Olson and Nancy Torrance, eds, *Modes of Thought: Explorations in Culture and Cognition*, Cambridge: 34–52.

Tarde, Gabriel ([1895] 2003), *Die Gesetze der Nachahmung*, Frankfurt am Main: Suhrkamp.

——— (2009), *Monadologie und Soziologie: Mit einem Vorwort von Bruno Latour,* Frankfurt am Main: Suhrkamp.

Taussig, Michael (2014), *Mimesis und Alterität: Eine eigenwillige Geschichte der Sinne*, Konstanz.

Teuwsen, Rudolf (1988), *Familienähnlichkeit und Analogie: Zur Semantik genereller Termini bei Wittgenstein und Thomas von Aquin*, Freiburg im Breisgau, München: 102–18.

Thiel, Christian (1995), 'Ähnlich/Ähnlichkeit', in *Enzyklopädie Philosophie und Wissenschaftstheorie*, edited by Jürgen Mittelstraß, 4 vols, Vol. 1, Stuttgart, Weimar: 52.

——— (2005), 'Analogie', in *Enzyklopädie Philosophie und Wissenschaftstheorie*, edited by Jürgen Mittelstraß, 4 vols, Vol. 1, Stuttgart, Weimar: 117f.

Thom, Martina, ed. (1989), *Moses Mendelssohn, Schriften über Religion und Aufklärung*, Berlin: Union Verlag.

Thorpe, Kathleen, Anette Horn, Alida Poeti and Véronique Tadjo, eds (2014), *Hospitality and Hostility in the Multilingual Global Village*, Stellenbosch: Sun Press.

Track, Joachim (1978), 'Analogie', in *Theologische Realenzyklopädie*, Berlin: 625–50.

Trouillot, Michel-Rolph (1991), 'Anthropology and the Savage Slot: The Poetics and Politics of Otherness', in Richard G. Fox, ed., *Recapturing Anthropology: Working in the Present*, Santa Fe: 17–44.

Tversky, Amos (1977), 'Features of Similarity', *Psychological Review*, 84 (4): 327–52.

Valéry, Paul (1989), *Cahiers/Hefte*, 3 vols, edited by Hartmut Köhler and Jürgen Schmidt-Radefeldt, Frankfurt am Main.

Weber, Max (1972), *Wirtschaft und Gesellschaft: Grundriß der verstehenden Soziologie*, fifth, revised edition, commissioned by Johannes Winckelmann, Tübingen: Mohr/Siebeck.

Weigel, Sigrid (1997), *Entstellte Ähnlichkeit: Walter Benjamins theoretische Schreibweise*, Frankfurt am Main.

Weingartner, Paul (1977), 'Analogie: Ein Versuch, verschiedene Arten der Analogiebeziehung zu präzisieren', in Günther Patzig, Erhard Scheibe and Wolfgang Wieland, eds, *Logik, Ethik, Theorie der Geisteswissenschaften*,

Vol. XI (Deutscher Kongress für Philosophie, Göttingen, 5–9 Oktober 1975), Hamburg: 500–11.

Welsch, Wolfgang (1999), 'Transculturality: The Puzzling Form of Cultures Today', in Mike Featherstone and Scott Lash, eds, *Spaces of Culture: City, Nation, World*, London, New Delhi: 194–213.

——— (2005), 'Transkulturelle Gesellschaften', in Peter-Ulrich Merz-Benz and Gerhard Wagner, eds, *Kultur in Zeiten der Globalisierung: Neue Aspekte einer soziologischen Theorie*, Frankfurt am Main: 39–67.

Westermann, Rainer (1996), 'Die Anwendung von Merkmalsmodellen zur Quantifizierung der Ähnlichkeit zwischen analogen Problemen', *Zeitschrift für Psychologie*, 204: 317–99.

Willer, Stephan (2000), 'Metapher/metaphorisch', in Karlheinz Barck *et al.*, eds, *Ästhetische Grundbegriffe: Historisches Wörterbuch in sieben Bänden*, Stuttgart: 89–147.

——— (2008), 'Herkunft und Ähnlichkeit: Genealogisches Denken in der Vormoderne', in Ohad Parnes, Ulrike Vedder and Stefan Willer, eds, *Das Konzept der Generation: Eine Wissenschafts- und Kulturgeschichte*, Frankfurt am Main: 40–63.

Wirth, Uwe (2011), 'Kultur als Pfropfung: Pfropfung als Kulturmodell: Prolegomena zu einer Allgemeinen Greffologie (2.0)', in Uwe Wirth, ed., *Impfen, Pfropfen, Transplantieren*, Berlin: 9–27.

——— (2014), 'Between Hybrid and Graft', in Naomi Segal and Daniela Koleva, eds, *From Literature to Cultural Literacy*, London: Palgrave: 232–49.

Witt, Hermann de (1972–83), *Analogik: Grundlagen einer Wissenschaft der Analogien, ihre Gesetze und Anwendungen*, 3 vols, Luzern.

Wittgenstein, Ludwig ([1953] 2001), *Philosophische Untersuchungen*, Kritisch-genetische edition, edited by Joachim Schulte, Frankfurt am Main.

——— (1969), *Philosophische Untersuchungen*, in *Schriften*, Vol. 1, Frankfurt am Main.

——— (1989), 'Bemerkungen über Frazers Golden Bough', in *Vortrag über Ethik und andere kleine Schriften*, edited and introduced by Joachim Schulte, Frankfurt am Main: 29–46.

——— (2006), *Philosophische Untersuchungen*, in *Werkausgabe*, Vol. 1, Frankfurt am Main: Suhrkamp.

Woodfield, Richard (1992), 'Resemblance', in David E. Cooper, ed., *A Companion to Aesthetics*, Oxford: 369–72.

Zadeh, Lotfi A. (2005), 'Toward a Generalized Theory of Uncertainty (GTU): An Outline', *Information Sciences*, 172: 1–40.

Zahra, Tara (2010), 'Imagined Non-Communities, National Indifference as a Category of Analysis', *Slavic Review*, 69 (1): 93–119.

Zedler, Johann Heinrich (1751), 'Ähnlichkeit', in *Grosses vollständiges Universal-Lexicon aller Wissenschafften und Künste*, 64 vols, 4 supplementary volumes, Supplementary Vol. 1, Leipzig: 624.

Zirfas, Jörg and Benjamin Jörissen, eds (2007), *Phänomenologien der Identität: Human-, sozial- und kulturwissenschaftliche Analysen*, Wiesbaden.

Contributors

Ravi Ahuja is Professor of Modern Indian History, Centre for Modern Indian Studies (CeMIS), University of Göttingen, where he joined in 2009 after teaching at the South Asia Institute, Heidelberg and the School of Oriental and African Studies (SOAS), London. He has researched various aspects of India's social history from the eighteenth to the twentieth century, including urban history, the history of infrastructure and the social history of war. His current research projects examine the social history of South Asian seafarers and the emergence of a labour-centred social policy in mid-twentieth-century India. His publications include *Pathways of Empire: Circulation, 'Public Works' and Infrastructure in Colonial Orissa* (2009), *'When the War Began, We Heard of Several Kings': South Asian Prisoners of War in World War I Germany* (co-editor, 2011) and *Working Lives and Worker Militancy: The Politics of Labour in Colonial India* (editor, 2013).

Aleida Assmann is Professor Emeritus of British and General Literary Studies, University of Konstanz. She has held visiting professorships at Princeton, Yale, Chicago and Vienna universitites, among others. A focus area of her research is cultural memory studies. Her publications include *Der lange Schatten der Vergangenheit: Erinnerungskultur und Geschichtspolitik* (2006), *Das neue Unbehagen an der Erinnerungskultur: Eine Intervention* (2013), *Ist die Zeit aus den Fugen? Aufstieg und Fall des Zeitregimes der Moderne* (2013) and *Im Dickicht der Zeichen* (2015).

Jan Assmann is Professor Emeritus of Egyptology, University of Heidelberg and an honorary professor for cultural studies and religious theory at the University of Konstanz. In addition to his archaeological fieldwork, his research spans the areas of Egyptian religion and culture from a theoretical and comparative perspective, cultural theory (especially the aspect of 'cultural memory'), religious studies (polytheism and monotheism), and the reception of Egypt in European intellectual history. Among his recent publications are *Exodus: Die Revolution der Alten Welt* (2015) and *Totale Religion: Ursprünge und Formen puritanischer Verschärfung* (2016).

Anil Bhatti is Professor Emeritus, Centre of German Studies, Jawaharlal Nehru University, New Delhi. He is a Research Awardee (*Forschungspreisträger*) of the Alexander von Humboldt Foundation. His fields of research encompass German Studies, Comparative Literature and Cultural Studies. He is the co-editor (with Dorothee Kimmich) of *Ähnlichkeit: Ein Kulturwissenschaftliches Paradigma* (2015). His recently published essays include 'Heterogeneities and Homogeneities: On Similarities and Diversities', in Johannes Feichtinger *et al.*, eds, *Understanding Multiculturalism: The Habsburg Central European Expe-rience* (2014); 'Plurikulturalität', in Johannes Feichtinger and Heidemarie Uhl, eds, *Habsburg Neu Denken: Vielfalt und Ambivalenz in Zentraleuropa* (2016); and 'Some Reflections on Marxism and an Aesthetics of Resistance', in C.P. Chandrasekhar and Jayati Ghosh, eds, *Interpreting the World to Change It: Essays for Prabhat Patnaik* (2017).

Johannes Feichtinger is a historian and cultural theorist at the Austrian Academy of Sciences and Lecturer of Modern History, University of Vienna. His areas of specialization are the history of science, the late Habsburg monarchy and Austria, and culture theory. His publications include *Wissenschaft als reflexives Projekt: Von Bolzano über Freud zu Kelsen: Österreichische Wissenschaftsgeschichte 1848–1938* (2010), *Wissenschaft zwischen den Kulturen: Österreichische Hochschullehrer in der Emigration 1933–1945* (2001), *Understanding Multiculturalism: The Habsburg Central European Experience* (co-editor with Gary B. Cohen, 2014), *Experimental Biology in the Vienna Prater: On the History of the Institute for Experimental Biology 1902 to 1945* (co-editor, 2016) and *Habsburg Neu Denken: Vielfalt und Ambivalenz in Zentraleuropa: 30 kulturwissenschaftliche Stichworte* (co-editor with Heidemarie Uhl, 2016).

Rüdiger Görner is Director of the School of Languages, Linguistics and Film, Queen Mary University of London, founder of the Centre for Anglo-German Cultural Relations, and founding member of the College of Classics in Weimar. As an author and literary critic, he writes for the *Frankfurter Allgemeine Zeitung*, *Die Zeit*, *Tagesspiegel*, *Die Presse* and *Neue Zürcher Zeitung*. His research focuses on the theory of poetry, the turn of the century, literary motifs of repetition and the late Romantic period in Germany. Selected publications include *Thomas Mann: Der Zauber des Letzten* (2005), *Ästhetik der Wiederholung: Versuch über ein literarisches Formprinzip* (2015) and *Hat man mich verstanden? Denkästhetische Untersuchungen zu Nietzsches (Selbst-) Wahrnehmungen* (2017).

Andreas B. Kilcher is Professor of Literary and Cultural Studies, Eidgenössische Technische Hochschule (ETH), Zürich, and on the board of directors for the Zentrum für Geschichte des Wissens of the ETH and the University of Zürich. He has held visiting professorships in Jerusalem, Princeton, Stanford and Tel Aviv universities, among others. His main research areas are Jewish literary and cultural history, knowledge research in the areas of literary and cultural studies, as well as Kabbala and esotericism studies. His recent publications include *Franz Kafka* (2008), *Max Frisch* (2011), *Lexikon der deutsch-jüdischen Literatur* (editor, 2012), *Die Wissenschaft des Judentums* (2015), *Writing Jewish Culture: Paradoxes in Ethnography* (editor, 2016) and *Deutsche Sprachkultur in Palästina/Israel* (with Eva Edelmann-Ohler, 2017).

Dorothee Kimmich is Professor of Modern German Literature, University of Tübingen. Since 2004, she has served as the Director of the 'Tübinger Poetik-Dozentur'. Her research focuses on culture theory and modern literature. Her recent publications are: *Texte zur Literaturtheorie der Gegenwart* (co-editor with Bernd Stiegler and Rolf G. Renner, 1995); *Wirklichkeit als Konstruktion: Studien zu Geschichte und Geschichtlichkeit bei Heine, Büchner, Immermann, Stendhal, Keller und Flaubert* (2002); *Einführung in die Literatur der Jahrhundertwende* (with Tobias Wilke, 2006); *Kulturtheorie* (co-editor with Thomas Hauschild and Schamma Schahadat, 2010); *Lebendige Dinge in der Moderne* (2011); *Ähnlichkeit: Ein Kulturwissenschaftliches Paradigma* (co-editor with Anil Bhatti, 2015); and *Ins Ungefähre: Ähnlichkeit und Moderne* (2017).

Thomas G. Kirsch has been Professor of Ethnology and Cultural Anthropology, University of Konstanz, since 2009. Earlier, he taught at the Institute for Ethnology and Philosophy in Halle, Saale and in the Department of Anthropology, Goldsmiths College, University of London. His research interests span religious ethnology, security and the prevention of criminality, and Southern Africa. His publications include *Spirits and Letters: Reading, Writing and Charisma in African Christianity* (2008), *Domesticating Vigilantism in Africa* (co-editor with Tilo Grätz, 2010) and *Regimes of Ignorance: Anthropological Perspectives on the Production and Reproduction of Non-Knowledge* (co-editor with Roy Dilley, 2015).

Ulrike Kistner is Professor, Department of Philosophy, University of Pretoria, South Africa. She teaches mainly aspects of social theory and political philosophy. Her research interests include the fields of aesthetic and psychoanalytical theory, and the history of medicine and psychiatry. Her recent publications include: 'Rassismus und Aberwitz: Überlegungen zur Frage nach dem "kolonialen Unbewussten"', in Heinz-Dieter Assmann, Frank Baasner and Jürgen Wertheimer, eds, *Grenzen* (2014); 'Common Purpose: The Crowd and the Public', *Law & Critique*, 26:1 (2015); and 'Trading in Freedom: rethinking conspicuous consumption in post-apartheid political economy', *critical arts*, 29:2 (2015). In 2016 she translated the first edition of Sigmund Freud's *Three Essays on the Theory of Sexuality* (1905) with an accompanying commentary.

Albrecht Koschorke is Professor of German Literature and Literary Studies, University of Konstanz. His fields of research are German literary history from the seventeenth to the twentieth century, as well as culture and narrative theory. Since 2006, he has been a board member of the Excellence Cluster, 'Cultural Foundations of Integration'; and since 2010, a spokesperson for the graduate programme, 'Das Reale in der Kultur der Moderne'. His recent books include *Despoten dichten: Sprachkunst und Gewalt* (co-editor, 2011), *Wahrheit und Erfindung: Grundzüge einer Allgemeinen Erzähltheorie* (2012), *Hegel und wir: Adorno-Vorlesungen 2013* (2015) and *Hitlers Mein Kampf: Zur Poetik des Nationalsozialismus* (2016).

Andreas Langenohl is Professor of Sociology with a focus on 'general societal comparison' at the Justus Liebig University, Gießen. From 2007 to 2010 he was the director of the research group, 'Idioms of Societal Analysis', in the Excellence

Cluster, 'Cultural Foundations of Integration', University of Konstanz. His research fields comprise social and culture theory, epistemology of the social and economic sciences, financial and economic sociology, and transnationality. His publications include: 'Verknüpfung, Kontextfiguration, Aspiration: Skizze einer Kulturtheorie des Übersetzens', in *Zeitschrift für interkulturelle Germanistik*, 5:2 (2014); *Town Twinning, Transnational Connections, and Trans-Local Citizenship Practices in Europe* (2015); *Transkulturalität: Klassische Texte* (co-editor with Ralph Poole and Manfred Weinberg, 2015); and *Idioms of Stability and De-Stabilization* (co-editor, 2015).

Gurpreet Mahajan is Professor at the Centre for Political Studies, School of Social Sciences, Jawaharlal Nehru University, New Delhi, where she teaches courses in political philosophy and philosophy of social sciences. She is the author of *Explanation and Understanding in the Human Sciences* (1992, 1997, 2011), *Identities and Rights: Aspects of Liberal Democracy in India* (1998), *The Multicultural Path: Issues of Diversity and Discrimination in Democracy* (2002) and *India: Political Ideas and the Making of a Democratic Discourse* (2013). She has also written extensively on issues of multiculturalism, minority rights, secularism and civil society. Her recent articles in these fields are: 'Religious Diversity and Multicultural Accommodation', in Sonia Sikka and Lori Beaman, eds, *Multiculturalism and Religious Identity: Canada and India* (2014), and 'Living with Religious Diversity: The Limits of the Secular Paradigm', in Anna Triandafyllidou and Tariq Modood, eds, *The Problem of Religious Diversity: European Challenges, Asian Approaches* (2017).

Jürgen Osterhammel is Chair of Modern and Early Modern History, University of Konstanz. From 2007 to 2014, he was the principal investigator in the Excellence Cluster, 'Cultural Foundations of Integration'. His fields of research comprise international and global history since 1750. His publications include *Die Entzauberung Asiens: Europa und die asiatischen Reiche im 18. Jahrhundert* (2010), *Die Verwandlung der Welt: Eine Geschichte des 19. Jahrhunderts* (2010), *Kommunikation im Musikleben: Harmonien und Dissonanzen im 20. Jahrhundert* (co-editor with Sven Oliver Müller and Martin Rempe, 2015) and *Die Flughöhe der Adler: Historische Essays zur globalen Gegenwart* (2017).

Klaus Sachs-Hombach is Professor of Media Studies (with a focus on media change and media innovation) at the Eberhard Karls University, Tübingen. His research interests encompass image, symbol, media and communications theory; aesthetics and culture theory; philosophical problems in psychology; the history of psychology; and cognitive science. His publications include *Das Bild als kommunikatives Medium: Elemente einer allgemeinen Bildwissenschaft* (2003), *Wege zur Bildwissenschaft: Interviews* (2004), *Bildtheorien: Anthropologische und kulturelle Grundlagen des Visualistic Turn* (editor, 2009), *Origins of Pictures* (co-editor with J.R.J. Schirra, 2013), *Krieg und Konflikt in den Medien: Multidisziplinäre Perspektiven auf mediale Kriegsdarstellungen und deren Wirkungen* (2015) and *Verstehen und Verständigung: Intermediale, multimodale und interkulturelle Aspekte von Kommunikation und Ästhetik* (2016).

Naoki Sakai is Goldwin Smith Professor of Asian Studies at Cornell University. He has published in the fields of comparative literature, intellectual history, translation studies, studies of racism and nationalism, and the histories of semiotic and literary texts and phonographic traditions. His publications include *Translation and Subjectivity* (1997), *Voices of the Past* (1991), *The Stillborn of the Japanese as a Language and as an Ethnos* (1996), *Politics of Translation*, Vol. 4 (co-editor with Sandro Mezzadra, 2014), and *Translation, Biopolitics, Colonial Difference* (*Traces*, Vol. 4, co-editor with Jon Solomon, 2013). Sakai served as the founding editor for the project 'Traces', a multilingual series in five languages (Korean, Chinese, English, Spanish and Japanese), and served as its founding senior editor (1996–2004).

Rudolf Schlögl is Professor of Modern History, University of Konstanz. His fields of research comprise religion in society and social history of the early modern period. His publications include *Alter Glaube und moderne Welt: Europäisches Christentum im Umbruch 1750–1850* (2013), *Anwesende und Abwesende: Grundriss für eine Gesellschaftsgeschichte der Frühen Neuzeit* (2014) and *Die Krise in der frühen Neuzeit* (co-editor, 2016).

Johan Strijdom is Professor of Comparative Study of Religion, University of South Africa, Pretoria. In his research he focuses on religious nationalism and violence, critiques of indigenous claims and practices, and critical approaches to material aspects of religion. These areas are analysed in a comparative and historically nuanced way, by elaborating a critique of class, gender and ethnic power relations from a postcolonial location in the global south. He has been co-editor of the journal *Phronimon*, which has as its goal the promotion of dialogue between western and African philosophies.

Levent Tezcan is a private lecturer in the Department of Cultural Studies, University of Frankfurt, Oder, and teaches sociology of religion at the Ruhr University, Bochum. In 2010, he was a fellow in the cultural studies postgraduate programme in the Excellence Cluster, 'Cultural Foundations of Integration', at the University of Konstanz; and in 2014–15, in the Käte Hamburger programme, 'Dynamiken der Religions geschichtezwischen Asien und Europa', at the University of Bochum. His fields of research encompass religion, lifestyles, body politics, the institutionalization of Islam in Germany and Turkish modernization. His publications include *Konfliktfeld Islam in Europa* (co-editor with Monika Wohlrab-Sahr, 2007) and *Das muslimische Subjekt – verfangen im Dialog der Deutschen Islamkonferenz* (2012).

Uwe Wirth is Professor of German Literature and Chair of the Study of Culture, Department of German Literature, Liebig-University Giessen. From 2005 to 2007 he was the scientific coordinator of the Centre for Advanced Studies in Literature and Culture (ZfL) in Berlin. He has also been a Fellow at the University of Konstanz in the Excellence Cluster, 'Kulturelle Grundlagen von Integration'; Visiting Professor at the University of Tokyo and at the 'Deutsche Haus', New York University; and Max Kade Professor in the German Department, University of California Berkeley. One of his main research interests is editorial fiction in German literature of around 1800, with a focus on media conditions (especially 'scenes of writing') and notions of authorship. Other research areas are the history of dilettantism, theories of humour with a focus on performativity and stupidity, and theories of hybridity with a focus on the cultural technique of grafting. He is the author of *Diskursive Dummheit: Abduktion und Komik als Grenzphänomene des Verstehens* (1999), *Die Geburt des Autors aus dem Geist der Herausgeberfiktion: Editoriale Rahmung im Roman um 1800: Wieland, Goethe, Brentano, Jean Paul und E.T.A. Hoffmann* (2008), *Bewegen im Zwischenraum* (co-editor, 2012), *Rahmenbrüche, Rahmenwechsel* (co-editor, 2013) and *Nach der Hybridität: Zukünfte der Kulturtheorie* (co-editor, 2014).